MEMORIES AND FORGETFULNESS

ABOUT THE AUTHOR

COLIN J REED WAS BORN in Southampton, Hampshire, towards the end of 1943 when WWII was finally taking a turn for the better.

His first taste of adventure came when he joined the Junior Civil Defence in 1956, and one activity was to recover life sized dummies from under the remains of the roof of a four story bombed-out building opposite the main railway station. When that closed, he joined the Southampton Sea Scouts, and learned to sail, and row, a 27ft Montague Whaler, the standard ship's sea boat of the day.

He served in the Royal Navy from 1960-70, and his first ship, *HMS Albion*, was the cornerstone of the Borneo War in 1963. During time onshore, he developed a passion for racing dinghies of various classes. After he left the RN he spent 40 years in the upstream oil and gas industry in various categories, and was one of the first crew members on BP's most successful offshore production platform in 1974.

A keen sailor he gained two sailing championships in dinghy racing in the 1980s, and in 1990 orchestrated the historic visit of the Royal Findhorn Yacht Club to Russia, the only UK yacht club to visit and race in the USSR.

He met his second wife in Rio de Janeiro in 1983, two years after losing his Scottish wife after a long illness, in only her mid-30s. He has two daughters from his first marriage. He is now semi-retired, living in the UK and Rio de Janeiro.

MEMORIES AND FORGETFULNESS

COLIN REED

Also by Colin Reed

Dangerous Voyage
Danish Gold
Time to Visit a Lady

First published in 2018
Copyright 2018 © Colin Reed
All rights reserved

Published by Boatswain Books • boatswainbooks.uk

ISBN: 978-1-912724-09-3

Designed and produced by Robert Deaves

All rights reserved. No part of this publication may be reproduced, stored in a retrieval system or transmitted in any form by any means, electronic, mechanical, photocopying, recording or otherwise without the prior written permission of the publisher, the author and any other copyright holders.

CONTENTS

Preface	Just Me	7
1	Being Born	9
2	School Days	12
3	Joining the Royal Navy	26
4	HMS Albion	33
5	Home at Last and My First Car	82
6	Twelve Months of Qualifying Course	85
7	HMS Gurkha	90
8	The Home Coming	121
9	PO Course and the Queen Mum's Parade	129
10	A Posting to Singapore	132
11	Time for Demob	154
12	Civvy Street and Decca Radar	159
13	The UK Atomic Energy Authority	164
	Gallery	173
14	British Petroleum – Forties Field	184
15	Going Contract	209

16	McDermott-Hudson	212
17	St. Fergus, Scotland	237
18	Two Short Contracts and a Big Surprise	268
19	Matthew Hall	277
20	Marathon Oil	315
21	The Survival Period	321
22	Going Subsea	324
23	Getting Married	335
24	Back to Brazil	342
25	Back to Blighty	345
26	Back to Brazil Again	351
27	Pegasus Int	354
28	Chevron	364
29	Total SA	370
30	BP	372
31	The End of a Working Life	375

PREFACE

Just Me

ANYBODY WHO MANAGES, OR RATHER is lucky enough to live a long, hopefully happy, life, will accumulate a lot of memories. Some memories may be unhappy but they can be forgotten in time. That's life.

These are my memories. The best reason that I can think of why I am putting pen to paper, or digits to the keyboard, is that in my seventy plus years the changes in everyday life on this planet have been fundamental. The population of the world has more than doubled. Computer technology unknown just a few short years ago has multiplied at such a rate that science has overtaken religion. Mankind now has so much information about the universe it's hard to get everything into perspective.

There are no earth-shattering achievements to boast about, just the quiet satisfaction of having lived a useful life and doing quite well for myself, and my family, all things considered. I have helped many people along the way, which is as it should be.

I

BEING BORN

SOUTHAMPTON, 'THE GATEWAY TO THE Empire'. Well, it was then but now it's not. Things are different, aren't they just?

("Although it is generally known I think it's about time to announce that I was born at a very early age." - Groucho Marx)

There was no fancy hospital for me with pretty nurses to gurgle at. I was born at home in October 1943 in a house the German Air Force had managed to miss. However, they didn't miss the houses on the other side of the road, which overlooked the steep slope down to Commercial Road just one block from Southampton's Central Railway Station.

This area remained as open ground for many years. Nature provided the grass and a mulberry tree, which grew in the middle of it. I haven't seen a mulberry or its tree in many a year. My younger brother and I used to pick the leaves to feed to silkworms from which we made silk thread. Bugger the Punjab we had it made except there was only one tree.

Just a short distance away the Luftwaffe didn't miss the general area surrounding the railway station though. Persistent buggers the Germans.

So what was going on in October 1943? Well, Vera Lyn was singing about the *White Cliffs of Dover* presumably because a Mr A. Hitler had seen them through his binoculars but that was as far as he got. Bless!

By the autumn of 1943, the war in Europe was turning against Germany. The German forces were retreating in North Africa and Russia, and the RAF was busy bombing the living daylights out of Germany

The USA was sending massive aid and IOUs to nice Mr Churchill including 2,600 aircraft to aid everyone, including Joe Stalin's Russian forces, who probably burnt the IOUs to keep warm. Why didn't Mr Churchill think of that?

The Italians found out about the aid. In an attempt not to miss out on the free handouts, plus avoiding a likely defeat, Italy reversed its course and declared war on Germany. That must have had Hitler shaking in his boots for sure.

So, all in all, my parent's timing was about right. Milk was in plentiful supply, English classes hadn't started and I didn't have to listen to or rather understand Mother's 'we only got one egg and two rashers of bacon a week' speech until much, much later.

Prior to 'D' Day, the streets around our area housed large numbers of US Soldiers; the original Airbnb. It was a win-win situation and the Americans didn't have to go camping in the New Forest where it rained incessantly most of the time, if not all of the time.

The US soldiers had their PX, a sort of early version of Tesco's-online cum Marks and Sparks food counter. They were not, so I found later, rationed to one egg a week. Far from it.

During the run-up to D-Day, everybody wondered about when, but they knew the time was coming. In between training, the Yanks in our street would spend a lot of time playing cards. The game of choice was Pinochle a kind of American version of bridge requiring clever bidding followed by making points with cards that had no strength.

Then one day the soldiers just…vanished…never to be seen again. Or so my parents thought.

Dad knew the time was close. He worked at a marine aircraft base on the other side of the estuary at Hythe repairing American Consolidated PBY Catalinas. He was one of the few workers with a pass to cross the water from Southampton each day where he could see the unbelievable amount of shipping waiting for the invasion. Security was very, very tight.

Dad used to joke about the sign hung up in the factory '*Don't tear your overalls on the flush rivets*'. In reality, it was no joke. Overalls were very hard to replace. Mending overalls required materials that were not easy to obtain and if the rivets on the aircraft wings were popping up above being flush, the aircraft were being seriously overworked. News about aircraft that flew out into the dark Atlantic Ocean to search for the enemy, and who never returned, was hardly ever spoken about.

A DIGRESSION - THE STORY OF THE HYTHE PIER RAILWAY.

THE 1878 ACT of Parliament made provision of a tramway along the 700-yard long pier although it was not originally installed. In 1909 a narrow gauge railway was installed with hand-propelled vehicles.

In 1922 the railway was electrified, which is still working to this day. The narrow gauge track is electrified at 250 V DC by a third rail. The line consists of a single track with no passing loops.

The line is operated by a couple of four-wheeled electric locomotives built in 1917 by Bush, crudely numbered № 1 & № 2. A third locomotive was used for spares.

Two of the four passenger cars have a driving cab at their seaward ends. In normal operation, the single train is made up of one of the locomotives, three passenger cars and a four-wheel flat car for baggage. The locomotive is always at the landward end and the seaward passenger car has a driving cab. The line also has an oil-tank car used to carry fuel to the Hythe ferries. The railway is the oldest continuously operating public pier train in the world. I am absolutely amazed that an electric railway of this age, which provided such fascination for us youngsters, is still working well and serving the public.

*

THERE WAS A massively cold winter in 1947, but downhill skis for three year olds were in short supply so no doubt I was kept indoors wrapped up safe and warm. And, before I forget brother Graham arrived in January.

On July 4, 1954 the UK ended 14 years of food rationing in Britain. It ended at midnight so that restrictions on the sale and purchase of meat and bacon could be lifted. This was nine years after the end of the war.

However, Mother's 'we only got one egg a week' speech lasted much longer, decades longer. I had to join up just to miss it.

2

SCHOOL DAYS

I WENT TO SCHOOL; THEY WERE all approved. A very old joke; almost seventy years old in fact.

One day on Feb 6, 1952 at St Marks Junior School, next to the former Saints football ground the headmaster toured each class, in turn, to inform that the 'King is dead, long live the Queen'. The school curriculum had not, up to that point, included irony in the syllabus so nobody asked if it was serious.

I find it quite strange to have this remembrance stuck in my mind for all these years.

*

BOTH MY PARENTS kept busy after WWII. No doubt they had to make ends meet to feed the four of us. Quite often I was pointed in the direction of Granny Pound's home. My mother probably attached a label in case of need and I would set off on my own. I was 12 years old.

It was an easy walk through the park after filling a bag full of conkers, then down Above Bar past the Bargate, then down the High Street, up the short rise to the square where sits St Michaels Church, past Tudor House then to Granny's at 2 Bugle St.

Granddad Pound did not survive WW1. Granny Pound had this huge WW1 picture hanging in her living room depicting British cavalry with huge lances charging over dead horses to get at the enemy. Very gloomy for a youngster, not quite my cup of tea at all.

*

ANOTHER LONG-TERM MEMORY when toddling down to Grannies was the 'open to the sky' cellars of the many bombed building in Southampton's *Above Bar*. At times I can still smell the odour of a bombed building.

Southampton was originally a Roman settlement, one square mile in area, the same as London. The *Bargate* was a fortified structure that served as the main north entrance. Below the *Bargate*, towards the harbour, exists the High Street. The street above *Bargate* was called *Above Bar*. Just so you know. The *Bargate* still exists today as a museum.

*

The Port of Southampton

THE PORT OF Southampton is blessed with four high tides a day in pairs, the second high tide following the first by about two hours. This marvel of nature is caused by the tidal wave that crosses the Atlantic Ocean, and divides as it reaches the British islands. One part of the wave travels around the north of Scotland; the other travels up the English Channel. The two tidal waves combine in the port of Southampton giving the two high tides, two hours apart.

The most magnificent ships of the era were the *Queen Mary* and the *Queen Elizabeth* both flagships of the Cunard & White Star Line. They used to berth in the specially built Ocean Terminus, which was famous for the first (and last) sailing of the Titanic.

To service the golden age of the big liners, special trains from London came directly to Southampton Terminus and the adjacent South Western Hotel (originally named the Imperial Hotel).

The station was authorised on July 25, 1834 as the London & South Western Railway which was the London & Southampton Railway until the line opened). The station opened on June 10, 1839 as Southampton Terminus. The station building was designed in the Italianate style by Sir William Tite

The grand and elegant South Western Hotel adjacent to the railway terminus offered the best hotel service in the city. Here travellers could rest before boarding their ship, mostly to the Americas. The hotel was eventually converted into apartments with the original windows that rattled in the wind, and kept the condensation safe on the inside.

Many other famous shipping lines used the port. A Union Castle liner used to sail at 4 pm sharp every Thursday from 101 Berth in the New Docks bound for a round voyage to South Africa and the British colonies along the East African coastline.

Holland American lines and the Peninsula & Orient (P&O) also used the port

*

ONE EXPERIENCE THAT lingers well was the arrival of the *USS United States* as she docked in Southampton's 'Ocean Terminus' on her maiden voyage in July 1952. Mother had a dear friend on board. Mother and I were thrilled to be ushered aboard this grand ship.

There was a big celebration as the ship had broken the transatlantic speed record (the Blue Riband) held by RMS *Queen Mary* for the previous 14 years by over 10 hours making the maiden crossing from the Ambrose lightship at New York Harbour to Bishop Rock off Cornwall UK in 3 days 10 hours 40 minutes at an average speed of 35.59 knots (65.91 km/h; 40.96 mph). She was the last liner to hold this famous record.

The record was never challenged again as the shipping lines already knew the time had passed. The era of transatlantic air travel was soon to commence to end their days.

*

TWO SMALL INCIDENCES come to mind. The first, a summer's day outing at Lee-on-Solent beach, which at high tide was mostly shingle. Low tide greeted our arrival. My brother and I, bucket and spade in hand, enjoyed what young children do on a sandy beach.

Later that day, the *Queen Mary* passed at a very sedate speed, the waterway as ever being very busy with many yachts, motor boats and ferries to and from the Isle-of-Wight. About fifteen minutes later father ushered us two kids up to the top of the shingle beach where he had moved the deck chairs, picnic basket and ground blankets.

Before we could complain father bid us sit down to watch. What? I thought. Other families also relocated to higher the ground.

The favoured area where we had been playing on the sand was rapidly occupied by other families despite father's low-key advice not to sit there. Then the sea receded and then whoosh and back it came with a rush almost as far as to where we were sitting. Now we knew why the great liner had passed so slowly on its way to the open sea.

Now then, if the *Queen Mary* sailed by at slow speed, caused such a fuss on Lee-on-Solent beach considered the following. Dad had a good friend at the sailing club, one Jerry Lapworth, who served on the *Queen Mary* during WWII. He had many good stories to tell and how the ship always sailed alone at very high speed.

The power-train of the *Queen Mary* consisted of four boiler rooms, one for each propeller shaft each containing six massive Yarrow boilers which fed the steam for the massive turbine. From memory, each boiler had 30 sprays to feed the fuel.

In standard service, normally forty-eight weeks a year, the ship could maintain her standard cruising speed on half the boilers with just half the sprays. Her top speed was rumoured to be well in excess of her service speed, which, during WWII kept her safe.

The ship was due to make a nighttime departure from Rio de Janeiro harbour. Brazil had entered WWII, contributing, amongst other assets, two air-groups flying P-47 Thunderbolts (ground attack fighter/bombers) stationed in northern Italy where they performed magnificent service whilst sustaining heavy losses. The US President presented them with a famous commendation.

Anyway, Jerry recalled that the ship went to full steam on all boilers, raised anchor and then backed-up in the harbour, the ship fully darkened. German submarines were expected outside in the Atlantic Ocean waiting for a shot at the mighty prize.

When all was ready the ship was aimed at the narrow gap between the fort on the east side of the harbour entrance, 'Ponto de Santa Cruz', and the small island of 'Ilha Laje' which gave the deep water channel just over half a kilometre wide. The Captain ordered full steam ahead and the *Queen Mary* quickly built up a high speed to reach open waters. Later, after I had spent some time in Rio de Janeiro I always wondered what the effect the ship's departure would have had on the surrounding coast and beaches.

*

MEMORIES AND FORGETFULNESS

FINALLY, I REMEMBERED the Port of Southampton was also an important cargo port importing many products mostly food from the Commonwealth. Ships in this era did not use shipping containers as they do today. Ships were unloaded by manual labour called 'dock workers', a gang of ruffians at the best of times.

One could always tell at the local Saturday market at St. Denys what ships had unloaded that week, as fruit and vegetables allegedly damaged in their unloading made their way into the public domain. Mother would take great advantage of the prices and she always had a huge stock of bottled fruits that lasted the year round.

*

SOME YEARS LATER Mother insisted I join the Sea Scouts. A uniform was provided and off I would go by bicycle to deepest Northam on the east side of the city on the Portsmouth Road.

The 25th Northam Sea Scouts was run by Scoutmaster Stan Fright. Stan was the police sergeant-in-charge of the Southampton Police River Patrol launch keeping a wary eye on the docks, not forgetting the many fiddles going on in this age before containers. You would not be amazed by the number of items that fell from conveyor belts to order during the unloading of any ship. Stan Fright was a large kind man but when he was on duty you wouldn't fancy your chances.

Training on the water was conducted in a 10' rowing boat and a 27' Montague Whaler donated by the Royal Navy during their change-over to the newer 'three-in-one' whaler, which had an engine.

Rowing the whaler was hard work for grown-up men so for us 'nippers' it was even more hard work. The oars were long and very heavy. See any Hollywood movie about Queen Cleopatra and her famous ship. The same damn oars.

However, sailing the whaler was fun. Stan knew how to rig it properly, and Dad gave me a book to swot-up so I could too. Thus, I got more than my fair share of helming.

Dragging the beast to the scout hut at the end of the season was a chore. Not many parents came to help either. Then we would spend all winter scraping its bottom, re-riveting the hull, repairing ribs, insert caulking where needed, then painting it a delicate shade of Pusser's grey.

*

COLIN REED

FAMILY DAY-TRIPS ON the paddle steamers in the 1950s, was one of the more memorable treats my brother and I enjoyed. The paddle steamers departed from Southampton's Royal Pier. In its hey-day, the Royal Pier was a wonderful place to visit. It provided excellent views of the docks and the great liners of the day as they arrived or departed from the Ocean Terminal or the New Docks.

The pier opened in 1883, but like so many of the piers along the south coast of England has since fallen into disuse. Our favourite paddle steamer was the *PS Balmoral*.

The only surviving paddle steamer of this type today is the *PS Waverley*, which is still in service, ably supported by steamship enthusiasts.

The day-trips would take us down Southampton Water to a number of destinations on the Isle of Wight. For some reason, I remember a day trip all the way to Poole, which turned out to be rather a long day. Both fathers and their sons were fascinated by the reciprocal steam engine. All that bright shiny brass work, big pistons driving the paddle wheel, plus the wonderful smell of steam.

My wife and I enjoyed a similar voyage many years later, on the *PS Waverley*, as we took advantage of a very special day out to watch the start of the last Whitbread Round the World Race (now called the Volvo Round the World Race).

*

The Sea Scouts visited the USS Forrestal in 1957

THE GREAT SHIP arrived earlier than expected in Southampton. At 80,000 tons she was big, huge in fact, at just under the displacement of the two *Queens* belonging to the Cunard Line. At over one thousand feet long she was moored in the New Docks occupying almost three berths (107-109).

By comparison, the Royal Navy's largest carrier *HMS Ark Royal* occupied the top left-hand corner of the KG-V dry dock, looking much more modest by comparison.

USS Forrestal was the first US Navy super-carrier, commissioned in 1955 and was the lead ship of her class. Unlike her sister ships, she was conventionally powered. The Sea Scout troop felt very privileged to be invited aboard.

The troop was being shown around the flight deck, between the frequent showers of rain, when a huge puddle became the subject of an interesting conversation. We asked our guide about the huge puddle.

Scoutmaster Stan Fright was most insistent that members of his troop didn't go paddling in the puddle.

Our US officer guide told us that the ship had been participating in a large NATO exercise in the deep Atlantic Ocean, when the remains of a strong hurricane had interrupted proceedings, prompting the various national naval fleets to scarper for safety.

USS Forrestal, unfortunately, had one of its larger twin propeller long distance recon aircraft aloft. By the time it had returned the ship was being battered by large waves and the conditions were extremely marginal for a safe landing.

The problem was the aircraft did not have sufficient fuel to divert to Ireland or anywhere else for that matter. Ditching and recovering the crew by helicopter was out of the question, so they had to land it aboard. Wow! What a challenge.

Anyway, after a few trial passes, so the story goes, the aircraft did manage to 'land' on board, its hook catching one of the arrestor wires and not actually breaking it which was always a risk.

However, at the instant of the actual landing, the aircraft had high vertical descent at the same time as the stern of the ship was ascending rapidly.

Whack, or was it crash. The aircraft pancaked very hard into the deck, it's under-carriage completely destroyed, badly deforming the fuselage and forming the large indentation in the armoured flight deck soon became the puddle of the year. The crew were safe, no doubt shaken and definitely stirred. The aircraft became available for spare parts and its remains probably dropped over the side at a later date.

I still remember looking down from the top of the ship's island at my home city. The visit to this ship was most impressive and we did enjoy the ice cream and sodas later on.

*

Fun at the Junior Civil Defence Training Site

AFTER WWII, THE *Civil Defence* was formed to combine the organisations that did such sterling work rescuing civilians during the war.

During the German air raids, the ARP service along with the Auxiliary Fire Service (AFS) took on key and often dangerous roles helping the public to find shelter, searching for survivors after bombing raids, assist in fighting fires, stretchering casualties to safety and dealing with incendiary devices.

That the *Junior Civil Defence* force existed was new to me, and my father. Mother, a district nurse had sources of information denied to Prime Ministers and so I was enrolled without my knowledge. Still, it was better than watching the single TV channel at home we now know as BBC 1. The alternative was ITV, which was banned by my father who detested advertising. Period.

The Civil Defence training site was the remains of a bombed building directly opposite the main railway station. The whole block was a bombsite bounded on both sides by streets that led up to Commercial Road just a three-minute walk away from our home.

The building was a shell with all four external walls shored up both externally and internally. Interior beams were placed where the four floors would have been plus a very small amount of roof remaining in the south-west corner. There was some floor space on the ground floor level but the basement loomed below as a dark mysterious cavern. People had died down there and the 'bombed building' smell was everywhere. It infused itself into all our clothing, which no soap powder could remove.

*

IT IS AT this juncture I would warn pedantic members of the HSSE industry to miss the next memory. The very thought of teaching young adults below the age of 16, the age when you can join the military services, how to perform vital rescue services, will be injurious. The actions described here cannot be performed whilst using a smartphone.

The training class for us juniors was once a week. I forget the name of the grumpy old bugger that taught us, but he had been a leading light in the rescue services during the 1940-41 blitz. Let's call him Grumpy Bert. It fits just who he was.

Armed only with tatty overalls, gloves and a WW1 tin hat, we would climb all over the building rescuing dummies of various types and religions, applying first aid as required. The ladders were tall and heavy. At least three would be needed to reach the highest level.

Lowering a stretcher from height needed care and a good knowledge of ropemanship. Fortunately, some of the older juniors, who came from the rough part of the city, had the strength and fortitude for the more strenuous tasks.

After six months we were told there would be a rescue exercise attended by one of the local commissioners, a pass-out test in fact, so we could be issued with our Civil Defence Badge.

Needless to say, the exercise combined all the different facets of rescuing an injured person. What would Grumpy Bert have us do? Surprise, surprise his pet rescue dummy, a female allegedly her late 40's called Rita, was put in the worst place possible, under the remaining vestige of the roof. God, it looked a long way up there.

Hey Ho, the team set too, installed the ladders up to the very small floor area under the roof. Two of the strong lads plus myself ended up attending to Rita. I had the job of giving first aid before preparing Rita for the descent down to ground-level.

Getting Rita onto a stretcher was a near-on impossible and it took some time to figure out what to do next. The district commissioner seeing we are all doing a good job gave Grumpy a 'well done', so as to bugger off home to a loving wife and a much needed evening meal.

The two stronger lads said 'bugger this', and tied the rope around Rita's neck. We gently lowered her down to the ground level. When we ourselves managed to reach ground-level we were expecting a big telling-off from Grumpy. He stared us down for two long minutes as we waited for the tongue-lashing we deserved and was bound to receive.

With that Grumpy smiled and said 'Now there's a good idea, now bugger-off home and well done'.

It was much later when his replacement arrived on the scene that we discovered his wife's name was …you guessed correctly…Rita.

It was only later when I learned that during the war, youngsters as young as 14 and 16 did serve in the AFS, so our training followed on from what really happened. Fascinating.

*

MY FIRST SECONDARY school was Deanery Secondary Modern located in the choice part of the city down by the River Itchen not too far from the coking plant that processed imported Welsh coal into town gas for the city and coke for the fire. When the wind was in the wrong direction breathing in deeply outside was not advised.

I had to bike to school in all weathers and now they have school buses.

Our class teacher was one Mr Barnes teacher and hero. He had served as an RN Petty Officer on board *HMS Cossack*, a magnificent Tribal Class fleet destroyer in the early part of the war. He was Captain of 'X' Turret, the aft main 4.7" turret on the ship.

The *Altmark* incident occurred on 16-17th February 1940 in neutral Norwegian waters. The *Altmark* was the supply ship supporting the German pocket battleship *Graf Spee* in the South Atlantic Ocean. On board the Altmark were some 300 allied prisoners taken from the ships sunk by the pocket battleship.

British naval forces cornered the tanker in a Norwegian Fjord. *HMS Cossack* boarded the German ship to free all the prisoners and in the process killed eight German seamen with firearms and wounding ten others.

PO Barnes (our hero) led the boarding party and judging from the German casualty list the British sailors were in no mood to mess about. In the classroom, however, Mr Barnes was quite tranquil; it happens if you survive a war as bad as WWII.

*

Playing cards when Lt Chuck Berry knocks on the door

ONE EVENING AT home in Southampton the family was playing cards, Pinochle. I was, for a change, winning. There came a knock at the front door. Mother sat nearest so Father asked her to see who it was. Mother opened the front door; there was a loud squeak and the sound of somebody falling to the floor.

Father laid his cards face down on the green baize, with his 'don't you two look at my cards' look, opened the dining room door looked down the hall and invited Chuck to come in. I think my brother went to help Mother to her feet.

Sergeant Chuck Berry was an African-American who had stayed in our home prior to 'D' Day. He'd brought gifts of scarce foods including eggs and more importantly American Rye in exchange for a dry comfortable camp bed that was not in a New Forest tent being hammered by the rain.

He remained in the US military after the war making it to the rank of Lieutenant in charge of two companies of Negro soldiers with their regiment based in Frankfurt. A rare honour.

Chuck took Mother's cards whilst she made the tea and brought homemade current cake to the proceedings. Chuck turned some pretty average cards into a winning hand and I had to hide my annoyance as I thought I had a 'lay down' hand until the unseen cards in the middle of the table were flopped over.

No matter, Mum and Dad were very pleased to see him, asked how he survived the war as it was known his outfit had some tough days against the Germans. A bottle of Canadian whisky appeared as we kids were packed off to bed.

The reunion continued well into the night. Afterwards, Dad told us that the family had been invited to visit him in Frankfurt Germany the following summer.

*

Going to Frankfurt and the Return through France – 1957

FOR MANY YEARS during my youth, father preferred driving a motor-cycle/sidecar combination. He liked big bikes and tried them all. The road tax on motorcycles was low plus Dad could repair any motorcycle ever made.

His favourite supplier was a company called 'Lawton & Wilson' and their premises were based on the Millbrook Rd going out of town to the New Forest.

L&W were both ex-IoM TT riders. For many years father stuck with his Brough Superior SS80 which one year returned all the way home to Southampton on one cylinder from Bridport, a distance of 75 miles.

Its time came, and there was a succession of big bikes including a Vincent 'Black Shadow'. Then, one day, Dad took me to see the new Royal Enfield 750cc. The engine was particularly powerful. Ideal for sidecar work.

Mr Lawton revealed that the bike frame of the Royal Enfield wasn't so good for competition work, so they had developed a 'special', shoe-horning the Enfield engine into a Norton 'featherbed' frame. Dad was tempted but the price was too high.

Following Chuck Berry's visit, plans were made to make the long journey to Frankfurt. The family only took camping holidays so the family would camp overnight going out and coming back.

To say that the motorcycle combination was overloaded was an understatement. It was on the autobahn when Dad's skill as a motor-cyclist saved the family from a nearly dreadful accident. The mudguard for the sidecar managed to shake itself loose, wrapping itself around the wheel in a huge shower of sparks. Despite the high cruising speed Dad managed to keep the motor-cycle combination in a straight line to reach safety at the side of the road.

The mudguard and the sidecar wheel were locked together. It took some effort to free the two. The family had a very close shave. If we had flipped my parents would have been thrown in the air and I doubt if the sidecar would have offered much protection to myself and my brother sitting in the back, despite the two of us being wrapped-up sitting on top of blankets and sleeping bags.

Still, we arrived safe and sound in Frankfurt to enjoy the luxury of US Army officer's quarters on the main camp.

It didn't affect Mum and Dad at the time but white US soldiers seeing white folk staying at a Negro officer's home caused some unnecessary racial comment which Dad definitely did not like. He said little; good for him. Racial segregation was bad in the US Army and no further comment from me is required.

Dad was a great jazz fan and I seem to remember him going to a Negro jazz club on the camp that he enjoyed greatly, getting on famously with everyone.

Now in 1957, Southampton was still a mess from the wartime bombing, and rebuilding was a slow and haphazard process. The area around Central Station remained, as was, until the early 1970s.

By comparison, Frankfurt had been rebuilt looking brand-new almost everywhere. It looked as though there had been no bombing at all. Everywhere was bright and shiny. The cake shops were to die for.

All too soon it was time to return to Southampton. The homeward journey would take us past Paris on the way to Le Havre and the direct ferry to Southampton. Dad's motorcycle combination was, even more, overload not sure why.

The back wheel started breaking spokes despite having the strongest spokes fitted before the adventure. Part of the problem came from driving on the right-hand side of the road, the back wheel carrying more load than normal due to the reverse camber of the road.

The roads would not have been to the same standard as present times. Dad had spare spokes and so started a running battle with the back wheel. Garages along the way helped but somewhere along the route it became clear the back wheel would never make it to the Channel Ferry.

I forgot what actually happen, but on the outskirts of Paris at the start of a major bank holiday weekend, the back wheel almost collapsed. So, we had to set up camp again. Brother and I were packed off to bed in our little tent and next morning it was obvious that Dad, hacked off with the turn of events, had gone to the local bar in whose field we were camped and whatever the locals were drinking did it in for Dad.

Somehow, Dad managed to contact the 'Royal Enfield' agent, who very kindly offered to work on Saturday rebuilding the wheel with super strong spokes probably using sports car spokes from either Aston Martin or Jaguar sports cars.

Our family meanwhile took the chance to visit the main tourist spots in Paris, the Arc Triumph and Tour Eiffel.

Job done, the family was able to continue to Le Havre and home.

*

SHORTLY AFTER THIS adventure, the results arrived of an exam I took before the summer holidays confirming acceptance to change secondary schools to Southampton Secondary Technical College. Apparently, I was one of 30 out of 300 hopeful applicants allowing me to escape from Deanery Secondary Modern.

The new school concentrated on more mainstream subjects and the two years was geared to getting pupils into local apprenticeship schemes. Dad was a master craftsman in metals so I chose woodwork for the six hours a week workshop practice. At the beginning of the last term, the pupils had to choose a project to make a 'useful item'. Dad suggested a large pair of steps to help when he redecorated the house.

I overdid the large bit and getting this pair of steps home was a real struggle on the back of my bicycle. They lasted well and are currently lying outside at the back of my daughter's house full of woodworm.

*

BEFORE I END this chapter there was a 'small' incident between my father and his brother, Uncle John, who lived in Porchester, near Portsmouth. In their early days, they both enjoyed owning and riding Brough Superior motorcycles, which in those days was the Rolls Royce of motorcycles.

Father had moved on but Uncle John had kept his SS100 hidden in his garage under a pile of old junk for many years. It was safe there or so Dad thought as Uncle John was an Olympic champion in untidiness.

During one of the monthly Sunday visits my brother and I had been sent to pick blackberries along the railway path at the bottom of the garden, when we heard our father shout very loudly indeed "You did bloody what?" We hurried back in time to hear 'Don't you remember whose bloody name was the 'blankety blank' log book?'

I looked at my brother and said 'Oh no don't tell me'. And so it turned out to be, not only that, it was the motorcycle on which Col. Lawrence of Arabia was killed.

(Funnily enough, I still have the full- size photograph.)

The motorcycle was sold, so the records state, for the princely sum of two quid. The last the family heard was the new owner spent a fortune on its restoration and was busy hawking it around the USA for a great deal of money.

3

JOINING THE ROYAL NAVY

I JOINED THE RADIO ELECTRICAL BRANCH of the Royal Navy on 5th April 1960. Pay was the princely sum of £4.18.6p fortnightly.

A Digression - The Navy is also referred to as 'Pusser', 'the Andrew' or 'the mob'.

"The Pusser" is Royal Navy slang for a ship's supply officer now called a 'Logistics Officer'. The word came to mean "One hundred per cent service," as in "Pusser's issue." "Pusser's issue" applies to anything supplied by the Royal Navy such as a "Pusser's grip" or a canvas bag used instead of a suitcase.

Pusser is also the name of Caribbean rum supplied to the Royal Navy, issued daily at lunch time as a 'Tot of Rum' as 'Grog' (or 2 in 1) to the ratings. The ceremony included the officer of the watch (OOW) observing the drawing of the exact volume of the neat rum (in accordance with latest crew list of ratings over the age of twenty years) and then escorting the ship's butcher to the rum barrel in the main mess hall, adding the water sometimes not so exact but never under, then issuing the 'grog' to the 'cook of each mess deck' in a container known as a 'fanny' who takes the 'grog' to the mess deck. Any extra was called 'Queens' and passed around the waiting mess deck members.

The senior rates (Petty officers and above) were issued 'Sipper's (1 in 1). Sometimes rum was issued as 'Neaters' or sans agua.

'Splice the Mainbrace' was the issue rum, (as above) for a special occasion.

The Andrew - The Royal Navy continues to be known as the 'Andrew' but there is no conclusive answer to the derivation of the nickname.

Some say the nickname 'Andrew' derives from a man called 'Andrew Mille' a zealous officer of the Impress Service during the French Revolutionary and Napoleonic Wars. Miller 'recruited' so many men to His Majesty's ships that the navy was said to belong to him.

Earlier 19th-century sources suggest the origins of the nickname derive from one Andrew Miller who supplied provisions to Royal Navy warships with such a monopoly that Andrew Miller was said to 'own the navy'. However, the origin of the Royal Navy's nickname remains obscure.

*

I WAS POSTED to *HMS Collingwood* for 'new entry' training which lasted a short six weeks, to learn the language, how to polish boots and shoes, wash, then iron clothes, press one's uniform and learn to march with/without seven kilos of Lee Enfield Mk2 rifle.

Learning to shoot a Lee Enfield Mk2 rifle required as much padding as possible for the shoulder. My 'new entry' class was taken to the butts on some miserable down somewhere on some miserable hill far from farmers and their easy to spot sheep.

Fortunately, it didn't rain. I managed to hit what was quite a large target at 300 yards. Fortunately, the target didn't shoot back.

A member of the class with previous shooting experience showed he could hit the target, showing his propensity to a 'pain in you know where' by shooting at the side of the target and collapsing the side of the target support structure. The Chief GI was not impressed. Still doubling with a rifle over your head for half an hour was seen to be such a relaxing exercise.

HMS Collingwood proved to be a handy posting as it was an easy motorcycle ride to my home in Southampton.

After new entry training our class was joined by a class from *HMS Vincent*, the boy's entry establishment. The lads in the joining class came mostly from the North of England particularly Yorkshire, a part of the UK us Southerners were unlikely to have experienced.

Pusser, in its wisdom, kept half their pay and purchased Post Office saving stamps (remember PO saving stamps? – I thought not), glueing them firmly into a saving stamp book which was issued to each junior rating on the day they stepped on the bus that brought them to *HMS Collingwood*.

In those days, pubs in the south of England would only have any trade worth bothering about on the weekends say Thursdays to Sundays. Then, I discovered the difference between the English cultures, mainly in this case North v South.

Our Northern friends, aided and abetted by few Jocks, set about, at the tender age of 16 years to quickly turn their savings into pints of 'black & tan', 'mild & bitter' and other beverages produced by the local breweries (Strongs of Romsey and Brickwoods of Portsmouth) not forgetting Watneys Red Barrel, a fleet favourite. This ceremony of underage drinking was conducted exclusively in the famed portals of the Naffi.

(NAFFI - Navy Army & Air Force Institute, a civilian-run organization providing canteens shops and bars for British military personnel at home or overseas.)

They also smoked to excess. 'Pusser' issued a duty-free cigarette ration of 200 fags a month, the ultimate in tradable currency. The cigarettes had a blue line printed on the length of the paper and surprisingly enough they were always called 'blue liners'.

I tried one once (don't tell my Mum), survived the horrible experience and so my monthly ration was traded in every time I had a duty weekend, enabling an unbroken run of going sailing and enjoying the more interesting race programmes.

Anyway, back to the navy and its ten months of training in understanding the mysteries of electronics, Ohms Law, power distribution theory, radio transmitters and receivers, radar systems plus all associated test equipment. In those days all electronic equipment had valves – known as thermionic valves (or vacuum tubes in American) – that glowed in the dark giving off quite a lot of heat. Learning to test these valves was a fundamental cornerstone of our training.

In the few months I spent at *HMS Collingwood*, I was surprised at how much one had learnt. Better still was the chance to meet so many people from all different parts of Great Britain. I even met two guys, a Liverpudlian and a full-on Welshman, who were the last of the National Servicemen, completing their mandatory two year's service.

*

AT THE END of the technical training course in the spring of 1961 most of my class were posted to *HMS Albion*, an Albion class aircraft carrier, recently returned to Portsmouth dockyard to be converted into a Commando Ship.

The ship, laid down in 1944, and commissioned in the early 1950s, was no spring chicken. She was originally designed to operate propeller-driven aircraft. At 24,000 tonnes she was too small to operate the new modern jet aircraft but she was fitted with hydraulic catapults, an angled flight deck and the famous landing mirror system, all British inventions.

She did go to sea for two commissions flying both jets and propeller-driven aircraft. Life expectancy of the Fleet Air Arm pilots flying jet aircraft, including the Super Marine Scimitar, was never considered good and the writing was on the wall for these ex-WW2 fleet carriers.

Digression: The test flight version of the Scimitar showed it was it was something of a rocket ship of its day. Dad had a friend on the test programme up in Wiltshire. By the time they had finished, the aircraft, now somewhat slower, had been equipped to land on an aircraft carrier and had become quite heavy but very strong. To prove its landing capability the final version was hoisted thirty plus feet in the air and dropped onto its wheels without damage.

After WW2 my father worked in aircraft production at a sub-contract firm in London making the jet engine air intakes and other parts of the fuselage for Supermarine Aircraft whose factory was based in Southampton. (I think it was on the rebuilt site of the Spitfire factory destroyed during the war.)

Occasionally these parts would pass inspection before being dispatched down to the main factory, but would not pass the 'goods inwards' inspection on receipt. Dad and his two buddies would be sent down by the grumbling company owner to fix things.

*

And finally, the pub opposite Southampton Central Railway Station

THE LAND OPPOSITE the railway station was eventually cleared of any remaining bomb damaged structures and the cellars filled in. There was a very small building on the site no bigger than a public loo. But no, it was a pub serving excellent beer, especially Whitworth draft IPA, with the best steak pies with gravy known to man.

Like many public houses in Southampton, their owners and/or managers were ex-Cunard Line stewards, an interesting section of the population and well worth listening to. The pub was a roaring success. When it became time to redevelop the site the owner purchased a substantial, rather famous, public house deep in the New Forest where he prospered greatly.

The pies came from a pie shop down a side street next to the Grand Theatre directly opposite the Southampton Civic Centre.

Its claim to fame in its final years was its nude shows in the late 1950s and early 1960s, similar in style to the Windmill Theatre in London. During school days, after swimming lessons, the class would make it up the hill to the pie shop for pies that were piping hot straight from the oven and munch away whilst looking at the Theatre's glassed-in billboards showing what was on next week. Food for the mind, food for hungry tummies.

*

ADJACENT TO THE London side of the main railway station was a similar building to the bombed building used for civil defence training, except it had survived the war.

The building, a hotel, on four floors had an interesting and valuable collection of paintings adorning the walls of the stairways going up to the bedrooms. The décor was all original, well maintained serving excellent fare and well-kept beers.

The owner, one of the local characters and ex-Cunard steward, drove an Aston Martin DB 2/4. That he was 'limp-of-wrist' was all too apparent. That every second Thursday he would take time off from his hotel and pop down to Portsmouth for the weekend was only something we learnt much later.

*

Learning to Race Sailing Dinghies

I HAD LEARNT to sail with the Southampton 25th (Northam) Sea Scouts. When I joined the Royal Navy, Dad introduced me to racing dinghies. It was love at first sight. Now at 74 my time has come to listen to my doctor who has a list a mile long suggesting tiddlywinks is a better sport. Pah! We will see!

Father joined Southampton S.C. located adjacent to the Millbrook Sewage Works and its discharge pier (now call water treatment works for the more delicate members of the community).

Originally, club the site was bounded to the west by the treatment works and to the east by the King George 5th Dry Dock (built to service the two Cunard Queens). The site had also been a wartime hospital. The existing wooden huts, now in a much decrepit state, remained where boats could be stored and/or repaired. There was a much needed hard because as the tide went out it went out a very long way.

In 1960, Father bought me a 12' Graduate racing dinghy, which I used to sail with a Yorkshire man Richard Tarpey who became my oldest friend until he died of cancer in 2004. A truly sad loss.

In June 1960 – very much the new boy, I entered the Southampton Town Regatta. Its entry fee was a massive five bob for the general handicap fleet. My only previous experience in sailing was with the Sea Scouts so it was all very new.

Tarpey joined in the fun. He joined the RN as a junior entrant at *HMS Vincent* and had become proficient in handling an RN 32' cutter that could be rigged for sailing.

On race day the westerly wind was light and variable. The course started at the Royal Pier and took the fleet up the River Test with the Southampton New Docks to leeward and the New Forest shoreline to the west. Our start was better than I expected but in the light conditions we sagged off badly to leeward over to the New Docks as our more knowledgeable competitors managed somehow to lee bow the tide and creep up to windward.

Anyway, the wind dropped, but when it filled in it came to us first at an angle most favourable. We steamed ahead rounded the Number 8 swinging ground buoy and held the lead to win the magnificent prize of five quid (£5) thereby providing beer 'coupons' for the next few weeks.

During my early days at Southampton Sailing Club, I spent my off-duty hours from the RN competing in the club's race programme, learning how to make my Graduate racing dinghy go as fast as everyone else's.

This expended a lot of effort, which needed refreshment at the end of each race. As an under-aged member of the sailing club, I was barred from purchasing alcoholic drinks except when my good friend Derek was duty bar person.

My favourite refreshment after a hard race would be to tie-up alongside old Frank's Six Metre cruiser named Ruthless, for Frank's version of a mug of tea. Frank was an old-timer whose wife Ruth had left him some time ago.

Frank spent his days resting on his substantial laurels. He'd been there and done that several times over. Quite what would always be a carefully guarded secret but there were rumours. Frank was a scruffy old bugger, just like his yacht. He wasn't short of a few bob but where he kept his bob's would also remain a mystery as he claimed to be always skint or so he said.

Frank had retired, liking nothing more than to sit on his beloved yacht watching the tide go in and out, the bird life on the waterway plus the comings and goings of great ocean liners at Southampton's New Docks.

Frank's tea was legendary and had been since the outbreak of the war. For sure it was strong. The 'tea' always served with generous helpings of sugar usually a wartime week's ration and condensed milk.

I tried to emulate the style of Frank's tea. The navy had the ingredients but it still didn't taste quite so good. Perhaps the difference was Old Frank's collection of battered enamel tin mugs rarely cleaned and incapable of formal recovery to total hygiene. Everyone knew Frank's view on hygiene, that it should be practised sparingly especially when it came to his drinking utensils.

Frank's other famous collection was his drawer of assorted cutlery. Every item bore the mark of a long lost airline. The only items that formed a complete set were priceless, to Frank anyway, BOAC desert spoons some still in their original plastic cover. The knives in the drawer had been 'donated' by Pan Am, Caledonian Airways, TWA and Imperial Airways. Despite all attempts by visitors to grab a memento from the past old Frank always knew to the nearest millimetre where every item lay.

One of the more humorous incidences came from a guy called Nigel. He raced a single-handed dinghy called an 'OK'. A hard-chine craft with a single unstayed wooded mast. When going about, or changing tack as it is known, he developed a curious technique of hopping from one side of the boat to the other. He was very proud of his 'bunny hop', until the day I caught him on out in a port/starboard meeting of our two boats, he 'went about' very quickly so as to end up under my bow and forced me to tack away.

His bunny hop was a tad too vigorous, as he hopped straight over the side of his boat into the water.

4

HMS ALBION

(March 1961 - May 1964)

HMS ALBION WAS A BIG part of my life and growing up. We were all youngsters when we joined her. When we left her it was as proud professionals that could tackle anything the navy gave us to do.

*

Portsmouth Naval Barracks

BUILT AT THE dawn of the twentieth century, the ceilings were tall, nearer to God than anything else. Tall windows let in a lot of light in the summer. In the winter they let in a lot of condensation. During summer the barracks were pleasant light and airy. In winter, yep you guessed, it was bloody freezing.

The ship's company was accommodated in the barracks whilst the dockyard tore the ship apart. The planned ship's compliment would be small for a ship of this size but finding space to accommodate just under a thousand 'Bootnecks' (Royal Marines to you and me) would take some doing.

One example of making space for accommodation was stripping out the hydraulic catapults ram-room to enable the creation of an electrical/radio department mess deck for about a hundred men, shoe-horned into Compartment 5F, directly under Compartment 4F, the main aft dining hall, a handy location indeed.

Removal of the hydraulic rams was filthy work for the dockyard workers. The hydraulic ram cylinders had very thick walls. Cutting them up with blowtorches was hot filthy work producing a continual outbreak of fires as there was a lot of grease and other congealed substances on the deck. Horrible.

The ship's hull plating had to be removed on both sides of the compartment to enable the cut-up pieces to be moved outside. A real dirty, dangerous and unpleasant job for the dockyard workers, and not much fun for us fire-watchers, our main duty for many months

At the time we all wondered what our accommodation would be like once the compartment was fitted out with bunk beds, seats, foot-lockers and personal kit lockers. It turned out not to be too bad; kind of cosy in places but the ship, originally a fresh-air ship, had its ventilation systems fully upgraded with full air-conditioning and recirculation, and unlike my second ship, the atmosphere in the mess deck was always pleasant no matter the outside weather.

The mess deck was also quiet. Being a good distance from the bow it didn't suffer so much from the ship's motion in a storm, unlike the officer's wardroom accommodation at the stern of the ship, which suffered from the ship's motion plus strong propeller vibrations at high speed, which was common during the commission.

*

NOW, HERE A wee story comes to mind. One week I was assigned fire-watch duties in one of the main engine rooms. Large diameter steam pipes entered from the adjacent boiler room. As you might expect they were heavily lagged with insulation covered in heavily painted canvas. In a quiet and dark corner of the compartment, the lagging was well worn, quite soft and clearly someone had been sleeping there.

I must admit I did take the occasional snooze myself. Anyway, one morning at the start of another long day, I arrived in this engine room compartment to find a dockyard 'matey', as they were called, fast asleep in my favoured spot. His foreman was doing the rounds so I thought it best to wake him and keep him out of trouble.

'What's the f..in' time?' he asked.

'Eight-thirty,' I replied.

'Wot at night. Why are you down here at this hour? There is no evening shift in this area,' the dockyard matey replied.

'Err. It's morning,' I replied.

'Oh my F....in' God,' he replied and rushed off.

My partner in crime who had previous dockyard experience told me the dockyard matey was in real trouble.

'And pray tell me why,' I asked.

'The clock, of course', he replied. 'He didn't clock-out yesterday. Now he's still here and he hasn't clocked-in. He's lost pay assuming, he doesn't get the sack.'

Poor chap. He'd taken an afternoon nap the day before and slept all the way through to the next morning. No doubt his mates couldn't find him and thought no more about it.

*

BACK TO THE ship, which had a fully riveted hull so the replacement of worn or rusted plating required the 'platers' and their 'riveting gangs'.

The riveting gangs would set up their braziers as close as possible to the area required as the platers wrestled new plates into position with words of inventive encouragement using traditional dockyard language. It certainly increased my vocabulary.

Then white-hot rivets are 'heave-hoed' through the air by the rivet gang using their long metal tongs. At the work site the rivet was caught in mid-flight, inserted into the awaiting hole, then two rivet guns one on either side of the plate banged away as the rivet is formed into a never to be moved again fastening. The noise is incredible. It is one of the most dangerous dirty and skilled jobs in the dockyard. Their wages were not commensurate at all.

(Local News; The government, via the local council, generally refused planning permission for new businesses to move or set-up shop in the Portsmouth area citing 'the national interest or some other concerns'. Thus the Dockyard was the main employer in the city and with few other alternatives, folk had the choice of working in the dockyard travelling away from home or moving away. Wages in the Dockyard were kept quite low.)

Anyway, walking unintentionally into the flight path of a white-hot rivet was not advised. I'm sure you will understand. Had a few close calls myself. The riveting gang would always offer advice in the usual brusque manner. The 'F' word featured prominently in this advice.

*

Portsmouth Field Gun Team

RNB PORTSMOUTH WAS the home of the Portsmouth Field Gun Team, one of the premier events at the Royal Military Tattoo held in London each year. I was fascinated to be so close to such an amazing experience.

The Field Gun Run was a tribute to the Royal Navy's action during the Boer War in 1899 when cannons from *HMS Powerful* and *Terrible* were hauled to the town by the ship's naval brigade to defend Ladysmith against the Boer forces. On returning to Britain the guns were paraded through London and their actions demonstrated at the Royal Naval & Military Tournament.

The first competition took place at the Royal Tournament in 1907. After WWII the competitions took place between teams from Her Majesty's Naval Base (HMNB) Portsmouth, HMNB Devonport and the Fleet Air Arm. The competition has been described as the toughest team sport in the world. It is certainly one of the most daring.

The last official competition took place on 2nd August 1999, killed off by the pen pushers at the MOD (Ministry of Disasters), so taxpayer's money could be wasted in other directions. A proud and unique British naval tradition has been lost to the nation and even now this history is being cast aside.

The spectacle was one of the best performed by men with courage, strength and a hundred per cent team spirit.

The RN Museum information sheet describes the competition: The 'gun run' is divided into three sections. The first second is the 'run out'. The 'second section' is the 'run back'. The third section is called the 'run home'.

The combined weight of the gun barrel and gun carriage is 1,250 lbs. As soon as the last man (nicknamed the flying angel) is across the chasm the rig is collapsed and three rounds are fired to simulate a rearguard action.

A four-minute run was first recorded in 1948 and a three-minute run in 1962. In the latter days runs just under three minutes were achieved. Just magical.

Being a spectator during the training period in Portsmouth barracks I was able to see why this magnificent competition was so special. Every component of the gun and its limber is very heavy, testing the strength of each team member. The lightest components are the iron-bound oak wheels (120lb) carried singly by one person on the shoulder as he holds onto the traveller as it crossed the 'chasm'.

The secret is to keep every component moving so as to reach a condition approaching levitation. The strength of man has the force to keep it in control, but if the component ever stops moving, especially the gun barrel, the full force of gravity takes over crushing and maiming anybody in range.

Thus, during the 'run' in front of the public audience, the true sense of the potential danger is missing to a large extent. During training, all is revealed.

Another very important secret of achieving a fast time is the tension in the wire across the chasm. I saw the Portsmouth team sling the barrel across the chasm for more than two days whilst the Chief GI adjusted the wire tensioning bottle-screw until he was happy that the wire would stretch no more and the calibrated tension gave the performance he was looking for.

The bottle-screw used to apply the tension is, or rather was, a very accurately machined item capable of precise calibration. The Chief GI in charge of this part of the 'run' kept his secrets very close to his chest.

I was taking lunch in the barracks on the first day their season training commenced. The dining hall had an area reserved for the Field Gun Run team as they all came marching in 'fit as a fiddle' in their new attire putting on the style. A special diet was provided with lots of eggs, thick steaks and massive amounts of hydrocarbons.

Fast forward one week, after a gruelling experience out on the cinder track, and oh what a transformation. Many were hobbling and many obscure parts of the body were wrapped up in bandages, plasters, plaster-casts, et al. Not so 'jack-me lad' now. The cinder dust was ingrained into all exposed skin and head bandages were much in evidence.

At the same time as the Field Gun Team set about their training programme, the navy introduced a new event to the Military Tattoo, the Naval Hornpipe a throwback to Admiral Nelson's day.

It is thought the hornpipe, as a dance, began around the 16th century on English sailing vessels. But the dance probably became associated with sailors in 1740 when the dancer Yates performed a hornpipe in the character of a 'Jack Tar' at Drury Lane Theatre.

The movements were those familiar to sailors of that time: 'looking out to sea' with the right hand to the forehead then to the left, lurching as in heavy weather and giving the occasional rhythmic tug to their breeches both fore and aft.

The hornpipe dancers started their training programme a few weeks later and shared the same reserved area in the dining hall with a similarly enhanced diet.

Needless to say, the field gun crew started to take the Mickey and after a few weeks the situation started to get a bit tense. The Chief GIs in charge of their respective teams decided to nip this nonsense in-the-bud. Each team was invited to experiment with the others team's event.

The hornpipe dancers gave it much thought and it was no surprise when their collective voice said (and here I quote with great accuracy), 'You must be fuckin' joking.'

However, the field gun crew Chief GI insisted that his boys should attempt the hornpipe dance programme. After all, it had been described as 'sissy boys stuff' fit for only those 'weaklings', 'those big girl's blouses'.

And so it turned out that after an hour, just one miserable hour of training, dancing the naval hornpipe, the members of the field gun crew collapsed on the floor of the gymnasium panting for breath, surprised at their fate. At least they had made the attempt.

To say that the field gun run event was dangerous was the understatement of all time. Only real men were chosen to take part and in truth, it was more like a club than anything else. Team members I recall rarely competed in two sequential events although the officer and Chief GI (Gunnery Instructor) were there for every event.

Finally, rumours about field gun run members' wives did the rounds. Their menfolk were super fit and super strong. You can probably guess the rest.

*

'Tug' Wilson and the Norton Specials

TUG D. WILSON was a special person, a nice bloke all round. He was a motorcyclist and amateur TT rider of the highest order. He was the leader a like-minded group of bikers. Pompey Barracks, at the time, could put on a display of the best of British, including BSA 'Gold Stars, a Velocette Venom, two Matchless G85, a Triumph Bonneville T120 and an AJS 7R racer. The cream of British motorcycles.

Tug returned from his last posting in Australia with two very special motorbikes, a 350cc Manx International and 500cc Manx Special.

These were ex-works machines, consumed high-octane petrol, the engines lubricated by Castrol 'R', that wonderful vegetable based oil that gives off that very special smell on the race track.

These racetrack Norton's could only be jump or bump started. One guy who Tug reluctantly let have a ride had the unnerving experience of performing the jump start, the bike shot forward and he was left just holding on to the handlebars. That a bad outcome did not result was an act of God. These two motorcycles were undoubtedly the real deal.

Tug had an interesting story. He had been based in Australia with his two bikes. At the time he was a Pomey better known as Petty Officer Mechanical Engineer (POME).

During holiday time he applied for extended leave to take part in the Australian GP. He was told he could only have extended leave for approved: sports: rugby, cricket and at a pinch, football. His divisional officer was the usual upper-class twit, one of the many that hide hopefully unnoticed in the ranks of the RN.

Tug being Tug said 'Fuck it,' and went anyway. His shipmates did not expect to see their rebellious friend again but the Military Police, 'the crushers', noted that a certain Mr Wilson had come third in the said GP. So they travelled a considerable distance to arrest him and bring him back

Now he had been demoted to just an ordinary ME1 but he didn't care. He treated himself to the last of the new Norton 750cc Dominators in bright red. He was very pleased with it until he discovered the recently released upgraded model came with a sexy black frame and stunning silver tank with black lines.

Not to be outdone, his new pride and joy was completely disassembled. The engine was smuggled down to the ship for some serious TLC. The cylinders were bored out, the head skimmed and the inlet and exhaust ports polished to excess. All the component parts of the engine were 'blueprinted' and if there was two of anything they were made to weigh exactly the same to improve the balance of the engine and reduce vibration.

The Radio Department inherited the fuel tank where our resident three 'badgeman' (a 12 year man) did the honours making a very fine paint sprayer and spending hours mixing and matching different paints until he achieved exactly the colour required.

When the Dominator had been rebuilt it looked perfection but more importantly, it had been upgraded almost to ex-works status. Tug Wilson was careful to give his pride and joy time to settle down to get the engine run-in and bedded down.

At the next long weekend, Tug took his Manchurian chum, another

ME1 known as 'Goofy' who looked and acted the part to perfection.

Tug's journey to Manchester involved using the dreaded A34, the main road from Southampton to the Black Country known as the 'World's Longest Lane'. It sure was a pain then. Today, it's still hard work. That the A34 connected the industrial heartland of the UK with one of the biggest ports in the country did not seem to connect with those in government.

Anyway, Tug reached Manchester in the same journey time that most sensible people using this route would take to reach the southern outskirts of Birmingham. Remember there are no motorways or dual carriageways in this story.

On the many bends in the road, as Tug pressed his pride and joy hard into all the corners, Goofy amused himself picking daisies from the roadside verge and just as Tug Wilson was about to enter his home city Goofy draped a huge daisy chain over his good friend's shoulders.

*

The guy with the 'Vincent Black Shadow'

DURING THIS ERA in Pompey Barracks, there was a little known midnight competition by the more adventurous members of the motorcycle fraternity. The barracks had a 'south gate' the official manned main gate plus a 'north gate' only used to provide easy access to the Dockyard during working hours.

The competition consisted of the challenge to depart the south gate, reach a hundred miles per hour and then brake before hopefully not crashing into the locked unmanned north gate.

Needless to say, the regulators did not approve, but tough on them. Attempts made on the record were few and far between. Even waiting for the right conditions required patience. Braking hard on wet cobbles was considered stupid by anybody sober enough to evaluate the problem.

The Vincent Black Shadow was a 1,000cc monster of a bike. Dad had one attached to his sidecar combination. Dad was 6'2" and even he had trouble kick starting it.

The owner, an SNCO, or senior non-commissioned officer, was a recluse compared to the free spirit of the gang but he had listened to the stories that started off being true, but given the time they morphed into the most unlikely of legends.

One evening having listened to the booze-fuelled bullshit over the preceding months he saw the conditions were just right, collected a couple of his chums as witnesses and completed the challenge. Just. He stopped micro-inches from the north gate. Everyone scarpered sharpish as the duty night guard rushed to arrest everyone. And that just about ended the days of the competition.

*

Fun at Bank Holiday Weekend – Southsea Beach - 1962

THERE CAME ONE Bank Holiday weekend, a bit of a scuffle concerning the two groups in the English community known as the Mods and the Rockers who had used Southsea Beach on a number of occasions as a convenient meeting place for a ritual known as a good punch-up.

The congregation making up these two groups were generally Londoners and violence was accepted as a means to an end. The Portsmouth Police were well aware of what was about to happen and were not well pleased.

What happened on this occasion did not follow the normal pattern because the day before the event, believed to be a Thursday, a new recruit to the Royal Marine's Eastney Barracks, at the far end of the beach, complete with his new haircut, was mistaken for one of the Mods and given a good going over by the Rockers.

The RM Commandos in the Barracks were not well pleased. It was their turf that the incomers were playing on. And so what happened next, according to legend, was the Warrant Officer, the senior SNCO in the Barracks, let it be known, unofficially of course, that the coming long weekend leave should be voluntarily delayed. Apart from a few urgent cases with family needs, the Commandos, not at all happy about one of their number being done over, 'volunteered' to be available for whatever was being planned for the weekend.

So, it came to pass, that the Mods and Rockers duly convened on Southsea beach, but did not notice the extra number of badly dressed 'tourists' in the vicinity wearing scruffy rig and military hobnailed boots.

Before the Mods and Rockers could engage in their planned violence competition, the tourists, aka the men of the Royal Marines Commandos, got stuck into both groups with a vengeance. There is violence, and there is professional violence.

The mayhem was in full swing when the heavy mob from the Portsmouth Police Force arrived, anxious to put this event to bed. As the Police

Superintendent alighted from his truck, a size sixteen hand landed on his shoulder, the Warrant Officer introduced himself and please could the police give his boys a few more minutes to clear matters up.

The Police Superintendent, no doubt smiling to himself, spent a few minutes reorganising his force until he received a nod and a wink from the Warrant Officer, who loudly blew his whistle, his men melted away, leaving the visitors from out of town in a sorry state, who then received the attention, believed not to be too gentle, of the police as they were rounded up and arrested.

And, so it came to pass, that Southsea Beach was removed from the list of venues that the Mods and Rockers liked to hold their annual get together.

*

The 1952 Victor Mature Movie – RNB Cinema

SUNDAY, LATE AFTERNOON. It was winter, it was cold, it was rain, sleet, hail, it was the second Sunday known as blank week and nobody had a red bean to their name. Just plain bloody miserable.

Somebody suggested going to the Barracks cinema.

'What's on,' came the reply.

'It's a Victor Mature' special,' came the answer.

'Oh, bollocks,' came the final verdict, but we all went anyway. The movie had all the signs of being truly dreadful. The plot, what there was of it, set in Roman times. The usual format; saving Christians from the lions, making the lions go hungry and saving the leading lady with big tits from danger with not a blonde hair out of place. Yawn.

We all sat at the back of the cinema so that if the film was that bad we could all make a quick escape. The film started to roll. The sound reproduction was awful and the colour of the film was grim. Before the rush towards the exit, the crew from a newly arrived submarine arrived in the cinema having bathed (submariners do stink when they come from the diesel boats) changed into civvies and grabbed a late lunch.

They proceeded to sit in the front row anxious not to miss anything. The scene was transformed. As the film plodded its way through the dreary plot these guys set too and sent it up big time. I mean it was hilarious, side-splitting in fact.

Their comments were, in no particular order, obscene (naturally), sexist (ditto), highly observant, irreverent, anti-Christ, anti-most other things including other religions, including his holiness the Pope who did not escape various comments. It was all very, very intelligent stuff. (Peter Cook standard and higher.)

My group tried to join-in but matching the leaders in the send-up was near impossible. How I wished I could have filmed the proceedings from the back of the cinema.

The next morning, the ship's company mustered outside the barrack blocks on another miserable day ready to march to the ship for another exciting day.

However, instead of the order to turn left towards the North Gate the ship's company turned right towards the South Gate. How exciting we all thought.

The ship's company marched in columns of three to.... the Barber's shop, where three masters of the thirty-second-haircut were waiting. Actually, they were just a tad quicker; mine was twenty seconds. The all-original basin haircut without the basin. God, it was cold around the ears as the ship's company marched the weary route down to the ship and another day's fire watching.

*

Part 2 – The Commission

THE MUCH-ANTICIPATED DAY arrived when the ship's company mustered by division on the parade ground of RNB and marched to the ship. The days of being accommodated in barracks had come to an end. The ship's company would now live onboard, the smallest and youngest ship's company the navy had ever assigned to one of their larger and more important ships.

The scope of the dockyard's work was well behind schedule but a week later five hundred workers were released from *HMS Triumph* and rushed aboard *HMS Albion*.

Vital decisions like the layout of the radio room whose mock-up varied daily over many months were suddenly confirmed by the dockyard superintendent who saw that navy had no real complaints and said 'just build it as it was'. Time-up.

I was there and this is what happened. What was the prevarication all about?

Thus, the ship's rebuild programme went from being three months late to two weeks late. Our chief, Chief Procter, a bearded Scot with a dour sense of humour that actually worked providing you understood where he was coming from, informed us youngsters that this was the natural way the dockyard worked.

In no time at all ship's systems were being brought on-line, the dockyard workers hurrying-up to finish, grabbing what overtime they could before being assigned to the next ship. The crew was left to pick-up the pieces. The long slow slog to clean, wash down, scrub and paint all the obscure compartments not visited by the dockyard began. The process took many months, well beyond the work-up period.

And thus, the great ship came to life. The radio department welcomed its divisional officer and department head Big Jack, an ex-Chief Radio Artificer who had made it into the wardroom as a sub-lieutenant SD through sheer hard work and dedication.

Big Jack became a very influential officer on-board as he became the captain of the officer's deck-hockey team.

After he had spent some time with his department, he called a meeting in the workshop. We were told we had to go through the formal process of volunteering for the forthcoming commission, which was to be a Far East, eighteen-month assignment. Now, in the navy, a volunteer is someone who didn't understand the question and this was a question we all understood very well.

We all knew this moment would come from the rumours circulating in the ship. One of the married men told Big Jack that eighteen months from home was a tough call.

Big Jack smiled reminding everybody that we had all enjoyed well over a year on easy street, a home draft. If we did not wish to volunteer we would be returned to Commodore Naval Draft (CND) for an active assignment. This meant a ship going on operations.

The Radio Department, mostly us youngsters from my class at *HMS Collingwood*, were not too concerned. The ship's programme was to sail for the Far East with Christmas in Singapore, and New Year in Australia. Then visits were planned to the Philippians, Japan and Hong Kong.

Gosh, a 'Wagon Lit' or 'Thomas Cook' special. 'Join the navy and see the world' or so the posters said. Hum, we all thought; tempting.

The final piece of information, deliciously slipped into the conversation, was *HMS Eagle*, a real beast of an aircraft carrier close to finishing refit in Plymouth and that the press gangs were out in force. There was just the tiny, tiny chance (i.e. 100%) of us all being sent there. Someone on our ship had been having discrete conversations with CND. After all, the crew that had been involved in the refit and conversion knew the ship very well, a big bonus for the department heads.

I looked at Tarpey, who had his hand raised high. We all followed his example. Better the devil and all that. Big Jack thanked us for our support. I added the line (stolen from one Spike Milligan) 'that we would wear it always'.

*

The Ship's Commissioning Day

1ST AUGUST 1962 was the ship's big event, Commissioning Day. HRH the Duke of Edinburgh (commonly known in the navy as 'Phil-the-Greek', no disrespect of course) flew his helicopter on-board, heaved his flying gear at his ADC, was welcomed on board by Captain Colin D. Madden and with the immortal words, 'This shouldn't take too long, then the bar can be opened.' How sailors love a man who understands.

The ship's company was lined up by divisions on the recently painted flight deck with its eight sexy helicopter landing rings (known as 'spots') painted in bright white. The Royal Marine band played suitable nautical music during the inspections, the ceremony began, fine speeches were made, the ship's 'Sky Bosun' or Padre blessed the proceedings and invited God to look after everybody and keep us all safe forever.

Jolly good show, what!

Then it was down to the hanger for tea and sticky buns for the ladies and pints all round for everybody else.

Now the ship was ready to do stuff, i.e. work-up. More like hard bloody work starting very soon.

*

Refuelling with Avgas Fuel

ONE WEEKEND, THE Captain cancelled all leave as the ship had to be refuelled with Avgas or aviation gasoline or spirit as it is sometimes known. The ship slipped out of the harbour to anchor in the middle of the Solent off Spithead to await the tanker bringing the dangerous cargo.

The ship would receive two Fleet Air Arm Helicopter Squadrons 845 & 846. The latter squadron was equipped with Westland Whirlwind HAS-7s, a 1950s design with piston engines. 845 Squadron had the more modern Westland Wessex HU.5 helicopters powered by gas turbine engines.

Onboard aircraft carriers, Avgas is treated with the respect it deserves. It's a very high octane fuel for high compression piston engines and is highly flammable.

Ex-WWII British aircraft carriers stored their Avgas inside a very thick walled armoured tank deep inside the ship. The tank is hidden inside a flooded armoured cofferdam. During the refit and conversion, I found exactly where and entered the cofferdam to look inside the Avgas tank. These areas were only ever opened up during major refits.

To deliver the Avgas to the flight deck, seawater is pumped into the bottom of the Avgas tank. Armoured pipelines, laid in armoured conduits, carry the Avgas from the top of the tank to sophisticated filtration systems at the side of the flight deck.

The fuel is checked for quality before being pumped into the aircraft. After fuelling the aircraft, the fuel lines are flushed with water back down to the Avgas tank. Avgas readily floats on water and the two fluids keep separated.

The Avgas tanker moored up alongside with the ship locked down in 'Damage Control - Condition One', all compartments sealed with very little movement allowed on board. Restrictions including no smoking or naked lights, all strictly enforced.

Before fuel transfer commenced two dockyard picket launches patrolled the area to maintain a five hundred yard exclusion zone. The operation completed just after lunch, and the ship returned to normal.

*

Work-up

IT WAS SOON afterwards that the ship began 'work-up trials' based in Portland, firing guns at towed targets, exercising fire crews, damage control and repair crews, refuelling the ship at sea and a host of other training exercises. Helicopters arrived and landed on-board; some stayed.

Next, the ship went to Plymouth to embark the Royal Marines of 41 Commando and their impedimenta as well as the 145 Commando Regiment Royal Artillery. Military work-up commenced, beaches were invaded, the 'enemy' routed and the 'wounded' recovered to test the ship's sickbay facilities.

So what is it like to live on a warship at sea? The accommodation is crowded and cleanliness and tidiness is paramount. Almost as bad as being at home with Mother in a bad mood.

The ship's company is divided into two watches Port and Starboard. Each watch is further divided into two parts, 1st & 2nd. Watch-keepers are required 24/7 when at sea and in harbour to look after ship security, the steam boilers when fired up utility systems and electrical power generation systems.

At sea, all being well, only one part of one watch is required for duty including the officers and seamen on the bridge, the operations room and communications, the manning the ship's seaboat, fire party and damage control parties, the engine room staff and the electrical staff monitoring the ship's generators not forgetting the Royal Marine posted on the quarter deck in case of man-overboard.

Otherwise, the crew in each department work days from early morning to the time for the evening meal unless they were required after-hours to turn-too for any number of reasons no matter how long it is going to take.

In the morning, in the mess decks, one person is assigned as cook to clean, polish and to make sure everything is ship-shape. Mess decks have to be kept clear if the damage control teams need to fight fires and pump seawater from a compartment.

During the refit and conversion all the mess deck accommodations were equipped with sprung fold-up bed frames and bedding including the mattress contained in a bed-bag, zipped closed when not in use.

The ship was also upgraded for entering a nuclear fall-out zone so the ventilation systems could be reset to full recirculation. The bonus was the ship was fully air-conditioned and a strict programme of keeping the air filters clean meant the internal atmosphere was generally pretty good.

One of the senior chief mess decks was always too hot especially as it was high up under the flight deck forward. A hunt was ordered and the related air filter, installed in an almost impossible to find location, was replaced. From then on the chiefs froze their tits off for the remainder of the commission.

*

AFTER WORK-UP AND foreign service leave, and with the ship fully loaded with Royal Marines, squadron's pilots and aircrew, RA gunners' et al, the ship finally sailed for the Far East.

We headed for Gibraltar with a bumpy ride through the Bay of Biscay, my first time at sea. Sitting with my back against a nice warm funnel on the lee side helped me become accustomed to the movement of the ship. The ship's motion was a great sleep aid, very relaxing and better than being seasick.

At Gibraltar, we all took photographs, sent postcards home to Mummy and avoided the Watneys Red Barrel, a beer which did little but cause headaches in the morning. Anybody that bought those damn Spanish castanets was invited to use them on the aft round-down of the flight deck.

Two days later the ship sailed to take part in an exercise in Libya, Royal Marines v The British Army (we won) and then to Malta.

Here it is useful to know the general format of an 'assault' by the Royal Marines. The basics are, assuming air cover is not a problem, the helicopters drop half of the force in a location of maximum disadvantage to the enemy. The marines are equipped with Land Rovers of every description including a few armed with the 120mm recoilless rifle which is a fearsome weapon in its own right.

When the enemy, usually a much larger force, has organised its defence and got its sorry act together, the helicopters drop the remaining force of marines behind the enemy lines in the rear and this multiplies the force being applied by the commandos.

The ship was also equipped with four landing craft used for ferrying troops ashore, bringing back the wounded, but more importantly taking 'Jolly Jack' to a nice secluded sandy beach for a 'Banyan' equipped with the necessities of life, cold beer, beer, more beer, suntan lotion, pick-nick hampers, sun umbrellas etc. etc.

Malta was fun. The US 5th Fleet was in town. So was *HMCS Bonaventure*, a small ex-British WWII aircraft carrier manned by the Royal Canadian Navy. The radio department went ashore to sample the delights of the Maltese nightlife. Naked ladies were promised and inviting bars. It was early so the first bar welcomed us all until it was time to leave to for the promised venue of entertainment.

When it was time, having settled our dues in the bar, the team departed only to run straight into heavily armed Shore Patrols. We noticed the street intersections being guarded by Maltese Police riot squads. Clearly, something was amiss. We were told we could stay in the bar or be escorted back to the docks to take the ferry back to our ship. Sod it, we all voted to go back but what was wrong?

Well, it seems the Royal Canadian Navy was involved in something of a major conflict with their American cousins. Being outnumbered ten to one did not seem to be a problem and there was a real punch-up going on that transformed itself into something more serious.

So, that was all we saw of Malta. We didn't even get time to take happy snaps to send back to Mummy. The ship sailed to catch a southbound convoy in the Suez Canal. The ship arrived at Port Said only to be delayed by fog in the canal.

Ancient joke: 'Err excuse me Mate. Where are the bleedin' heads (toilet).'
'Port side,' the standard reply.
'Bugger that. Can't wait that long.'
This is, of course, a northbound convoy joke

The ship was delayed. During the wait, a large searchlight was placed at the front of the flight deck by the Canal authorities. Eventually, the ship joined the southbound convoy which met up with the northbound convoy waiting in the Great Bitter Lake about two-thirds of the way south. Seawater flows freely through the canal. North of the lakes the current flows south in summer, north in the winter. There are no locks in the canal.

It took two frustrating days to reach the open sea at Suez. Personally, I found the experience fascinating, very scenic. Our department had no work as all radio and radar systems were shut down except for the small navigation radar, due to the Russian monitoring stations perched upon the hills to the west overlooking the canal.

This was my first experience of electronic warfare. The British are very good at it. It was a major part of the WWII Bletchley Park story, otherwise known as Station 'X' (meaning ten). During WWII, the 'Y' Stations dotted around the UK would monitor every electronic signal sent by the Germans. The operators wrote down the transmitted Morse code, which was then sent to Bletchley for decryption

By the time I joined the navy the game had moved on. Many were the occasions when I was woken up in the middle of the night, usually midnight UK time, to insert some small components into a radio transmitter just to make it sound different from the previous record held by others i.e. the USSR.

Anyway, next stop was Aden where the ship discharged 41 Commando and inherited 40 Commando from *HMS Bulwark*, our sister ship thankfully on her way home to Blighty.

Aden was OK, with its many duty-free shops willing to make a good deal. I bought a decent SLR camera and an Omega wristwatch. It was quite safe so in the evening one could visit the military clubs serving ice-cold beer and decent seafood snacks.

The ship sailed for East Africa. The next exercise with 40 Commando would be at Malindi, Kenya followed by a brief visit to Mombasa where the ship took on bunkers (the heavy fuel oil for the ship's boilers), and diesel for the electrical generators.

*

EARLY DECEMBER 1963, *HMS Albion* set sail for Singapore. We all looked forward to a fascinating visit to the Far East. It all sounded very exotic. Then everything changed.

On the second morning after the ship's departure from Mombasa, I was working in the Island's lower assault operations room, where the planning and conduct of an assault by the marines would be carried out. The centre of the compartment contained two large cabinets with glass tops. Inside the cabinets, a projector shone the display of a radar transmitter so that maps or charts could be overlain on the projected image to gain accuracy in the operations.

Having finished my task on the first unit I went below for stand easy, better known as a break for refreshment. I returned to find Lt Cmdr Miles busy with papers spread all over both units. He apologised but I said it was no problem.

I looked up at the compass repeaters noticing the course being steered was zero zero five, or almost due north.

Lt Cmdr Miles, the ship's Intelligence Officer, was well known aboard ship. He had a great skill as a cartoonist and could draw very accurate cartoons capturing every detail of the subject person. He drew with the style of the very famous British cartoonist Giles and he signed his work 'by Smiles'.

'Excuse me Sir,' I asked. 'A question if I may.'

'Of course,' he replied.

'If the ship is headed for Singapore should the compass repeaters not show a course of 'zero nine zero or thereabouts?'

'Absolutely.'

'So there is a slight change of plan?' I suggested.

'Indeed,' he replied

'A secret then?' I suggested.

'Absolutely,' he said smiling.

'On this ship that's something new: a 'rumour mill' failure. This should be recorded.'

He laughed telling me the ship was heading to rendezvous with a fleet tanker. I replied that I had seen bunkers being refuelled from lighters in Mombasa. He smiled, and put his fingers to his lips, before resuming his work.

Sometime later an ageing RFA Fleet tanker hove into view her reciprocating engines flat-out, smoke pouring from her funnel. The RFA came alongside the ship's starboard side, and two hoses for bunkers (FFO) were quickly rigged, plus a third hose way up forward for diesel fuel.

Tarpey joined with me on top of the Island to spy on what was going on. Rumours were starting to spread. One of the intercoms from the bridge suggested that the engine room staff were getting busy. What with we thought? After what seemed a considerable length of time all but one refuelling hose was recovered.

I returned to my duties in the Lower Ops Room to find the Lt. Cmdr was still busy with his paperwork. He asked if refuelling had finished? I told him just one FFO hose was still pumping vigorously adding just where was all this fuel being stored?

A question for Commander 'E', he suggested.

'I'll try and perhaps catch him at dinner this evening,' I offered.

'Doubt it, he will be too busy.'

It was at this point that I remembered during the ship's conversion I was on duty in one of the engine rooms on fire watch. There was a gang of men under the deck cleaning out the accumulated filth of the ship's double bottom compartments. A truly dreadful and uncomfortable task. It would be in the ship's double bottoms that all this FFO was being stored.

At that, the intercom burst into life 'Engine room – bridge, thirty minutes notice for eighty per cent full power, thirty minutes.'

'Oh Shit,' I muttered to myself. 'Someone has started a war somewhere and the ship's been invited.'

The intercom from the electrical switchboard control to bridge burst into life announcing three of the four diesel generators were 'on the board' and the more reliable steam driven generators were being disconnected. This confirmed the preparation of the ship for a high-speed dash to somewhere. The ship disconnected the last hose from the RFA and set a fast course to the east.

Back in the radio workshop our illustrious Chief Procter, always connected to what was going, on informed that the ship would be going to ninety per cent full power in two hours' time and all steam driven services were either being disconnected or severely reduced including the ship's main freezers.

An hour later the captain made a broadcast to the ship's company to inform us that the Borneo War was now in progress. So-called rebels, known to be regular soldiers from the Indonesian Army, had attacked positions in various locations in Brunei and that some losses had been sustained by defending forces including a detachment of Royal Marines.

From that moment on the ship moved into high gear. The reduction of defect lists in all departments became top priority, none more so than the Radio Department. Big ships require a lot of communication channels during operations.

The Royal Marines began training to build-up their battle readiness, both mentally and physically.

Two days later the ship came within range of another RFA waiting to discharge dry stores. No time to slow down so the replenishment was carried out by 845 Squadron flying the larger Wessex type S61 helicopters. The ship passed the RFA at a fearsome rate and the helicopters were having a hard time catching up with the ship with a large sling carrying stores hanging beneath.

It appeared to be touch and go for the last helicopter as it reached the landing spot just in front of the aft hanger lift, then without any ceremony, dumped a wire sling full of broom handles and large containers of detergent amongst other vital supplies on the empty landing spot before expiring on the next adjacent landing spot. Rumour was he was running on vapour as he reached the ship. From my favourite goofing position on top of the ship's Island, it was quite a show.

Occasionally one could sneak onto the bridge without getting chased away. As the ship hurtled down the Malacca Straits the tension was very high at night in such a crowded waterway. It certainly was in the ops room, with twice the number of operators staring at their radar screens.

The next morning *HMS Albion* entered the channel that led around Singapore Island to the Naval Dockyard. It was clear the captain was still in a big hurry. Speed limits? What speed limits? The local fishing community perched at the side of the waterway on their rickety huts standing on stilts in the water would have all felt the passing of this large warship. That they didn't get washed away was a relief.

A few of the department had sneaked into the Admiral's Bridge just below the main bridge. I didn't know a lot about large ship handling in a confined waterway but given the speed at which the ship was approaching the dockyard I sensed the captain was about to perform an infrequently executed manoeuvre and awaited with interest. As the ship approached the naval dockyard the captain already had the helm hard down to port with the port engine building up to full astern.

With the stern of *HMS Albion* swinging hard to starboard she began to shake and spin about her axis. With the ship nearing a 180-degree change in heading the captain achieved a fair amount of sideways movement as the ship drifted sideways into the fenders protecting the harbour wall. Further bursts of engine power brought a successful end to the manoeuvre.

Four harbour tugs moved quickly to push with their bows to hold the ship against the harbour wall as the dockside gang concentrated on getting the fuel oil hoses connected up. As the fuel oil hoses started to snake vigorously under the pressure of refilling the ship's depleted tanks the dockside gang completed the docking of *HMS Albion*.

Looking down at the crowded dockside the Royal Marine 3rd Third Brigade HQ was waiting to embark with a large assortment of heavily laden transports. Other troops of various persuasions were also seen waiting to embark. Quite where they would all sleep that night was a mystery but any spare deck space on the ship would have been the only option.

The ship sailed just after midnight. Everybody not on duty grabbed some much-needed rest to prepare for the coming busy day. I doubt if the cooks in the galley had any rest at all. With a ship bursting at the seams with hungry troops and helicopter squadrons' maintenance teams preparing and arming their aircraft, it was a busy night for all.

The ship arrived in Brunei the next evening and there was a great departure of all our guests. The flight deck aft of the aft hanger lift became empty when up to the present it had been a large parking lot for army Land Rovers of every description including first aid, communications, the large recoilless rifles, troop carrying, and the RA pack howitzers et al.

*

FROM THEN ON the ship spent most of its commission trooping to/from Singapore. Not very exciting at all. Sometimes we were given leave in Singapore, which we found to be a fascinating island, scruffy, dirty, old-fashioned and fun. Bugis Street was the main attraction, a community full of street traders selling everything from the freshest Chinese food, exotic silk bedroom attire for those with wives and girlfriends plus the usual junk for tourists.

MEMORIES AND FORGETFULNESS

The other community in Bugus Street concentrated on promoting the world's oldest profession. The girls were everywhere, clearly the main tourist attraction. Some years later when Prime Minister Lee Quan Yew had transformed the Island, he tried to close the trade down but the fall in international tourism prompted a return to a more ordered and somewhat revised situation.

However, in the early sixties, there were certain things one had to know. The really beautiful exceptional females were the in-betweens, neither boy nor girl. Some of these transvestites were so extreme so it was hard to tell. A group from my mess deck were investigating the delights of Bugis Street guided by someone's relation who was stationed on one of the many RAF airbases. His experience was, to say the least very valuable. He advised:

Trick #1, refrain from putting a hand up the mini-skirt as that did not always give the required information.

Trick #2 could generally be relied upon, which was to sit said person, allegedly a female, on one's knees. Then, place an open hand on one knee and stroke downwards. Smooth as a baby's bottom was good. Anything else, err! Not so good.

Next, stroke hand in an upwards motion returning to the knee. Any sensation other than the first was the signal that all was err, different.

Far safer to stick to enjoying the Chinese food and a few beers. I guess we all know that these types of communities can handle any trouble themselves. They always had their minders lurking in the background.

In the 1960s, Singapore was not entirely safe as the locals could riot at any time but if one kept the peace and spent one's hard earned pay, all was well. The Chinese like money.

One time, as the ship returned from Brunei to Singapore Naval Dockyard I enjoyed the delights of being 'volunteered' for the ship's anti-riot squad. So, at some godforsaken time in the morning after a rushed breakfast, the anti-riot squad mustered on the flight deck fully booted and spurred carrying a trusty rifle (no bullets) to be flown ashore to an army base for a day's training in dealing with the locals.

I guess us anti-riot squad volunteers thought this was all a bit OTT until we were shown a movie of a full-blown Chinese riot in a crowded Singapore street. Very, very violent indeed.

So, we trained how to march in protective columns and manoeuvre in a closed-in street in a square formation. I was placed on one side, my appointed task was to look-up and over to the other side of the squad to shoot at any threat from the higher floors of a building. Me, fire a Lee Enfield rifle without huge amounts of shoulder padding? I don't think so.

Anyway, the ship's squad did quite well, or so we were told by our army instructors, but before we could all feel pleased with ourselves we were shown a second movie on how the Army's Black Watch regiment did it.

Oh dear, we didn't even come close. Would you face a load of hairy Jocks in their kilts 'sans' knickers, clearly at one with their rifles and a dedicated love of violence. Self-preservation would surely reign; 'absence of body being better than peace of mind'.

Singapore had, still has, many interesting tourist attractions including the Tiger Balm Gardens. The Cold Store in Orchard Road, where it was really cold and a favourite Mecca for shoppers. It was well named. Tourist ladies in their flimsy dresses couldn't wait to rush in to sample the delights of shopping.

Among the more offbeat things to do in Singapore was to go and look at Changi Jail. During the Japanese occupation, it acquired a truly dreadful reputation with its treatment of British prisoners-of-war. I was told that if I went to look at the outside of the Changi Jail I would feel some of the horror. And so it was. A truly hideous looking building with a truly hideous history. Now it had been returned to being a state prison. The new prime minister of Singapore had many of his political rivals inside, just to keep them safe.

*

HMS ALBION SPENT over a year trooping between Singapore and Borneo. Entertainment at sea, and in harbour, was a matter of using one's own time to do things one normally had little time for. Some boxed, the gym was well attended in the main hanger (most if not all of the ship's helicopters were deployed ashore). I received from my parents a marquetry set with two pictures to complete and I still have one kept safe after all these years.

The other diversion was the cinema using a temporary collapsible screen and a Bell & Howell 16mm projector. Cinema operators were required. The ship's welfare fund would pay five bob a show. So, I became a cinema operator.

Once, during the time in Singapore, it was blank week so nobody had a bean to their name and being unable to visit the local dockside Naffi bar, an evening movie was organised. I received the call to show a truly dreadful Cliff Richard musical, all three reels of it.

As I was preparing to show the third reel the credits came up on the screen. Nobody had noticed the missing reel, the plot was that bad. The audience thanked the lord for a short movie. They didn't know how short. Anyway, I still received the five bob for showing it, so all was well.

*

THE SHIP MADE a few visits to Hong Kong for R&R, mainly because Hong Kong had an aircraft factory that could repair helicopters. The jungles of Borneo were very hard on the ship's squadrons and miracles were performed in keeping them flying no matter what.

Generally, they would return to the ship for the more important maintenance procedures to be carried out or for the replacement of failed equipment. It was not unknown for the Chief 'Waffoo' in-charge of aircraft maintenance, as we general service types used to call our brothers in the Fleet Air Arm, to order a suspect Wessex helicopter to be placed at the bow of the ship on #1 spot and shackled tightly to the flight deck for a full engine power test.

The chief would stand in front of the aircraft directing the actions of the pilot. Everybody else was cleared from the flight deck all the way back to the Island and it was not unknown for the engine to shed its turbine blades all over the passing ocean.

Any component on any aircraft has a specified service life. Many were the helicopters flying with life extensions on many of the more important components. One helicopter had a life extension on the airframe, a sure candidate for TLC in the Hong Kong aircraft factory.

For many months 845 and 846 squadrons were the only helicopters engaged in the Borneo War. Where was the RAF became another question? That was a question that would be answered the next time the ship visited Hong Kong.

And so, on the ship's first visit in 1963 Hong Kong looked very different from today. There was a naval dockyard and *HMS Albion* was just able to go alongside the dockyard wall. Outside the dockyard gate was the RN China Fleet Club, a large building used and owned by the men serving in the Far East. The China Fleet Club had small cabins where one could change into civvies and get a really cheap meal, the cheapest being curried eggs and rice with plenty of mango chutney. Some folk even had this for breakfast.

A short walk from the Fleet Club was the district of Wan Chai, which commenced where the business districts of Hong Kong ended. Wan Chai had a street, I think the name was Lockhart Road, which spanned the whole length of Wan Chai from east to west. In the 1950s and 1960s, the road was complete with girlie bars. Nightclubs existed close-by in the red-light district of Jaffe and Lockhart Road.

The challenge for the drinking classes was to start at the end nearest the China Fleet Club and drink one small beer, usually San Miguel, in each bar on the left-hand side of the street to see how far one would reach before returning back-up on the other side of the street. It was considered an impossibility to complete both sides of the street in one attempt but this didn't stop sailors from trying very, very hard.

I think I made the turn at the bottom of the street, once. My friends and I made it into a bar, the Green Bar, with the intention of getting something to eat and try and refresh ourselves with some alcohol dilutant.

I remember it well as in the back of the bar two large apparently very drunk stokers from our ship, definitely able to handle themselves very well in any altercation, were unable to persuade the bar owner to give them free drinks.

They discovered a jukebox in a corner, where for two Hong Kong dollars you could get twenty tunes. They scrapped together four Hong Kong dollars in very small change then invested all of it on Lonnie Donegan's (the King of Skiffle, remember? - I thought not) hit song 'Does Your Chewing Gum Lose Its Flavour on the Bedpost Overnight'.

After about eighteen plays, so we were later told, the owner tried to disconnect the jukebox from the electrical socket on the wall but he decided against it on the grounds he could see the two drunks just spoiling for a fight and did not wish to call the navy shore patrol or the police. So he gave them a bottle of whisky to relocate somewhere else and allow his regulars to return.

We had just one beer with our food and watched the proceedings for as long as we could put up with the repeats of the same damn song before calling it a night to return to the China Fleet Club for a late night meal of curried eggs and plenty of mango chutney.

The next day the US Navy's 'Formosa Patrol' arrived in Hong Kong harbour. Many were the crew numbers that took up invites to visit what was a very old WWII aircraft carrier complete with a wood-lined flight deck. Good food though. Plenty of ice cream and sodas.

Jolly Jack made a sport of hustling the Yanks for all they were worth. Taking advantage I called it. The US sailor's shore leave was restricted to midnight so in our favourite bar we would let the American sailor's muscle in on our favourite bar girl and buy them drinks, which is how they made their money. The drinks were, of course, coloured water, very expensive coloured water. The head bar lady, the Mamma San, made sure her girls stayed on duty. It was virtually impossible to ask a bar girl to take you to her place for some horizontal tango lessons.

Nobody could afford a hotel room, the China Fleet Club was definitely off-limits to females in general and the local bar girls in particular. In polite Chinese society fraternisation with Jolly Jack was never going to happen without a formal invitation.

*

ANOTHER EVENT I found fascinating was the visit of a Hong Kong master tailor and his assistant as they toured the many mess decks in the ship. Just one look revealed the master tailor had been in the business for a very long time. And what wonderful offerings he brought too. Using the very best of British cloths rarely seen in the UK, he could make the most elegant suits, jackets of all descriptions, shirts and all manner of other garments.

Tarpey was the first to stand in a long line to make an order. He described the suit he wished with all the latest fashion details. These were recorded by the master's assistant. To my surprise, he was told the first fitting, of three, would be during the next day at lunch hour. Tarpey protested that he had not been measured by the tailor's tape.

He was shown the order sheet with his the details recorded complete with measurements. Being as the writings were in Chinese it was kind of hard to check the fine detail. The assistant read out the measurements in English as the master tailor ran the measuring tape over Tarpey's frame. All were correct. The master tailor knew the measurements without using a tape. An amazing skill and necessary show to the waiting customers.

*

Jenny's Side Party

WHEN A WARSHIP visited Hong Kong the opportunity arose for the ship's exterior (the hull) paintwork to be touched-up and the ship generally made to look its best. This service was provided by Jenny and her girls. She was a much-loved living legend who for all the colony's constant changes remained the same incomparable institution for over half a century

Much of her life was an enigma. It is generally agreed that she was born in a sampan in Causeway Bay in 1917. Her mother, Jenny One, according to one surviving Certificate of Service, provided sampans and services for the Royal Navy. She brought up her two daughters to help her.

But what Jenny lacked in education she made up more than a hundredfold with her immense experience of ship husbandry, unfailing thoroughness, apparently inexhaustible energy, her unquestionable loyalty, her integrity, her infectious enthusiasm and her innate cheerfulness.

Officially, she volunteered in 1928 until 1997 when the colony became a Special Administrative Region of China and the Royal Navy moved out. She and her team of tireless girls once numbering over thirty unofficially served the Royal and Commonwealth navies by cleaning and painting their ships, attending their buoy jumper's and when dressed in their best Chinese dresses, waiting with grace and charm upon guests at ship's cocktail parties.

Captains and executive officers would find fresh flowers in their cabins and newspapers delivered daily. For all of this, she steadfastly refused ever to accept any payment. Instead she and her side party earned their keep selling soft drinks to the ships' companies and accepting any item of scrap not wanted on board.

Sometimes I had the chance to watch them at work for much longer than I should have. Of great interest was the manner how such slim petit ladies could paint the side of a warship. Using only a small sampan they would tie up along-side no matter how rough the water from the incessant passing marine traffic, wash the salt from the ship's hull with a freshwater hose provided by the ship, then when dry, apply the paint using rollers attached to long bamboo poles.

Using great dexterity the bamboo poles were made to flick the paint-laden roller up and down with great skill. It was said that Jenny and her girls could paint the side of a destroyer in a day's work.

Jenny received many awards for years of long service. She put together an amazing collection of photographs and letters of reference all filled with praise and affection for her. One was a commendation by the Duke of Edinburgh when the Royal Yacht visited the port in 1959.

She was awarded a Long Service and Good Conduct Medal presented to her in 1938 by the captain of *HMS Devonshire* but her most treasured award was the British Empire Medal given to her in the Hong Kong Civilian List of the Queen's Birthday Honours in 1980 and formally named Mrs Ng Muk Kah.

*

DURING MY FIRST visit to Hong Kong, a letter arrived from Mother asking me to visit my godparents, of whom I knew virtually nothing. I probably only met them sometime after my birth. I almost forget the name now but Uncle and Aunty Peggy Gough comes to mind. He was an army major, officer-in-charge of Stonecutters Island, an island quite small and close to the Kowloon side of the bay the mainland side.

The directions advised me to take the ferry to Kowloon and then find the water taxi for the island. These days Stonecutters Island is now part of the mainland. Anyway, I phoned ahead and on the appointed day I reached the island without getting hopelessly lost. As I stepped off from the water taxi I was met by a servant. As we turned the next corner to the OIC's residence I was scared out of my wits by a huge dark figure that turned out to be a Sikh guardsman.

My godfather explained that Stonecutters Island had seen many changes. The Royal Navy established a Radio Interception and Direction-finding Station on the island in 1935 until it was surrendered to the Japanese in WWII. From 1935 to 1939 the base was also the main radio interception unit for the Far East Combined Bureau.

After World War Two, the island became host to British Army units including a maritime unit, but its main purpose was a rather large ammunition depot deep underground. Uncle and Aunty, as I called them, were most welcoming but a return for a longer daytime visit was not possible as the ship was due to sail the next day on the tide.

*

NEXT DAY, AT the height of the tide, two harbour tugs gently pulled the ship away from the dock. The ship slowly got underway heading towards the sea but turned into Junk Bay and anchored. Watching from my favourite goofing position up on the island my shipmates and I wondered quite what was going on.

Anyway, it was at lunch where we learnt that the bottom of the ship, when alongside the dockyard wall, got rather too close to the harbour's muddy bottom at low tide and the ship's many seawater intakes could pick-up goodness what. This required the ship's divers to check the intakes and make sure the protective grills were clear.

It was mid-afternoon when the divers gave the all clear. The ship headed back to Brunei to deliver the repaired helicopters and release them back into the wild.

*

MID-TERM WAS GENERALLY the same routine for months but when operations in Brunei and elsewhere started to settle down the ship returned to Singapore and went into dry dock.

The ship's company moved into *HMS Terror* and its old style, but quite comfortable, barracks. No air-conditioning of course but the barracks had high ceilings. The night breeze made conditions bearable considering that Singapore has a hot and humid climate.

The junior rates lived on the top floor of the *HMS Terror* barrack blocks. Our main run ashore was to Johor Bahru (JB) where we used Amy's Flower Shop & Bar. Then there was Wai Lee Sun Restaurant & Bar, the Rina Restaurant and my favourite of all, The Three Rings.

Anyway, the main reason for dry-docking the ship was to carry out vital repairs and modification to the ship's main engine's high-pressure steam system. This work could not be carried out earlier due to the many operational requirements that were imposed upon the ship. Few knew that the ship had this major problem with connections on the main steam lines. I wondered why this work had not been completed in the refit and conversion, but the subject was very hush hush on board ship.

There were rumours that a sister ship of the same class had burst a steam pipe killing the watch below. One should know that superheated steam is one of the most dangerous gasses that exist. Steam at six hundred degrees centigrade is invisible, as it has no water vapour. The method to search for small leaks is to use the humble lollypop stick.

Steam turbines engines do not tolerate what is call saturated steam as it affects the turbine blades. Really wet steam, when fed to a turbine at full power, the water droplets can strip the turbine blades. That the ship's engine room staff had continued to perform their duties was another unsung moment of bravery.

Still, the time ashore was useful to recharge our batteries. Tropical routine was introduced, which meant an early start to the day when the outside temperature was more pleasant and the sun not so high. Lunch was provided slightly later than normal but that signalled the end of the working day. So, time for the swimming pool or going ashore on a rabbit run, 'rabbit' being navy slang for presents for the family, girlfriends, et al.

One of the must do's was to get a crowd of your chums to cram themselves into a 'fast black' (taxi) and go to the southern end of the island which was downtown to take afternoon tea in the Raffles Hotel which is still famous, even today. Raffles Hotel is a colonial-style luxury hotel in Singapore established by Armenian hoteliers the Sarkies Brothers in 1887. The hotel is named after British statesman Sir Thomas Stamford Raffles the founder of Singapore. To compliment this treat we all went to the hotel's barber shop for a classic wet soap shave with a cut-throat razor, still in common use in that era.

*

Singapore Grand Prix

DURING ONE STOP-OVER in Singapore came the opportunity to enjoy the Singapore Grand Prix, held over a weekend. This was not the current Formula One event, but a yearly event held by the Singapore Motor Club for all comers.

Half of the course consisted of an original winding roadway that passed through a wooded area. The second half consisted of a new bypass built to improve traffic flow. The start and finish line were close to the end of the long bypass.

First up was an invitation event for motorcycles, attended by privateers and Japanese works team keen to improve sales of their products.

Of great interest to us Brits was the main event, unlimited big bikes. An entry of a privateer, a Royal Marine sergeant, had prepared an immaculate British bike, a Norton Dominator, equipped with uprated brakes and a modified twin cylinder blueprinted engine of 750cc.

The Japanese were using the latest multi-cylinder works engines with a smaller capacity than the big British bike, but were much lighter and more nimble. They also had a much higher engine rev range to play with as well.

So the long straight along the bypass up to the Seletar Roundabout favoured the big British bike, but the forest section of the course favoured the smaller Japanese works bikes and their professional riders.

An epic battle ensued. As the big bike entered the fast section of the course, its rider opened it up full. Viewing from a good vantage point halfway along the fast section the sound of the big bike was thrilling.

The big bike trounced the smaller Japanese works bikes on the long straight, but it was a losing battle. However, our hero still managed a third place to mighty roars from the crowd.

With the motorcycle events completed, the competition turned to other main event, an open, all-comers race for motor cars. What a menagerie of cars turned out.

The local rich Chinese boy racers turned out with their 'E' Type Jaguars, hardly race prepared, except for putting more pressure in the tyres. There was a Formula Three entrant, assumed to be race prepared, a couple of little Lotus Elites in John Player colours turned up, plus three works Mini-Coopers from Australia. Hey, but wait, these three Australian cars looked very different. A visit to the pits was required.

What we found were three Mini Coopers fitted with bored-out British Leyland Maxi 1,750cc engines fitted with truly exotic carburettors with long trumpets on the inlets. To fit the inlet trumpets, lightweight bonnets in glass fibre were first strapped on each car so the trumpets could be screwed in through holes in the bonnets. When asked how effective this arrangement was, the Australian mechanic just grinned a huge grin.

The race started in a squeal of tyres. The 'E' type Jaguars made a decent showing up to the roundabout but the winding forest section was not their cup of tea. The end of the winding road ended in a particularly tight reverse hair-pin bend, before the start of the long straight. The lighter more nibble cars soon made it to the front of the pact.

Halfway through the race, the Formula Three car was leading, no surprise there, but snapping at his heels all the way around the course were these three works Mini-Coopers. It was magnificent stuff. At the finish, the Formula Three car just made the line first, but they had been pressed every inch of the way by the Australians.

*

MEMORIES AND FORGETFULNESS

AND SO, THE time ashore was most enjoyable but in no time at all the ship was readied to go to sea. Back to more hard work. One of the occasions was when the ship embarked a very famous Gurkha regiment, the 7th Duke of Edinburgh's Own Gurkha Rifles.

Looking down from my vantage point the Gurkha's were lined up on the dockside their white tropical uniforms beautifully enhanced by the famous colours of the Scottish Black Watch clan.

In front of the drawn-up parade was the regiment's Pipe Band and to this day, having heard many famous Pipe Bands, they were by far the best.

By this time the Brunei Revolt had morphed into a war between an expansionist Indonesia and the new Malaysian Federation backed by Great Britain and the Commonwealth. The conflict became known as the Borneo Confrontation fought largely in the mountains and swamps of Sabah and Sarawak, without much publicity, lasting from 1963 to 1966.

The lack of publicity was considered a great bonus by those in the know. In the jungle, the Gurkha is the most fearsome warrior. You just can't see them until it's too late. The Kukri, that odd looking short weapon with the heavy blade, is the signature weapon of the Gurkhas. The head of an enemy soldier could easily be separated from its shoulders; the Gurkhas have no fear of death.

If a Kukri is drawn, tradition says it must draw blood before being sheathed. The Gurkhas would nick their finger, so I was told.

The following experiences come to mind regarding the Gurkhas

One day the ship prepared for an operation to retrieve a force of Gurkhas from an area which existed of very thick jungle. The operation would be carried out by sending the ship's four landing craft, heavily armed, up the river. The ship anchored offshore as the ship's four landing craft prepared for action.

With a full crew of Royal Marines, four heavy machine guns mounted in the corners of each landing craft, with a full load of fuel and plenty of ammunition, this small fleet set-off up the jungle-lined river to the pick-up point. The marines wondered how the pick-up could be achieved given that the impenetrable jungle came right down to the water's edge.

When the leading landing craft reached the given map reference they found the river formed a long slow bend. On the inside of the bend existed an area of tough knee-high grasses. After checking the area appeared to be safe, but remaining very much on their guard, the lead landing craft beached, lowering its ramp on to the land.

The coxswain-in-charge went to the edge of the ramp, his weapon very much at the ready, when less than two yards away a Gurkha sergeant stood and bid him welcome. Until that moment the Gurkha was not seen. One by one, the Gurkhas stood up and filed onto the landing craft. The Royal Marines were astonished, as the entire space of the grassy area appeared totally deserted.

A second landing craft quickly beached and picked-up the remaining force of Gurkhas and their equipment. The four landing craft quickly returned safely to the ship.

Another occasion was on a Sunday just after lunch. I was the duty bod for the weapons and radio department, a new categorisation of the radio department. I was enjoying my after-lunch snooze when the pipe called for the duty W&R hand to report to the operations room to process incoming troops and receive the relevant instructions. I was told that the ship was rushing up the coast to rendezvous with helicopters that were busy extracting a force of Gurkhas who had been in a ten-day firefight and needed to be withdrawn.

Here I should mention that when troops came aboard they kept their weapons but definitely no ammunition. I headed off to the seaman's mess collected my duty party, instructing them to bring a handcart with a few empty ammunition boxes up to the flight deck and wait at the aft end of the island.

The first helicopter landed and disembarked twelve Gurkhas who proceeded to unload over two hundred plus rounds a man. After I had checked that their weapons were clear, a seaman arrived to guide them to their accommodation. With two further helicopters due to land, there was a short moment of panic as I sent my men to bring extra empty ammunition boxes.

The next helicopter arrived, the same thing. The chief PO from the ops room came down to see how things were going and I asked why the incoming troops had so much ammunition. No reply.

The last helicopter arrived with just eight Gurkhas plus a British Army Major and his British Army sergeant. I processed the major first, double checked his weapon was empty, just to impress, then completed processing the remaining Gurkhas. The sergeant was the last so I asked had they been in a long fire-fight. He affirmed a yes, quite a tough one too. I pointed at all the ammunition on the heavily loaded handcart and the sergeant said smiling, 'We don't like to use our weapons they make far too much noise and you could get a nasty headache.'

'OK,' I thought. 'Learn something new every day.'

*

MY FONDEST MEMORY of the Gurkhas was onboard the ship. I was working for the 'between decks' party, at the time helping to keep the ship clean. There were insufficient non-technical staff onboard ship so the technical divisions, electrical and radio amongst others, had to contribute a volunteer (there's that word again) and so one by one the members of the radio department took it in turns to down tools and pick-up a mop, or a scrubbing brush, or a paint brush, and always a large can of metal polish and clean rags.

During my stint as Mr Mop, I was assigned a section of the main thoroughfare on Four Deck, which went the whole length of the ship. My patch started at the Bomb Hoist compartment, next to the sick bay, down aft to the start of the wardroom, including four separate side compartments each with their own difficulties to keep clean.

The first area containing the bomb hoist system, which connected the munitions magazines on Nine Deck to the main hanger on Two Deck. There were two hoists one from the magazines to Four Deck then a second hoist from Four Deck up to the main hanger. In between the two hoists was a horizontal track for the carriage carrying the munitions. Of course, this complicated system was designed to keep the ship safe with lots of interlocks to prevent doors and hatches being opened when the preceding door or hatch had not been fully closed.

I normally worked on my own and it would take just about a week to keep the basics shipshape. When the Gurkhas were on-board I would be given two happy smiling couples. The Gurkhas always seem to go around in twos, generally holding hands. I guess if you are halfway up Mount Everest it's handy to have a chum with you. The Ghurkhas were a very close-knit community.

And boy, did they work hard. Just show them what to do and stand back. With Admiral's Inspection still to come on the ship's programme, the Gurkhas were a heaven-sent opportunity to get ahead of the game.

Living with them onboard ship up close we all got to know their little ways, like meal times these little fellows could eat and some. The cooks had to stop them from 'going around the buoy', a naval expression for eating two meals at the same sitting. They also received a daily rum ration.

I remember when a small barrel of Ghurkha rum found its way into the hands of a certain group of seamen. They took it to their secret hidey-hole for a Sunday afternoon drinking session. The rum was too strong and tasted truly horrible. That you could run your car on it for a week was a given.

*

IN THE RUN-UP to Christmas, I returned to the normal duties, working once again in the ship's island. The next big event was fleet exercises with ten other Royal Navy ships, when most of the crew thought some time off would have been more appropriate. Anyway, the exercises went well as did the Admiral's inspection.

My next memory was the visit to the Island of Penang located on the north-west coast of the Malaysian Peninsula. The capital city, George Town, is located on the island and is steeped in the history of many different cultures.

The visit was short but with friends, I enjoyed a pleasant journey using the rack railway up the hill to visit the Kek Lok Si Temple, a Buddhist temple situated facing the sea and commanding impressive views. It is one of the best-known temples on the island and is said to be the largest Buddhist temple in Malaysia. It is decorated with reverse swastika emblems. The swastika as an emblem has existed in many formats over many hundreds if not thousands of years. The swastika has two shapes with its arms facing either right or the left. The left facing swastika had been a Buddhist or Hindu symbol for many centuries. Many cultures believed the swastika derived from the swirling arms of the jet streams of passing comets. Comets throughout the ages meant amongst other things a lucky or auspicious object.

*

ALL TOO SOON the ship was back to Borneo carrying more troops but then followed another visit to Hong Kong. Some of the helicopters were proper poorly and in need of some advanced TLC in the Hong Kong aircraft hospital. As the ship passed the northern end of Sabah, a helicopter was sent ashore returning with a solitary soldier, a Royal Marine in fact.

His very scruffy fatigues were close to falling off his back, he stank to high heaven and his last bath had been a long time ago.

I must add here that during operation in Borneo the British made a point of contacting all the remote villages deep in the jungle and coming to some positive arrangement with the native leaders.

Many of the villagers could be genuine headhunters. I once saw such a person on the flight deck complete with a long thin bamboo stick stuck through his nose carrying a blunderbuss that would definitely attract the attention of a Christie's auctioneer. These villagers could smell a European for up to five miles away in the jungle. Troops were issued with an anti-deodorant spray but how effective it was I have no idea.

Anyway, the ship's new guest was certainly detectable from any range as he was hustled into the nearest shower room stark naked whilst the RM Sergeant went to the stores to find fresh kit for the man.

After the man was restored to his personal comforts he started to entertain the ship's company with little pranks, like standing outside of the Naffi shop pretending it would open soon for business. A queue would form behind him at which point he would make his excuses asking the second-in-line to mind his space.

Next, an officer would come upon the queue, generally the ship's Commander, asking what the devil was going on. The Commander could get quite short at times but he was a busy man with a huge job to do.

When the ship arrived in Hong Kong our little friend, as he became known, upped his game. He wasn't a particularly big man, very lean in fact. There were rumours he had a Celtic background, but definitely a man of mystery.

One afternoon a group from my mess deck were wandering along our favourite street in Wan Chi when we came across a large altercation in the middle of a road junction. No need to get involved, the participants were all US sailors.

We leant on the pedestrian barrier with a couple of stokers to await the fun, which arrived in the form of a US Navy shore patrol comprising an Ivy League Officer, his faithful Chief Petty Officer, and a gang of large tough negro sailors all carrying large nightsticks.

The shore patrol got stuck in with a gusto, biff, bang, wallop, crash etc. As they dragged the mealy apart they found in the middle of all this confusion our little friend. The US officer picked him up, dusted him down, apologised profusely on behalf of Uncle Sam and gave him twenty US bucks in compensation.

As the US Navy shore patrol dragged away the guilty, the stoker next to me said 'That was quite strange.' We all asked why? He said, 'The Royal Marine wasn't losing.'

Two days later just before the ship was due to sail our little friend was involved in something quite serious. Being a loner he was drinking in a bar when a huge US Marine master sergeant came in on his own sat close by, took his cap off dropping it on to the bar counter. Our little friend, feeling playful, picked up the US Marine's captain, placed it on his head and started to show off examining the effect in the mirror behind the bar.

The US Marine master sergeant made it known to everybody that anyone touching the goddamn cap of a US Marine master sergeant would soon be in deep dodo. At which point our little friend, in an absolute blur of movement, hospitalised the US Marine master sergeant, very seriously.

The bar owner hurriedly called the police and two members of the ship's company rushed to collect our little friend to whisk him back on board ship as fast as possible. The aftermath was never revealed and it was fortunate the ship sailed the next day.

*

THEN, OCCURRED AN amazing event. The ship's rumour mill labelled each rumour as a 'buzz'. No matter how secret it was supposed to be, I was always impressed how the rumour mill would decipher the 'buzz' faster than you could say 'Bletchley Park'.

However, on the evening before the ship sailed there was 'Super Buzz'. After one hour it had not been cracked. In fact, it was not cracked by breakfast time the next morning.

The whole ship's crew became alive; what could it be? In the radio workshop, we pressed our Chief Procter very hard but he denied all knowledge, which nobody believed because his best chum on the ship was the senior chief in the signals department, one of only three or four persons on board that were authorised to decipher top secret messages.

As the ship was pulled away from the dockside, rumour fever reached a very high pitch. So, when ship anchored in Junk Bay for the divers to make their inspection the captain announced, 'clear lower deck - muster in the main hanger'.

The ship's company mustered, waiting for our captain to arrive,

MEMORIES AND FORGETFULNESS

which he did with a flourish. He waited for calm and silence then without any drama, informed the ship's company that the conflict in Borneo required more helicopters. The only ones available belonged to the RAF, who were henceforth invited to join-in and assist.

The helicopters were being mustered at an RAF airfield near Tobruk. After dropping-off sections of the ship's crew in Brunei, the ship would sail to Singapore then to Port Suez, transit the canal then anchor at Tobruk to receive said helicopters.

He also informed that this change in the programme was classified and the ship's company was not to start writing home or, for that matter, to anybody else. Everybody stood still stunned into silence. Many tried to remember exactly where Tobruk was? Someone asked the question out loud. A voice replied that there was one in North Africa, must be a different Tobruk.

The captain smiled and confirmed our destination. A voice from the back started to sing, 'so near and so far away'. Everyone laughed, the mood lightened but it had been a long hard year away from home. Getting that close to home to then suffer the disappointment of having to return all the way back to bloody Borneo caused the mood to darken.

The ship's company went back to its duties, everyone with different thoughts. That evening a list of personnel who would be transferred to a temporary base onshore in Brunei was published. All the ship's aircrew staff, some stores-men, along with a whole load of stores from the ship's inventory of spare parts for all things aerial, two staff from our radio department and half the ship's complement of Royal Marines to enhance security plus a range of other odd bods. Volunteers (yes, it's that word again) would be required from certain departments. I slid to the back of the queue feeling glad two of our department had put their hands up. I kept mine firmly in my pocket.

On the return voyage to Brunei our little friend was released back into the wild from whence he had come, still dressed only in fatigues and with little or no equipment. It was some time before someone figured out who he might have been; SBS (Special Boat Squadron) which most of us had never heard of.

*

AFTER DISEMBARKING THOSE personnel who had been selected to stay in Brunei, the ship sailed to Singapore to refuel, pick-up stores and supplies. The ship felt empty, the main hangers were silent as the grave as the ship set off for what was a marathon jog around the planet there was little to do except the boring routine of finding something to occupy our time.

I discovered the ship had received from a service foundation, three sailing boats delivered in flat pack form. The boats, called piccolos, were little more than a flat skiff type craft with a single unsupported mast and a triangular mainsail. With the help of a friend, I managed to complete the construction of these three craft in our enhanced spare time.

They were fun to sail but hardly offering the type of sailing I had become used to at home.

*

SO, AS THE ship began its marathon journey, the only bonus as far as most crew members were concerned was that with little to spend one's pay on, one could repay the Mess Deck Welfare Fund operated by the leading hand of each mess deck. These welfare funds were used to smooth out the finances of mess members in times of stress, like arriving at a port with bars that served ice-cold beer and one was suffering from the medical complaint of boracic lint, or skint, as it is more commonly known. Remember, t'was before the era of the credit cards.

So, all being well there was not a lot to go wrong. Not quite. Sailors, like all servicemen of the era, relied on the certainty of receiving mail from home or loved ones or both. It was the *only* medium by which contact could be maintained with the outside world. Totally unlike today; think about it.

Because of the sudden change of the ship's programme the military mail service struggled to keep up, except it didn't keep up at all. The ship's company was told that our letters from home kept arriving at places we had just left. So there was no mail. The harder the system tried to deliver the mail, the worse the situation became. The ship's company joined as one in their disapproval of the situation. Even the Captain expressed total dissatisfaction, sending an urgent 'shit-o-gram' to that effect to the powers that be.

The ship missed the mail in Singapore, Aden, Port Suez and Port Said, and the sop offered was that HM Forces Mail Service just gave in and sent the huge number of mailbags direct to the Army Base in Tobruk.

Due to delays in getting through the Suez Canal; in the era, there were always delays in transiting the Suez Canal, the ship was forecasted to arrive at Tobruk Harbour very early on a Sunday morning. The ship actually received a message from the Army confirming that the mail had indeed arrived at Tobruk, and had been processed for delivery first thing Monday morning. This did not go down at all well.

The captain requested a Sunday delivery but the army replied that their Army Post Office did not open on a Sunday. The captain's reply, apparently, informed the army that the ship still had a detachment of Royal Marines, a naval boarding party, and he felt certain that they certainly would be able to assist with the opening of the said post office and that it would not be a problem.

Sunday morning came with many of the ship's crew not involved with entering harbour and the subsequent anchoring, watching with interest. I was certainly one of them, as two landing craft headed for the shore full of the ship's company specialists at opening things, like closed army post offices, crowbars and other delicate equipment, sledgehammers for example, at the ready,

I believe the army actually opened the post office seconds before the ship's 'Recovery of the Very Late Mail Party' was about to. Complaints were received from the Army but rumour had it that the captain had advised the army to contact Sir Charles Madden, C-in-C of the Home Fleet, a member of the Admiralty Board, in the event of any complaints. The communication was signed Colin Duncan Madden, Captain, *HMS Albion*. How convenient it was to have a senior member of the family in the right place at the right time.

*

THIS LITTLE BIT of fuss set the tone for the rest of the day. Yes, the Royal Air Force had mustered a wide range of helicopters scrounged from bases all over Europe, about twenty-five aircraft including two twin-rotor Belvederes but there were only five bloody RAF pilots to fly them onboard ship. The other pilots having been rudely awoken from their slumbers had applied for Foreign Service leave and buggered off home to the UK.

Our captain and commander 'flying' were not amused especially as a quick embarkation and turn around was necessary to meet the allotted time for the planned southbound convoy through the Suez Canal.

Matters got a trifle testy, so we all heard later on. The ship had been flat-out operational for just over a year, overcoming every obstacle, now the RAF wanted to lean-on-their-oars and take their time.

Still, it was an interesting spectacle as five helicopters arrived from the inland RAF airfield, then watch four of the pilots scrambled back into the fifth helicopter as it took-off to repeat the process.

Eventually, all the RAF helicopters were on-board along with some of their flight crews and handlers. There was more anxious waiting on the bridge as the ship waited for a quantity of cargo the ship was supposed to take to Singapore. I cannot remember quite how this moment progressed but I suspect that the ship waited until the last possible moment before up anchoring to make a mad dash for Port Said and the convoy south.

Apart from all that, Tobruk and its protective harbour proved an interesting sight. The WWII history of the city is a classic struggle between two great armies. If you look carefully at Google Earth you can still make out the original defensive line established by the British Army.

Looking at the landscape from the top of the ship's island this part of the world is almost certainly an ideal place in which to conduct violent battles. It doesn't matter who wins at the end of the day, the remains of the equipment employed can be removed, the wind-blown sand will soak up all the spilt blood and the landscape will remain as is, just a flat featureless rock-strewn desert. Oh, there was a small fort. Perhaps it sells postcards to lost tourists?

*

THE VOYAGE BACK to Singapore went as advertised. The crew devoured their letters with the usual range of emotions. I received a 'Dear John' from a girl called Christine that I had forgotten all about until I wrote this piece.

The ship arrived in Singapore and discharged the RAF helicopters to RAF Seletar where they spent some time being modified for service in the Borneo Jungle.

The next important milestone was my birthday and I started to receive my daily rum ration. Lunch never tasted as good as after gently sipping a nice glass of Grog, or two-in-one.

The ship's last visit to Hong Kong came just in time for Christmas. Christmas Day dinner was a grand affair on-board with roast turkey with all the trimmings, crackers and things that went pop, funny hats plus the naval tradition of the officers serving wine to the men. The youngest person on the ship just sixteen and a half years old was installed as captain of the ship for the day all dressed-up in a captain's uniform.

The previous Christmas (1962) had been spent at action stations somewhere offshore Borneo. The combined electrical/radio mess decks compartment had held a suitable party with beer that had been carefully hidden behind the outboard bed screens, which the nightly officer-of-the-day inspections had been careful not to look at too closely. Our nightly beer ration was two tins per day per man so saving up for this party involved real sacrifice.

However, Christmas 1963 was a great improvement. The captain gave a week's local leave to each part of the watch so that his crew could relax and unwind.

Next morning, Boxing Day, a Sunday no less, Tarpey and I were having a late lie-in. Our bunks were opposite each other on the top tier. A young officer arrived. I opened one eye to understand whatever question he may have. The good news was he was carrying his cap, a sign he was not on duty, a social visit even.

He asked my name and was I one of the ship's sailing team. I wasn't aware there was a ship's sailing team but I mumbled a yes. The officer asked about a similar team member called Tarpey. I pointed a toe in his direction.

'Sorry for the intrusion but the Royal Hong Kong Yacht Club has issued an invitation to take part in their Boxing Day Regatta. Tarpey opened an eye. The Officer arranged for us to meet at the gangway in twenty minutes dressed in smart but casual gear carrying a large grip full of waterproofs and other clothing to go sailing.

Hong Kong in mid-winter is cold and if it's not raining that's considered a bonus. There was no bonus. The weather blessed our day out on the water with good old-fashioned drizzle, which no neck towel was going to keep out. Also, there was little wind and with the thousands of small vessels crisscrossing the bay it was going to be a bumpy day's sailing.

Our officer met the two of us at the gangway and we were ushered into a waiting taxi. The RHKYC was all I expected it to be, old-fashioned, comfortable old school, classy and rich. It was located to the west of Causeway Bay, a typhoon shelter and fishing village, in this era, full of Chinese sampans where the boat people were born, lived and passed to the great beyond.

This community was famous in its own right. Books were written, newsreels broadcasted and now all gone and forgotten. The demand for land changed the Hong Kong waterfront, which is now totally different than it was at Christmas 1963.

Tarpey and I were introduced to our host for the day, a nice old gent who needed a race crew to help him do something he rarely did, racing his very comfortable 20ft open day boat.

Our friendly ship's officer warned that guests were not permitted to purchase anything in the club as no cash could be used. All items and services were noted on a chit with the club member's number. So we were asked to take it easy on the drinks during the buffet that was to be held after the prize giving.

Tarpey promised our friendly officer we would not be giving our host the chits, a throwaway remark that did not register for some moments. The officer turned and smiled, laughing to himself.

Having changed, we went afloat. Our host asked if we could set his craft up for racing, asking advice about how to make a good start. He almost managed to make a good start but having spent a lot of money on new paint he declined to push his luck on the start line.

Still, we got away cleanly but the wind, what there was of it, became very variable, so a long slow drifting match resulted. Halfway through the race, we managed to be third last but our host gave me the helm to see if matters could be improved.

Luck was needed, quickly. Tarpey spotted some wind away to our left, which we reached but nobody else did. We made third position behind the leader but the wind decided to die altogether. A club race official went around the fleet saying 'well done', gave each boat its position before bidding a Chinese boat boy in another craft tow us back to the mooring.

A hundred metres from the club mooring the wind picked up. Our host was busy fiddling about up at the bow of his ship. Seeing the chance to use some skill I entered the club mooring up area at full bore under sail. I nodded to Tarpey and headed for an empty berth as near to the club building as possible. I then executed a magical three quarter turn stop with the boat nicely drifting in the desired mooring berth. If 'high fives' had been invented that would have been the time to celebrate. Our host was impressed and so was I. It was a do or die type of manoeuvre that worked. Yee ha!

The rest of the afternoon was most enjoyable inside a warm clubhouse, where we were plied with pink gins before the buffet was ready.

MEMORIES AND FORGETFULNESS

The buffet was rather special a mix of traditional UK and Chinese foods. By the time we returned to the ship we were both ready to hit the sack.

*

THE NEXT DAY, the pair of us went walkabout. Having changed into civvies at the China Fleet club, we headed west from the dockyard in the direction of Kennedy Town. The weather was still overcast so the visit to the Peak, the mountain behind the city, was held over for a better day.

First, we passed through the main city buildings, tall glass-clad skyscrapers dedicated to making money, making street-level very uninteresting until three drop-dead gorgeous American Chinese air hostesses passed by all dressed-up for a day in the first class cabin of Cathy Pacific Airways.

The street slowly changed to more traditional buildings. We came across a Chinese Emporium full of the very best Chinese artefacts. There was the whole range of what Chinese culture is famous for, the chinaware, the furniture, the jade statues and a lot of ivory carvings.

I was fascinated with the Chinese puzzle balls, which have been around for hundreds of years, made exclusively from ivory. Most balls have between three and seven layers but the largest known example is made up of 42 separate balls.

Usually, puzzle balls are symbols of good luck. The ones I saw you would need a lot of good luck just to make one. They were highly decorated, varied between seven to twelve layers and cost an absolute fortune. I noticed the Jade was also very beautiful in dark greens with very high prices. The sales lady seeing our interest in the best of Chinese art and knowing full well we could only look was very kind to show us all the very best.

Tarpey took an interest in the cultured pearl necklaces, hoping something might be in his price range as a present for his mother but credit in this era was very hard to come by.

We wandered all the way down to the dockside at Kennedy Town. The buildings got smaller and poorer. We found one craftsman sitting on his doorstep with a large piece of ivory in one hand and a beast of a band saw in the other, cutting the ivory into thin slabs and then into perfectly straight chopsticks.

In Chinese culture, when the rich host a big banquet, the honoured guests receive their own highly decorated set of chopsticks. We saw some in the emporium with prices still too far from our reach.

The street was also the home to many shops that produce speciality Chinese foods many of which hung outside in baskets that stank to high heaven. You won't find these Chinese foods in a Portsmouth Chinese take away.

At the end of the street, we reached a dock area with many sampans unloading a wide range of goods. One sampan was unloading rice. The bags spilt rice onto the ground if roughly handled. Starving beggars were sweeping up these few grains of rice for something to eat. Welcome to the real world.

The remainder of the week's leave was spent looking around Hong Kong and buying LP jazz records from the Verve label that were unavailable in the UK. For some reason, I never made it to the other side of the island and the floating fish restaurants in Aberdeen Harbour. Other distractions plus a shortage of the readies no doubt.

*

ALL TOO SOON the ship was on its way again. Help was needed in Borneo so the ship sailed four days early. The ship engaged in operations in some unpronounceable location, supporting the helicopter squadrons configured for battle with machine guns and rockets, rather than providing an expensive taxi service for the troops.

On the return voyage to Singapore, having emptied a rather small tanker, *HMS Albion* undertook one of the longest and heaviest food replenishments at sea, all two hundred tons of it, in only three and half hours.

No one was spared the ultimate get-fit-quick exercise. I remember it well. The whole of the ship's company not actually on duty was invited to volunteer and participate. From the flight deck down into the hanger (quite easy using the hanger lift and trolleys), then from the hanger through a large hatch nobody knew was there into the main mess hall (sliding down temporary ramps - harder) and then by hand down the companion ladders to the dark caverns under our combined mess deck – very tiring.

The ship's main refrigerators and freezers took up the whole of the ship's section known as 6F. Yours truly spent most of the time half-way up (or down) a ladder as a seemingly never-ending stream of beef, chicken and other meats in hard to handle cardboard boxes were passed hand to hand. When we were finished, knackered was not the word for it.

*

THE NEED FOR more helicopters in Borneo drove the need for one last visit to Hong Kong to recover repaired Wessex aircraft and their crews who had needed hospital treatment. The return to Singapore was the last chance to buy 'rabbits' for family and friends and then the ship became a commando ship again as we set off for the east coast of Africa, arriving back in sunny Mombasa.

A second opportunity presented itself in the form of an invitation from the Mombasa Yacht Club to those with the necessary skills to crew a racing dinghy called the 505.

Now the 505 was, and still is, the sexiest racing dinghy ever to grace the planet. It should have been the Olympic dinghy of choice and in trials, it was superior to the dinghy that was chosen. But it wasn't a girl's boat, and the dinghy chosen could be raced by either of the sexes.

Anyway, Tarpey and I set off for the club ready for a good day's sailing. We took long sleeve shirts to sail in, loads of sun cream and big floppy hats. We were asked if we had crew experience using a trapeze which is standing on the side of the boat with a harness around the waist connected by a wire up to the hounds on the mast. Yes, we lied convincingly, although we knew the basics.

Our arrival at the club was met by total tranquillity. We were ushered to the poolside and enjoyed a very pleasant swim. No wind disturbed the waters of Mombasa Harbour. The racing dinghies were still covered over from the hot rising sun. Just after eleven a.m. a light lunch with lots of salad was served at the poolside with cool shandy if you wanted a beer or one of the many local beverages.

As lunch slowly came to an end a slight breeze developed. The boat boys prepared the 505 racing dinghies, took them down to the water fully rigged and all ready to go. Midday arrived and it was time to go. The building breeze took us gently past the Arab Fort, out into the Indian Ocean with a perfect Force Four wind, steady as a rock.

I asked my helm how many days a year did they enjoy these conditions. 'About three hundred days,' came the reply. Despite a lack of sailing practice, the race went well. I crewed with reasonable competence and trapezing off the side of the boat was a blast. The sensation of speed was fantastic and being able to coordinate closely with the helm a bit of a triumph.

All too soon I was back ashore The sailors from *HMS Albion* were treated to great hospitality, an outdoor Bar-B-Cue, drinks and interesting colonial conversation. The club members were third or fourth generation British immigrants, many had built good businesses and farms. The country was doing well and in this colonial-era support from London was always available via the Governor, or his vice, who lived in Mombasa.

As the darkness descended, we all settled in for a most enjoyable evening up until the point when the Club Commodore arrived asking 'Does anybody know what a 'general recall' actually is?' Tarpey looked at me and whispered 'Are we suppose to rush back to the ship?'

'No idea,' I said. 'Play dumb and see what happens.'

Someone asked why? Only to be told that there was a lot of 'toing and froing' by the military and all the warships were raising steam at a fair old rate.

Someone shouted out that it was time to go. The fact that the Commodore had already ordered taxis soon told me he already knew the answer to this question long before he asked it. It is the way these old boys work. I just love it, keeps one on one's toes every time they speak.

Our group arrived at the dockside where a landing craft was waiting. An officious official asked 'What ship?' In a very brisk manner. Somebody offered *HMS Victory*, which did not go down well with the officious official.

Tarpey whispered 'Let's chose a different ship they could have better food,' but a look around the harbour showed that there was serious business going on and being a funny sod was not about to gain any brownie points.

What we did not know was that in December 1963 Zanzibar Island had received its independence from the United Kingdom as a constitutional monarchy under the Sultan, a short-lived state of affairs as the Sultan and his democratically elected government were overthrown in January 1964 in the Zanzibar Revolution, led by a Ugandan citizen, who wanted to get his hands in the till, and who organized and led the revolution with his followers on the island.

Several thousand ethnic Arab and Indian civilians were murdered in the traditional manner of the region. Thousands more detained or expelled and their property confiscated or destroyed.

The ship's company were given very little information and there was no access to the news. (Remember the era before the internet. Do you? You must be an oldie like me)

Anyway, Her Majesty's Royal Navy came to the rescue and quite a big fleet of ships sailed as soon as they had sufficient crew. Many stragglers were left behind.

The next day the fleet gathered out of sight offshore. One of the larger destroyers arrived at full speed with the stragglers. This large destroyer executed that time honoured 'Officer-of-the-Day' manoeuvre by announcing 'Hands to dinner – port thirty'. You could hear the chaos in the dining hall.

That night, no doubt, the grownups were busy planning tomorrow's exciting instalment. So it came to pass, that at five a.m. the next day two destroyers rushed into the small port of Zanzibar bombarded the city with overhead flares and wiz-bangs followed immediately by four of our landing craft plus an assortment of ships boats transporting the Royal Marines and boarding parties from all ships.

Tradition has it that when they got ashore all they saw was mostly brown bottoms sticking out from whatever table their owners were hiding under. Job Done. Hooray for our side.

In April 1964 the mainland colony of Tanganyika united with Zanzibar to form the United Republic of Tanganyika and Zanzibar but this lengthy name was compressed into a portmanteau, the United Republic of Tanzania, in October 1964, just after my twenty-first birthday. It was unbeknown to me, as I was at home on a course at *HMS Collingwood* and celebrating my coming of age in the Southampton Sailing Club, and a good night it was too.

*

THE SHIP RETURNED to the UK in May 1964 after a mad dash through the Bay of Biscay in very bad weather that started to roll up the sponsons alongside the forward part of the flight deck. The ship slowed briefly to allow work-crews to cut away the bent steelwork, which was consigned to the deep waters of the cold sea.

The ship arrived in Plymouth to a large crowd comprising families, girlfriends, loved ones and mistresses all anxiously waving on the dockside with many children about to get their first sight of Daddy.

And, so after three years and two months, and many fond goodbyes, I was discharged from the ship that meant so much to me. I had joined as a junior and left as a leading hand, with many skills and about to learn a great deal more on my qualifying course, which was expected to last just over a year of very hard study and many exams.

It was a long train journey from Plymouth to Southampton, which gave a lot of time for reflection.

5

HOME AT LAST AND MY FIRST CAR

THE FIRST PRIORITY ON MY foreign service leave was to learn to drive and pass my test as soon as possible. The Car Mart next to the Southampton New Docks had auctions twice a week. My father introduced me to the Lions' Den to teach me how to buy a car at an auction without being burned. A very useful lesson indeed.

So how did this car auction business operate? Well the basics for car owners not in the trade, and being unable to sell their car or get a good trade-in deal, would be to dump their pride and joy on either the Wednesday session (cars under four years old) or the Saturday session (cars over four years) So, cars were known by the day they were to be sold.

The general public could go to either session to bid on any vehicle. The bid price would creep up to the reserve figure set by the seller. Just below his perch, the auctioneer had two light boxes, one which said 'Close to Reserve' in red, the second light box would say 'Being Sold' in blue.

Sounds straightforward, eh? Wrong. Provincial car auctions are home to that part of our society who do not wish to rest at Her Majesties pleasure. These gentlemen were called traders, selling second-hand cars from one of Southampton's many corner bombsites. Cash was the name of the game. Cheques?

'Look loverly on a suit,' they used to say.

Cheques made out to cash were acceptable but only if trade was not as brisk as it could be.

So what goes on? In this era, this auction house was supplied, in the main, by two Irish Brothers using their car transporter, would scour the countryside for cars the main dealers were not that much interested in. After, say a good bank holiday weekend, the main dealers would have quite a few trade-ins they wanted to dispose of. It took time and money to shift trade-ins, which is where Paddy 1 and 2 came in.

The main dealer would have, say six Wednesday cars and four Saturday cars. Haggling would take place, very advanced haggling indeed, but after rolls of tenners had changed hands, the ten cars to be sold would arrive at the car auction premises by Tuesday or Friday morning. The brothers could shift around four hundred cars a week and they were only looking for a fiver a car. As Paddy #2 told my father 'I buys 'um, I shifts 'um and no disappointed punter (the eventual purchaser of the vehicle) will be knocking on my door in the middle of the night.'

So, Father took me to the Wednesday auction. Stares of hatred rained up at from the floor in front of the auctioneer. Punters invading the afternoon session were definitely not welcomed.

A chap Dad knew quite well was trying to buy a pretty, three-year-old, Riley in black and red but the auctioneer knocked it down to one of the traders with a strong family resemblance.

An even better car came up for auction, an MG Magnette, a rare car today. Dad went to sit next to this chap, offering him the use of his police whistle and a rolled copy of the Daily Torygraph newspaper. He whispered some instructions.

The bidding reached the halfway stage. Dad's chum was being ignored yet again. The bidding reached the reserve price and the auctioneer's light went on.

'Now,' said my father, as his chum raised the newspaper high in the air and blew the police whistle. Laughs all around. The other traders were enjoying themselves at someone else's expense.

The trader in question upped his bid but Dad's chum responded with an improved bid as the sound of the police whistle rang around the building. Some of the traders dashed for cover thinking it was a police raid. Almost.

The trader in question muttered something quite unprintable but sat back to await the next opportunity. No point in paying over the odds and reducing one's profit margin. There would always be another car coming along soon.

The next car to come on to the blocks was an ageing Mk9 Jaguar

Saloon in surprisingly good condition. A Saturday car, so what was it doing here on a Wednesday? It was being actively examined by four students. My father engaged with them to discover they were language students in their third year. They wished to go to Europe for two months to immerse themselves in the languages and cultures they were studying.

Dad had a quick look at the car which had four brand new tyres, there was little smoke coming from the exhaust, the engine oil looked OK and it had four months valid MOT remaining.

He told them to bid for the car, their upper limit being the cost of four new tyres. After their holiday any decent scrap-yard would give them at least what they paid for it. The upside was the car could be broken for spares or even restored at the very least. He also gave them his thirty-second course on bidding techniques in this auction house and left them to it.

The Jaguar stopped on the block in front of the auctioneer with four students sitting directly opposite staring at him. The car had no reserve, so any bid was a winner. The leader of the students butted-in after the third bid with the right price as suggested by father and the car was theirs.

Next to come on the blocks was the car father was interested in for myself. A dark green Austin A30 van, very clean, few miles and ideal for the purpose. Father followed the example of the students, sitting directly in front of the auctioneer who looked at his trading mates on the floor of the auction house saw little interest and quickly knocked the car down to father with a wry smile.

Although a more upmarket first car could have been desired, this little van was perfect. Cheap to buy, cheap to run, cheap to insure (my first car). Easy to convert with back seats and windows. Ideal for ping-ponging between camp and home and ideal for carrying all the junk required to go sailing. At a push, one could sleep in it overnight at a weekend competition away from home.

When I finished the course, I was informed that I would be posted to Scotland. Someone offered me good money for the Austin, so with profit in hand, I bought a 1952 gentleman's car, a Sunbeam Talbot Mk II with a four-cylinder, 2.2 litres engine with the clean body in very shiny black. A good and very comfortable long-distance means of travel to the other end of the country.

6

TWELVE MONTHS OF QUALIFYING COURSE

AFTER TAKING MY FOREIGN SERVICE leave I returned to *HMS Collingwood* and volunteered to be the leading hand of a new entries mess hut. (Hut 14B) This meant no weekend duties and home each weekend to go racing in my new sailing dinghy.

As for the coursework, the navy in its wisdom did not provide the training of its highly specialised ratings using civilian courses, HNCs and HNDs for example, which would have been useful when servicemen returned to civvy street (and which the RAF did).

The syllabus was divided into two-week or four-week courses comprising of pure theory, then actual equipment and system work. The course exam at the end of the two or four week period was always held on a Friday morning which by chance always followed a payday Thursday.

Seeing as how everybody was skint during blank week it was a tough decision whether to spend Thursday evenings swotting-up for the exam next day or take one's hard earned pay to the Naffi bar. The Naffi usually won. Still, my course marks averaged out in the mid-seventies, which was good going as we later learned that the whole course was equal to the third year at university.

At the end of the course, I discovered my planning had been all wrong. Having completed an eighteen-month foreign commission on *HMS Albion* nearly everybody, when sent to their next draft, were given a one-year cushy appointment, and then I could have done the qualifying course.

Tarpey was posted to a very pleasant posting at *HMS Mercury* (the

RN Signals School) located in some very pleasant surroundings at the back of the hills overlooking Portsmouth. An easy life, surrounded by pretty Wrens learning Morse code and signal handling. There were also some decent pubs serving very acceptable scrumpy. It was here that Tarpey met Linda, a chief Wren, and in due course, they married.

One summer evening towards the end of the term, I enjoyed a very pleasant evening drive to see the lad in my recently acquired 1952 Sunbeam Talbot Mk II. Its dark black finish, when polished, looked very posh.

I met Tarpey in his workshop, mentioned the words 'opening time' and so we set off to the Ye Olde George Inn, a 15th-century local pub in East Meon. The pub food was good and the scrumpy quite delicious, although this was a beverage I rarely drank. After a few pints, I felt quite mellow and quaffed a couple of strong coffees to assist in the recovery for the return journey.

On the drive back to *HMS Collingwood* the country road out of East Meon up to the main road the line in the middle of the road seemed rather wiggly, although I remember it being quite straight on the way in. I stopped the car and had a word with the wiggly line in the middle of the road, which is when I realised that scrumpy had a different effect on me than feeling sick after too many beers. I felt really great but a re-examination of the facts suggested that I should park the car in a lay-by and rest awhile. Maybe a short walk would help. Anyway, the wiggly line in the middle of the road started to become straighter so I completed my journey back to camp in a calm and much slower manner.

Time flew and as qualification course came to an end I surprised even myself at the good marks obtained in the many exams. I was duly confirmed in my promotion and put on the roster for draft.

*

Social Life during Qualifying Course

AFTER MY RETURN the UK from the Far East, it was time to go sailing once again. I purchased a 14ft racing dinghy called a Zenith, a pretty double chine dinghy designed by Ian Proctor who designed many famous racing dinghies. The Zenith was destined not to become famous despite its many qualities. There were so many new designs coming on the market it was hard to keep up.

It had a deep bow section, she was strong in the chest, just in front of the mast, ideal for chopping through the kind of waters that existed in the Solent on a windy day. The sail area was quite large and she had both spinnaker and a single trapeze. An easy rig made it possible to set her up for most weather conditions.

Because only one hundred and thirty were ever constructed, she remained in the secondary yardstick section of the Portsmouth Handicap Tables. Her number of ninety-two was based on the countrywide results of only a few overall numbers. I soon proved that given a good start, I could race this class of dinghy well below her handicap number. This made her an ideal pot hunter for the many famous regattas and their handicap races that were held around the country.

In the club races, I had Susan as crew, a tall attractive girl with a ready smile. She learned quickly and soon became a good crew. She was very nimble on the trapeze too. We won our fair share of races and series club competitions.

I remember one glorious evening race; the wind was light and variable. The heavier dinghies were not making much of the conditions. After a strong tussle with my father's Albacore 15' dinghy, we reached the penultimate mark just in front and no more, probably a minute behind on handicap, when I found a special wind, just forward of the mast. Susan managed to set the spinnaker on what was a very tight reach, the Zenith very gently lifted up on to the plane and we just sailed away, not daring to move in the boat or make any adjustments to the rig. We won by six minutes on handicap, wonderful.

*

THE SAILING CLUBS in Southampton Water formed an association, the SWSA. Dad became the Secretary on the basis he had the time to organise their affairs and he liked to race as well. Dad was an expert sheet metal worker (from the aircraft industry) and eventually left his industry to be a craft teacher in one of Southampton's secondary school. Turning sheet metal into a jet engine air intake plus or minus two thousands of an inch took real skill. He was an absolute wizz at making copper coal scuttles, but repairing broken metal masts was the real feather in his cap.

Each year the SWSA organised a series of six handicap races for all members of the associated clubs. Each club would send teams of five boats. Hamble River SC and Weston SC never did join in as their clubs concentrated on class racing, which did not require a complicated handicap system.

At the start of the new season in 1965, the club asked me to lead the second of two fleets of four boats that the club wished to enter for the SWSA Championship. I had form in this area, as I used to take part in this championship before *HMS Albion* sailed for the Far East in November 1962, racing in the club's second team of mixed handicap dinghies.

The championship consisted of three weekends shoehorned into the yearly racing programme after the Easter Holiday and before the Summer Bank Holiday weekend. We raced on the Saturday and the Sunday. With our club being situated at the top of Southampton Water, our team members had the chore of the early start, sailing down river against a flood tide to the venue, racing, the stay over-night, and the next day, another early start to get our team boats to the second venue.

Following the Sunday race, and the prize giving, and the buffet, and the beer, the team members would have the task of sailing all the way back up to our club, arriving a low tide and then the long haul to get our boats up the very long hard into the dinghy park.

Having done that, I would drive back to camp, as no way I was going to mess with the Monday morning traffic getting out of town.

One of the races, at Netley SC, if I remember correctly, was great fun. The wind was light, and after the first windward mark, the dead run to the next mark became very slow. The slow boats from behind started to bunch up on the faster boats in front, with everybody trying hard to steal what little there was of other boat's wind.

As I neared the bottom turning mark, a very strong oak post, part of the estuaries secondary navigation system, a National 12 dinghy, crewed by two sweet and very pretty teenage girls came in from one side of the course, finding wind that nobody else had, and aimed for the mark, with absolutely no right-of-way according to the racing rules.

I wondered what would happen next; a mighty crash looked the best option. At the last moment, the crew girl lifted her tee-shirt up to her neck, revealed the lack of any bra, and shouted out, 'Hey boys have a look at these.' All the male helms lost interest in their position rounding the mark, a gap appeared, goodness knows where from, the girls dived into it, rounded the mark, leaving everybody behind. Wonderful. You may wonder why nobody entered a formal protest to the race committee, demanding to see err, the evidence.

My best race and absolute favourite was the SWSA at Warsash. It was an end of season race, on a cold windy Sunday. Susan had a cold, so I took Graham, my brother. There's nothing like having a tall brother on the trapeze in windy weather.

The competitors to beat were the Warsash SC Hornets, a slim sixteen-foot dinghy with spinnaker and a sliding seat for the crew. One of their numbers was the South Coast Champion. I could ill afford to give away too many places if I was going to win the yearly overall SWSA series prize for the best helm.

I tracked him at the start, as he would have the sixth sense of where the course marks were. Off we set on the first beat. Graham set up the rig for heavy weather, and once I got the Zenith settled down, I took a long hike out to the left with tide giving me a lee bow, with Graham full out on the trapeze. We hung on grimly in the building seas as our target competitor slowly opened up the gap between us. Now we were racing on a handicap number of 92, and the Hornet was sailing off 88. I told Graham our time had to be inside four minutes a hundred, or one minute every fifteen minutes.

We rounded the windward mark. The Hornet had set his spinnaker for the broad reach, but I could see he was having trouble holding it. Graham asked, 'Up Spinnaker?'

I shouted, 'Put some more power into the mainsail, then park your arse on my shoulder.'

The Zenith flew downwind. I could see the Hornet's crew was too far forward sitting on his sliding seat for the conditions and he was unable to adjust his position aft. In contrast, Graham and I were both positioned as far back in the boat as we could go.

The deep bow of the Zenith smashed the awkward waves aside, rising high into the air. With only a little centreboard down, the Zenith flew like the wind. By the turning mark, we were very close behind the Hornet and I saw its helm getting frustrated.

The gybe mark came and went, the Hornet almost lost control of the spinnaker, whilst we just sat behind letting the Hornet show us the way around the course, giving early warnings of the next gust of wind to hit us.

And so, the race continued. The other Hornets started to close the gap from behind, but why worry. I was minutes ahead on handicap, so just enjoy the ride. We were the second boat to finish and miles ahead on handicap.

After the prize giving, we raided the hot sausage rolls and very a welcome hot drink, before setting off for home. We found more sheltered water as we rushed upriver. I shouted, 'up spinnaker', and had a really fast run home. It was a wonderful day's sailing, and the SWSA Championship was in the bag.

7

HMS GURKHA

A Tribal Class Frigate of no fixed abode

FOLLOWING A HAPPY YEAR AT *HMS Collingwood* and enjoying some very good racing in Southampton Water, I received a posting to *HMS Gurkha* in sunny Scotland, the fifth ship to be so named, a famous name for a small general-purpose frigate.

The preamble regarding the ship looked inviting, modern living conditions, all bunk beds, air-conditioning et al. This was a first for smaller ships in the RN, but *HMS Albion* had been so equipped four years earlier.

HMS Gurkha came in at under three thousand tons displacement, equipped with steam and gas turbine propulsion; the gas turbine enabled the ship to leave harbour at very short notice.

She was equipped with two refurbished ex-WW2 single barrel 4.5" guns, one three barrelled anti-submarine mortar (the anti-submarine frigates had two), anti-submarine sonar and a little helicopter. She had arrived in Rosyth Dockyard for refit and turn-around to go back to her happy hunting ground, the Persian Gulf.

The ship did, however, have a full suite of radar systems including a long-range bedstead radar, a general purpose radar, navigation radar and the latest gunnery radar system, least that's what they said. It was enough to keep me busy at sea if nothing else.

*

FIRST, I HAD to make the long journey to Scotland. I had no previous experience to guide me as to how long it was going take. At least the Navy provided a mileage allowance in lieu of the train fare.

From Southampton, there was nothing for it but to head-up the dreaded A34, known as the 'Longest lane in the World'. Nothing much had changed and Newbury was still the monumental pain in the bum it always was. Dad used to say, 'If 'Jerry' had invaded the south coast during the war, the flanking movement to the west to surround London would have been halted at Newbury'. Whoever designed that damn bridge did a bloody good job in the defence of the realm.

Next, the route getting around the west side of Birmingham was slow. Then on to parts of the new M6, but with so much work still in progress, it took a lot of time.

Progress to the Lake District could have been worse but getting through the Lake District was grim going. There was one small bridge with controlling one-way traffic lights and the queues were bad in either direction. I have never seen so many cars towing those damn caravans in all my life. And as for the rain!

North of Carlisle, the rain turned to light snow then heavy vertical snow. Time for a stop at the nearest roadside garage and greasy spoon to rest a while. It was now early evening and the chances of making it to Edinburgh were not looking good.

I still had a way to go up the A74, the Glasgow road, before turning onto the A702, the Edinburgh road, to pass through Biggar, then on to Rosyth via Edinburgh.

By the time I reached the Beattock Summit the weather had started to clear and as I turned on to the A702 at Abingdon I enjoyed one of the best drives in my life. The sky was clear with a strong full moon shining on a still landscape. The road was covered in fresh snow two inches deep. The Sunbeam cruised in total silence with only a muffled exhaust behind me. The tyres made no noise on the road, the snow crisp and providing good traction when driving as smoothly as I could. The memory lives with me as strongly now as it did then.

Chugging along at a steady forty to fifty miles per hour through deserted villages and along open roads, the moonlight providing all the illumination I needed. It was just a magic experience. As the road started to descend down into the outskirts of Edinburgh the snow petered out, the ring road around the city was clear and fortunately empty.

MEMORIES AND FORGETFULNESS

Tired but happy I crossed the recently opened Forth Road Bridge to reached the naval base to be directed to my accommodation for the night.

*

THE NEXT DAY I reported to *HMS Gurkha* only to find that she would be in dockyard hands for a few months and during this time her crew would be accommodated in the dockyard shore base know as *HMS Caledonia*, or the *Chevron Hilton* by those with a queer sense of humour.

The *Chevron Hilton* consisted of three old ships the navy considered surplus to requirements, *HMS Girdle Ness* (an old RFA converted as the testing platform for the Sea Slug missile system), the *RFA Fort Dunvegan*, plus an old WW2 C-Class destroyer born in 1943, the one and only *HMS Chevron*.

(HMS Girdle Ness had an interesting moment when testing a Sea Slug missile which managed to lose its radar guiding beam. It reacquired the radar beam only flying towards the ship at very high speed. A quick-thinking Chief PO lowered the radar beam to the minimum horizontal position and pressed the emergency 'Off' button. The missile roared its way between the ship's two masts at a very low level to disappear into the distance.)

Depending upon which ship you were accommodated on, the conditions were described as, err, less than perfect. Those of you who remember the 1973 movie Papillion starring Steve McQueen will have some idea of the real conditions. The movie is a semi-fictional account of Henri Charrière's time in the penal system in French Guyana on the infamous Devil's Island, and he was one of the few to escape. This movie was a true representation of what was going on in the *Chevron Hilton*, except the escaping part took a lot longer.

I quote from a published letter from husband to mistress:

(Half the enjoyment of a commission, a cruise or even a run ashore is being able to reminisce and it would be interesting to discover how many can recall their thoughts on that fateful day in September '66, when with our goods and chattels, we found ourselves unceremoniously dumped at Inverkeithing station.

One's immediate thoughts must have been many and varied but uppermost in our mind must have been transport! The wise and crafty of us cajoled an RN Staff Car driver to take us to the 'yard while the less wise but equally crafty caught a bus and claimed a taxi fare on their travelling expense form.

Whatever our means of conveyance our reaction on our arrival is unprintable!

The 'Chevron Hilton' came as a shock to us all; no water, no heating, no drying facilities and in one particular case no sleeping billet (he was the chap who eventually sought refuge in the galley) and these were only a few of the snags encountered.)

I ended up being billeted on the *RFA Fort Dunvegan* in what would have been one of the main holds. Terrific.

'Hammock or camp bed,' I was asked by the Chief PO dishing out the places to sleep.

'Camp bed please,' I replied.

'OK, you're a lucky man,' came the reply. 'You get to sleep under the mess deck table. One of the seamen gets to sleep on top of the mess deck table.'

The Chief wasn't joking. Numerous complaints had been made to FOSNI - Flag Officer Scotland and Northern Ireland and numerous local MPs but the navy was dragging its feet building the promised barracks due to be completed next year or the year after, who knows.

Hundreds applied for extra pay called 'hard layers' but all were turned down. Only submariners actually living on a submarine received this less than generous uplift in pay.

Still, one had to make the most of it until the ship was ready to receive its crew after the dockyard hands had completed the refurbishing work. There was a debate as to whether it was in their scope of work to actually finish work. We soon found out, so it was alleged, that the dockyard workers knew how to finish work and go home, generally forty minutes before time, with someone staying behind to work some fiddle on the time-clock. I never did find out the truth of the matter as the dockyard pay was just as bad as Portsmouth. The more the refit continued the more ship's equipment became U/S.

I cannot remember how many months I spent billeted in the worst accommodation I have ever experienced, but in the navy, one has to cope. One experience that was completely new to me came in the form of obscene graffiti universally adorning all toilets and washrooms. The messages generally invited His Holiness the Pope to perform certain actions I am sure he never completed. Having sex and travelling seemed to be the most popular.

MEMORIES AND FORGETFULNESS

During the day, the crew of *HMS Gurkha* would muster on-board ship to work alongside the civilian workforce. Lunch was provided by kitchens, built some millennia past, located on the dockside. Actually, the food was prepared that morning for the midday meal, so at times, we dined very well. Fresh chips was the most popular, ten grades above what was served in the *Chevron Hilton* complex, where food was prepared and half cooked many hours before and then reheated before being served.

*

THERE IS LITTLE to record during this period except for one fundamental life-changing experience. Surprisingly it happened and it went like this. The nearest city to the town of Rosyth is Dunfermline, the capital of the county of Fife and one of the original capitals of Scotland. Scotland is awash with history, most of it bloody and violent.

The city had a large ballroom called the Kinema and still has. Wednesday night was the highlight of the week, usually with a visiting band of some stature, *The Who*, for example, and their performance would be preceded by a local band. These gigs were well attended and in company with the inmates from the *Chevron Hilton*, I enjoyed quite a few evenings there. I usually parked the car some distance from the Kinema Ballroom if only to throw the local Bobbies of the scent.

The evening in question was, as always, all very tribal, brought about by Scottish licensing hours with closure mandated at 10 pm sharp. The first band would make a start with the men folk crowded around the bar drinking at a fearsome rate. The ladies would form small groups on the dance floor jigging and dancing around their handbags piled-up in front of them like a mini-pyramid. I laugh to myself every time I think about it.

By 10 p.m. the men were well lubricated and some of the ladies too, who mostly drank the rave drink of the era, Brandy and Babycham. Then, when the bar did close there was more drink outside the shutters than on the inside.

As the main event of the evening started it all became very jolly. The strong and invisible magnetic force holding the ladies against the walls of the auditorium weakened and eventually diminished to zero. Boys and girls began to pair off to start dancing or rather their version of dancing. It got very crowded on the dance floor, especially during the slow numbers.

A chum of mine who had a part-time job as a bouncer told me how he enjoyed himself 'splitting the atom' as he called it, which we all took to mean dividing vertically copulating consenting adults and showing them the door. I always wondered what the aroma was in the dance hall and it wasn't cheap perfume.

Anyway, I asked this nice young lady to dance, which went well and we spent the rest of the evening together. Names were exchanged and I asked to see her again following evening, more in hope than anything else.

'Outside the Coop seven pm,' she suggested. 'Fine,' I said. 'See you there.'

Then, it was time to take the troops back to the *Chevron Hilton*. That night having made up my camp bed and turned-in under the mess deck table, I didn't sleep a wink all night. A strange feeling pervaded my every attempt to get to slumber. Love at first sight? Surely not? However, I knew the next day was going to be very special.

So there I was leaning on my shiny Sunbeam Talbot outside the Dunfermline Coop. The town hall clock struck seven pm and no date. Oh dear! Then the name Cowdenbeath flashed before my eyes. I had heard the name just once and it must have been last night in the dance hall. I had absolutely no knowledge of its location or how far away it was.

An elderly man wandered by, clearly having partaken of a suitable quantity of courage in the local pub before going back to the happy homestead with a broken pay.

'Excuse me Sir,' I asked. 'Does a town called Cowdenbeath have a Coop?'

'Aye aye laddie, so it does.'

'Which way?' I asked in some haste.

'Oh, Gae straecht doun yon road, left at Crossgates, then left when you 'it town, into the High Street. It all be on the right afore' the railway brig.'

With absolutely no idea where I was going, the Sunbeam set off at a fearsome rate. I missed the early evening drinkers wandering across the road at Crossgates, a dark sombre village whose only claim to fame was the butcher shop that sold every kind of pudding known to science.

On I charged, made the left turn into Cowdenbeath High Street pulled up at the Coop She was still waiting, hiding in the shop entrance trying to keep warm.

I wound down the window and shouted a 'Hi' to receive the reply 'you're late' the manner of which told me all was well, just don't do it again.

I made my excuses, parked the car and together we headed to the nearest lounge bar. Two brandy and Babychams later all was well. Her name was Johan, a high-class hairdresser and champion highland dancer so I found out later and the rest as we say became history.

It was not long before I was invited to tea with her parents Jim and Margret Anderson. Jim was an underground mechanical engineer in the Fife coalfields. A very tough and dangerous occupation for sure. Margret was a housewife who taught highland dancing to championship standard. A very nice family; very welcoming for a stranger from the South of England. (Think about it.)

We had a very nice courtship following her father's bidding to the letter, always returned his daughter at 10 p.m. sharp, not a minute later. The two of them were very close and my time in Scotland became? Well, you can guess.

I enjoyed my time with Johan's father. He told stories of working underground in truly grim conditions; three feet high coal seams with two feet of water that needed pumping out was one of the many. The lack of changing facilities, until the Coal Board was formed, was another.

His best story was during the construction of the Forth Road Bridge. The miners were invited to walk the wire, and the bridge workers were taken down a coal mine to chip-away at a couple of tons of coal. In the social event that flowed, the two industries declared the other was..... too dangerous and stupid.

One special evening after we had been going out for some weeks Johan asked me to drive into the wilds on the back road from Fife over the hills towards Rumbling Bridge then on to another back road towards Glen Eagles to see an ageing uncle and aunty. I was warned I would be unable to converse with an uncle as he had only spoken the Scottish language for the last few years, having spoken the Gaelic for all his life.

Johan and aunty soon got down to some serious chit chat, disappearing into the kitchen for the well-known ritual of making a strong pot of tea for all and filling a huge cake stand with delicious home-made Scottish cakes.

Johan was astonished when she returned to the living room to find her uncle and myself in deep conversation. Afterwards, on the journey home, she asked what on earth it was that we had to talk about.

'The Royal Victoria Hospital or the Netley Military Hospital,' I replied smiling.

To cut a long story short The Royal Victoria Hospital was located on the east bank of Southampton Water, a huge Victorian building with the longest corridors in Europe. It received the broken bodies from the many wars of the era, including WWI and earlier.

As a young man, he had fought in the Crimea War and been evacuated there when he was wounded. His memory of the hospital remained crystal clear. As a young sailor, I had sailed passed it many times.

My intended was suitably impressed. I didn't mention that I had absolutely no idea what else he was talking about.

*

IN DUE COURSE the ship's company reluctantly (sic) left the *Chevron Hilton* and moved to our new home on board our ship

Once on board *HMS Gurkha* I was detailed off to be the leading hand of the weapons and radio mess deck, which meant the radio staff, the seaman gunners who were the captain's of each gun or other mountings and looked after their maintenance as well as being the lead operator, plus a few electricians involved with the ship's armaments.

The mess had amongst its numbers three of the Portsmouth field gun crew, all individuals to a man. Jesse Owen was captain of 'Y' turret. Jesse looked to be average sized and height but he was the strongest, hardest man I had ever met. No bulging muscles, just a genuine hard-man from London. He was tranquil if you didn't get on his wrong side and he never, ever suffered fools no matter what their rank. He had 'tread carefully' written all over him.

His opposite number, Big George, a Scot, was the captain of 'A' turret, a much bigger guy, equally as strong, but wasn't as hard and quite an easy going sort of guy.

Then, there was Wee Jock from the Glasgow Gorbals. His claim to fame in the field gun crew? He was the 'Flying Angel' the man that flew across the chasm on the end of the long piece of rope carrying the post that held up the wire on the other side of the great divide.

And, so it came to pass twas a Sunday afternoon on a blank week. Nobody had a red bean to their name; there was nowhere to go to and in any event twas raining. I was trying to sleep on my bunk with little success; everybody else was just plain bored to death.

Wee Jock made a tour of the mess deck being a complete pain, scrounging every Playboy, Frolic and Penthouse magazine he could. All were well-thumbed, some were triple thumbed. I asked him what on earth he was going to do with the ship's supply of high class classic reading literature.

He said, and here I quote him one hundred per cent accurately, 'I'm going upstairs to the heads for the 'Shit of the Year'. Expect me back in at least two hours, about meal time.'

So, off Jock went and I thought no more about it.

Twenty-odd minutes later there was one hell of a crash, the ship shook violently and the lights went out for a few minutes

'Some shit,' offered Jesse Owens and we all laughed.

Ten minutes later Wee Jock returned; a shadow of his former self. He was white as a sheet and clearly in shock. As I sat him down on the nearest bunk he keeled over. I called the duty medic but by the time he made it to Jock's side, some colour had returned to his normally rosy cheeks. He took a long time to fully recover.

What happened occurred in the compartment above the heads, wherein the ship's secondary diesel generator was located. It had been on a test run with Wee Jock sitting unexpectedly below. The diesel engine had split its crankshaft at one of the journals under heavy load and produced one hell of a racket.

It was not long after this incident when another event occurred this time caused by carelessness when the ship's boiler had steam up and the main steam turbine driven electrical generator was being tested, connected to the ship's load.

Towards the end of the test, the main diesel generator was fired-up to be brought into service as the steam generator was shut-down.

To achieve this (sorry for the techie talk) the second generator is controlled so that its cycles are slowly matched to the first generator. This is called 'paralleling'.

This requires the use of a meter that has a pointer. When the pointer rotates very slowly clockwise to the five to midnight position the electrical breaker is closed with the usual bang and this connects the two generators together. The electrical technician then fiddles about with the two engine speeds to transfer the load to the second machine so that the first machine can be disconnected.

Get it wrong and the stronger machine will cause the weaker machine to go walkabout, which is what happened in this case. Seriously wrong, the breaker closure was mistimed with the pointer somewhere round about twenty past midnight, or so we were told.

The diesel generator lifted off its bed as it attempted to relocate to another area of the engine room. The hapless technician had an even bigger shock than Wee Jock. Everybody heard the commotion as the ship shook and shuddered so badly that crew members started ringing their loved ones to say the ship would not be going to sea that weekend.

To save the day, the ship's refit programme, a sister Tribal class frigate arrived in Rosyth for refit and it became a donor-ship for all our ship's troubles. Some smart arse suggested just swopping the two ship's nameplates; just transfer the two crews from one ship to the other. The Captain was not amused.

*

DURING THE DELAY to get the ship ready for sea trials my relationship with Johan powered ahead so we planned to get engaged at the next leave.

Eventually, the ship was ready to go to sea for trials to see if it would actually work and reach the open sea from Rosyth and back again without anything going too wrong.

Following successful trials, the ship sailed for the Portland Naval Base on the South coast for work-up, which went surprisingly well. I was assigned to the ship's Gunnery department looking after a quite clever piece of kit (the Gun Positioning System or GPS) which collected all the information about potential targets garnered from the radars sets and various 'mark one' eyeballs located around the upper deck.

It processed the information and presented it to the officer-in-charge of the display consul in the Operations Room, whose task was to prioritise the targets before sending them down to the TS (transmitting station – a big mechanical computer) in the depths of the ship. The TS passed the information to the gun radar turret so it could lock to the target, and the guns would engage the target ensuring its destruction.

The GPS system did have one very useful piece of kit mounted on a pedestal on the open deck above the bridge. A very powerful motorised binocular unit ideal for watching young ladies on any passing beach, Weymouth for example.

*

WHEN WORK-UP HAD concluded, the ship had the rather interesting experience of being assigned as the guard-ship for the 1965 Cowes to Torquay Power Boat Race, a premier event in anybody's calendar.

MEMORIES AND FORGETFULNESS

The Cowes-Torquay race was launched by Sir Max Aitken; the first offshore powerboat race in Britain in 1961. It became the longest-running offshore powerboat race in the world.

This was one tough event and the race boats were the best of the best. Racing boats with twin four hundred horsepower diesel turbo engines and were strong enough to pound their way through the rough waters of the English Channel over a course exceeding a hundred miles.

That their race crews could stand the pounding was incredible. It was very easy to break both legs if momentarily locked in the standing position. Most of the competing racers had heavily padded armchairs with strong safety straps.

The other RN guard-ship was *HMS Brave Boarder*, an MTB weighing in at over one hundred tons equipped with three gas turbine engines not too dissimilar to the engines used on Concorde.

She was more than able to keep a close eye on the competitors from the front of the fleet to the rear. This race was dangerous and many competitors did not finish the course. Lady Aiken's cruiser split her transom. At speed, the cruiser was not going to sink but as it arrived at Torquay Harbour the speed restriction sign (five knots-max) became redundant as Lady Aiken drove her cruiser up the nearest sandy beach. When asked about the damage to the hull she was quoted as saying 'Bugger the hull, I had to save the engines.'

*

AFTERWARDS, THE SHIP returned to Rosyth so that foreign leave could be given to the crew before proceeding to the Persian Gulf and the ship's base at Bahrain.

Johan and I became engaged and a great family party was held. Following this, I took the opportunity to return my car to my parent's home in Southampton and for them to meet my fiancé. My Sunbeam Talbot left the dockyard for the last time. The duty policeman saluted as always, a courtesy for officers, as they did not expect a rating to be driving such an iconic motor car.

The return journey by train back to Rosyth included a couple of nights in London; the highlight was the chance to see Spike Milligan's stage play *Son of Oblomov* at the Comedy Theatre, where it was collecting rave reviews. The story was about a Russian noble who spent all his time in bed. All you ever heard about this wonderful comedian is true.

He ad-libbed every show, the cast never knew what to expect. It took a few shows for them to, as we say, 'get with it'. The show became famous later on, so it was very hard to get tickets.

We returned on the night sleeper to Edinburgh and then by local train service to Cowdenbeath. The ship sailed a week later on and it would be nine months before the return and the planned wedding.

*

The Second Commission of HMS Gurkha

THE OUTBOUND VOYAGE was not as tranquil in the Bay of Biscay as I would have liked. The ship refuelled at Gibraltar where little had changed. I had hoped that *HMS Gurkha* would visit Malta but no such luck. However, to the delight of all, the Wasp helicopter made a quick flight ashore to pick-up the mail. The ship's passage through the Suez Canal went smoothly and the voyage down the Red Sea was without incident.

The ship put-in at Aden to refuel and it did not take long to discover matters ashore were not as stable as before. Nationalist insurgents were causing problems. Shopping and relaxing in Aden required crew members to keep together and look-out for one another.

Aden has an excellent natural harbour but the landscape is strictly desert, mountains and the odd volcanic crater. An ideal location for a honeymoon, Ha! Ha!

Two events come to mind, the first when relaxing on top of the bridge when an RAF transport aircraft was seen to make a perfect landing in the sea a hundred yards short of the airfield runway. Quite what happened who knows but by using the GPS power binoculars I could see the crew had scrambled out of the aircraft via the windows in the nose of the aircraft and were sitting somewhat forlornly on top of the cockpit awaiting rescue.

The second incident, so rumour had it, concerned the all-important BP oil refinery on Little Aden, located on the other side of the large bay. It seems that the insurgents were making a nuisance of themselves and someone in authority was concerned for the continuing operations of this vital facility.

Someone, so it was further rumoured, had come up with the bright idea of using the Gurkhas based at Aden to see if they could solve the problem, which they did almost overnight. A week later the authorities sought to visit the refinery to see what steps had been taken. They were glad they had made the visit but were totally shocked, as it seems that the Gurkhas had caught a few insurgents, dissected one completely then wired his remains up on the boundary fence and let the others return to where they had come from to spread the news. If anybody had taken a photograph of this rumoured incident there would have been hell to pay.

Before the ship departed for the Gulf, the ship spent time towing 'splash' targets for the RAF Hunter fighter aircraft to shoot at. The pilots had great skill as their main task was supporting SAS patrols inland. So, while the RAF fired their cannons at the splash target, the ship's gunnery team took the chance to get some much-needed practice acquiring fast moving targets and getting the time from acquiring the target to being ready to open fire down to acceptable limits.

At the end of the exercise, the RAF squadron leader made a pass at the towed splash target using two-inch rockets and whoosh! There was little left to reel in. Still, they did supply the splash targets in the first place.

Two days later the ship completed replenishment at sea and more importantly the mail had arrived. Johan wrote twice a week, everything at home was fine and now she had a new focus in her life, which she was getting used to.

As the ship proceeded along the Yemen coastline the Captain kept our course some distance from the rugged mountainous shoreline. The weather is very clear in this area making it very hard to judge distance without radar. The ship kept outside of the shipping lanes to avoid the many commercial ships and tankers heading towards the Red Sea and the Suez Canal.

We reached the border with Yemen and on to Oman with little change of scenery. As the ship slowly turned north we reached Al Hadd the turning point for entering into the Gulf of Oman and up into the Straits of Hormuz, a natural choke point for the hundreds of huge tankers transporting crude oil to the world markets.

The passage through the Straits of Hormuz was interesting. Due to the clear air, it was quite easy to see both sides. The friendly side to the west, the doubtful side, the Iranians, to the east. There was little going on, unlike the present day when political matters are in a state of flux.

It was a short thirty-hour voyage to the shared naval dockyard at Bahrain. The dockyard was quite modest in size but it had a few facilities including a club with a swimming pool. The ship had long reverted to tropical routine meaning an early start to the day and an early end of the day just two hours after lunch at midday.

First thing in the morning I found the deck to the ship covered in water, condensation from the night air. As soon as the sun peeped above the horizon the temperature quickly rose, and became unbearable by mid-morning.

After work, I joined a group from the mess heading towards the swimming pool for exercise and relaxing. Next to the pool stood a tall tower covered in a white slatted wooden structure. We wondered what its use might be. I dived into the pool and soon found out. The water was freezing. I almost came out of the pool feet first. Anyway the hardy managed a short swim and fortunately, a local attendant came to open the pool bar to serve cool sodas and local snacks.

In the evening we all went into town, wandered around the souks and saved our scarce pennies for another day. There was little to do in Bahrain, so little to write home about. The letters to Mum and Dad were easy enough but finding suitable words to write to Johan was hard. She wanted to know all about the great outside world. Bahrain did not provide much to write home about.

I once wrote a spoof letter describing an exciting day-out swimming with the camels and saving beautiful Arab princesses from danger. She replied she didn't buy into the saving beautiful Arab princesses from danger story on the basis the only place one would find beautiful Arab princesses would be in the lady's department in Harrods, London.

*

NEXT UP, THE festive season. The ship was programmed to visit an Iranian city called Abadan some miles up the Shatt al-Arab waterway that forms the border between Iraq and Iran. The focus of the visit was the expat community that supported the operations of a truly huge oil refinery, at the time the largest in the Middle East.

I found myself ahead of the game as this community had schools for the expat children. Father sent me a letter to let me know that four very attractive young teachers, former members of the Southampton Sailing Club were teaching there. Dad was rather fond of them. The teacher's secret circle in action. I did meet them a couple of times in the sailing club during the time when I joined the Royal Navy in 1960.

The ship navigated its way up the waterway with care, tied-up at a jetty positioned on the division between the refinery and the area of the expat housing estate.

An important request had been received from our hosts, cigarettes: American or British. The word smuggling was not used but imported cigarettes had a huge duty imposed upon them by the State of Iran in an attempt to protect the home market. Smoking an Iranian cigarette was later described as smoking a ten-year-old Woodbine that had been dropped in the 'john' and allowed to dry sitting on top of camel dung. (Interesting flavour.)

The exit from the jetty onto the street was guarded by a couple of truly bored Iranian security guards who made no attempt to involve themselves in what was being taken ashore. Duty-free cigarettes in the Middle East were amazingly cheap.

I vaguely remember the festive programme. First up was a day visit to the refinery. After forty years in the upstream side of the oil and gas industry, I only ever took one assignment in a refinery, Esso Fawley, and never felt comfortable in the environment. I only took the contract because there was not much going on and it was close to my parent's home in Southampton.

The Abadan refinery was working flat out. The most impressive feature was the four massive pipelines feeding the complex. Each had a mechanical flow-meter measuring the crude oil flowing into the storage tanks. The counters spun around so fast it was hard to read the numbers. Each digit was one barrel of oil or forty-two gallons.

The first evening was a meet and greet session in the main community hall. Someone had thoughtfully stacked some empty cardboard boxes that were the right size for collecting packets of two hundred 'ciggies'.

I soon met the ladies from my badly missed sailing club, quickly brought them up to date with the club gossip and passed on my parent's well wishes. The evening soon achieved its purpose dividing the ship's crew up in a more or less equal fashion between the competing expat groups.

The next evening was carefully arranged and I remember going to four parties in one evening. It was all very jolly. My group arrived at the last venue slightly late and the only beverage remaining were cases of Drambuie, a sweet Scottish liqueur based on best whisky. Now, I do like Drambuie but a half-pint glass full of this golden liquid is a bit much. Still, I continually slipped as much ice into my glass as possible. The evening was getting late, so I took the chance of a large mug of coffee and carelessly 'forgot' where I had left my half full half pint glass.

The next event must have been Christmas Day, USA style. In the morning my friends and I arrived at a huge bungalow where our host, an American professor, lived with his British wife and daughter. The daughter was quite pretty, married to an Iranian naval officer, a Lt. Commander if I remember correctly. We relaxed in the garden while the host's wife and maid prepared the biggest turkey I have ever seen.

We took bets as to whether it would fit into the oven but clearly American ovens are sized for American turkeys. The professor was a very interesting host. He'd travelled widely across the vast history that is Persia, now called Iran. He described the wonderful mosques containing magical interior decorations, with great spans that covered huge floor areas far greater than anything built before in the west. It would be centuries before the west could build cathedrals with comparable covered floor areas. He'd explored the ancient Persian cities plus the forts some of which had been built high up on cliff faces or on the top of impossible mountains.

The turkey took a long time to cook to perfection but by late afternoon a wonderful spread was laid out on a huge table located on the veranda overlooking the garden. By the time the Christmas feast had concluded everyone was full so full that further activity was not possible.

To complete our tour of Persian culture our host laid on a spectacular photographic slide show of the places he had visited. Confusingly he had mixed up his Persian presentation with photographic slides his wife had taken of Wigan's Botanical Gardens, one of the finest in the UK. The evening silently crept up upon us all. After a light tea and many fond farewells, we made our way back to the ship.

*

THE SHIP RETURNED to Bahrain and occasionally went on patrol. The focus was the gold trade between the Gulf States and India where gold is used in many of its traditional customs. The rulers of the Gulf States were keen to have their legal trade protected. An illegal trade existed and when the ship came across on Arab Dhow without any signs of being a sailing or fishing craft but equipped with a stonking great MB diesel engine, an inspection invariably took place.

The Arab captains, noticing our ship had two funnels, apparently thought our ship could go twice the speed, at least that is what we were led to believe. Actually, the ship was equipped with a Wasp helicopter, a small but effective aircraft.

Later on, in Bahrain, Sir William Luce, Political Officer for the Persian Gulf, arrived onboard with his daughter Diane, and social secretary Victoria, for a short voyage to Abu Dhabi. The two ladies took to sunbathing on the small deck in front of the bridge, which kept the bridge look-outs focused on looking ahead.

The captain was keen to demonstrate what a mighty fighting warship we were (sic) and so the main gun was fired at nothing in particular but the demonstration of our anti-submarine capability proved most interesting. The Asdic boys, hidden up in the bows of the ship, found a huge shoal of fish. The anti-submarine mortar was fired to wake them up. There was a magnificent underwater explosion at a shallow depth and thousands of stunned fish floated to the surface.

The captain called away the ship's sea-boat to collect some fish for the evening meal. And so it came to pass that the sea-boat came back quite a few times loaded with more fish.

So the ship's company had fish for the evening meal, breakfast, lunch, the evening meal again, then fish cakes became a regular feature of the menu for some time. The ship's Supply Officer was well pleased as he had to live with a fixed budget for food per person, believed to be eight bob a day.

The ship's final exercise in the Gulf was to take part in a shore bombardment shoot at Das Island. There must be two Das Islands as the other one is full of oil refinery. The ship arrived at the target area staying three miles offshore in calm seas. The map of the area, engraved on clear plastic sheet, was overlain on the GPS radar display, to give the necessary range and direction. The ship, whilst still moving, engaged the target and from my vantage point using the GPS system binoculars, the ship's shooting was quite effective.

As if to put us in our place, the army was cleared to complete their part of the exercise. A Chieftain tank came barrelling along the beach at speed, the hull leaping and bouncing over the sand dunes, its stabilised main-gun rock steady in comparison, fired three rounds and the target disappeared. Our gunnery officer made a mental note not to engage with any modern army tanks. If nothing else, their gun was big than ours.

Finally, the ship said a final goodbye to Bahrain and the Persian Gulf, or so we all thought, and headed out of the Straits of Hormuz to make a courtesy call at Muscat, the capital city of Oman. On the voyage to Oman, the ship entered a famous inlet known as Elphinstone Creek at the tip of the peninsula that forms the narrow waterway at the Straits of Hormuz.

Both sides of the Creek towered three thousand feet on either side and the area was known for being one of the hottest locations on earth. The day we entered, it was only 45 degrees centigrade (113ºF)

The Creek was famous for Telegraph Island a truly barren lump of rock sitting in the middle of the channel for safety. The company, Cable & Wireless, installed a telegraph repeating station to boost the telegraph signals, which faded over distance on the longer routes.

There were living quarters for the telegraph operators and their servants, but the dangers, the tremendous heat and the sheer monotony of living on the island caused the operators to go mad and Telegraph Island became the source of the phrase 'going around the bend'.

When *HMS Gurkha* visited the area the island had long been abandoned. It was, however, a great experience especially in the late afternoon giving fabulous colours on the extremely rocky landscape with stunning topography to photograph.

*

AND SO, ON to Oman, an absolute monarchy. The country covers some interesting real estate, which over the years has attracted the attention of several colonial powers. The Portuguese held it for a century, fought the Turks for it and there were challenges from Persia.

A civil war and repeated incursions by the Persian King Nader Shah in the 18th century destabilised the region, further straining relations between the interior and Muscat, producing a power vacuum in Oman leading to the emergence of the Al Bu Sa'id dynasty who have ruled Oman ever since, absolutely.

Muscat's naval and military supremacy was re-established in the 19th century by Said bin Sultan who signed a treaty with the U.S., which is why when the crew went ashore there was plenty of Coca-Cola but no beer. Many visited the American Hospital to give blood for which a small reward was given in cash.

The ship anchored in the fine protected harbour, which annoyed a very large whale shark that made its presence known. It actually bumped against the ship and I did feel the movement. The duty Seaman Leading Hand in charge of the ship's sea boat decided on an attempt to chase it away which was a strange idea as one flip from the tail of such a large mammal would have relocated the sea boat to an unplanned location. After all, was it not the shark's bay?

One side of the bay was protected by a fort with a very tall mast. Our American guide in the hospital recalled the mast was once used on a sister ship to Admiral Nelson's *HMS Victory*. How it survived the harsh weather plus the sandstorms for all those many decades was a question that crossed my mind.

And finally, Muscat was home to that marvel of automotive engineering, the Land Rover. I did not see any other kind of vehicle, but Muscat in the mid-1960s, was more sleepy hollow than anything else. Given the heat, I'm not surprised.

Following the visit to Oman, the ship sailed for Mombasa, on the East African coast.

*

THE VOYAGE TO Mombasa was very relaxing. With the ship's anti-roll stabilisers safely tucked away out of harm's way I was able to sleep in the air-conditioned comfort of my mess deck without the infernal noise of the hydraulics that powered the stabilisers in the compartment below. The natural movement of the ship, as it gently rolled and pitched in a slowly building ocean swell, was bliss, I slept like a log.

Two days out, the purpose of the ship's assignment was revealed. *HMS Gurkha* was heading to the Beira Patrol, the blockade of oil shipments to Rhodesia (now Zimbabwe) through Beira, Mozambique, resulting from United Nations trade sanctions on Rhodesia.

Rhodesia's mostly white government had unilaterally declared independence in November 1965, after rejecting British preconditions for independence. The United Nations Security Council reacted by passing Resolution 217, to be used by the British as legal justification for the blockade.

I, along with many of my shipmates, knew little about the subject, but the collective opinion was it would become some long drawn out affair that would prevent us from doing something more useful, like visiting countries of interest. Harold Wilson was the UK's prime minister. If he was involved the opinion amongst us was not positive. Who was it who said, 'How do you know when he's lying? When his lips move.'

The ship arrived at Mombasa for a week's stay, which gave me the chance to visit the Yacht Club to see if there was any racing, but there was none to be had. Still, I enjoyed a few beers in the club and listened to the farmers complain about the situation in Kenya and in Rhodesia. Independence was coming to Kenya. The collective opinion was it would not help matters at all. There were many issues, all contentious, depending on your point of view.

The ship was ordered to escort *HMS Ark Royal*, one of the UK's largest aircraft carriers, tasked with the blockade. Six bloody weeks, watching a big ship work very hard, for very little result.

Our ship's area of activity was the same six long boring weeks, up and down, up and bloody down. The only activity worth watching was when *HMS Ark Royal* went to flying stations. Our captain requested the Fleet Air Arm Buccaneers to occasionally fly-by to give our operations room crew some practice tracking aircraft and handing off to the Gunnery TS so that our gun radar operators could get some practice.

This involved the equipment I was tasked with looking after so during the day and the occasional nighttime exercise, so I was kept sufficiently busy to pass the time.

*

EVENTUALLY, THE SHIP returned to Mombasa, enabling the captain to give Foreign Service leave of one week, to each watch. The choices presented to the crew were, a hotel on a beach somewhere just up the coast, but my friends and I chose the option to take the overnight sleeper train to Nairobi with a cheap deal on offer at the Nairobi YMCA. The train journey was interesting in as much the distance was under three hundred miles, so why an all-night journey?

We were soon to find out. The engine and the rolling stock were British, of course, but none of it was modern. Still, the ride was comfortable enough in the old-fashioned corridor carriages. Our group took the precaution to fill picnic bags full of drinks and snacks, plus our normal luggage. The train departed late afternoon. As it climbed out of the city up into the hinterland we all enjoyed a marvellous African sunset.

The smell of Africa was exciting. This was a very large continent that could hold so much promise. Talking of promises, we were at a loss to know where we would actually lay our weary heads down. With six of us in a compartment, sitting three each side, just where was the beds?

We soon found out after visiting the restaurant carriage. We returned to find the compartment transformed by the simple means of raising the seat back-rests to the horizontal, the middle bunk, and lowering a panel from high in the ceiling, the top bunk. Simple really. Crisp white sheets, a soft pillow and a folded blanket for later if it got cold during the night.

The facilities were located at the end of the corridor. I prepared for bed and bagged a middle berth, where I could lay to look out the open window, the fresh night air keeping us all very comfortable.

Going to sleep proved to be easy, as the train rocked and rolled its way up the ageing track at a very sedate speed. You could hear the engine working hard on the steeper gradients. Ah, heavenly.

I awoke just as the sun was rising. I lay in peace and tranquillity as the new day arrived with Africa slipping past outside the window. Later, the car attendant served morning tea and biscuits in bed, a well-timed service with the objective of getting the passengers up and about before the train arrived at our destination.

So, what did our party get up to during the four days we were there? Well, the YMCA was comfortable, if basic. Everybody had a room to themselves. The helpful staff provided a full range of information and suggestions. The safari day-trip was good, except the zebras, who all turned away from our cameras. When you've seen one zebra's arse, you have seen them all.

Then, there was a trip to the Karura Forest Waterfalls, followed by two days exploring the city. The railway depot was also interesting as Kenya used the Garratt locomotive, that magnificent giant of a steam locomotive that is articulated into three sections, with the boiler occupying the suspended centre section.

At night, as the daytime temperatures cooled off, several bars were visited and several ice-cold beers were consumed. OK, more than several beers and we may have engaged with the local female students studying at the local university.

*

ALL TOO SOON it was time to make the return journey to the ship. Just as the second watch was about to end their week's leave the Captain received orders to return to Bahrain to continue our presence in the Persian Gulf. I have long since cast any memories of this era into the waste bin of life. No doubt the ship chased a few Arab dhows and found very little for the effort.

During what was to be the ship's last visit to Bahrain, new crew members embarked, known as advance leave party. This was quite a clever idea the navy had come up with towards the end of a ship's commission. The new crew members would be the caretakers of the ship the minute it arrived back in the UK base so that the lonely hearts club, that is to say, everybody else, could rush ashore to be with their loved ones or wives and families, parents, et al.

The party was actually quite small but in my combined mess deck, we welcomed just two electricians plus one radio mechanic. His name was Terry but quickly picked up the handle of 'the entertainer'. Terry was a card magician, actually quite a good one. He was a popular fellow had a quick wit and made people laugh.

*

BACK ON PATROL in the Straits of Hormuz, the ship passed through Elphinstone Creek for the second time. Later that day, the Captain received orders to proceed to Seychelles to assist in some unrest that had occurred among the local population.

This would be the second long leg of the ship's programme and evening entertainment generally defaulted to playing cards. This required care. Playing cards was a very popular evening entertainment, but gambling was definitely not allowed. I always ensured my mess deck followed the ship's rule on this subject. My favourite game was crib and I was quite good at it, as my father was a very good player and an excellent instructor.

One evening, the pressure reached the point where Terry was pressured to demonstrate his card skill playing poker. Terry's card tricks were all very good, but human nature gravitates to gambling. Something Terry would never do on board ship. So, a poker game was set up using matchsticks, with a guard on the gangway coming down into the mess deck.

Three players with alleged poker skills sat around the mess deck table and the game began. It crossed my mind that Terry must know how to play poker, how else could he demonstrate what to do and what not to do. The game followed the course you can imagine, Terry started losing, then recovering his lead, then loosing again. He knew just exactly where every card was, an amazing skill. He showed how crooked players could deal from the bottom of the deck, plus all the other tricks of the trade. His party piece was yet to come when one of the players thought he had a winning hand and Terry laid down five aces, just to prove what could be done. In all, it was a very entertaining evening.

So what there to know about our destination, this island paradise? Seychelles is archipelago in the Indian Ocean with many small islands, home to numerous beaches coral reefs and nature reserves as well as rare animals such as giant Aldabra tortoises.

The islands were a transit point for trade between Africa and Asia and occasionally used by pirates until the French took control in 1756. The islands were named after Jean Moreau de Séchelles, Louis XV's Minister of Finance. The French took root and a French Creole community developed.

The British helped themselves to the islands later in their history and it became a Crown Colony at the beginning of the twenty century. The ship's crew, always interested in history, took an interest in that other expected species on the island, pretty French Creole ladies.

*

THE VOYAGE OF just over one thousand miles took just under a week. When the ship arrived all seemed to be well. Beach parties were organised and I took the chance for some scuba diving. The beaches were wonderful, the island being largely unspoilt at this time; free from the tourist industry that now blights this far away wonderland.

In the evening, a ship's dance was held in the island's community hall, with music from a local band, drinks and local cuisine from our hosts. This turned out to be the highlight of the visit.

My mess deck attended in full force except for the duty hands. The dance proved to be a very nice evening. Gentlemen outnumbered the ladies, although some stalwarts managed to dance with the local ladies who came in pairs, the sweet young Creole girl and Mummy. The mothers were, err, quite large, and more than a few were Benny Hill ready.

Still, it was a good evening sitting with my messmates including the three field gunners who were always good company. Jesse Owen was quiet that evening, saying little, nursing his beer for longer than usual.

On the other side of the dance hall, a group of stokers were overdoing the jollification including one large fit sort of guy who might have been a boxer in his day. It was just the way he flung his arms around. He was one of the new boys and didn't we know it. Laughing too loudly, being a complete pain with the ladies and generally looking like trouble.

As the evening wore on this person became more objectionable. Just as night follows day he just had to come over to our side of the dance hall. What happened next was classic. He started berating Jesse, a man he did not know: was he the ship's hard man etc, etc.

Jesse turned his back and ignored him. That made things worse. Big George and Wee Jock cleverly moved out of Jesse's way but when the taunting became too much Jesse suddenly stood up, spinning around in one fabulous body movement as he hit this objectionable person just the once with all the efficiency of his brute strength he could muster. The power was there to see. Crikey!

The stoker flew across the dance hall, collapsing on the table he had just vacated, unmoving, out for the count. Big George and Wee Jock quietly took Jesse by the arms to lead him outside into the cool night air. The rest of the table followed behind. As I left the dance hall I saw the stokers were sitting there just stunned.

One of the Chief POs went to the stoker's table, told them 'that was that' and if anybody asked they saw nothing. To be fair only a few people actually saw the body sailing across the room. Well, that was the end of the evening for us, time to invoke that classic phrase, 'Absence of body is better than the presence of mind,' before the shore patrol arrived.

Did the shore patrol or police arrive who knows? My group was long gone as we quietly made our way back to the ship. Sometime later I heard that someone had thanked Jesse because the stoker he put on the floor had been making a nuisance of himself in the junior stoker's mess deck.

*

NEXT DAY, SHORTLY after lunch, the ship sailed for Aden and the start of the long voyage back to Blighty. Johan's letters were still regular as always telling me about the arrangements for our wedding as they pushed along at a respectable rate. I wrote to my parents advising them of the intended arrangements, the locations and hoped to see them soon in Southampton.

The evening passed quickly so my mess deck took the chance of an early night. The visit to Seychelles had been enjoyable but hectic. The officers and men of *HMS Gurkha* had all enjoyed themselves with just the one noticeable exception.

I turned in early and slept soundly; a welcome change. Then, about two in the morning I woke up. Everything was quiet, too quiet. The ship was not moving, just rolling slowly from side to side. I switched on my bunk light. Nothing? I tried the bunk light of the adjacent bed still nothing. Then I heard footsteps, urgent feet moving quickly on the deck above; the main through-deck for the whole ship.

I found my torch and saw everyone in the mess fast asleep. I rose, dressed and found my shoes in the foot-locker. The small green light on the small mess deck refrigerator was unlit, confirming the lack of power. I moved to the centre of the mess deck and as I went to climb the gangway up to the next deck I avoided braining myself on the underside of the closed hatch.

I opened the small emergency hatch, the 'Y' hatch, in the middle of the main 'X' hatch and stuck my head through the 'Y' hatch and saw much orderly confusion. Fire hoses everywhere with ghostly emergency lighting showing what was going on.

The damage control officer rushed by. I shouted out the loudest 'Oi you' I could manage. The officer stopped dead in his tracks looked around at me with a big question on his face.

He shouted, 'You are?'

'The leading hand-in-charge of this mess deck down here. I have everyone fast asleep about forty-five men.'

The words 'Oh fuck me,' flashed across his lips. Nobody had thought to rouse the alarm for my mess deck.

He said, 'Boiler room fire, serious.'

'That's the adjacent compartment to the mess deck.' I said. 'Want to share some thoughts?'

I didn't manage the usual greeting of 'Sir' but never mind.

The damage control officer told me the forced lubrication pump had split a connection flange, the resultant high-pressure leak had flashed into a very serious fire.

He added, 'OK, Leading Hand, get your men up, get them dressed, bed bags zipped up and bunks stowed in the 'up' position. Footlockers to be cleared away and stowed on the top bunk. Then, get your men forward out of the way. The mess deck must be ready to spray the boiler room bulkhead from the mess deck side if necessary OK?'

I indicated an OK and disappeared down below. My bunk was on the far port side of the compartment. I chose Jessie Owen to help me. His bunk was on the opposite side of the compartment. I woke him gently and received a staring eye.

'Jesse,' I said. 'Fire, fire, fire in the boiler room. I need you to clear this side of the mess deck. Get the men up, get them dressed, bed bags zipped up and bunks stowed in the up position. Footlockers to be cleared away and stowed on the top bunk. Tell them to move forward and keep out of the way. When you've finished stay behind with me to double check.'

'Nothing too serious then,' he said, his London humour shining through.

Together, we quickly and without drama, led our the members of our mess deck to safety. Men from above opened up the 'X' hatch. Someone told me that the steam in the boiler had been emptied at high pressure into the locked down boiler room and the bilges were being flooded with foam.

'Is the fire out?' I asked

'We have to sit on it and pray, otherwise, the boiler room will have to be flooded.'

'Christ,' I thought. 'What a to-do.'

Jesse and I double checked the mess, and then went forward just as the fire team rushed down into the mess to spray the boiler room bulkhead just as a precaution. Shit, that was my side of the mess deck.

An hour later the fire was declared extinguished as the electrical department set about bringing the ship's electrical power supplies back on. The ship slowly got underway powered by the 'G8' gas turbine that enables a dead ship to sail without steam for the main engine.

The galley started serving corn dog sandwiches (navy slang for corn beef) with lots of hot coffee. The fire and damage control parties were fed first but a few of us tagged along afterwards. I went back to the mess to find members of the mess cleaning up the last of the seawater used to spray the boiler room bulkhead. Big George and Wee Jock brought a large fanny of fresh water to remove the drying salt on the deck.

The ship's mess decks became too hot for comfort making any attempt at further sleep difficult. There was no power available for the air conditioning system and a ship that ran on eighty per cent air recirculation was always going to get too hot. It was a fitful night for many of the crew of *HMS Gurkha*. The electrical and mechanical departments were both working double watches. There was much to do.

The fire in the boiler room had damaged some of the main electrical cables including one of the two confirmed supplies to the ship's steering motors. Emergency cables were run to make up for the shortfall.

The engineering officers were trying to assess the damage to the boiler as some tubes had burst during the emergency discharge of steam to quell the fire. The whole compartment was a mess. The engineering watch below spent a long time trying to restore order and cleanliness.

With the boiler still needing to cool down before repairs could commence there was not much else that could be achieved. By now the midnight watch had become the morning watch but few of the crew took any rest. The electrical department had managed to get some of the ship's services restored. There was no power available for the armament systems and only the small navigation radar was operating. The ship's lighting was fully restored and partial power to the food storage systems was another priority.

Now, could the ship's 'G8' gas turbine engine continue in service until the main boiler could be repaired? A big ask as the ship did not carry sufficient diesel fuel for long duration service.

I managed a few hours uncomfortable sleep in the mess. The air-conditioning was partly operational but it was very hard to ventilate the ship with fresh air.

A frugal breakfast was served the ship's galley, being short of electrical power and the lack of steam. In this era, many navy ships used steam to cook foods, soups being one of them. Fresh steam fed to a large forty-gallon cauldron filled with new or other ingredients could feed a hungry crew very quickly, traditionally between brief rest spells when in battle. A well-fed crew could always fight a ship much better than a hungry crew. Even Admiral Nelson knew this.

I made my way to the department workshop. The radio department had little to do so I went to explore the damage in the boiler room, entering at main deck level from the sea boat station. I climbed down to be confronted with an eerie sight. The compartment was lit by hastily installed necklaces of emergency lights. The glass wells that protected the main lights up on the deckhead had all melted. Long thin strands of glass hung down waving slowly with the motion of the ship.

It was very hot, the pungent smell of the fire and burnt cables was almost overpowering.

One of the stokers told me an amusing story about the previous night. It had humour only because the man involved was not injured. The ship's engine room and boiler room were separate unmanned spaces but a combined control room sat above the dividing transverse bulkhead with two adjacent ladderways down into their depths. A duty member of the control room crew made a tour of these two important compartments every fifteen minutes.

The crew member in question was passing the forced lubrication pump and saw the flanged connection starting to give way. Well aware of what would happen next he activated the emergency shutdown for the boiler room then made much haste up the ladder to safety. The flange burst and a big ball of fire chased him, and his bottom, up into the control room.

As he shot up into the control room the duty chief dryly welcomed him with a 'Hello Nobby Clark' as he slammed the boiler room access hatch firmly closed behind him. The shaken crew member lost his balance, fell down the access hatch into the Engine Room, followed by a 'Goodbye Nobby Clark' from the Chief. More London humour at its best.

On my way out of the boiler room , I ran into the Chief Electrician, enquiring if there was anything the radio hands could do. He suggested doing something about the lighting but added the fire had vaporised almost three feet of steel ladder. The molecules of molten steel had invaded every electrical circuit in the compartment and everything was shorting out.

I said I would gather my team to see what we could do. I collected four radio technicians and headed to the electrical stores for supplies of new cable, fittings and cleaners. I explained it would be easiest to chop the existing cables from light fittings grouped in one area, remove the remains of the glass wells and metal guards strip, clean the internals, then rewire this cluster of deckhead lights in a daisy chain fashion with new cables from the nearest lighting fuse box.

It took little time to make good progress and soon the first four lights in the corner close to the boiler room entrance were ready for testing. The electrical resistance to earth was poor, possibly acceptable, but only switching on would tell.

The Chief Electrician arrived to see the progress. Explaining the situation I switched on, the fuse didn't blow and the new cables stayed cold.

The Chief said 'And the Lord said let there be light.'

A voice behind him replied 'And you could see fer fuckin' miles.'

We all laughed; it did us all good. The Chief gave a well done and asked when the other areas would be completed. By late afternoon all that could be done was done. The engineering black gang preparing to repair the cooled down boiler were more than grateful.

Back in the mess, I found cooks-of-the-mess had finished restoring our home to orderliness. I took a shower and turned-in for a couple of hours. The evening meal menu was reduced to two choices, take or leave. At least the AC was back on and the mess managed a comfortable night's rest.

The next day one of our submarines appeared from the depths to replenish the ship's diesel tanks. Diesel submarines carry a lot of diesel. I assume they can flood some of their buoyancy tanks with the fuel, diesel being lighter than seawater.

As the fuel was being pumped aboard, the submarine opened its main hatches to ventilate the vessel's interior and the smell was wow, you can't believe the stink. The submarine crew cannot smell it as they live in it.

The good news of the afternoon was that the boiler repairs were well underway with completion expected in thirty hours. It would have been a long way to Aden powered only by the ship's gas turbine, assuming a sufficiency of diesel for such a long journey.

So, for the next two days, I retreated to my little world and concentrated on revising for my PPE exam to gain promotion to senior rating. The specialised trades in the RN had a shortage of personnel and their rosters were dry. Time to take advantage. The other trades were not so blessed, especially office hands and services. Those ratings could wait a long time to get the chance of advancement.

Eventually, the repairs to the boiler were completed, a truly difficult task at sea. The mess had to suffer the noise of the hydraulic pressure testing pump in the adjacent compartment as it banged away, mostly during the night. Hard to complain though. I was in a comfortable bed with AC. The engineers in the boiler room were working hard in very tough and hot conditions.

The engineers raised steam very slowly with constant checks to ensure all was well. Steam is a very dangerous gas and superheated steam is just downright dangerous as it is quite invisible.

The warm-up was successful and after some hours the ship resumed full power, steaming on its main engine. Next, normal electrical power was restored; time to get the armaments and radar systems back online. As the ship passed the Horn of Africa we all knew this part of the Middle East presented real and present dangers.

*

THE SHIP DOCKED at Aden to refuel, replenish stores and catch-up with the mail. I wrote to Johan with the latest news, but that all was well, hoping to be home soon.

Shipyard workers with a team of engineers from the UK came aboard to complete extra items on the big repair list but the general consensus was that the ship would make it back to the UK more or less as is, but a lengthy refit would be essential to replace all the electrical equipment and rewire the entire boiler room.

I took the opportunity in Aden to buy some presents for the family and my fiancée Johan, but going ashore was tense as the local population was forever being stirred-up by the disaffected. After the short stay, the ship sailed for the Suez Canal and the last leg of our return voyage.

*

The 1966 World Cup Saga

THE RETURN VOYAGE through the Red Sea and the Suez Canal must have been tranquil, as I remember very little about it.

The voyage from Port Said to Gibraltar became more animated as the subject of the World Cup became a hot topic. England was in the finals at Wembley Stadium. England v Germany on 30 July 1966 at 15.00 hours. What a match this could be.

As a quick diversion, I would mention that football is not my game but in the era, the matches were much better than they are at present. How tough could those footballers be? Remember Nobby Stiles? 'If you can't stop them, drop them,' was his reputation, true or false, I couldn't say. However many years later I was drinking at a bar in Rio de Janeiro which was a favourite of Pele's chum Jairzinho, who although in his early sixties, was still one tough looking guy. He bore all the signs of a lifetime of playing hard.

Anyway, the subject of navigation became of great interest, just where were we exactly, what was the distance to run, could the ship go a little faster, was the Captain sure we would reach Gibraltar in time for the Cup Final?

Two days out the Captain confirmed that all being well the ship would reach harbour in time to allow most of the crew ashore to watch the game on television. To most people, this meant getting to a bar or an outside broadcast venue.

And so, the ship reached Gibraltar in time but the port sent a signal saying that as the ship was not 'whole' and in the interests of 'safety' (sic) the ship had to enter harbour with the assistance of the harbour tugs.

It was midday and just where were the tugs? Another signal advised the tugs would be available after 19.00 hours. If there was a reason it wasn't shared with the crew. The ship's company knew where the tug crews were, in the bloody pub waiting for the match. The ship's company was livid from the Captain downwards and although the match was broadcasted throughout the ship it was not the same.

Eventually, the ship was cleared to dock just after 3 p.m. so all was well. I stayed on board the ship and listened to the match on the radio. Later, I received a telephone call from cousin Peter serving in the Royal Marines as a bandsman aboard an RN frigate painted in 'bright white', the Admiral of the Mediterranean Fleet's Yacht. Some people get all the luck.

The celebrations that night were as you would expect, it certainly was a memorable occasion.

8

THE HOMECOMING

3rd August 1966

TEN DAYS LATER THE SHIP returned to Rosyth to a right royal welcome. Johan was waiting on the dockside with her father, James. By this time, James had left the coal mining industry in Fife, where the pits closed at a steady rate, taking a job on the tools in Dounreay, the nuclear fast reactor research establishment outside of Thurso in the far north of Scotland. He had taken leave to be with his family and help with the forthcoming wedding.

Laden with presents, the three of us jumped into Jim's car to head up the back road to Cowdenbeath. Johan was looking a million dollars as more friends and family arrived. The coming home party grew. One of Jim's friends took me back to the ship and I slipped under the covers in a half-empty mess.

The next two weeks were hectic, between getting to grips with the wedding arrangements, getting my family in Southampton organised, and finding a short-term rental to set-up our new home.

The apartment finding exercise was not that easy, being as how I needed to be close to the naval base at Rosyth. Eventually, a furnished one-bed apartment in an old tenement building in the Scottish style was discovered and the deal is done. The loo outside in the hall and centuries-old brown lino covered the floor, but it would do.

The view to the front of the building was the railway embankment carrying the line to the Forth Railway Bridge. The view at the back was a ship breakers yard. Hardly romantic, but who cared. During our short stay at this apartment, *HMS Lord Roberts*, a shore bombardment monitor arrived to be scrapped.

Although built in the early part of WWII, she led a useful life supporting a number of land invasions, Operation Husky (the invasion of Sicily) and the Allied landings near Salerno (Operation Avalanche). During the D-Day landings, she was positioned off Sword beach.

The ship looked very odd and top heavy, with a massive 15" gun turret and barbette positioned in front of the bridge. It wasn't until the turret and barbette were removed, and the guts of her engine room torn out, that the wide underwater form of her hull became evident.

One of the *Lord Roberts*' 15" barrel's (originally from the WW1 battleship *Resolution*) is mounted outside the Imperial War Museum in south London, together with one from the WW1 battleship *Ramillies*. This ship type will never be seen again.

*

The Wedding

THE WEDDING WAS preceded by a rather spiffing evening, a show of the wedding presents. I forget if there was a Scottish name for the event, perhaps it was simply 'A Showing of Presents'. In other cultures, it is called a 'bridal shower'. Johan and I were overwhelmed. The hall was chock full, mostly from Johan's long list of customers. She was always a very popular lady.

Johan's parents laid-on a fine spread, as most folks arrived with their contribution. Result? One fine evening's entertainment, and a great party. What would the wedding feast be like I wondered? Distant family relations from the four corners arrived. I had little chance to remember all their names.

My family contingent also arrived in time for the show of presents. Tarpey took time off from defending the nation behind his desk in that cosy posting that he had, driving north with brother Graham to keep him company. Mum and Dad arrived by train. Fortunately for Dad, Mother cut down on the complaining about her why didn't her son marry a nice girl from the next street.

Talking of a girl next door. There was a very attractive sexy Maltese lady living in the next but one house. She was however married to six foot three, eyes of blue, a retired member of the Parachute Brigade. He had an unfortunate experience when his parachute failed to open over the

Malaysian jungle. The trees saved his life, just, but he took a long time to heal the many broken bones.

The story was, after he had recovered he had been posted to Malta, had met and married the lady in question. About a year later, he came home from camp to find his wife fending off the local priest who was engaged in God's work trying to increase the population as no offspring were forthcoming after one year of marriage.

The parachutist threw the priest out of the window, just one storey up. The army quickly moved him and his wife on to the camp. At first light the next day they flew back to the UK by RAF Transport Command, to head off the unwelcome attentions of the local police and the Church. Trying to defend his actions with accusations of rape would not be in the interests of anybody.

My parents were doubly impressed if a little confused by the Fife and the other Scottish accents. That evening Johan and I spent the night together in our new home, just to get the feel of it. Anyway, her father needed her bedroom for Great Aunt Annie and her friend.

Two days later, the wedding went very well and I was looking forward to another great party. Halfway through, came the time to leave for the short journey north to Dunkeld, in Perthshire.

Johan's Great Aunt Annie, a great old girl and dedicated spinster, had offered the use of her small terraced cottage in the street leading up to the Dunkeld Cathedral, which stands on the north bank of the River Tay. The cathedral was begun in 1260 and completed in 1501. The entire street was taken over some years before by the National Trust, to restore and maintain all original buildings to preserve them for the nation. Only true locals are considered as tenants.

We were very lucky to receive this special favour. Dunkeld is a very special place, deep in the Perthshire countryside, vastly improved ever since the main highway, the A9 to Inverness, was routed away from the town. It is a great location for a spot of salmon fishing, assuming you have a very thick wallet that needs some severe thinning out.

Our honeymoon was very pleasant, as well as romantic. On the Tuesday after the wedding, Great Aunt Annie returned home, so the two of us set off to tour Bonnie Scotland by driving over to the west coast to visit Oban for a few days. Then we wandered up to Inverness, returning to Fife, via Aviemore and its famous ski slopes.

*

BY CHRISTMAS, GOOD news arrived, a trifle early, but not to worry. We would be three by June at the latest. In February, I received a new posting, which proved to be very interesting. The RN had been assigned one of three new satellite stations to be installed, one in Singapore (army), one in Cyprus (RAF), and one at Christchurch, in Hampshire, not too far from my parent's home in Southampton.

Whilst I was away in the Middle East the old lady who lived in the top floor of what was a large house, had sold it to my father who was a sitting tenant. It had its own entrance, with two large rooms and a kitchen in front. The room at the back was shared by brother Graham and his beer making factory, which once sprang a leak, much to mother's annoyance.

So, with Johan in confinement, we moved into the family home. It would have been strange surroundings for my wife, as she had never lived away from home before. Still, it seemed to be a suitable arrangement and the satellite station had an easy routine based on its development programme.

The station was located on the beach just east of Mudeford with its narrow entrance into Christchurch Bay. A private road connected the adjacent housing estate to the site. The road was also designated as a public footpath to the beach. A big sign at the entrance to the road said, 'Ministry of Defence – No Unauthorised Cars'.

The site consisted of four temporary buildings plus the large air-inflatable radome, which housed a sixty-foot diameter satellite tracking dish. The set-up was quite cunning, as the dish did not only communicate with military satellites in space but also could send and receive signals, bounced off large pieces of space junk, the second stage of a USSR rocket being the object of choice due to its size.

In this configuration, the returned signal back to the station would be very weak, collected by the large dish antenna, and then passed to a cryogenic amplifier operating just a few degrees Kelvin above absolute zero, which is -273.15 centigrade.

The advantage of this system of signal transmission is that it is virtually impossible for the other side to intercept the signal, thus giving much needed total security.

The station was not generally operational and with the 24-hour police guard at the main entrance less than fifty metres away, it was quite common for the station to shut down thus enabling the watch-keeping staff to go home. It was a very pleasant twenty-five-mile drive to/from the station through the New Forest, although wriggling through Lyndhurst could be a pain at times, and nothing has changed.

So, some history. The Signals Research & Development Establishment (SRDE) originated in the Royal Engineers Wireless Telegraphy Experimental Section founded in the very early part of the twentieth century. In 1916 it settled into its own premises becoming the Signals Experimental Establishment, and then renamed SRDE at the start of the Second World War. Now it had a strong focus on developing military satellite communications using the three earth stations Singapore, Cyprus and the UK.

The top end of the site disappeared into a wooded area high up on a cliff. It was a very secure area. Deep in the woods, clever scientists developed new and secret technologies. One turned up at the satellite station, a true beatnik. Scruffy beard, hair all over his face, sandals no socks, a 'ban the bomb' tee shirt, torn jeans falling from very thin legs, and horn-rim glasses. He was the dish expert. His task was to get the same performance out of a thirty-foot diameter dish as the sixty-foot diameter foot dish on the main station. His eventual goal was a ten-foot diameter dish, with performance suitable for a mobile unit.

Underneath his strange appearance was one very bright scientist, who could explain anything in a manner where the details would infuse themselves into your brain and remain there for a very long time. I figured his dress was just an act so that the management would leave him alone to his work. I was proved right sometime later.

*

The Locals

DUE TO THE close proximity to the upper-class residential housing site bordering the site, there was a big restriction on noise. Mustn't upset the local Tories. (Conservative & Ratepayers Association, Independent Conservatives, and of course, the Conservative Party.)

One Saturday morning, a site contractor had urgent repairs to finish with permission to complete the work. I was on duty that day, chatting with the MOD police on the main gate. They were all ex-army sergeants or sergeant-majors, all twenty plus year men, with amazing stories to tell, most of them unprintable.

Next thing we all knew was a Jaguar roars up to the main gate and the driver jumps out to start to haranguing and complaining at length about the work being performed on a Saturday morning. The policemen moved into Dixon-of-Dock-Green mode, (after a famous TV series, evenin' all, bend the knees, where's me notebook) and proceeded to have some fun.

'Dis your car, sir,' the driver was asked, as its details were taken and recorded.

An almost unprintable reply was the result, (you stupid little man etc, etc) in a hideous hoity-toity tone of voice.

'Can't yur read the notice at the top of the road, *No Private Cars?*'

Another almost unprintable reply, again in a hoity-toity tone of voice.

'Yur knows that it will hav' to be towed?' said the policeman. 'Quite expensive for an emergency tow by the security police.'

Another reply, possibly printable, but not so hoity-toity tone of voice.

By the time the police had read the UK Secrets Act then quoted all sorts of obscure regulations, all made up on the spur of the moment, reports to be sent to the Royal Navy's regulators, the Police Special Branch, possibly MI5, the hoity-toity neighbour had switched to Mark 1 grovelling, name-dropping, in a voice very close to total panic.

It was cruel, but we all enjoyed the show – with a straight face. The neighbour crept away, never to be seen again. It did a lot of good, as complaints to the head of SRDE just seemed to go away.

Winding up the locals was actually quite easy. One weekend, I was called upon as responsible duty person, to accompany the duty police sergeant to walk along the beach. Security check? Right! More like let's take a walk along the beach, show our faces, perhaps look at the girls sunbathing.

So, the two of us are walking along, just in front of the Radome, when we were accosted by one of the councillor's from the local parish council. We had been looking out to sea. I had pointed at a rather nice yacht that was attempting to enter the harbour against a full spring ebb tide, not easy as the current was very strong.

The councillor demanded to know what we were talking about in a very rude voice. The sergeant moved into action.

'Well, Sir,' he started, lowering his voice. 'It's a bit hush hush, but just offshore at the spring tide low water mark, it is intended to build a tower with a calibration beacon on top to aid in the setting-up of the satellite station. No planning permission is required because it's a military objective so not many folks need to be informed.'

I kept a straight face as the councillor rushed away in complete panic. We heard later he had called an emergency meeting of the Parish

Council, then, first thing Monday morning, the leaders of the Parish Council marched into Christchurch's Main Municipal offices and raised holy hell. Oh dear.

*

ONE OTHER PIECE of fun came when the scientists were trying to conduct an experiment to check the response of the main aerial dish by positioning the dish in front of the expected path of a satellite to watch the rise and fall of the incoming signal as it passed through the apogee. They almost succeeded, but by the simple method of switching the aerial drive motor to automatic the dish moved a fraction and a small difference was recordable. The scientists argued about what to do. We, the navy, waited impatiently for them to finish and go away so the station could be shut down, so we could all go home too.

My partner butted, saying he could get the result they wished in five minutes. The scientists wanted to know how. He switched the station to automatic, the dish locked on to the apogee, then he pressed the stop button and watched as the signal from the satellite dropped to zero on the graph recorder.

'But that is only half a curve,' the scientists wailed.

'Make a copy, turn it over, attach it to the first half and you will have the whole curve, simple.'

I tried not to laugh, but some of the scientists were smiling at the obvious, the others shook their heads muttering. Still, job done, and soon I was on my way home.

Somewhere among these memories, I became a father, and my daughter Carolyn was born. Johan's confinement had passed, if slightly late, with few worries, and a lovely baby daughter, all seven pounds and a few ounces drew us ever closer together. I wangled a week's compassionate leave as the station was undergoing a few changes.

My stay at SRDE lasted until the early part of 1967. I greatly enjoyed this posting. Something well out of the ordinary, walking along the beach to Mudeford, right on the tip of the point for truly excellent fish and chips. Driving through the New Forest to get to and from work was a pleasure, and finally learning to cope with being a father and trying hard to be a good husband. Who would have thought?

*

MEMORIES AND FORGETFULNESS

MY FINAL RECOLLECTION of SRDE came in the form of a visit by a famous rigging specialist from the famous yachting harbour of Lymington. The chief of the station had contracted him to check the wire rigging that stabilised and supported the sides of the inflatable Radome. The south-west side of the Radome took a lot of hammering from the Atlantic storms that came barrelling up the English Channel. I was instructed use my yacht racing experience to provide assistance aloft as necessary.

I spent my morning aloft helping, fetching and talking shop about sailing, and we were finished by lunch time. He thanked me profusely, gave me a twenty-pound note as he now had to attend an urgent call from a rich client where he would undoubtedly make very good money.

He invited me, and brother, to come to Lymington to show us around and have lunch. Two weeks later we both enjoyed a most interesting lunch time in the Ship Inn where we got an in-depth exposé on who, in the upper classes, was doing what to whom, mostly under the covers or even without covers, who knows? I am sure a certain British Sunday newspaper known as 'The News of the Screws', would have been more than interested in his detailed knowledge.

At the end of the year, I passed my PPE exam for promotion to senior rate, and I was told I would be sent on qualifying course within a few months.

9

PO COURSE AND THE QUEEN MUM'S PARADE

AND SO IN EARLY FEBRUARY 1968, I moved to *HMS Collingwood* to receive my promotion and brand new uniform. I could not wait to get a photograph taken with my lovely baby daughter. And it all seems like yesterday.

Now, I cannot remember if I lived on the camp or did I go RA (or ration allowance), which gave extra pay in lieu of living off the camp. Southampton was quite close to the camp, but the heavy traffic, need I say more. I guess I went home each night, why wouldn't I.

By this time I had to change cars. Once again the Southampton Car Auction came to the rescue. I bought, for the huge price of thirty quid, a Commer Cob Van, ever heard of Commer? Thought not! Commer was the commercial arm of the Rootes Group, another forgotten name.

Founded in 1913, they ceased operation in 1971. With the financial support, the two Rootes brothers bought some well-known British motor manufacturers, including Hillman, Humber, Singer, Sunbeam, Talbot, Commer and Karrier, controlling them through their parent company. They produced, as their base range in motor cars, the Hillman Minx and the Hillman Super Minx, two standard four-door cars of the era.

I discovered their entire car range had only two floor pans, no matter what the different badges from the above range they placed their cars. This led me to think that an underpowered and very basic 7 cwt van could easily be modified by picking up bargains at the local breakers yard.

A van was an ideal vehicle for families in Her Majesty's service. There was always the danger of being posted. It is far easier to pack one's goods and chattels into a van than on the back of a camel. So, first off, the van was fitted with an anti-roll bar and uprated brakes that did wonders for the handling, such as it was.

One Saturday morning I was raking around my local breaker's yard when the owner came out of his office and shouted, 'er nipper, interested in a Sunbeam Rapier engine?'

'Tell me more,' I shouted back.

'Yer van has the 1300cc engine that couldn't pull the skin off' a rice puddin'. I got a Sunbeam Rapier, Series V, bin wacked up the back, with the 1725 cc engine, almost a 'undred horses'. Yers fer forty-five quid.'

I shouted back, 'how much will you give me for my old engine, very low miles.'

'Appens I ave' a customer fer it,' he replied. 'Say thirty quid and yer motor.'

And so the deal was done. Father helped me swop the engines over, and my van was transformed. Wow, what a difference. With a low ratio back axle, I could stay the course at the traffic lights with the Austin Mini Coopers that were all the rage. Scared a few of them too. Scared myself once, so it was necessary to keep things cool especially with the wife and bairn on-board.

*

THE QUALIFICATION COURSE passed without any problems, A bit short of time here and there for revision, but my course marks held up OK. I took lunch each day in the combined senior rates mess. I met up with Tarpey, who by this time had signed-on to take the two-year 'Mechanicians' course, which would fast-track his promotion to Chief PO.

During this time, the combined senior rates mess had an 'In Crowd', mostly comprising of that superior race, the Apprentices, who from a young age completed a four-year course that propelled them upstairs at a rapid rate.

Tarpey, not to be outdone, formed the 'Out Crowd' and it did not take long before its numbers overtook the opposition.

During this time, the camp was preparing for a royal visit from HRH the Queen Mother, which involved a grand parade on *HMS Collingwood*'s enormous parade ground, (the largest in Europe, apparently).

This required an honour guard, so four classes of new entrants were volunteered (it's that word again). To get them up to standard, *HMS Excellent*, Whale Island, Portsmouth, the cultural home of the RN, sent two of their very best Chief Gunnery Instructors (Chief GIs).

The In Crowd, with little knowledge of the deep historical culture of the RN, started to take the 'piss', whereas Tarpey and I knew professional grade when we saw it and welcomed them to the mess and to engage with them.

Both were twenty-seven year men and Chief GIs always had a fearsome reputation. We all watched with great interest as they slowly but carefully brought the youngsters in the new-entry classes forward to being one of the best guards anyone could remember. Both Chief GIs could whisper well over a hundred yards. They kept the squad in two halves, thus generating a strong measure of competition between them.

Within four weeks, the honour guard of just one hundred men, plus the officer-in-command in front, and a senior rating behind, became as one, pride bursting from their chests every time the chief GI muttered a 'well done'.

The parade itself was held on a Friday afternoon. Everyone looked forward to an early finish followed by the rush to the main gate to go home. The parade itself was under the command of the camp Chief GI, and things seemed to go OK. As the parade came to an end, it was necessary to get the men assembled on the parade ground relocated to line the main road to the main gate for Her Majesty's departure.

This turned into a bit of a shambles, aided and abetted, mostly, by the In Crowd. Then, came the fun part. The Chief GIs from Whale Island reported to the camp Chief GI, telling him in no uncertain terms that they would take charge, which they proceeded to do. The In Crowd had now met their match. These two professionals had the whole camp ramrod straight, eyes to the front, don't you dare move a muscle unless ordered. Soon, all was in order for the Queen Mum's departure.

It was an experience just to watch. The Queen Mum waved majestically as she left, the Captain of *HMS Collingwood* smiled in relief it had gone so well but the In Crowd, anxious to get home, found themselves on the parade ground for some advanced lessons in marching. Oh dear.

Tarpey and I slipped into the mess for a coffee to let the crush at the main gate die down before slipping into Southampton where his Mother was due to arrive from Yorkshire.

10

A POSTING TO SINGAPORE

THE NEXT PERIOD OF TIME was an unhappy one at home. Mother, who had always interfered with matters she should have stayed clear of, finally upset Johan to the point of no return.

Johan had had some health problems, and mother, being a nurse, would lay down the law no matter what. It all became rather serious, Johan's health suffered even more and it became time to take action. The atmosphere in the house had become unnecessarily bad.

I took the decision to leave this sad situation behind. I had been discharged from *HMS Collingwood* at the end of the first week in July, with a posting to Singapore.

I had a new wife and beautiful daughter and they had to come first. I prepared all our belongings for an early getaway the next morning. The long journey from Southampton to Thurso would take at least two days.

The total distance was just under seven hundred miles and Great Britain's road system was short on motorways. Leaving a short note of explanation to Father, we left soon after five in the morning. It was an easy run out to Winchester followed by a rush up the A34 to pass the bridge at Newbury before the traffic built up. My route took me around the south side of Birmingham, then on to the new M6 motorway, which was now half complete.

During the early part of this marathon journey, Johan, fortunately slept, as did Carolyn in her cot immediately behind the two front seats.

As I ran into heavy traffic in the Midlands it became very tiring and the roads were not built for overtaking. Realising I had to pace myself, I took the opportunity to stop at least every three hours. Nappy changing increased the frequency of stops.

The hard work started in the Lake District, always bedevilled with heavy commercial traffic and many underpowered cars towing caravans. In the great tradition of British caravans, they would drive in convoy and with passing places in short supply, one could but fume at their thoughtlessness.

Johan started this long journey feeling not very well and her spirits were very low thanks to my mother's behaviour. I tried to think what more I could have done, but getting distracted from my driving was not a good idea so I put my thoughts away.

We took a long rest in the Lake District, which fortunately held back from providing the usual wet weather for the campers. As we continued we reached Gretna Green on the Scottish Border where runaway lovers used to escape to so they could evade the law on marriage at the age of sixteen without parent's consent. I guess not many people remember those days.

Now we were back in Scotland and Johan cheered up feeling more at home in her own country. She had arranged for us to make a stopover in Fife, which we reached late evening. We arrived at one of her Auntie's home and I was immediately handed a large dram which I certainly needed. Carolyn, having gained her freedom from the cot in the back of the van started to run around enjoying being made a fuss of by Aunty and her children.

I slept well that night and thus did not see the need in starting too early the next day. I guess we started on the final leg of our long journey about mid-morning, but with two hundred and forty miles still left to go, most of it through the mountains of Scotland on the main road north, the A9, loved by all who travelled on it (sic), I had to get a move on.

Inverness was the usual trial to get through but the road up to Thurso is very scenic, if you are not in a hurry, and hard work if you are.

I remember little about this second day, but we arrived in Thurso safe and sound in time for supper. I was so pleased to see Johan's happy reunion with her beloved parents. Carolyn was quickly rushed up to bath and bed, which seemed to take a very long time. A lot a splashing and laughter was heard downstairs which made everyone feel much happier. The bathroom floor was very wet when I struggled up for a long hot shower.

Johan and I spent the rest of my foreign service leave in Thurso. Johan recovered well, her parents spent many hours with their granddaughter. Johan and I enjoyed walks along the beach or visiting the shops just to see what they had.

I told her father not to worry. We could look forward to two years living in the Far East. I had a favoured position with a good posting. The accommodation was not going to be a problem, although Johan didn't quite know how to react when I mentioned that most senior rates on station hired a maid to help with the chores at home and help with many everyday items, like shopping in the local markets. The language would not be a problem either, Singapore and Malaya were both at one with the British.

There was plenty of time to plan the return journey south to Tarpey's place in Fareham. Before the journey, we went through all that we had brought with us. Although the baggage allowance for the flight to Singapore was generous, it was necessary to leave quite a few items behind.

With long farewells behind us, the journey back south went well, and we spent two days at Tarpey's place getting ready for the long flight to Singapore on the 18th July 1968.

I left my Commer van with Tarpey for a small consideration. Apparently, it did sterling service as Tarpey spent two years commuting between Fareham and the navy's atomic submarine base in west Scotland, clocking up in excess of three hundred thousand miles.

At last, the day came and the three of us checked in at *RAF Brize Norton*. Senior rates with families enjoyed a fast track service and we were made very comfortable. The RAF would use their version of the VC10 to fly to Singapore.

The RAF aircraft was the standard VC10 fitted with the Super VC10 tail, which included more powerful engines. Inside the cabin, we discovered the seats faced the rear of the aircraft. The RAF's thinking was that this was a safer configuration than with seats facing forward. This gave the strange sensation on take-off when we were left hanging in our seat belts as the flight took-off and gained height.

Otherwise, the flight was comfortable the service much better than I had expected. The aircraft stopped at Cyprus, to unload some passengers and to take on-board a full load of fuel. However, Singapore is a long way around the world so we arrived very tired and having to cope with the twelve-hour time difference was difficult.

We were quickly taken from the military airport to a transit hotel, where we would stay while I searched for our new home. Our guide had the details of my appointment and quickly told me that most of the navy staff stationed in and around *HMS Terror* and the adjacent naval dockyard on the north side of the island, were living in dedicated housing estates on the other side of the causeway in Johore Bahru, just inside Malaysia. The houses were a better quality and much cheaper because the RAF and Army preferred to live in Singapore to stay much closer to their many bases.

I struck lucky, as the third house I was shown was a detached property on two floors with the houses behind shielding it from the late afternoon sun. The road was a quiet residential street and my next-door neighbour would be a Chinese school teacher with a young family. At the top of the road, there was Forces Medical Centre and Administration Office, an office for the Military Police, and opposite stood a well equipped medium-sized supermarket run by the Naffi.

In being introduced to everybody, I quickly learnt that a Chief PO from the dockyard submarine support unit was due to move out in two day's time and did I wish to buy all his furniture and other household items?

Deal done, as I followed the well-trod path to getting set-up. Johan and I spent a relaxing two days in the transit hotel, resting up after the long flight, trying to readjust to the time difference. With two years in front, we thought best not to start rushing around sightseeing as there would be plenty of time later on. Carolyn enjoyed splashing about in the hotel pool but getting used to the hot weather started to take its toll on the third day.

Then, as if by magic, everything fell into place. The lease was signed, we moved into 15 Jalan Keruing, Kebun Park, Johore Bahru, the furniture arrived, as did our luggage from the transit hotel. Being a tropical posting, I had received my all-white uniform, which actually fitted. A new found friend in the local office recommended a very nice Chinese girl called Suzie to be our 'Amaha'.

And just in time before starting my new duties, I also acquired a cute little car, a Triumph Herald convertible in a lovely light blue metallic.

*

Singapore and its Many Changes
GENERAL ELECTIONS HAD been held in Singapore a few months before our arrival in April 1968, the first as an independent state following the island's expulsion from Malaysia. PM Lee Kan Yew ended up with all fifty-eight seats in his Parliament and soon got to work.

What I noticed when I first arrived were the dramatic changes. 'Keep Singapore Clean' was a campaign that was enforced with great rigour. Drop a sweet paper, someone would report you or a policeman would appear from nowhere with an instant fine.

Large roundabouts, long overgrown, became tropical gardens bursting with colour from exotic plants. More importantly, vast numbers of apartments were being built at pace and hills removed as landfill for the swampy areas to gain much-needed development land.

When new housing was ready, a Kampong's, (Malay for a natural village) still full of wooden shacks, pigs playing amongst the children and chickens running around, would mysteriously catch fire. Usually at night. By chance, the emergency services and the Singapore Army would just happen to be in the area to rescue the Kampong people and their livestock.

Fortunately, the Kampong people were quickly given housing in the new apartments close by. All their goods and chattels would also be transported that very night, without loss and all livestock found a new home too.

The kampongs would burn to the ground and the ground cleared the next day. As my favourite Chief PO used to say, 'Now that's what I call direct action'.

The UK military, at the time, held over twenty per cent of all usable land on the island. Clearly, this was going to change. A four hundred acre industrial park was built on land inside the naval base area, and you wouldn't know it was there because the naval base was that huge. There were RAF airfields aplenty and even the Fleet Air Arm had its own airfield.

But, despite having over twenty thousand service men and women in Singapore, when troops were needed to go up-country to help out with the on-going activity on the northern Malay border, fighting troops had to be brought in from the UK. The army had less than two thousand front-line soldiers on the island and most of these were Ghurkhas.

The Singapore economy grew apace and still does to this day. I must visit one day to check it all out.

*

Royal Navy Wireless Station 'Suara' – Singapore

RNWT SUARA WITH the motto 'Kami Chakap Sama Dunia'– 'We Speak to the World' came under the administration of *HMS Terror*, which had the barrack accommodation, medical and other facilities for the men of the Far East not assigned to any ship. It could also house, on a temporary basis, ship's companies when their ship was required to undergo repair or refit.

HMS *Terror* was familiar territory. In 1963/64, *HMS Albion* had drydocked during the Borneo War and the ship's company moved into barracks.

The main entrance to RNWT Suara was directly opposite the main gate of *HMS Terror*. The station was responsible for five point-to-point high-frequency services to major centres of naval communication. The UK, via Mauritius, Australia (Perth and Melbourne), Hong Kong (of course) and the USA navy base in the Philippians (Subic Bay). Suara operated the latest self-tuning 30 kW Marconi HF Transmitters for these services.

As one entered the station, the road to the main building was just over half a mile long and was surrounded by a large aerial farm. Large steel masts supported a confusing array of wires. These were the Rhombic Aerials and here is a brief technical description:

The rhombic aerial is an array of two wires arranged as the name implies, directional in the way that the long diagonal points. The height above ground is important, as the angle into the sky of the main lobe depends on this. The main lobe points skywards to be able to bounce the signal off a layer in the upper atmosphere called the ionosphere. Radio waves transmitted at the correct angle into the sky are reflected back to Earth beyond the horizon at, in our case, transcontinental distances. This technology is called 'skywave' or 'skip' propagation and is used by amateur radio operators to talk to other countries, and shortwave broadcasting stations that broadcast internationally.

For each service route, the operator is presented with an IF Curve, (one of the many layers in the upper atmosphere) which displays the best frequency to be used on that particular service at the particular time of day. As there is a big difference between the day frequency and the night frequency, two separate aerials are rigged from the same masts, but at different heights.

Surprise, surprise, these two aerials are designated the upper or the lower aerial, or they can be considered the day aerial and the night aerial.

This all sounds very technical, but Singapore has a very dynamic environment. It's hot, humid, and huge thunderstorms are frequent. The upper atmosphere layers in question move quite a lot too, due to many reasons. Add interference from other stations, always present, and keeping any service in service required a skill approaching a black art, relying on guesses, hunches, perceptions, shots in the dark, inspiration, perspiration, experimentation (with different frequencies) and in many cases, pure luck.

Of course, this Marconi age technology has all but disappeared around the world with the advent of satellite communications, or land or sea lines with high-speed optic fibres.

The remainder of the aerial farm was equipped with single wire vertical aerials hanging from a strong cable strung between two large towers on the east side of the station. These were used for the many fleet broadcasts over a wide range of frequencies; the transmitters being much smaller units with considerably less power.

One of the first pieces of advice I received was not to go walkabout in the aerial farm as there were many snakes living there. The roadway from the entrance gate to the main station building had deep open storm drains on either side. It was good to know the snakes could get into them but could not get out. I saw quite a few cobras in the storm drains in my time on the station, always from inside my car.

And so now came the moment when I joined the merry-go-round. First day, introduction to the OIC and his number two. Then the more important person in the shape of the Station CPO, who looked after all matters technical, maintenance routines and major repairs that the duty watch could not, or did not have the time, to complete.

I met my relief, a fellow Petty Officer with the station title of Watch Systems Supervisor (WSS), responsible for all matters to do with station operations. He had just six weeks left to serve and I would be his shadow until he departed for the UK. Fortunately, he lived with his family in an adjacent housing estate and there was an established car school to share the chore of commuting.

He reported and was responsible to, the Watch Systems Controller who wielded his power over both the transmitter station and the receiver station located on the west side of the island at Kranji. Where the Singapore station used Petty Officers for these two important posts, the larger RN stations in the UK or other foreign countries had officers performing the watch-keeping duty. I guess we senior rates were cheaper. Singapore was an expensive place to post an officer on station.

The watch keeping system was kind of strange. As it was explained to me that the civilian technicians in the Communications Centre, or

Comcen for short, worked shifts the normal way, a week of days, a week of evenings and a week of nights, followed by a week off, to recover.

The RN's system was an afternoon shift, followed by a night shift, followed by an evening shift the next day, then a morning shift the day after. Then, 24 hours off, followed by a repeat of the merry-go-round and then three days off.

I guess the powers that be couldn't stomach the idea of ratings getting a week's holiday once a month, plus normal station leave. This routine did not promote the best possible efficiency in the workplace, as the body was always trying to catch up with a disturbed sleep pattern. Trying to sleep during the day when it was at its hottest was something I always struggled with.

Anyway, the WSS had two hands to assist him, a leading hand (LREM) and what the seaman would call an AB, or in this case a REM1. The station routine was exactly that, routine. We would all three of us take it turned to patrol the three main halls, 'A', 'B', and 'C', and when it got busy at least two persons were required to bring transmitters on to a new frequency and/or change over the designated aerial(s).

'A' Hall housed the main long-distance transmitters, (A-1 to A-6) plus two old multi-stage high power Marconi transmitters (A-7 & A-8) that were a pain to tune and bring online correctly. Fortunately, they were assigned to static fleet area broadcast duties.

So, was there any excitement when on watch? Generally no, but if a decent sized lighting storm decided to pay a visit, the lightning would enter into 'A' Hall and cause a bit of a fuss. One time it left transmitter A-8 a smoking ruin, and two other transmitters tripped out when it was too dangerous to venture down the hall to enact a reset. The WSC at the time was not amused when I told him my watch was hiding under the main control desk.

*

THE OTHER INCIDENT of note was the monthly diesel run when the station would revert to its standby power supply for the day. The change-over in the morning could be accomplished without shutting down the station, but in the evening it was necessary to reconnect to the main Singapore grid. On this occasion, the big electric motors that fed a large AC system failed to automatically disconnect when the station supply was shut down.

So, with these substantial motors still winding down, they ended up by back feeding the newly restored Singapore supply with a large out of phase voltage and there was the most tremendous bang. The Station Chief who had a hold of the breaker handle took the full force of a breaker cabinet exploding and bursting into flames. There was a lot of molten copper inside what was left of the breaker cabinet.

We were all very glad he was not badly injured, but his golden locks got a little crisp at the ends. The rest of the shift was hard work, as without AC a lot of the new electronics in the station did not take kindly to the outside heat and humidity. I was glad I only had the evening watch.

*

LAST, BUT NOT least was the sage of Little Tommy. He was my watch REM1, an old hand, very competent, who refused all efforts to be promoted from being just a radio mechanic first class. He smoked heavily and lived in barracks in *HMS Terror*.

During one evening shift, Tommy did not look well. I ordered him to return to barracks and report to the Sick Bay. He cycled back, refusing transport. His arrival at the Sick Bay disturbed the duty Sick Bay person who was more interested in giving him a couple of aspirin and turning in for the night.

As luck would have it, the head surgeon had been working late, caught sight of Little Tommy and suggested to the duty bod to get him into the emergency ward PDQ.

When the duty bod asked why he was told, and here I quote with accuracy, 'Because he is having an f…in' heart attack, you damn fool.'

Phew, that was a close one.

Tommy survived and next day I took my watch to visit him in the recovery ward and deliver thanks for his survival with flowers, only to be told he wasn't dead and didn't need the flowers just yet. But did anybody have a 'ciggy' he could cadge? That's Mancunians for you.

*

Comcen Blues

MY TOUR OF duty at Suara W/T Station came to an end approximately ten months after my arrival in Singapore. One of the Watch System Controllers had his discharge date firmly in sight which required my move up to the Communications Centre inside Naval HQ,

Fortunately, this WSC was also a member of the car school, as was my new assistant, one Taffy Pugh. Taffy Pugh was a good hand, very experienced in the Comcen, and played football for the navy. He was to be my mentor for many a month.

Using the same watch system as the W/T Station, the job entailed controlling all radio communication circuits, be they long-distance communication links or ship/shore area broadcasts. I also discovered that the RN radio communications system was a part of a much larger organisation known as DCN, or Defence Communications Network, which included all Army and RAF communication system, wherever they were located around the world.

The DCN system also linked into the communications systems supplied by the UK or NATO allies. For instance, the RN long-distance link to Mauritius was one leg of the RN communications link to the UK. But signals to ships at sea on the west side of the Indian Ocean could be sent to Mauritius for re-transmission by Ship/Shore (S/S) area broadcasts, all the way down to South Africa and part of Antarctica.

Similarly, the long distance links to Perth, in Western Australia, and Melbourne in Eastern Australia could perform the same service in their areas.

Our long distant link via Mauritius and then to the UK was also the backup link for the Army and RAF based in Singapore, who had the luxury of direct sea cable communications to the UK.

The other two long distance links to Hong Kong and the USA Navy at Subic Bay in the Philippians completed the coverage required to maintain contact with all naval ships within the alliance.

To say it could get hectic and stressful in the Comcen was an understatement. The added workload of keeping the five fixed services online, including the need to connect the primary traffic of each service through NSA encryption equipment. Normally, the duty civilian technician was responsible for this work, but when activity became hectic, it was necessary to help out.

There was a lot of jargon to learn, and the circuit to the US Navy was full of it. It would take over three months to learn all their fun words.

So, what excitement was there in the Comcen? Aggravation was most of it. What could go wrong invariably did. Sky Failure was the big one. I'll explain. The fixed services, all five of them, had a day frequency, a night frequency, and a muddle of frequencies on the way up or down.

For instance, to Mauritius, the day frequency would be 18.8 MHz, and the night frequency 9.1 MHz. But when the 18.8s as we used to call it started to fade, the trick was to double up using the lower Mauritius Rhombic aerial on say 13.3s.

When Mauritius started to get good reception with the lower frequency, the 18.8s would be taken off the air. Remember, there were only six of the self-tuning high power transmitters for five services. If the other fixed services all started to fade at the same time a juggling act took over and swopping services around the system became very complicated.

Still, that's what we got paid for. Occasionally, the sky would drop-out altogether. All the engineering and the traffic teleprinters started to chatter at once, the system had to shut down and the operators just had to damn well wait.

I remember one time; the receiver station supervisor over at RN Station Kranji rang me up and said that it would be a long wait. The drop-out wasn't totally unexpected, but its severity was. The Wrens in the adjacent traffic hall next to my control centre all sloped off to do other things; mostly going outside for a cigarette, but one rather attractive Wren called Sheila would come and sit with Taffy Pugh and myself. She even made a much-welcomed pot of coffee. Not having had a break from the start of the shift and now it was gone three a.m. in the morning, feet up and being served hot fresh coffee was a welcomed treat.

Secrets were exchanged. Sheila lived with many of the other girls in the Wrenery. Their Sick Bay person in the shape of an old battleaxe of the Chief Wren who figured the only medication her girls would ever need was the birth pill and the aspirin, both issued in large doses. I asked what aliment the birth pill was used for. Answer? Anything a couple of aspirin couldn't cure.

Sheila laughed out loud when Taffy asked did the birth pill prevent pregnancy. The answer, only when secured tightly between the knees. A golden oldie from comedy land.

We also discovered or rather received confirmation of, a certain traffic hall Petty Officer, male, who used to mysteriously vacate the premises during the quiet spells. A certain Wren, female, would also be absent at the same time. The girls giggled and we men kept a stiff upper lip. Such talk could go down the wrong corridor very quickly.

Sheila asked me why either Taff or myself hadn't made a pass at her. Well Taff had married a local Welsh girl from his valley, he was newly married with a baby boy, and the thought never crossed his mind. I later explained to Sheila that the Welsh were a very close-knit community and such antics were definitely frowned upon.

As for me, well I was newly married too, to a wonderful Scottish lady, love at first sight, and we had a wonderful baby daughter, now in her second year, bringing joy to our lives. Sheila complained about the lack of suitable men and being as how she was a cut above the average, I could see her problem.

'Darling,' I said. 'It's so sad, there is just so few of us good un's to go around.'

The conversation was fun, but before we could inquire into her love life the damn sky returned and there was a mad rush to get all services back online. The normal early morning frequencies used on all of our five fixed services were being aired (transmitted) but they were still unheard at the distant ends, so Taff and I concentrated on getting the service to Mauritius back online, and left the other services airing their day frequency until such time as they came in.

*

THE OTHER MOMENT of interest came one evening when a telex, about a hundred yards long, started to spew out of one of my engineering control teleprinter on the circuit from the RN receiver station at Kranji. It consisted of three columns of numbers, clearly radio frequencies.

Then the duty Signal Officer rushed in, a person known as the Third Man, because nobody ever knew if he actually existed, to remove the top copy of the telex roll.

I asked 'What's it all about Alfie?' and in a hushed voice he told me excitedly that *Apollo 13* was hurtling back to mother earth and the yanks (i.e. NASA) were preparing for an Indian Ocean splash-down if they needed it. The list contained all the frequencies to be kept clear until further orders. Taff thought that by the time anybody waded through this huge list of frequencies, *Apollo 13* would either be home safe and sound, or not, as the case may be.

Anyway, there was no mention of our valiant part in this saga in the subsequent movie. I did check, many times.

Repeats, that's all that's worth watching on TV, repeats.

*

MEMORIES AND FORGETFULNESS

THE LAST INCIDENT worth recording was the saga of the Error Detection and Correction equipment that arrived on an unusually quiet morning shift. The idea was to install it in the space where the coffee machine was located. What would it do?

Well, here comes more technical guff again. Channel Two on the main circuit to Mauritius was used for the coded traffic. Any errors in the system were a pain, as it was not until the message had passed through the decoding machines at the far end in the UK did the errors become obvious and retransmission of messages on a busy route took valuable time.

So, this equipment would chop the message up into packets, transmit an outgoing packet, which was returned from the receiving machine in Mauritius to the sending machine, in Singapore, for comparison, and if all was well, that packet would continue its journey.

To save money, the equipment was 1st generation, powered by thermionic valves and by testing the system back-to-back via Mauritius the system worked just fine. But be damned if it would work with the equipment installed in Mauritius.

The experts (naval description - a small squirt of water under pressure) buggered about for days, taking up my time, and others, in the quest for the Holy Grail.

The next time I came on the morning shift, they were still at it. I suggested the problem was simple and did they want to hear the solution?

'No,' they said, 'Bugger off.'

Taffy Pugh and I sat down for a stiff coffee and just smiled at the 'small squirts of water under pressure', until out of sheer exasperation, one of them said, 'OK Chief and what is your solution?'

Smiling, I told them that a system based on valves would never talk to the 2nd generation equipment at the other end in Mauritius because the equipment at the other end was based on solid-state technology, i.e. transistors, fast entering the electronics world at that time. Best to splash some cash on the new technology.

'Bollocks,' came the reply. 'All the wave-forms match perfectly.'

I smiled and attended to my duties. When I arrived for the next morning watch, the equipment had been removed and replaced by the much smaller solid-state units, allowing the table with the coffee pot to be restored to its rightful position.

My watch was warned not to say anything by the senior civilian engineer, but just to get a dig in, I asked if sniggering was acceptable? They deserved all they got.

Word of this saga went upstairs. To the man. Later the Commander-in-Charge-of-Far-East Communications arrived and gave me a wry smile. Taffy and I feigned innocence, but not very convincingly.

Uniformed RN Staff 2 - Civvy Technicians 0. A great result.

*

THE SOCIAL SIDE OF LIFE IN SINGAPORE

AND, SO TO the social life of Singapore. During my off-watch periods, what did we do? Well during the first 24-hour rest period, not a lot. Getting home from duty after lunch did not leave much time for anything grand.

Generally, I would have lunch, a few beers, play with daughter Carolyn and then get some much need sleep. The next morning there was just time for a lazy get-up, and then to the station for the afternoon watch and the second merry-go-round. Stupid system really, too much wasted time and too much commuting.

During the three days off, I generally I took Johan and Carolyn downtown for shopping and a look around in the afternoons. The street stalls served excellent Chinese food straight from the wok.

The second day would provide time to explore Singapore, the Tiger Balm gardens and other areas, but Johan did enjoy going to the Cold Store, in Orchard Road, a large department store in the downtown part of the city, where it was always freezing. Every time we left the store my spectacles would steam up for at least ten minutes.

Of course, the big treat for Carolyn was to visit the combined Senior Rates Club in *HMS Terror* and its excellent swimming pool. Occasionally we would visit one of the beaches that were attached to UK Military bases on the east side of the island.

Another area we used to visit was the local shops in Sembawang, mainly an Indian village on the east side of the island just outside the east entrance to the naval base

The east side of the island had a famous road that is now named Yishun Ave. I remember it was called the Yishun Kan, but I could be wrong. It was a winding road that linked the eastern extremity of the island, Changi, with Sembawang and the Naval Dockyard. Once I took the family for a drive along its entire length, as at that time it had not been rebuilt.

The road had been constructed by the British POWs during WWII. The Japanese did not recognise its design was contrary to the requirements of safe passage, which is to say all the bends and corners, of which there were many, all constructed with the slope of the road in the reverse of what they should have been.

In dry weather, the road was uncomfortable to drive along, but it was difficult to see why. However, in the wet weather, at the slightest provocation, vehicles would fall off the road into the deep monsoon ditches on either side. It was reckoned that this road killed more Japanese than during the defence of the island, and this could even be true. During my time in Singapore, many were the public buses that ended up in the monsoon ditch, where they would be dragged out and put back on the road, bent chassis or no bent chassis.

*

Mr Song, Our Chinese neighbour in JB and the Sultan's Palace

OUR NEXT DOOR neighbour was a Chinese school teacher who taught English, among other subjects. Mr Song lived with his ageing mother, his wife and his son, a little boy called Sonny. Both he and his family were charming. Occasionally he would invite his neighbours from both sides of his home for a Chinese banquet, usually in honour of his ageing mother.

Looking forward to a genuine Chinese banquet was one thing, but nobody had any idea of the various dishes that would be served. Well, I can inform of one thing, it wasn't a meal for five from your local Chinese in Portsmouth. A Number Six through to Number Fifteen it wasn't.

A vast array of different dishes and aromas greeted us, and some of them looked and smelt, err, challenging, to say the least. It would be impolite not to try them all, but damn it, I for one was hungry. The soups were OK, the funny looking dried chicken, other bits of animal and many other dishes were the complete opposite. Some of the dishes had funny smells, and not very pleasant ones at that. Still, despite the culture shock, Johan and I made progress with a pork dishes and the fried rice, which was wonderful.

Mr Song had a hobby of making busts of famous people and had received a commission to make a bust of the last Sultan of Johore Bahru. Song, as I used to call him, would make a bust in clay which when fired would be used to make a mould for casting in the local foundry in bronze.

To aid in his research, he had access to the main palace, which is now a museum, the Royal Abu Bakar Palace, overlooking the waterway at Singapore Island, close to the interconnecting causeway. The present Sultan's residential palace could be found further along the coastline to the west.

I was invited to visit the palace with him one morning. He regretted that he could only take myself. Johan was kind enough to say she didn't mind being left behind. Torn between two options I went and what a visit it turned out to be.

The Sultans of the differing states in and around Malaysia have been wealthy for a very long time, centuries in fact. The official Sultan's Palace was all I thought it might be, not huge but definitely not too small.

Beautifully manicured gardens surrounded the main building and on a hot day walking under the canopy of a covered garden walkway of carefully tended plants and flowers was a delight.

Inside the Palace, Song showed me around a number of large rooms, the first of which was full of junk with a capital 'J'. The stuffed tiger was a huge beast with claws so big you cannot imagine. Tiger hunting is the Sport of Kings and despite being sat on the back of a huge elephant, it was necessary to be an excellent marksman. This tiger would have been well able to jump that high. This tiger sported a large bullet hole in one of his shoulders, and in an adjacent covered in gun-rack, I could see the type of rifle used, a big safari rifle at least a 0.345.

Another item being stored was a huge piece of silverware, about one and a half hundredweight, a present from the British Royal Family for some occasion in the 1930s, donated by the Prince of Wales, two dukes and an earl.

Other artefacts would have been presents from visiting dignitaries, members of other royal families from around the world and friendly governments.

Next, we entered the main hall at the foot of a magnificent staircase. This area was used for state dinners and dances. In the cloisters surrounding the main hall I came across wall to ceiling glass fronted cabinets made of the most beautiful rich mahogany, the workmanship was beyond perfect. But what was inside these many cabinets?

Stacks of thick heavy metal plates made from Russian pink gold in all sizes. Song told me this was a twenty piece dinner set for three hundred guests, plates various, bowls various, side plates, saucers, cups, et al. The cabinets were not locked and Song retrieved a couple of items for me to examine. I wondered if we were being watched, but every time I quickly turned around I knew I had just missed seeing the servant who was keeping an eye on us.

We made our way up the staircase into the ante-room for the main throne room. The furniture was all made from crystal glass. I dinged a coin on a lampshade teardrop and the sound was pure and strong, the best lead crystal glass you could ever hope to see.

Magnificent carpets covered the floor, and ornate curtains covered the windows. Inside the throne room was more of the same but without furniture except for the two thrones, one slightly larger than the other, placed on a plinth.

Fascinating as it was time was pressing, and I suspected I had been shown all that was allowed. We made our way home and took Chinese tea under the veranda that would normally be a covered car parking space.

*

AFTER A FEW months based in Singapore, I found out that cousin Peter, the family Royal Marine, had been posted to Singapore at the Seletar Air Base, not too far down the road from the Naval Base. Peter had married Margret, a lovely cultured lady and an ex-model. She arrived with child and I seem to remember a child being born in Singapore. Anyway, her son was very young when we first met.

Peter worked in the Sergeant's Mess bar, where he and his fellow barmen made a decent living by being expert bar persons. Being very careful the way beer was served, the allowed for spillage was turned into sales that didn't make it into the till and those pesky records that the till machine would automatically make.

Impolite Sergeants, usually the worse for wear, would be plied with watered down alcohol drinks, easy in a hot climate where a lot of ice was used. This was described as a helping hand to maintain the health of Britain's finest. Ha, Ha!

One afternoon, I went to meet Peter as he finished a lunch time shift at the Sergeant's Mess. 'Golf?' he asked. 'Not for me, thanks.' Together, we wandered over to the driving range, which had a fair downward slope to the perimeter fence. Outside was the main road and on the far side a bus shelter with passengers waiting for the next bus.

A Royal Marine of some size was practising his driving with a #1 wood, only he wasn't aiming at the targets at the bottom of the driving range, but at the bus shelter. He laid about twenty rather cut-up golf balls on the mat and commenced to bombard the bus shelter. Surprisingly accurate too. The passengers quickly hid behind the shelter as the golf balls started demolishing the wooden structure.

'What's up with him?' I asked Peter.

'He's just been demoted from Corporal and he's not a happy bunny.'

'Best to be absent then, someone is bound to cause a fuss,' I replied. 'Good range, what distance was he getting?' 'Bout three hundred yards, he's a strong lad and some.'

We headed to the camp swimming pool and hid amongst the bathers and their noisy children.

*

OCCASIONALLY, THE ROYAL Marines were sent north to the border with Thailand where there was a long history of insurgencies. We used to visit Margret when Peter was away. Sadly, we discovered that Cousin Peter would go downtown to visit bars with his mates, bars not generally frequented by loving husbands.

I remember him aged fifteen, a tall gangly kind of person with no physical attributes at all. In Singapore, he was the model of a Royal Marine, tall, very strong, and a member of the RM's boxing and water polo teams.

I watched him in a boxing tournament once. The constant swimming had caused an ear infection which he'd kept from the Sergeant-in-Charge of the boxing team. He protected the infected ear by leaning his head to that side that gave him an awkward stance that actually served him well in the match.

But he was a tortured soul. He left the service not long after I completed my term in the Royal Navy. He moved back to Southampton, his family living with his mother-in-law who ran an old folks home on the west side of town. It was a large property, having been built by a Northern industrialist in the last century. The business had potential and there was plenty for Peter to do, but he never settled. He took a number of jobs as bouncer at a few nightclubs in town, became depressed and one day overdosed and died soon after. It was all very sad. Shocked both his father and mine.

*

ANYWAY, BACK TO Singapore. Normally life in the service family ghettos continued without incident. Occasionally, one of the other housing estates had issues with Indian males stalking lonely wives and vulnerable teenage schoolgirls. The MPs kept a close but unobtrusive eye on matters.

Their modus operandi was to collect the more insistent of the Indian stalkers after sundown and take them for a little ride up the Kota Tinggi

Road, through remote rubber plantations, away from JB towards the eastern Malay coastline.

Fifty kilometres, or thereabouts, the MPs would release their charges into the wild, shoeless and with very recent memories of what would happen, only more severely, the next time they were invited for an evening ride back out into the remote rubber plantations.

There were, however, two serious cases that caused quite a stir in the British community in Johore Bauru.

One occurred in late 1969, in an adjacent housing estate. One evening a serving SNCO came home from duty to find his wife in bed having sex with an Indian businessman. Being a member of a shooting club, he fetched his shotgun and emptied both barrels into his wife, killing her stone dead. He reloaded and then waited for the almost naked Indian gentleman to make a very rapid escape.

Many were the thoughts, 'had he got it the wrong way around?' least that's what the Red Caps thought, allegedly.

Some months later, in 1970, not too far from where Johan and I lived, came another tragedy. This time the wife was the perpetrator. Every Wednesday was a lady's club evening when their card school played bridge without fail. Any interruption to this evening had never been known, but on this occasion, it happened.

The wife returned home to find hubby giving the young Chinese maid some serious attention in the missionary position. The wife let herself out of the house without being seen or heard and went next door for a cup of tea to commiserate with her friendly neighbour.

Then she returned at the normal hour to find hubby showered and naked, smoking a cigarette in bed. The story continued. She asked her husband if he would like a refreshing cup of tea or coffee. Offer accepted, she put the kettle on, then returned to the bedroom and poured the full contents of a boiling kettle over her husband's private parts. The shock killed him instantly. The next door neighbour heard the scream and sent for the Red Caps. The matter was hushed-up, and the wife was UK bound within the hour.

*

IT WAS TOWARDS the end of 1970 that the British Military began a long slow pull-out of the Malaysian area of operations. Not too many miles out of town, up the main road to Kuala Lumpur, existed an army base vehicle depot, BVD #221, often described as many rows of trucks and other equipment, two miles long by half a mile wide.

The Malaysian military was offered the bulk of the inventory, but the Malaysian military was very difficult to deal with. I remember a ten ton Bedford army truck had cost the UK taxpayer something like ten quid each, although just where that number came from who knows?

Eventually, the British Army said something along the lines of f...-it and became as one with the Chinese businessmen in Singapore who knew a good deal when they saw it. They had ready customers throughout the Far East. When the Malaysian military found out they had overplayed their hand they were not at all amused.

One afternoon I was driving my watch from our homes to the Causeway and into Singapore. We all wore uniform when going on and off duty – it certainly helped coming back through the Malaysian immigration post on the Causeway. Anyway, we came up behind a British Army convoy moving a huge road making machine into Singapore for disposal. The Malaysian military would have really wanted to get their hands on this truly vital piece of equipment that was being towed by a huge tractor. The local motorists, well aware of the situation, we're trying to impede the progress of this massive machine loaded on the back of a long low loader.

What we saw next was actually quite fun. All around the load-loader, soldiers holding very large wheel spanners were banging large dents on the roofs of any car that came to close to cause an impediment to their task.

*

DURING OUR STAY in Singapore, Johan and I grew ever closer together. There were the usual ups and downs, safely put behind us. One evening, Johan got to talking about when we first met, and how she enjoyed my rather grand ye olde English car, the Sunbeam Talbot.

'Wouldn't it be nice if we had another one,' she murmured.

'Uh, oh,' I thought, 'Has someone seen an advert on the notice board up at the local medical centre?'

To cut a long story down to size, a friend of hers rather fancied our convertible light blue metallic Triumph Herald, and a good deal was intimated. I asked about the advert for the Sunbeam Talbot, followed by, 'Oh, didn't I tell you.'

So, a change of transport was arranged and a mid-green Sunbeam Talbot Mk II with a must-have modification, a floor mounted gear change. Although I ended up with cash in hand, the Sunbeam was far more expensive to tax. Local car tax was based on engine capacity and all cars imported had the smaller engines as a rule.

For instance, at the time, the hot rod of choice in Singapore was the UK built Ford Capri, but with the 1,300cc engine. No thank you. This model was a very poor selling car in the UK when the top of the range was the Ford Capri Guia with the three litre Essex engine. Now there was a machine.

Our new car did us proud. On our visits to Singapore, we would both dress up. Johan had a big floppy hat with a silk scarf around it. All very Mary Poppins. To celebrate, I bought an artificial chamois leather in a small round yellow container to help in keeping it shiny clean. To my surprise, I still have it, and I use it every time I wash my car. Amazing.

Having bought this classy British car I did worry though, about the time when I would have to sell it on to another classy owner. I had considered giving it a full restoration and take it back to the UK. This was not a practical proposition. I was due to finish my time in the RN, and together we would be setting up a new home once I found a new profession.

Tempting though. There was a Chinese row of workshops on the road into town. Their speciality was restoring ageing and battered 190 Mercedes Benz taxis into better than new. One of the UK civilian technicians spent big bucks on a special make-over on an up-market Vauxhall limo of the day, but then I discovered his home shipment allowance would include the car. No such luck in the RN.

Still, as luck would have it, I successfully advertised the car, and one afternoon a rather nice young man arrived in an RN Land Rover. It turned out to be a Lt Mark (forget the surname), the Captain's 2nd Secretary of *HMS Terror*.

We invited him in and served tea under the carport overlooking the garden. Mark told us he was looking for a car that stood out from the general offerings of small-engined and boring Japanese cars. He liked the Sunbeam, accepted the carefully pitched price, and agreed to pick it up the day we left for the transit hotel at the RAF airport at Changi in Singapore. The envelope containing the cash was skilfully intercepted by my smiling wife.

I asked him what duties a Captain's 2nd Secretary had to perform. Mark smiled and confided that he was the Captain's Lawyer. Other questions followed, some answered and some skilfully put to one side. Concerning matters with all service personnel who were stationed in the Singapore area, the higher up the tree, or was it a greasy pole, one existed, the more unfortunate the affairs that landed on his desk.

He declined all comment about the two murders that had occurred in our housing estates, but SNCO and officer wives, ever desperate to climb whatever social ladder they thought they were on, would borrow heavily from sources he described as unwise, which meant stupid. This I took to mean the Indian money sharks that existed in the village outside of the Naval Base eastern gate,

Mark did elaborate on one story, soon to be doing the rounds in the attempt to cool matters down.

A naval officer, with a social climbing wife, had run-up a huge account in the local cold store. Alcohol, it seems, had been one of the very popular purchases. To get out from under, the couple hatched a 'plan that could not fail', that was to repay small increments to the store owner, keeping him on the hook until it was time to return to the UK.

Then, a week before this couple and family were due to go to the transit hotel before boarding their flight, the family vanished into the home of a good friend that lived near downtown. No one would find them there. Really?

Halfway through this week of the great disappearance, a court official and the store owner arrived at the front door of the good friend who denied all knowledge of the errant family. The store owner pointed to one of the children playing in the garden and in his best broken English said, 'Dis Missy daughter'. The game was up, matters were communicated to the naval authorities and hence to the captain's office.

The officer decided to contest the huge outstanding account. Silly man. The net result was that his seat on the RAF flight was cancelled, but his family still travelled as per orders.

'To cut a long story short,' said Mark. 'The officer was found to be liable for the outstanding account. Also, he would have to pay for his keep in barracks, whilst he found the funds to clear the account, and then to add woe upon woe, he was also told he would have to pay for his own flight home, the full economy, last minute, one way fare.

Ouch! 1970 airfares were not for the faint-hearted.

Mark smiled as he finished his story, soon to be released into the wild as a warning to all.

11

TIME FOR DEMOB

AND SO OUR TIME IN Singapore slowly came to an end. I finished my duties at the Station, being asked many times why I had decided not to sign-on for another engagement (cos I didn't want another bloody wireless station posting – I wanted to say), but explained that one either completed the first nine years and start afresh in civilian life, or sign-on for twenty two years, and that was not my thinking.

I had free time at home and joined in the afternoon expat prayer mat session, kneeling on the grass in the garden clasped hands raised high, chanting ROMFT, as the daily British Caledonian VC10 flight flew overhead every day on its final approach to RAF Changi.

(ROMFT - best you work it out for yourself.)

With a bit of forward planning, the contents of the house were sold to an incoming senior rating, who made things even sweeter by taking over the lease on the house. The house agent duly paid a nice sum in commission and all was well.

The car was collected by Mark and the move into the transit hotel must have gone OK as I remember nothing about it. We did get a couple of days to go walkabout in downtown Singapore. Fortunately, our overweight luggage prevented the female urge to buy even more presents.

Well rested, the three of us arrived at the RAF terminal. Carolyn had grown up quickly into a strong good-looking three year making her collapsible pushchair almost redundant. (Push-chairs are useful for other items apart from bairns.)

The RAF VC-10 was late inbound from Hong Kong by two hours and the turn-around added another unwelcomed hour. Then, after we had taken-off the Captain revealed the flight would stop-off at some godforsaken island in the Indian Ocean. Forget which one, not surprising really.

When we took off once more for the long haul to Cyprus, three hours behind schedule, dinner was served and we all tried to get some sleep. I had smuggled a half bottle of Scottish restoring fluid onto the flight and it certainly helped to induce slumber. I awoke to answer the call of nature and the flight attendant kindly enquired if she could get the pennies back on the empty bottle. I smiled a thank you and dropped it in the bottom of an empty waste bin that was just about to be filled with the wreckage from the evening meal.

As I regained my sleeping posture, I seem to remember the engines had been gently wound up. I was worried, as a late arrival in the UK would dash my carefully laid plans for onward travel.

No need to worry. As the flight started its descent into Cyprus, breakfast was served with the news we would arrive twenty minutes early. The Captain made the welcome announcement and thanked the strong tailwind that had provided such valuable assistance. Those of us with knowledge of the VC-10 were not surprised. The aircraft, fitted with four RR Conway jet engines was, and still is, the fastest commercial airliner ever built. Only Concorde was faster across the Atlantic Ocean to the USA.

After Cyprus, the flight landed at RAF Lyneham, which was handily placed for the nearest railway station and the train into London. Johan and Carolyn were booked on the sleeper to Inverness, where her father, Jim, would drive down from Thurso to pick them up.

*

HAVING SETTLED MY family on the train to Bonny Scotland, I headed smartly for RN Barracks, Portsmouth to complete my demob. It was early evening when I checked in, and the bad news was the next day would be Thursday prior to a Bank Holiday weekend, and could I come back next week. NO, I said, Thurso, is too far away and it will cost Pusser money for the second return train journey including sleepers.

I was given a bed for the night with the advice to report as early as possible to the demob office, which I did. I phoned Thurso and very glad to hear that the family had arrived safe and sound and that grandma Margret was making a big fuss of Carolyn.

I believe the twelve hour time difference became something of an issue, as a bright lively three year old started her new day, just as grandpa and grandma were trying to go to bed. Knowing Johan, she would have taken a good drink of the local brew and gone to sleep without too many problems.

Next day, Pompey Barracks.

'What you want Chief?' I was asked as I reported at an early seven-thirty in the morning.

'Demob,' I replied.

'We're closing down for the holiday weekend can you come back next week?'

'Not from Thurso I can't and I have no travel warrants to do so.'

The rating called his chief, I explained the issues and the Chief PO, an old hand by the look of it, suggested that I should attempt his short version of his usually very long demob procedure. He took my papers and began putting stamps in all the right places.

'Toolbag,' he asked.

'In my shipment,' I replied. 'Two months before it arrives.'

'Well I don't think we need another well-worn tool bag full of tools,' he said and the stamp hit the relevant square on the paper.

'Right Chief,' exit, turn right, follow the yellow brick road, tell them I sent you, and just to stamp your papers as required.' This I did, including the Sick Bay, and in twenty minutes I returned to the demob office.

'Well done,' said the old Chief. 'I 'ave a Land Rover ready to take you to the station, you'll just catch the London train and then you will have time to catch the train for Edinburgh. Then you'll have to wait for the overnight train to Inverness, and then the mid-morning train to Thurso.'

'So how well do you know Scapa Flow,' I asked.

'The memories are scared on my brain, so you best be off, it's a long haul and some.'

I grabbed all my gear from the SNCO's mess, flung it all into the waiting transport, and whoosh, I was long gone. I caught the next train to London Waterloo, and then came the mad dash to King's Cross Station. I managed to get to the Edinburgh express in good time to slump into a half-empty compartment, put a paper on the opposite seat and stretch out. Considering the impending holiday, the train wasn't too full.

I was just plain lucky.

The train arrived on time in Edinburgh's Waverley Station and I made my way up to the North British Hotel, which was opened in 1902. But now it was 22.03.

I ordered a pint of heavy, only to be told closing time had just closed, so I ordered a large sandwich and a coffee. The barman smiled and told me my order had just made me a resident and did I want a 'wee haf' to go with the beer? I held out three fingers, which is just about two-quarter gills of best whisky.

He asked me where I was headed and I said Thurso. He suggested I drink-up and he would pack the sandwich and coffee as a takeaway.

'Ta train will be fair' full to nicht,' said the barman, 'Best get down thar the noo' and find a seat.'

His advice was well timed. I arrived at an empty compartment and feeling 'fair scunnered and wan' I crashed out along all three seats. I awoke ninety minutes later as the train made a start. I opened one eye very slowly and saw the entire human race staring down at me. They were even standing in the corridors that train was that full.

I carefully closed my eye wondering how long I could keep my more or less comfortable position. The chances were it wouldn't be very long. I was right; the ticket inspector came along, woke me up and said I couldn't sleep here all night.

He noticed my uniform as I stood up to sit down again next to the window.

'Where you cum' from,' he asked

'Singapore, the flight arrived in the UK yesterday morning. I've come from Portsmouth after demob.'

'Going to Inverness?' he asked.

'Thurso, on the ten o'clock flyer from Inverness,' I replied.

'Flyer my arse,' he said. 'best you come with me.'

I picked up all my kit, and I followed him to an empty first-class sleeping compartment.

'There you go Chief, this will do you,' he said.

I made to give him a tip, but he refused, saying he had done this journey many times during the war and one had to look after one's own. I crashed within minutes, dead to the world.

The next thing I became aware of, needing the wee basin under the sink to discharge what was left of the beer. I looked out of the window and saw the sign for Aviemore. My watch told me the train was more or less on time and boy did I feel a whole lot better.

On arrival at Inverness that most welcome of refreshments arrived in my sleeping compartment. A large mug of British Rail tea and two whole-wheat biscuits. I stayed abed for as long as possible, and then made my way to the station café for a cooked breakfast. That done, there was the longish wait for the ten o'clock flyer to Thurso, a four-hour journey that takes much longer than any decent motor car.

The train journey is actually quite interesting, as twice it is routed inland. The first diversion calls for the railway to be routed around a small mountain called Beinn Domhnaill, but this route follows the winding Scottish roads to and from Lairg, one of its many stops. This is a community train serving the many needs of the local population.

In Caithness, the railway cannot follow the coast road either. The route goes deep inland through some very wild country, an area with no roads before it drops back down onto the coast road a fair distance along the coast towards the north.

To add to the journey time, apart from all the stops at local stations, there is also the shuffle at Georgemas Junction, as the train divides, half to Thurso, on the north coast, and half to the town of Wick on the east coast.

On the whole, however, the railway still provides an important service, especially when the snow arrives. I write from experience, it's a bad road to Thurso when the snow comes.

I remembered to check which carriage I would need and eventually I arrived at Thurso after the longest train journey I am ever likely to experience. Jim and Johan were waiting at the station, and oh, it was good to be back.

Looking back I had departed Singapore on a Tuesday afternoon and arrived at my destination on a Friday afternoon. Three long days.

Time to rest, take stock, and build a new future.

12

CIVVY STREET AND DECCA RADAR

HAVING LEFT THE SECURITY OF the Royal Navy and with no opportunities to join Dounreay in 1970, I decided not to join the rat race working for military communication contractors. Father-in-law Jim suggested I find work in Scotland for one year as he was certain I would be able to join Dounreay the next.

So I took a position as a service technician with Decca Radar Ltd in their depot at the small fishing port of Buckie on the Moray Firth. The words 'jumping from the pan into the fire' came to mind but Johan and I coped. Decca Radar's main product was the Navigator; heavily used by the fishing community.

Sorry for the technical speak but here comes its description. The system invented in the US, then developed by Decca UK and first deployed by the Royal Navy during World War II.

A similar system was used by the RAF for their night time visits to Germany. The Decca Navigator was a post-war commercial version, heavily updated and improved. It was extensively developed around the UK and later around the world. Decca Navigator's primary use was for ship navigation in coastal waters, but fishing vessels were the major post-war users.

The Decca Navigator System is a hyperbolic radio navigation system allowing ships and aircraft to determine their position by receiving radio signals from fixed navigational beacons, using phase comparison of four low-frequency radio signals from 70 to 129 kHz. The signals were designated Black, master, and three slaves, Green, Red, and Purple.

The comparison in each of the three slave channels produced hyperbolic curves that could be drawn on a chart, crisscrossing each other. By knowing where you were at the start of a voyage, the display unit would count along the curves. Any intersection would give a position on the chart.

Now for ships travelling from 'A' to 'B', the system was sufficiently accurate to get you to the entrance of your destination, but it wasn't that accurate that you could not ignore the requirements of safe navigation for entering difficult harbours, e.g. taking sightings of lighthouses and the accurate use of your chart. The greater the distance from the transmitter, the less accurate the system became as the radio signals only travelled on their ground wave.

However, the system was very repeatable, i.e. it always gave the same position at the same spot, so the fishermen used it very effectively for fishing. They would survey an area of interest, shipwrecks, outcrops of rock and deep hollows in the seabed, anywhere the fish liked to hide, using sonar, usually called a 'fish finder' or 'fish loop', they would write down the numbers in a book that never ever left their person. A return to the same numbers would take you back to exactly where the fish where. These books were handed down father to son, but only once did the skipper show me his numbers.

So, what class of good people did I have to deal with? The fishing community along the Moray coast from Inverness to Macduff and part of the West Coast were mostly adherents to the Free Presbyterian Church of Scotland, known as the Wee Frees.

Sunday was their day to give thanks to the Lord above and their religion forbade working on the Sabbath, but at two minutes past midnight on Sunday, their boats would be quickly on their way to the fishing grounds.

They were a hardy breed and lived a tough life. At the time, I was told they were pretty cute when it came to finances. I knew one skipper who fitted the bill quite nicely.

The White Fish Authority was a government organisation to help finance the industry. The skipper I knew followed a well-worn trail.

He applied for finance for a new boat, to be built locally in Buckie or Macduff. An 80-footer would, in those days, run to about four hundred thousand pounds to, fully fitted with the latest equipment and electronics.

With this collateral, the skipper would visit his friendly local building society for a loan for a new home, normally four bedrooms, double garage, etc etc., Say forty grand.

Then, with the collateral from the new house, he would then slip into his local bank manager for a loan to buy a new Jaguar. No point in having a swanky new home without a decent car parked in front.

Then, all the skipper had to do was to catch plenty of fish, otherwise the White Fish 'manny', the mortgage society 'manny', and the bank manager 'manny' would have many sleepless nights.

Did the skipper worry, apparently not, he started off the merry go round with little and he could only end up back at the starting post.

Skippers came in all sizes, shapes and humour. I remember one skipper, not the easiest person to deal with, always complained about his Decca.

'It's nae workin' richt,' he would complain at length.

Everything was tried, new set, new aerial, new everything, but to no avail. Then one day I said, 'OK Skipper, show me on your chart just where the hell are you are trying to use your Decca. Otherwise, I cannot help you.'

The skipper was not pleased, not pleased at all, but with great reluctance, he made a sweeping stroke of his pencil on the chart. Ah, I thought, now I know what the problem is.

Taking him to one side, so that his 1st Mate wouldn't hear, I told him he was out of range. Christ, he was nearly going ashore in Norway.

I continued, 'Skipper, in the North Sea you use Chain 6C, but 6C doesn't cover coastal Norway. You should use Chain 5E' in Norway.'

A dinna kin!' he said. 'I've nae efin' numbers fer Chain 5 efin' E.,'

Well go and make another survey on Chain 5 efin' E, that's all that can be done', I said.

The skipper went away muttering, and rumour had it he went inshore inside the fishing limits and made himself a lot of money without getting caught. This time.

Phew, that description wasn't so bad, was it? I have added a picture of the display unit. The box with all the electronics (remember valves?) was installed somewhere else on-board. This was all there was before the days of microchips and GPS units.

No way would you be climbing up a mountain wondering if you were lost carrying one of these. And you would have needed a power supply to go with it.

Now your smartphone i.e. I-Phone, Blackberry, Galaxy et al. will do the job for you.

(By the way 'Blackberry is or was so I was told, American slang for 'ball and chain'. A great piece of humour.)

The modern devices that sit in your pocket weigh almost nothing, the battery lasts forever but if you do get lost but it will record exactly where, if you fell down a ravine, so your children would know where to find your remains should they ever find time to stop looking at their smartphones.

So, to recap, the Scottish fishermen used it extensively and this is how they used it. Fishermen know where the fish should be, (assuming a Russian trawler hasn't entered your fishing ground to 'hover' up all the fish, small, large, and newborn, barely leaving the salt behind, just to use their catch for animal feed).

The only real problem with the system, as the Decca engineer who was frequently called out in the middle of the night to fix the damn thing, was the earth bolt which was always down in the bilges so that it would connect directly with the sea outside. The Decca system relied on the earth as a base reference and unless the earth was clean, the system would wander just sufficiently to cause problems.

I would arrive on the boat. 'Aye aye skipper,' I would yell out.

'Ma Decca is neh workin' he would reply 'An were awa' in twenie minutes.'

I would press the test button and the three slave decals (meters) would go to zero.

'Can't see a problem skipper,' I would yell back.

'Oh eye, look at ma' nets, ripped to pieces,' would come the reply.

I would press the test button again and soon learnt how the three meters should move to zero. If the needles did not point exactly to zero it was the earth bolt. Time to put on overalls, my rubber gloves, take a spanner, a wire brush and a carton of petroleum jelly and dive down into the bilges with water always full of diesel, dead fish bits or fish scales. Strip the earth bolt cable connection, clean as required, reconnect and slap a large dob of petroleum jelly on the fitting. All for a basic pay of £19 quid a week plus overtime and car allowance.

Ten minutes later job done. The skipper would be happy he could rely on his next shoot where the fish were and he was able to be on his way. In the summer these guys would run their boats twenty-four hours a day. I used to enjoy driving in the midnight sun, as being this far north, the sun never set completely.

A happy skipper would give me a 'fry' of fish, about half a box of beautiful fresh haddock that took less sixty seconds a side to cook in the frying pan.

*

BUCKIE HARBOUR HAD three boat yards and could build excellent wooden fishing boats up to about 90' in length. They were very strong and they needed to be. The ribs in the hull generally comprised of steamed oak ribs, four inch square, with a spacing of about sixteen inches.

Herd and McKenzie, the largest of the three yards, received an order for the *Captain Scott*, a sail training ship, (named after explorer Robert Falcon Scott) in 1971 for the Dulverton Trust, run by the Loch Eil Trust which combined sail training with onshore expeditions.

She was constructed in the traditional style from Scottish oak and pine from Uruguay. Her lower masts were an aluminium alloy and her upper masts and spars were wooden.

At 52 metres long and 30 meters high she was a big ship and the largest ever built in the yard.

As a sail training ship, the rigging for the two large masts was specified to be in the traditional style (think *HMS Victory*), which was all very well but there were few specialists in the country who could do this work.

Eventually, Harry Spencer arrived on the scene and took charge of installing the masts and making the standing rigging in the old way of doing things. I briefly met the man during my time in the navy. He came to check on the wire rigging that stabilised an air inflatable Radome that protected the main satellite dish at SRDE in Christchurch.

One day, he dropped his favourite wrench, which he had used from his days in WW2, into the harbour between the schooner and the dockside. He was quite distraught. I dashed back to the depot and returned with a radar magnetron (a very strong magnet) and a long length of line. Ten minutes of fishing his favourite article was restored to him and Harry Spencer was overjoyed.

(Later the schooner was sold to Sultan Qābūs bin Saʿīd of Oman in 1977 and entered the Oman Navy as a sail training ship. Running costs were just too expensive in the UK.)

Anyway, a year later Johan and I left behind the council house we had been given, packed up and we were on our way back to Thurso and a new start at DERE.

13

THE UK ATOMIC ENERGY AUTHORITY

Dounreay, Scotland (1971 - 1974)

IN JULY 1971, I WAS accepted into UKAEA Fast Reactor Development Establishment Dounreay (DERE) located at the north of the Scottish mainland just west of Thurso. Many old navy hands will remember this bleak and remote location and its local harbour, Scrabster, which was the southern end of the ferry route to the main Royal Navy base during WWI and WWII at Scapa Flow in Orkney,

As described earlier it's a long train ride to Thurso. I did it from Portsmouth, once, thanks very much. So what about Thurso? Thurso is the most northerly town on the British mainland situated on the northern coastline overlooking the Orkney Islands

Its history stretches back to the time of Norse Orcadian rule in Caithness until 1266. Neolithic remains were found on nearby Shebster Hill and date back about 5,000 years. The town was an important Norse port and carried on trade with ports throughout northern Europe until the 19th century.

A major expansion occurred in Thurso when the Dounreay Nuclear Research Establishment (DERE) was established at Dounreay, in 1955, causing a three-fold increase in the population of Thurso, leading to 1,700 new houses being built in the town and nearby Castletown, a mixture of local authority housing blended with private houses and flats built by the United Kingdom Atomic Energy Authority.

The authority gave me one of the 1,700 new houses, a three bedroom property, with a garage just across the road. Quite a nice home actually.

And so to Dounreay itself and its many divisions. The purpose of the site was focussed on nuclear fast reactor technology. The future, so they said.

The first reactor was the Dounreay Materials Test Reactor (DMTR) in May 1958 and used to test materials under intense neutron irradiation.

The second operational reactor was the Dounreay Fast Breeder Reactor (DFR), housed in what looked like a huge golf ball. It used liquid sodium as a coolant for the reactor and the heat produced used to make super heated steam for the electrical generators.

It achieved criticality in November 1959. Its electrical power was exported to the National Grid from October 1962 until 1977 and produced over 600 million kWh of electricity. I remember the times of major UK strikes and the three day week in the early 1970s. Dounreay drastically cut its electrical power consumption to enable the level of exported power to Scotland to reach a much-needed maximum.

The last reactor to be built was the Prototype Fast Reactor (PFR) fast breeder reactor also cooled by liquid sodium. It went critical in 1974 and began supplying National Grid power in January 1975. The output of PFR was 250 MWe. There were many delays and reliability problems before reaching full power.

The reactor was taken offline in 1994 marking the end of nuclear power generation at the site. A remotely operated robot dubbed The Reactorsaurus was sent in to remove waste and contaminated equipment from this reactor, a task too dangerous for a human.

*

BACK TO THE story. By this time my father-in-law James, now promoted to foreman in one of the nuclear fuel reprocessing buildings in the Process Plants Division, recommended I ask for an assignment to Process Plants, which was granted.

A line of buildings were connected to either side to a long central corridor. There was only one entrance into Process Plants, via an entrance building where a clothing change was mandatory, from a shoe and sock change plus white overall coat to a full change of all clothing for staff entering any area that had radioactivity. Thus, 'little' Jimmy, an elderly ex-crofter, became the most important person in Process Plants. He ran the entrance facilities, and without them, one could not gain entry to the site.

Nowhere was there access to the outside except in an emergency. Starting at the bottom rung of the Dounreay ladder as an instrument technician I was sent to the building that assembled instrumented fuel pins for the DFR. The objective of these fuel pins was to measure conditions inside the reactor, as the fuel pins would swell with the intense radiation, restricting the flow of the sodium coolant, causing a hot spot in the reactor core. This was considered by the scientists as not good.

Anyway, I noticed that outside, between the buildings, the rabbits played with gay abandon on the uncut grass. I mentioned this to Jim, who laughed. I asked why, but he said, 'let's go to lunch'.

Who should we meet in the canteen behind the counter was Margret, Jim's wife.

'What's in the pie today, Mother?' Jim asked.

'Chicken,' she replied.

'Is that chicken chicken, or Dounreay chicken?' he asked.

Margret smiled a knowing smile and gave us both a double helping. It was very nice pie, which tasted like, err, Dounreay chicken. I wonder who caught them, must have been at the weekend when the site was almost empty.

Meanwhile, back in the fuel rig instrumentation workshop, I was getting bored and I wasn't learning anything about industrial instrumentation and control systems. So I wangled a transfer to the workshop that covered the uranium fuel recovery plant called Process Plants.

A nuclear fuel pin, made of highly enriched Uranium 235 would have a burn-up rate in the reactor of somewhere in the region of ten to fifteen per cent. It has huge heat potential. Get your head around this:

The fission of one atom of uranium-235 generates 202.5 MeV = 3.24×10^{-11} J, which translates to 19.54 TJ/mol, or 83.14 TJ/kg. This is around 2.5 million times more than the energy released from burning coal

Gosh!

So the recovery programme is quite simple. The uranium fuel pin is removed from the reactor and allowed to cool for a few months in a big pond. It is highly radioactive.

The actual fuel is enclosed in a stainless steel sheath and this is removed. The uranium is extracted, chopped up and placed in a basket. The basket is lowered into a vat containing nitric acid at sixteen times normal strength. The uranium dissolves into a liquor, with just a few grams of the metal per litre.

This is passed to the next building, where the weak liquor is passed into a sealed metal trough containing a very, very strong alkaline liquid. The acidic liquor flows one way, the alkaline liquid in the opposite direction.

For strange reasons known only to the mad scientists, the dangerous fission products in the acidic liquor transfers into the alkaline liquid, making the uranium carrying liquid safe to pass to the next process.

The dangerous alkaline liquid is passed to another building where it is chemically neutralised, condensed, and then safely stored for the next million years, either in a very strong deeply buried underground tank or it can be encapsulated in small glass spheres before reaching the underground tank..

Meanwhile, the uranium liquor is processed by condensing it and then turning it into a powder, processed twice more in ovens full of strange dangerous gasses resulting in a turquoise blue powder which is mixed with magnesium chips and fired electromagnetically in a very strong container. At a critical temperature, the magnesium fires and turns the blue powder into a uranium metal billet, about the size of a large doughnut.

It is quite weird handling a uranium billet, wrapped in nothing more than a simple plastic packet, as it is three times heavier than lead.

Two stories from these days come to mind. The first when, let's call him Joe, decided to get rid of the rust on his car. He found a source of clean nitric acid, at sixteen times normal, put half a pint into a glass jar and mixed an equal amount of demineralised water.

Sneaking the mixture home past the policeman on the gate, he spent a happy evening removing the paint from the rusty parts of his car, and wearing thick rubber gloves, used a thin paint brush to coat the rust with the mixture.

To give the mixture time to work, he went indoors for a cuppa and then the loo.

When he returned to his car the rust had disappeared, as had most of the metal. Now a car with no wheel arches or sills is going to look kind of, err, stupid.

*

THE SECOND TALE occurred in the building that made the uranium billets. The plant had been busy all day and there were a number of billets on the window ledge opposite the plant foreman's office, all carefully spaced apart.

When the foreman had finished filling out all the paperwork on each billet, a tiresome job, he asked 'Big Billy, a crofter turn process worker's assistant, to move the billets into the special safe inside a secure room. Inside the safe were slots, at a suitable distance from each other, for the billets to sit in.

Big Billy started to collect the billets into the cradle of his arm and was about to place the fifth billet into the cradle of his arm when the foreman came flying out of his office in the best rugby tackle around the legs I have ever seen. Big Billy went flying, as did the uranium billets.

Had the sixth billet been cradled into Big Billy's tender loving care, there would have been a 'blue flash' at criticality and there would have been an event. Jesus H, some event, (but not an explosion)

*

ALONG WITH EVERYONE else who worked in Process Plants, it was necessary to visit the Whole Body Monitor in the Medical Centre once in a while for an in-depth medical exam. Everyone working around the various plants had some exposure to radiation and this examination was to double check the totals derived from the radiation badges we all had to wear were correct.

Dounreay was very strict on this type of monitoring. And there was an interesting story about the monitor. In these early days of the industry, monitoring instruments became ever more sensitive, so that natural background radiation started to become an issue.

One of the managers had the bright idea of building a room with steel that predated the nuclear age. A ready supply existed on the seabed in Scapa Flow, just across the water in the Orkney Islands. Steel from the scuttled WW1 - 1918 German fleet was being recovered for such a purpose for clients everywhere.

So Dounreay ordered six steel plates with which to construct the monitoring room. The required steel could only come from a warship's armoured plating. The plating arrived on-site, and the metal workers got to work, or rather they didn't.

They found they had no method of cutting these thick armoured steel plates. Having expended a considerable sum on the material, they were at a loss until some bright spark suggested getting someone from the Krupp's steelworks in Germany to come and help.

Krupp's had no suitable person below pensionable age, so weeks later, a seventy-plus-year-old Krupp's steel chemist/scientist arrived to help out. Exactly what the method used was never revealed, but the old guy was making a good living out of it. Anyway, when the work was completed, the new body monitor was a great success, and one received a nice cup of tea while waiting for the monitor to complete its rather lengthy examination.

*

AFTER TWO YEARS in Dounreay, I achieved a much-welcomed promotion to charge-hand and a move away from the often dirty work in Process Plants.

I had learnt a lot and now I was assigned to the ETG group (Engineering Technology) in a more pleasant part of the site.

ETG possessed a number of mad scientists, who invented mad experiments that needed constructing. Quite often this required the workshop team to work some welcome overtime, as wages at DERE were not under any circumstances generous. I remember when the leader of one of the big trade unions came to the site to address the men. Fine words flowed, but as my foreman pointed out, a grey-haired short stubby and very sharp member of the Dundee mafia, the Union boss's silk tie would have cost more than the basic weekly wage of his workmen.

This was the first time I had met a senior union official because the Royal Navy doesn't have a union that needs officials. I wasn't impressed, but I held my counsel.

The main work that ETG performed was to investigate the area concerning the exchange of heat from the reactor to turn water into high-pressure superheated steam to drive the electrical generators.

The reactor coolant was liquid sodium, which under operating conditions has the same flowing characteristics as water at room temperature. This was very convenient, as pre-testing could be completed with demineralised water before putting the item to work.

The PFR reactor had three sodium cooling loops; the primary, which flowed through the reactor, obviously very radioactive; a secondary which transferred the heat to the tercery loop that contained the sodium/water heat exchanger. Pumping the sodium is achieved by using non-mechanical electro-magnetic pumps, which makes life very easy, and achieves very high safety standards.

This is the most sensitive part of the whole reactor system, as water has a lot of hydrogen (H20) and hydrogen can, in this environment, diffuse through stainless steel and hydrogen in very hot sodium is a very bad idea.

The process workers in our area used to help themselves to small amounts of cold clean sodium, a very soft metal. They would wrap it in toilet tissue and keep inside a small containment that would not allow the ingress of any moisture.

The sodium was used for salmon fishing. Just put some sodium chips into a dry clean coke bottle, stuff tissue paper in the neck, and when the coast was clear of the salmon gillies who were elsewhere, just drop the coke bottle into the salmon pool and by the time the bottle reached the bottom of the pool, the water would soak through the tissue and a satisfying explosion occurred, stunning any salmon in the pool.

It was best not to get caught poaching. The police would confiscate your transport, send it to the crusher and if they could prove slivers of sodium had been used, loss of employment became a strong possibility.

What many people did not understand was the landowners made a living by selling very expensive holiday packages to clients, mostly from Japan and the USA. The visiting clients expected to either catch something, or shoot something, and drink a lot of special whisky that came from the northern part of Scotland.

ETG group also had a covered-in concrete bay on the edge of the site for cleaning equipment that had clean sodium residue needing to be removed. The item was placed under two heavy steel plates forming a rudimentary shelter. Then a low-pressure steam hose was placed at the upwind end of the cover and then stand well back.

One Sunday afternoon, the two shift process workers had to clean the sodium from a length of pipework. They did everything correctly, pointing the pipework out to sea, but being in a hurry to finish early they applied rather too much steam. What they didn't know was there was more sodium in the pipework than they had allowed for so when they applied the steam there was a nice show of pyrotechnics. Over the sea. The next thing that occurred was the Thurso RNLI lifeboat turned up in a big hurry, accompanied by an RAF Rescue helicopter from RAF Lossiemouth, a hundred plus air miles away down on the Moray coast.

As you can imagine, there was a bit of a fuss, followed by a full-blown investigation where everybody seemed to get involved on what was otherwise going to be another quiet week.

The Social Side of life in Caithness

ONCE I HAD established myself at Dounreay and got my finances under some sort of control, it was time to return to my favourite sporting activity, sailing. The Pentland Firth Y.C. was based just a mile down the road at Scrabster Harbour. It wasn't a big club by any means, but it had a clubhouse, a bar, a dinghy park, and held three races a week during the summer.

The huge influx of workers into Caithness from all over the UK added to the number of sailors keen to go racing. I managed to buy an Enterprise racing dinghy and found that I liked it. It was a very popular class in the UK. I was lucky to get a good crew as well, a keen sixteen-year-old, Steve Arkley, the son of one of the senior management staff in Process Plants.

We did quite well in the racing, won a few, lost a few, but the best race was when just after an excellent start, a shackle failed and the deck mounted mast fell into the water. Furious, I grabbed the mast and in sheer bad temper pulled it upright and put it back into its place as Steve found another shackle to secure the shroud.

Rather than follow the fleet, I took a big hike out into the bay, tacked, and still with the furious temper, I forced my Enterprise past the fleet into second place at the first mark. I think we finished first, anyway, it was a series race and I gained sufficient points to win the series.

*

WITH THE EARLY warning that Steve would be passing his exams to go to college out of town, I took a fancy to sailing a single-handed dinghy and ended up building my first Phantom dinghy in the garage over the winter. It was a new boat in the marketplace, designed for homebuilders using plywood cut into predetermined shapes using a template, and then wiring the edges together in a process known as 'stitch and glue'.

When the hull is just held together by the copper wire, it is very fragile, and requires perfect setting-up on trestles, making sure it is square and has no hog or sag along its length. After taking many measurements and using a level to ensure the hull was square, I started the process of laying glass fibre tape along all the internal edges of the plywood.

By morning, the hull had become very strong, so rigid so it was possible to carefully turn it over so that the glass fibre tape could be applied to the outside seams. In all, it took just over a hundred hours to complete.

The boat was very light and comfortable to sail. From that moment on, I was in sailing heaven, and oh, what fun I had racing it.

*

MY TIME WITH the Phantom was all I expected of it. It was a very light craft, just under 60 kg all up. Getting it upwind was hard work. I never did find the groove I was told I should find. But off the wind, on the reaches, the boat just flew. I could get it to surf down waves at catamaran speeds. And if I stayed the course, good results made it all worthwhile.

In June 1973, I grabbed some days leave to go to the Scottish Phantom Championship at the Carnoustie SC, held over a bank holiday weekend. I was lucky to be offered accommodation by the club commodore.

Three hard days of racing were in front of me, and I felt a little nervous as my wet weather clothing did not include a wetsuit. These were quite expensive at the time, and I never really felt I needed one.

The first two days went well. I found I had boat speed and lots of it. There was a hotshot sailor from Edinburgh who was slated to win the Championships and I had a clear advantage over him. I was not that keen sailing from the sandy beach and the race course was laid on exposed waters just to the east of the famous golf course.

On the last day, the wind got up during the race and I was leading by a huge distance that surprised me. Perhaps racing in Thurso Bay was a good training ground. More likely it was because I raced three times a week.

The wind picked up quickly, well past limits. I looked around expecting the race officer to be calling for a shorten course and get everyone back on the beach for safety. I was getting tired but didn't realise how tired. I was on a downwind leg and only had to gybe to reach the bottom mark and hang on to the finish line. I should have worn ship, which is to come up on to the wind, tack, then bear away. I had plenty of time to do so. I didn't think to do this, the gybe went wrong and I ended up in the water.

Without any assistance, I manage to right my boat, but I didn't have the strength to get back into it. I made the beach and collapsed. Fortunately, help arrived. I was taken to the clubhouse and dumped into a hot shower, where it took a long time to recover from a bad case of hypothermia. My Phantom was brought back to the club by a rescue team, without damage thank goodness.

So, in the end, I only gained a third overall place, despite having lost the vital result that should have been. Ah well, there was always another year.

GALLERY

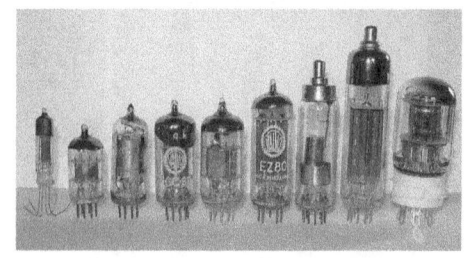

Clockwise from top left: Sailing a Montague whaler • A rather overloaded family motor cycle combination • Class of 1960 • Small thermionic valves • The £30 Commer Cob van • Wedding to Johan • On our way to #8 Swinging Ground Buoy and £5 • Sailing a Piccolo in Singapore

Clockwise from top left: Johan & Carolyn Overlooking Singapore City • Carolyn • Singapore 1969 • In new uniform with Carolyn • In French Waters Outwards Bound • A Decca Mark 12 display unit

Clockwise from top left: HMS Albion • At Tiradentes, MG, Brazil, HMS Cossack – Fleet Destroyer • a 500cc Manx Special • A typical Class 1 competitor • USS United States – Maiden Voyage

Clockwise from top left: HMS Brave Boarder at 50 knots plus Itaipu Hydroelectric Dam • National 18, No. 316 with Russian Crew, • Thurso Jan 1984 – Sonia with the Rover • Linda and Richard Tarpey with Andre from Russia at the wedding

Clockwise from top left: National 18 • Phantom 263 - My Pride & Joy
Exploring a gold mine in Minas Gerias, Brazil during Carnaval 1984
Carolyn's 16th Birthday with Sonia • Ex-T.E. Lawrence's Motor Cycle

Clockwise from top left: Wedding Day June 1992 • Sailing a Finn in front of Sugarloaf in Rio de Janeiro • Me – Trying to Remember z z z z z • 1937 Cord

MY OTHER NAUTICAL experience during my time in Thurso was to join the RN Sea Cadet Corp as I had three years reserve time that I had not expected to use.

So once a week I would put on my CPO's uniform and teach the sea cadets all they needed to know about rowing, sailing, and of course, safety. They were keen youngsters and it was great to pass on all the knowledge I had accumulated over the years.

I also managed to get special leave from Dounreay to attend training courses at the RN Sea Cadet Training Centre at Port Edgar, near Edinburgh, the bonus being I was paid full CPO's pay plus expenses, which certainly helped my finances at the time.

The first week I passed through three refresher courses to obtain my certificates for Rowing, Sailing, and Motor Craft. Very handy certificates for later on, especially when insurance matters needed attention. The second week, I spent teaching a Sea Cadet unit from Scotland, and that went well.

On the second occasion I spent two weeks in Port Edgar, a colleague and I had to teach a large Sea Cadet unit from Belfast. Now, this was at the height of the Troubles, and some of the young adults had experienced some very harrowing times. Because of this, they had a rather different view of life in general, and any navy bullshit was not going to go down well. I had to check my colleague a few times before he cottoned on to their situation.

So, I gave my classes as much humour as possible, stood for no nonsense in a friendly relaxed manner, and everybody got on splendidly. My classes received the most certificates so I was well pleased.

*

AS FOR FAMILY social life in Thurso and not being able to splash the cash as I had a young family to support, Johan and I would usually spend our evenings with Johan's father, James. Dounreay had its own social club called Ormlie Lodge, which had subsidised prices on snacks, meals and some beverages.

The only danger was getting involved with those members determined to talk shop. It eventually drove James to join the Thurso Club, originally formed by local businessmen and ladies. It was not easy to get a membership, as there was a definite divide in the city between the two communities. Occasionally this nonsense would come to the fore in the yacht club, but I always kept neutral and well away from any fuss.

The Thurso Club became that little home from home. James became good friends with the barmaid, and there is no better friend than a good barmaid.

Last, but not least, I remember a wonderful piece of gossip. It came from a new member of staff who joined my section in Process Plants. I forget his name, but he was Mr Handsome, ex RAF, and in his late thirties if I remember correctly. Let us call him Simon, an upper-class type, never married, not short of a few bob either. Quite why he turned up in Dounreay one will never know.

Simon slipped into the upper areas of social life of Caithness with little trouble. He was a favourite with everybody. He was a genuinely nice guy as well.

One evening, I met him in Ormlie Lodge and he was a bit low. He had discovered his social scene was quite restricted because of the low numbers in the circuit. After one year he discovered he was socialising with the same people time after time. He was, to be honest, looking for a life partner, but the only ladies he found taking an interest in him were ladies looking for a divorce, but they came complete with someone else's children, or they were too young and that held little interest for him.

He did, however, reveal a wonderful piece of gossip. It goes like this. At the time, Grampian Television was showing a very popular family medical programme during the week. The two doctors who hosted the TV show actually came from Thurso. One of the doctors was Scotland's leading gynaecologist who had a huge fan club.

It was during one of the more upper-class social events in Caithness when the said doctor was cornered by a rather loud, overbearing, overdressed lady, a social climber of the most hideous sort, who decided to use the occasion to ask the usual questions that gynaecologist really hate. How do you separate your work from one's normal relationship with one's wife?

The doctor, who had a really lovely wife, had heard it all before and evaded the question. But later, the lady, with far too many pink gins inside of her, came back determined to get an answer. The good doctor decided enough was enough, rammed his hand up her flimsy long dress into her area in question, with the words, spoken quite loudly, 'Madam, at the hospital, this is just work,' said he manoeuvring his fingers in a very professional way, 'But this evening it gives me great pleasure to give you great pleasure.'

The lady in question, who had started to blush bright red with great pleasure, now blushed in pure embarrassment and fled the scene in panic, never to be seen again. Everybody in the room agreed that the doctor had done a really good job of ridding their social scene of someone who really didn't fit in.

It was not long before Mr Handsome, tired of the limited opportunities to be had in Caithness, made a silent exit to pastures new, where we did not know.

*

BEFORE I LEAVE Caithness behind, two stories may be of interest. The first one concerns the BBC, who arrived in the county to erect a new TV tower to broadcast programmes to both Thurso, on the north coast, and Wick, on the east. To do so would require a tall tower to be erected high up on the moors between the two towns. The BBC engineers enquired, so the story goes, as to what wind strengths their tall tower should be rated for. Figures in the region of 150 mph (gust) and 120 mph (constant) were offered and rejected.

The standard tower was erected, capable of withstanding 100 mph winds. The next gale quickly arrived, deciding the tower looked much better lying on its side, rather than spoiling nature's wild beauty. The locals sniggered as the BBC removed the wreckage from attempt number one, sardonically applauding the erection of attempt number two, with snide comments about you can't beat a good erection.

*

TO ALL THOSE worthy cyclists that have peddled their way from John O'Groats to Land's End, the most northerly point of the UK mainland is, in fact, Dunnet Head, a short but dangerous seven miles from the Orkney Islands.

And so, on a blustery day, I took the family to visit the Dunnet Head Lighthouse, built in 1831 by Robert Stevenson, grandfather of Robert Louis Stevenson. The twenty-metre tall tower sits impressively on top of forbidding ninety metres tall cliffs. A total, if you're not a fan of metrification, three hundred and sixty-six feet altitude.

It was a perfect day. Strong gale force winds were much in evidence at the lighthouse, overlooking a west going spring tide whose velocity is enhanced by the two islands, Stroma and Swona. These tidal streams can reach up to eight knots and when combined with a strong westerly gale, the sea state becomes most impressive, best watched from the shore. It is extremely perilous if by any chance you are taking passage in these waters.

As we arrived, Johan suggested parking next to the coastguard's van, hiding behind a very strong, very high stone wall. The wind was rising and she had heard stories of cars being blown off the Head onto the rocks below.

We made our way into the lighthouse and climbed up to the gallery. What a sight we were presented with. Nature's fury in full force. The coastguard officer was searching the boiling seas with his binoculars. Somewhere in the tempest was a hundred foot steel trawler with a defective engine.

The question, 'Was it in danger,' almost crossed my lips. The coastguard was also looking for the Thurso lifeboat. 'My God,' I thought. 'How could this be?' Eventually, the emergency past and the fishing trawler limped safely into Scrabster Harbour accompanied by the lifeboat.

Inside the lighthouse, all was original except for the upgraded lamps that shone to keep seafarers safe. The rotating mirror assembly floated on mercury, making its rotation frictionless. A large cuckoo clock mechanism provided the drive to rotate the assembly.

A brief look outside on the gallery showed the large circular flutes on the glass had their sharp edges with big lumps knocked out them. The lighthouse keeper told me that the waves travelled across the Atlantic Ocean, crashed on the beach at the base of the cliffs, throwing up large stones that had caused the damage. Another good reason for hiding ones car behind the thick stone wall in the car park.

14

BRITISH PETROLEUM FORTIES FIELD

(1974 - 1977)

IN JULY 1974 I TOOK the family to Morayshire to take part in the annual Findhorn Regatta hosted by the Royal Findhorn Yacht Club. The drive down from Thurso was easy and the trailer carrying my racing dinghy managed not to fall apart.

We were fortunate to be hosted by a friend in Forres, a welcomed invitation as the year before we had camped and the weather was damp, Scottish damp. My friend was a bit fond of the water of life (whisky) and so a good day's racing was enhanced by lively convivial evenings.

One morning when I was recovering from a convivial evening I came across a notice in Aberdeen's favourite newspaper for candidates to join BP on the very first of their mammoth offshore oil fields. The suggested salary propelled the nearest pen I could find to paper and my letter in response was posted in record time.

The newspaper in question is the Aberdeen Press and Journal. Records show that it has two world beating headlines. They were: 'Titanic sinks, Aberdeen man drowned', and at the start of WW1 the headline read:- 'Giant neep found in Bucan'. Neep is Scottish for turnip in case you were wondering.

I joined BP towards the end of 1974 as a member of the initial *Forties Alpha* offshore production team, the first major oil-producing platform in the North Sea. The BP Forties project was a massive development requiring at the time the largest private loan of capital from the major UK and US banks: over one billion pounds at the time.

Johan was surprised at my decision, but I explained very carefully that Dounreay was never going to provide a good living over the many years we had left before us and the BP project was the start of a new massive industry. Better to get in early, work hard and see how far we could get.

She didn't like the idea of me working two weeks offshore, for two weeks at home, but to make ends meet, I was mostly working six days a week in Dounreay, so where was the family life?

We had enjoyed being in Thurso, but it was time to move on. Her father agreed. Had he not left the coal mining industry after all those years? Now he had improved his home situation substantially.

So, leaving the family with the grandparents, we drove down to Morayshire to search for a new home. Johan was against moving to Aberdeen, for whatever reason, and she liked the Forres area a lot. It was a pretty little town and still is.

The house I fell in love with was a large traditional property on the eastern outskirts of Fochabers, home of Baxters of Speyside, that marvellous company that make all things yummy in Scotland, including wonderful highland soups in tins and the best shortbread biscuits on the planet.

The property had four bedrooms, three public rooms, all in oak wood panelling, for the bargain price of £10,000 pounds. But the building societies were not interested in an older wooden house. They preferred the construction of a modern house, mostly chipboard, with a few decorative bricks around the outside. The standard Barratt offering.

And so, we bought a traditional cottage in the little village of Kingston on Spey. 'Moray View', Beach Road was a description, rather than an address. Its construction was strong but drafty, the wind whistled between the stone walls and the lathe and plaster interior, and a strong fire was needed in winter to keep warm.

Still, it had its good points. A Glasgow couple had taken over the local shop at the end of the street and could get their hands on most things. They did miss their hometown where items fell from local transport to order.

The doctor's surgery was held at the local hotel just a mile up the road. The waiting room was the lounge bar. When Doctor was running late, the bar would open for lunch and it was not unknown for the waiting patients to have a wee dram whilst waiting for their appointment. Quite often, the wee dram would provide the medical treatment required and the doctor, quite an old guy, would come out looking for patients who had healed themselves and vanished.

*

MY FIRST DAY at the office was interesting. BP had built a new headquarters In Dyce, just outside of Aberdeen over-looking the airport. The head of control systems welcomed the five of us. I often wondered what he made of us as a group. Two of us were ex-Royal Navy, one ex-RAF chap who had come down from ARTE, the Admiralty Reactor Testing establishment next to Dounreay, another ex-service man from somewhere I cannot remember, and an ex-BP guy, a Mr Russell, from the refinery at Grangemouth, just west of Edinburgh,

We were given the does and don'ts and although he stressed that when completing our expense reports our meal receipts should not show any alcohol consumption he certainly did not expect anyone in his division to be paying for their own drinks.

And so we hung around the office that day, collected an advance of expenses, enjoyed the hugely subsidised lunch, then slipped quietly away to our hotel in Aberdeen. First stop the lounge bar, where Russell corralled us into a quiet corner for his lesson on how to filling out a BP expense claim form. He was deadly serious. He didn't want any of us dropping him in the soup when it came for our little team to submit our expenses. I must say, it was one of the most valuable lessons I ever received.

*

WITH THE OFFSHORE construction programme being delayed, the company started a merry-go-round, by sending all the newly gathered team members, about fifty specialists, various, on a range of different courses. Round and round the country we went. The fire-fighting course, the first-aid course, the underwater helicopter escape course were just a few.

Then, came a round of vendor visits and one week we all ended up in The Hague looking at the modules being built for the *Forties Charlie* (FC) platform, the second of four platforms to be installed. We were told that they were ready for load-out, which kind of confused everybody. Our platform was *Forties Alpha*, known as sweet 'FA'.

Then, the big secret was revealed, the 'FC' modules would be installed on the 'FA' jacket, so perhaps we should pay attention rather than shuffle our feet and wonder where to go for lunch. I asked does that mean that the 'FA' modules would be installed on the 'FC' jacket. The Dutchman smiled and left us with our thoughts.

'Should be fun,' I thought. 'I wonder if they will change all the labels.' Seemingly not, so it turned out. All four of the Forties platforms would be identical except for the FC platform which would receive the exported oil from the other three platforms and connect them to the main pipeline to shore.

The Hague in winter is a dreary place. One of the team leaders led us to the red light district to show us tenderfoots how to get the best lady in the windows upstairs for some horizontal exercise at the right price. After some toing and froing, the team leader made his choice and proceeded to negotiate. The lady slammed the curtains closed and buggered off for a cup of coffee which rather left the team leader looking a bit perplexed.

It started to rain. The Hague was so boring, we all returned to the hotel and an early night.

*

WITH CHRISTMAS FAST approaching, two of us control and instrumentation types were dispatched to the refinery at BP Grangemouth, who didn't really know what to do with us.

The hotel was not up to the standard we were getting used too but it was OK except for one thing. The evening meal was the dreaded all-inclusive Xmas menu and who the hell was going to eat turkey for two weeks. Plus the fact, that the restaurant had full Xmas party bookings for every night of the week. Any chance they would go home early? Nope! The noise they made, and in Scottish.

After Christmas and New Year I returned to the office to join in the big discussion on when we would be going offshore. The news was inconclusive and the company was keeping the true situation very tight. I suggested it could be a while, only to be asked, 'How the hell would I know?'

I replied, that considering, as of first thing that very morning, the two halves of the main accommodation module were floating on a barge approximately one or two miles from my kitchen window as it looked over the Moray First, it could be a while. In fact, the weather was bad, the forecast was not very promising and that there were four other barges and their attendant tugs busy taking shelter in Spey Bay. I smiled and made myself another coffee.

*

LATER THAT WEEK it was announced that the whole of the offshore team would go to the City of Lincoln for a three-week course on Ruston Gas Turbines, of which the platform had six, three for power generation and three for pumping the produced product, via the newly laid pipeline, to Grangemouth.

There was a block booking at the White Hart Hotel, very old fashioned and comfortable in an 'olde worlde' English sort of way. This was where the clergy and visitors to the Cathedral next door were accommodated. It offered full service and an excellent restaurant with very old gentlemen waiters with starched high neck collars that could behead a normal person if his head moved too quickly.

Was the White Hart Hotel ready for an invasion by BP's finest? I don't think so. Every evening the team sat down to the formal five-course dinner. One of the offshore managers led the proceedings. He was a certified ship's Chief Engineer, known as Bob the Dog and came from one of those small Scottish ports in the North East that produce so many of the UK's finest seafarers. Many of the mechanical and electrical teams were also ex-merchant navy, dedicated drinkers all of them.

Any level of decorum in this exclusive refuge for the Holy Se did not make itself apparent. Lincoln Cathedral is the seat of the Anglican Bishop of Lincoln and its importance in the hierarchy of the English Church is very high.

It is to the credit of the staff of this hotel, who didn't turn a hair, when on the Thursday evening, Bob the Dog announced that the evenings five-course set dinner would be eaten in reverse, starting with the coffee's and 'after eights'. It was all very bizarre.

The second week, I took to eating out. I just cannot eat the same five-course meal every night.

And as for the training course? Well, actually, it was very interesting. The Ruston gas turbine is an industrial engine, one not derived from the aircraft industry. The instructors were all ex-RAF engine specialists, hardly surprising as the County of Lincoln is home to the RAF's Bomber

Command. They taught a good course, but I wondered why it took three weeks?

The head instructor, over a lunch time shandy, admitted that the course was structured for their Middle East clients, who, being good Muslims, would avail themselves of Lincoln's finest hostelries and any spare totty that was available. Apart from that, they expected any course concerning such a difficult subject to be suitably long, i.e. they liked coming to Lincoln a lot.

The only downside was the lack of sleep starting at five in the morning, when the milkman delivered the bottled milk and recovered yesterday's empties, in steel crates designed to make as much noise as possible when dropped on stone cobbles. (Anybody remember bottled milk being delivered to the front door?)

Then, at six-o-clock in the morning, the campanologists in the Cathedral would get to work in an infuriatingly energetic manner calling the faithful to prayers. Lincoln is famous for its campanology; they can be heard for f....g miles.

So for three weeks, I enjoyed Lincoln. The good news was I was almost top of the class when the instructors gave everyone an exam paper they were not expecting after a Thursday night on the tiles. I finished my exam paper quickly, receive my certificate and caught the early train back to Elgin via Aberdeen.

Finally, a wonderful story about the use of company expenses. One of the senior managers was hauled in before the Project Director, known as 'Dr No', about his expense report. The airport hotel was more motel than anything else, nice big comfortable rooms with comfortable American sized double beds.

One could check-in via the front desk, and ones beloved, or wife, could slip-in through the car park entrance on the far side of the hotel. The hotel also served fine cuisine in a sublimed and relaxing atmosphere. A full dinner would cost, and the wines were not cheap either.

It is at this juncture I can suggest that the two combatants were exactly that. Dr No was not a liked person, apart from any other qualities he may have had. So, back to subject in hand, the submitted expense report, which, amongst other things, had set a bit of a record.

It was blindingly obvious, that the submitter of the expense report had followed the well-known procedure of taking a member of the opposite sex for a romantic dinner and then received the female's energetic gratitude in the expected horizontal, or otherwise, position.

Legend has it, that the project director picked on this most expensive of items, although other items were not far behind, and explosively demanded an explanation.

The reply, 'Because I was 'expletive' hungry.'

The submitter of the expense report then just walked out.

*

AFTER A FEW months, life at home settled down, Johan, happy with my larger salary, was busy equipping our home. I changed my car for a BL Wolseley Princess HLS saloon, based on the Austin 2200. It was probably the most comfortable car I have ever driven and ideal for Scottish roads in winter with a big 2.2-litre engine sitting over the front wheels, it could plough through most snowbound roads with ease. I recently visited the UK's National Car Museum, and when nobody was looking, I had a quick sit down in the driver's seat. Just as good as it ever was.

*

APRIL 1975 ARRIVED and construction of *Forties Alpha* had reached the point where the onboard life support systems were able to accommodate some of the offshore contractor's workforce, and progress accelerated.

Within weeks came the call to report to the Heliport at Dyce Airfield. My first flight offshore seemed OK. Just sitting in the helicopter in a survival suit with nothing to do. I quickly figured the best place to sit was as close to the two pilots as possible on the basis if anything was going to go wrong I would be right behind them. But, of course, nothing was going to go wrong, go wrong, go wrong, otherwise why you would even get into the damn thing.

The arrival on the platform was an experience. Our cabins were not ready, and we were shown to the Quiet Room (the library), which had more beds in it than the Royal Navy's *Chevron Hilton* could have ever managed. Work was frantic. There was a huge push to get the platform ready for production.

The prime construction contractor was the American company Brown and Root. Now we would be dealing with the Americans.

We were not to know that BP was desperately short of cash. The drilling crews were already hard at it, and the platform had over three hundred Mexicans living in very cramped temporary living quarters. Quite where the Mexicans were housed was a bit of a mystery until I found the jumble of very second-hand accommodation containers hanging precariously from the outboard end from the drill rig pipe rack. It soon became clear the Mexicans were hot bedding, as one rose for a twelve shift; one would slump into an exhausted sleep. Their rota was twenty-five days on, five days off. Their transport to shore was by supply boat not equipped for passengers. A tough existence that would make them well-off for life in their poverty-stricken villages in Mexico.

One snippet of information that came my way was the revival of a certain industry in the Port of Peterhead, provided by the ladies of World War II coming out of retirement with their daughters.

On the platform, our team was soon put in its place. BP Projects were controlling everything, and we were BP Petroleum Development.

BP Projects was a group of dedicated construction and commissioning specialists with great experience who were tasked with completing very important projects on time. In other words, the heavy mob, rather like the Praetorian Guard.

The Pet. Dev. personnel were not particularity welcomed. The boss of BP Projects was Big Dave, and he soon told us we were there to work, otherwise go home, he needed the bed space for workers. Progress was all about bed space.

I had no problem with his thoughts and soon I was hanging from every ceiling in every module pre-commissioning the Fire & Gas system (FGS). Our very lives would depend upon this system to keep the platform safe. The technology for this system was very new, and BP had its own specialist in-charge of it. He had a touch of the mad scientist about him, but no doubt he was a very bright laddie.

What was quite strange about this guy was he had spent years developing the technology, using a new type of microchip that enabled a large and comprehensive system to be packaged into a much-reduced footprint (smaller cabinets), and I was very keen to understand more and learn as much as possible.

However, when the FGS system was declared fully operational, Big Dave gave him a well done. One platform down and only three platforms to go. The specialist took fright. He was not about to become a member of the great unwashed, 'a hewer of wood and carrier of water'. He was a scientist, a technocrat, only new things could keep his interest.

When he left the platform on his two-week break, he was never seen again. Later we heard that he had taken up medicine as a profession, training to be a brain surgeon. We all imagined him performing a brain transplant, dropping the brain on the floor, picking it up, giving it a quick rub on his scrubs and carrying on with the operation. He was a wonderful person, very easy to get on with but he was that kind of guy. It was a pity to lose him.

*

THE FIRST TWO weeks offshore flew by a blur and I was glad to get home. It was great to see that Johan had settled down. She even started taking the odd evening appointment with customers who liked the personal touch when having their hair restored to beauty.

Later on, one story came to mind when Johan was attending to a very nice rich widow in Elgin. The lady would send the taxi for her should I happen to be offshore. The skilful hairdresser soon becomes a confidant of the client.

This particular evening Johan returned home with a twinkle in her eye. The following story followed after a strong cup of tea.

The lady's husband had built a very successful business in Elgin. She classed her son as, unfortunately, being unable to take over the reins of the business, as he was 'a lazy sod' and drank too much. There were other relatives circulating around wondering what would she do? Would they be favoured in her thoughts or in fact her will? They knew her health could be better, the stress of running the company after her husband's death had left her feeling very unwell.

'Who was going to get what?' The lady could see it on all their faces.

And so, on this particular evening, when Johan had finished making her hair look very special, Johan was invited to sit down for a 'cosy cosy', and served a glass of homemade apple wine, that while delicious, was very strong.

'Mrs Reed,' started the lady. 'It has been a great pleasure to have you come to my home and give me the honest attention that I crave. You know the story about my family. I see you understand. I have a little secret to share with you. Tomorrow at six in the morning, a taxi will come to take me and my luggage to Aberdeen to catch the first flight too, err, somewhere away from my uncaring, grasping family.

I have sold everything, this magnificent home, the business, and the land, out from under this useless family of mine. Very few of them have helped me since my dear husband died and he would hate to see his life's work wasted. So, let us drink to our future, and many thanks, once again.'

'Good for you,' said Johan.

And so one bottle of homebrew later, a rather tiddly wife returned home.

*

ON THE OCCASION of my next tour of duty, there was a bit of a fuss at the heliport. Someone had given our flight to someone else. Not good. The timing of the BP crew-change flight was carefully set-up so that the crew returning to their families would arrive in Dyce airport in time to match the train schedules to Glasgow and Edinburgh, so that crew members would arrive home early evening at the latest, and for the late afternoon flights to destinations going south.

By lunch time, matters were getting out of hand. The heliport had few facilities for refreshment and the seating was poor. Considering how much money the oil companies were throwing at the helicopter company, it was a very poor show. By late morning the heliport was empty except for angry BP personnel. Enter from stage right the platform manager, tall, strong, every inch the oilman, Mr Ted Roberts, Mr North Sea himself.

Ted Roberts was quite famous in BP circles, he had been there, done that. Legends were based on his achievements, or so we were told. He calmed everyone down, informed that packed lunches were on their way as the heliport food service was worse than poor.

Then, he gathered everyone around him and quietly informed that the BP crew-change flight had been sequestrated by, as he called them, 'the Gentlemen from the City of London', two top-level chefs and a waiter from the Ritz, and a senior BP PR person from London office.

He continued, 'BP needs thirty million pounds, in cash, now, this week. The money men wish to see for themselves an offshore North Sea platform. The winter build has overrun, there are many unpaid short-term contracts, especially the tugs and barges that have been cruising around waiting for the right weather. Mr Reed here has seen them from his kitchen window overlooking the Moray Firth. At this moment, the money men are dining on haute cuisine with the finest of wines, on silk tablecloths and silver cutlery.'

Everyone was perplexed, wasn't BP one of the biggest and most innovated of the major oil companies? Ted Roberts read the mood of everyone and said all would be well, but there would be a tremendous push to get the platform finished and into production. This was vital for the health of not only the company but for the UK as a whole. He also added we should not repeat his words.

So there it was, BP Forties project, the largest and most expensive private financed operation ever attempted in the UK, teetering on the top of a slippery slope.

Much later the returning crew-change helicopter landed at Dyce and after a flight crew change and a fast turn-around, we were all on our way.

*

TALKING OF LUNCHES onboard the platform, an amusing memory follows. It was during the early days that the platform had, as a member of the galley staff, a genuine high-class haute cuisine chef. The meals he produced were just out of this world and everyone enjoyed them greatly except for a gang of Glaswegian steelworkers, led by their foreman known as Big Tam, or some such name.

I was in the queue for lunch, just about to serve myself when Big Tam shouts across at super chef, 'Hav' ye nae any decent grub cept' for this fancy cooking of yurn.'

The chef asked for their suggestion, only to be told 'mince and tatties, with plenty of neeps.'

So the next day, the chef laid-on exactly what he had been asked for. I was eating my lunch and I must say, the 'mince and tatties, with plenty of neeps' was exquisite, I had never tasted better and everyone at the table agreed.

We all waited for Big Tam to arrive with his merry men, who grunted a belated thanks to the chef, filled his food tray to overflowing and then covered the lot with tomato ketchup. The look on the chef's face did not bode well for the future. After the next crew change, we never saw him again. Probably he was in between contracts on the super yachts that linger in those wonderful locations with even more wonderful weather.

*

THE NEXT MEMORABLE event occurred a few months later. A mega storm was playing hooky with the North of Scotland in general and the North Sea in particular. I left home early that morning to catch my usual train through to Dyce and wondered if it would have been a good idea to take the car. Surely the day's flying programme would be affected.

I arrived at the heliport and it seemed that normal service was going to be the order of the day. Outside on the helipad, it looked bad. I could not imagine how they could start-up a helicopter in very strong winds. It is a matter of getting the helicopter blades up to their correct rotation speed, as the transition from a stopped condition in high winds is problematic.

There was a bit of a delay. Then the Captain of the helicopter brought his passengers together for a special briefing. The flight would go ahead. The helicopter would be wound-up in the hanger and then brought outside to load–up. It was going to be a bumpy flight and if anybody thought they would be airsick, they should remove the internals of their hard hat and use that to be sick in.

The flight time would be much shorter than normal as the wind would come from behind. The flight would land first at *Forties Bravo* and crew leaving that platform would board the aircraft first before crew joining the platform disembarked.

At *Forties Alpha*, the crew departing the platform would board and everyone should stay in their seats whilst the helicopter was refuelled. Then, the crew joining the platform would disembark. All movement on the flight deck would be controlled by flight deck crew who would be roped together for safety. When traversing the flight deck from the aircraft to the helideck stairs everyone should hold on to a safety rope that would be deployed. Absolutely nothing must be allowed to fly away in the wind, which would be quite 'strong'.

We all looked at each other and wondered should we get on the helicopter in the first place. From my perspective, the Captain and his First officer looked like ex-RN pilots, and if they thought the flight was doable, perhaps we shouldn't worry. Perhaps just display a little concern.

Anyway, ten minutes later we were in the air and the good news was that the standard one hour and twenty-minute flight would be approximately forty minutes. The Captain was as good as his word. The flight path followed the normal route over the fishing port of Peterhead, before heading out over a very angry sea. The flight was an experience that I promised myself not to repeat.

The aircraft landed on the Bravo platform, I say landed, but from my seat at the front of the cabin, I could see the helicopter was in full flight mode by a very busy 'pilot flying', the first officer. The white knuckles of his hands said it all.

The landing at our platform was a repeat performance. I could see very clearly the 'pilot flying' working very hard to keep the aircraft stable on the flight deck. The wind battered everything and everybody; the aircraft lurched and swayed but the pilot managed to keep it pointing slightly to one side of the wind direction. The departing platform crew boarded into a very crowded fuselage while the refuelling crew got to work in what little wind shadow of the fuselage the 'pilot flying' could create.

The 'pilot not flying', the Captain, came into the cabin to see that his instructions were being adhered too. I assume there was little room for error. Then it was time to keep a steady nerve and step outside the helicopter. I held on to the safety rope with all my strength and quickly made it to the helideck stairs down below to safety.

Ted Roberts greeted his joining crew with a 'nice flight boys' only to receive murmurings of discontent and one suggestion concerning an impossible manoeuvre in a sexual context. After check-in and the strongest coffee I could find, I heard the helicopter take-off. Apparently, the flight to the mainland took three hours and forty minutes, which was the maximum flight time before the aircraft would start using its twenty-five minutes emergency reserve.

In fact, the helicopter was ordered to land at the project airfield just outside of Peterhead to refuel, as Aberdeen air traffic control refused to allow any aircraft with only emergency fuel reserve on board to fly into commercial airspace over the city.

In all, that flight took four and a half long uncomfortable hours.

*

NEXT, THE TIME when the platform had just started production and there was the small matter of filling the 36" inch pipeline with crude oil all the way down to the BP Grangemouth Oil Refinery, a distance of 105 miles to the landfall at Cruden Bay and then a further 130 miles overland to the Kinneil Terminal.

Her Majesty the Queen was due to press the famous button during the inauguration scheduled for early December and as you can imagine, the Company Chairman was rather keen that this should happen without incident.

Just my luck, I flew on to the platform to start my regular tour of duty and after a hurried lunch I was called down to the gas turbine pump control room (or shack) on the lower deck to help with a 'bit of a problem'.

This problem turned out to be the 'poly ball' pig, a big tough plastic ball that had been inserted into the pipeline to be the interface between the oil being pumped and the water in the pipeline that had been used for pressure testing. The pig was getting stuck along the first section of the pipeline, which had been badly installed by one pipeline contractor. The second section had been installed by a second pipeline contractor and was known to be without restrictions. I assumed two contractors had been employed to shorten the construction schedule.

The problem for the production department was when the 'pig' became stuck, the level in platform's twin parallel separators would quickly reach the high-level alarm causing an automatic 'Yellow' shutdown of the production system. (Note: A 'Red' shutdown would kill the entire platform as all sources of energy are removed and isolated, used only for truly major events like a mega gas leak and possible abandon ship.)

Due to the complexities of the production control system, it was necessary for the platform's control system specialists, of which I was one, to quickly understand the fine detail how the system worked so that we could identify all faults and breakdowns. In these early days there was quite a bit of 'finger trouble' by inexperienced operators and when in trouble they naturally shouted for assistance.

I met with the production supervisor (PS) in the cramped turbine control room, or shack. Something drastic was called for, but what was it? There were no written procedures to guide us. A stiff coffee helped the thought processes, so I suggested starting the gas turbine pump at minimum speed with full recirculation back to the separators, a vital safety feature to keep flow flowing through the pump and protect it from damage.

Then, when we ready to go, I would ramp-up the gas turbine pump up to its maximum speed, whilst the PS closed the recirculation valve to its minimum setting. I would keep the pump at maximum for ten seconds, and then quickly reduce its speed to minimum. This, I explained, would send a pulse of energy down the pipeline and the 'pig' would deform and 'pop' by the obstruction and pumping could be continued anew.

The PS wasn't so sure, but what else was there? This was going to be a two-person job, so I offered to operate the gas turbine controls if he operated everything else.

We gave it a go, I took the gas turbine to maximum power, held it for those few seconds and then dropped back to idle. The noise of complaint from this powerful gas turbine engine, just outside the shack in its own insulted enclosure, was unnerving, to say the least.

The first attempt did not produce the desired result, so we tried again. This time it did work, the export oil flow meter shot up to maximum and there was a mad scramble to slow everything down before we emptied the separators and initiate a production shutdown on a low-level.

Having proved the method, we both realised we had let ourselves in for a long hard day repeating this complicated procedure until such time as the 'pig' reached the second smoother section of the pipeline.

Of course, nobody knew what debris was being pushed along the pipeline by the 'pig'. Pipeline welders were known to unfortunately drop objects, on purpose, into the pipeline during the welding operation. Empty tins of sodas were a favourite and this line had not been pigged by the usual 'cleaning pig' run.

By watching the export oil flow meter very carefully, it became possible to see or guess accurately when the next obstruction in the pipeline was getting near.

'Pigs' travel quite slowly, just about the only thing in our favour. This ad hoc procedure became some balancing act, as the choke valves that control the flow of oil from the wells had to be factored into our complicated ballet of callisthenics.

The platform engineer arrived in the shack, to see for himself just what was going on, but his visit wasn't at all helpful. Did we have a certified procedure, safety checks, blah blah blah?

I asked him did he want to 'stop the job', a phrase used without mercy in the early days of the platform. Such was the pressure to get the platform up and running, a lot of concerns were cast aside, safety concerns being in the forefront. Progress on the platform was everything, risk or no risk.

Getting the pipeline operational was vital. The PS and I knew the limits of the equipment and we had managed to stay inside those limits, just, but forcing a reluctant 'pig' down a badly constructed pipeline was hardly going to be a 'certified procedure'. Fortunately, the platform engineer made himself scarce.

The two of us spent all day and half the evening in the shack, a long and very concentrated day, not being unable to relax for a single moment, but at least the galley staff did a good service bringing fresh food and drink through the day.

Eventually, the 'pig' reached the second section of the subsea pipeline and at last, we could hand over operations to the new shift coming on watch with a long list of do's and don'ts.

*

ONE OF THE big concerns on any production platform is fire. To this end, the Fire & Gas System (FGS) is the first line of defence. However, it cannot be totally one hundred per cent as my next experience will show. During the course of one tour of duty, in the company of my colleague, we came across two very small fires that could have become major events.

The first was in the Separator Module. We were walking towards the large filter that prevented debris coming up from the oil wells entering into the two parallel separators. The production staff had just completed a small maintenance routine, which was to change the internal basket that caught the debris coming up from the well. Unfortunately, the circular trap door, although tightly closed, had nicked the sealing 'O' ring, which was leaking a small amount of gas. The gas had caught fire and the small flame was flickering unnoticed by either man or machine.

Taking no chances, my colleague rushed to the fire monitor in front of the separators, and shouted 'keep clear'. The fire monitor delivered a 150 psi of firewater, blasting the flickering flame to eternity. The act of using the fire monitor caused the main diesel fire pump to activate and at the same time activate a total production (Yellow) shutdown.

The action was well timed, as we noticed a grey fog coming up out of the open drains around the separator skids, which could only be gaseous condensate from goodness knows where. With a large squad of construction workers and welders, working high-up in the module, there could have been a very bad event. The Fire Team arrived en masse, as the Production Supervisor examined the separator oil filter 'O' ring to find it was very badly charred and ready to fail completely.

The Platform Manager arrived to take charge, saying he didn't see that we needed to use the fire monitor. I explained the logic of doing so, so he learnt something new.

The next day, my colleague and I were working in more or less the same area, when we heard the fire alarm and the tannoy announce that the diesel day tank was on fire.

Strange, I thought, the diesel day tank was just under one corner of the helideck. What could possibly be on fire? We legged up on to the roof of the separator module, then across the top of the adjacent LNG module, yet to be commissioned and arrived at the best place to view the diesel day tank. The top of the diesel tank was in full view of the platform's main flare, which was burning a huge amount of gas and in the calm weather that day, everything was very warm.

From our vantage point, we saw the mushroom vent on top of the tank was venting diesel fumes and had caught fire due to a passing welders spark from work in progress on the other side of the helideck.

The Fire Team at the base of the tank were attempting to spray foam up and over the mushroom vent, a process with no chance of success. With another fire monitor close to our viewing position, my erstwhile colleague shouted for everyone to stand clear and gave the errant flame a very quick two-second blast of firewater.

The flame immediately surrendered, the Fire Team, all covered in foam and sea water, started cursing in a non-repetitive manner.

*

DURING MY DUTY time on the *Forties Alpha*, everyone was always busy. The construction had been so fast a lot of loose ends had been left behind. I called these items the 'legacy items'.

One of the more unusual tasks was chasing down faults that occurred infrequently. Like the day when someone barged into the control room, ricocheting off the side of a large cabinet that housed many of the platform electrical relay systems.

This caused a Yellow shutdown, but I didn't put two and two together at the time. The same thing happened again, not soon after and another total production shutdown for no reason leaving everyone in the control room worried and perplexed.

One day, someone in the throes of a heated argument with the Duty PS, banged the side of this cabinet in disgust and stormed out of the control room. Again, another shutdown. Ted Roberts was to hand and thought he saw what was going on. He called me into the control room to discuss the situation.

'Could be a loose wire in the cabinet,' I suggested. 'Order the coffees, I'll go and fetch my pump handled screwdriver.'

I opened the cabinet door, tried tightening a few connections to find all were either loose or not totally secure. Ted suggested checking all the wire connections and I agreed with him. An hour later, having pumped thousands of connections it was obvious the contract installation electricians had cut and prepared each wire for connection and just poked them into the terminal block without checking the screw was fully tightened. Yet another legacy item.

There were other areas of the shutdown system that were giving the wrong actions. I told Ted that it would be best to chase these now; the true situation had just been revealed.

Four hours later, a strange collection of small wiring errors were resolved and I for one felt easier going to sleep better knowing that the safety systems were now fully in accordance with the specific details of the safety design. What was strange was that all the safety systems did actually work, so there was no real danger, just odd results that didn't add up.

*

AS WE ALL know, don't we, that living offshore, whether it is on a ship or a fixed offshore platform, accommodation generally provides cramped sleeping quarters and that cleanliness is twice as important as godliness. The *Forties Alpha* was no exception and in the early days, the two men cabins had been modified to become four men cabins.

On the level in the accommodation block where I shared my cabin, there were two cleaners who came from Newcastle, in the North East of England. A rare breed called Geordies, with their very distinctive local accent. They were both very good at their jobs, keeping our area of the accommodation blocks always spotless.

They were both very short, very thin persons. They were good fun too and also one hundred per cent limp of wrist. They could have been a stage act. I have never seen two homosexuals this queer. Pure ex-Merchant Navy stewards.

Just as the all too short lunch time zizz was coming to an end, we all heard the most violent altercation taking place outside in the corridor.

The corridor filled up to discover our two little friends in the most heated of arguments with the Tool Pusher, a huge Canadian gentleman, who was the boss of the drill floor. Tool Pushers are one tough breed of men and not to be argued with under any circumstances. This one had come down to his cabin to retrieve something important but he omitted to remove his considerably dirty drill floor boots, caked, as always, in drilling mud, oil, grease; leaving the pristine floor full of guilty marks.

Our two cleaners, having just finished cleaning the corridor floor, were extremely upset. The cleaner, with the very pronounced Mike Jagger lips, raised himself to his full height of 4ft 8ins to have a full-on face-to-face argument with the Canadian.

'Just who do you think you are?' he screamed.

'I'm the Tool Pusher,' came the reply in a deep Canadian accent.

'Tool Pusher, Tool Pusher,' screamed our little friend. 'I've sucked more tools than you've ever pushed.' He then proceeded to demonstrate on the empty coke tin in his hand.

At this point, everyone died laughing, it was so funny.

The Canadian turned on his heels, retreated back to his drill shack and the following day he took the first flight from the platform, never to be seen again. A coincidence? Who knows?

*

ONE DAY THE new head of Forties Field production made his first visit to the field, visiting the *Forties Alpha* platform first. This was a new and much needed senior management position now that all four platforms were on-stream and producing a lot of valuable and much needed crude oil.

Let me call him senior 'Sir', as his name has long departed from my memory. He was an up and coming executive with a great deal of responsibility. A pleasant fifty-year-old, easy to talk to, a person who had come to listen and learn.

It was early evening when Sir was chatting with the team in my workshop, drinking a much-needed coffee. The workshop was next to the radio room, which was next to the control room. We understood he was waiting for a radio call to the 'beach', as the world of the onshore was universally known.

Just as everybody was getting comfortable with everybody else, it went suddenly dark. It also went suddenly silent. The emergency lights came on as we just stood and looked at each other. I went into the control room, the same thing; everything was dead except for the emergency section of the Fire & Gas system showing no events or problems.

I conferred with my lead technician who suggested we had a 'Red' shutdown, but where was the emergency? Red shutdowns are a last resort, time to leave the platform, man the lifeboats. All power on the platform is shut down and isolated, all process plants are vented to atmosphere via the flare system, and the subsurface safety valves, which are installed in each production well tubing, deep below the level of the seabed, are closed.

The process operators and the fire team completed a quick survey around the platform, finding nothing, except for the process plant venting down via the flare, now shining brightly in the evening sky.

It was so quiet you could hear the people on the other side the platform as they stomped along the walkways in their steel capped boots to bring their reports to the control room.

Clearly, to my mind, there was a technical fault in the 'Red' shutdown system itself, but the PS wasn't so sure. He told me the sub-surface safety valves hadn't closed. Very strange.

The new Sir asked for an appraisal. I suggested there were two technical faults and I would divide my team into two groups, one for each problem. My lead technician remembered the Red shutdown box was behind one of the control room panels, which he quickly opened up to the aroma of burnt and smouldering cabling. I left him to it.

I asked the PS to start the never used before Black Start-up diesel generator. This generator could be used even in the potential presence of gas without causing an unwanted event. It provided emergency power for the fire and gas detection systems as well as emergency lighting and some ventilation in areas needing machinery to be started.

This caused a moment of delay as not many operators knew where it was; let alone knew the procedure for start-up.

I took senior Sir with me down to the wellhead gantry, where the wellhead control panels sat outside the 'egg' boxes containing up to six wells. The egg boxes were highly protected fireproof compartments.

The sub-surface safety valves were activated by hydraulic controls, but a common air header, when vented down to zero, would cause every hydraulic sub-surface valve to close. It was easy to see that the electrical solenoid that vented this common air header had indeed deactivated, but the air pressure had not been vented.

I took out a handy wrench, gave this solenoid a good whack and got covered in rust particles as the air pressure in the header vented its contents all over me. I suggested to senior Sir, that at installation, the lines had been pressure tested with water, instead of air, a much longer procedure, and the lines had not been fully dried afterwards. This was another legacy item; all part of the long saga of recovering from what had been a frantic hook-up and commissioning phase two years before.

I called for two technicians to come and complete a scope of work to check out the whole system, pass dry air through all the pipework and report back. I retreated to my workshop with Sir valiantly trying to keep up, to see how the repairs to the 'Red Shutdown' system were getting on.

Time for another coffee. I enquired if Sir had been brought up to date with all the issues we had faced on start-up and getting the pipeline filled before the inauguration. I told him *Forties Alpha* had highlighted many issues so that they would not be repeated on the three platforms following in our trail. He said he knew about them, but he was very new to the job.

Senior Sir praised everyone for the way they were working and asked how long they would be? Before I could answer, he told me that this shutdown was costing the company £3,000 pounds a second, more or less. Then I realised it was not crude oil the platform was pumping, but it was money. I smiled and suggested the oil wasn't lost per se' just a short delay.

'Can't pay today's bills with tomorrow's income,' he said.

I replied, 'I thought that was the basis of all big business?'

Senior Sir smiled and told me that the field was on track to repay the largest financial loan ever, the US$1.1 billion that the field development had cost, probably two years early. A truly great result. I replied that was just good to know. Perhaps the company would consider keeping salaries in-line with the ever-rising cost of living.

His reply was interrupted by his incoming radio call next door. Good timing, for him.

*

ONE OF THE more unusual results of the offshore platform working really long hard hours started to manifest itself from stories when the crews returned and landed back on terra firma at the start of their two-week break.

First stop for most people was the Station Hotel opposite the main railway station. The first pint of beer always tasted the best. The heavy drinkers had never heard of the phrase 'the marginal utility of satisfaction', and many of them boarded their train home somewhat the worse for wear, especially if there was a long wait for their train.

Only a few travelled north on the Inverness line, as most travelled south on the Edinburgh line. Tales of crew members waking up in either of these two capital cities started to become legend. One guy actually moved to Edinburgh, because he could never wake up in time to get off the train in Dundee.

I usually managed just two pints of Dublin's finest brew, along with a couple of hot sausage rolls from the counter. Fortunately, I always needed the loo, two stations before my stop-off at Elgin. Thank goodness for regular water works.

*

TO RECOVER FROM the offshore stress, exercise was a great recovery agent. I was always grateful that Johan made little complaint. The tides at Findhorn helped because high water during a suitable time of day occurred but fortnightly. I had been bitten by the National 18 bug and had bought the last wooden one ever built. It was a shining example of varnished boat building, but its lines did not match the performance of the latest fibre-glass boats that had, unbeknown to me, heavily modified. No matter, it was a joy to sail, and very comfortable.

Her name was *Ocotillo*, a strange name until I discovered it was a beautiful desert scrub that can handle the wide temperature ranges of the desert and requires little water to survive. The Ocotillo is not some sissy plant that requires pampering. It is one of the easiest plants to identify in the desert and, in my estimation, one of the most beautiful.

This beautiful boat needed pampering, every winter. All that lovely varnish to keep in pristine condition. She was a strong ship and survived many harsh conditions. National 18s are big dinghies, with a crew of three. Although heavy, the sail area is large and there is plenty of power. Equipped with a big spinnaker and a single trapeze, she was a challenge to sail in heavy weather. I was fortunate to have two lovely ladies crew. They only asked that I did not swear or shout, which I was not prone to do anyway.

However, I still had my Phantom, and I raced that too, winning when I had a clear run in a series race (usually five races spread out over the timetable). In 1976, I persuaded my club, the Royal Findhorn YC to host the Scottish Phantom Championships during Findhorn Week. I was very keen to have another go at winning the title.

The club acceded to my request, the event was held in much better weather than the 1973 attempt, and although pressed closely by a fellow club member, I still had the speed to cover any mistakes in tactics and become successful.

*

IT WAS TOWARDS the end of my second year on *Forties Alpha* that I was given the good news and the bad news. The good news was my promotion to Control Supervisor and a welcome increase in salary. The bad news was I would be transferred to the *Forties Charlie* (FC) platform, which was the premier platform of the four. The other three platforms pumped their production to FC, where the incoming pipelines connected to a common manifold.

By now, all four Forties platforms were in production, and BP was making a lot of money. More importantly so was HMG. I learnt that there was a special room in the Treasury with a single telex machine. It was only used once a day when BP Dyce sent the total production figures for the previous twenty-four hours. Such was the financial pressure on the British Government.

I was sad to leave FA. It still had many of the original start-up team onboard where everyone got on very well with each other. I found the situation onboard FC quite different. No matter, the team I had to work with were competent and hardworking and just keeping up with the maintenance of the vital control systems was more than a full time job. Information about modifications to various systems on the platform started to be issued for information, which could only mean one thing. There would be a major platform shutdown in the offing and planning became a priority.

The good news was the platform was producing at a steady rate, in fact, I remember one offshore tour where the export oil flow chart in the control room hardly varied, and even then, only in response to the other platforms adjusting their flow rate. It was necessary to remind the duty operators that our platform was pumping against the production of the other platforms. Operations can get a bit tricky when four platforms are pumping into the same pipeline to shore.

*

MY NEXT TOUR offshore included a forecasted platform shutdown. Fortunately, all the required materials were on board. The Controls &

Instrumentation group had lots to do, and four extra contract technicians were sent offshore to provide the necessary manpower. The fortnight tour passed in a flash. These shutdowns are programmed for a finite length of time, and any overruns are heavily frowned upon. The work was completed with minutes to spare, just before lunch time. We all took a long lunch.

My after lunch snooze was disturbed by the news that one of my contractors was required at home as soon as possible. His wife had been in a car accident, taken to hospital, and there were young children that needed looking after.

By luck, the afternoon flight was due shortly and a seat to the beach was available. I ordered a company taxi to meet the helicopter when it arrived at Dyce heliport, with a request to get the contractor onto the one train journey that could get him to Manchester quickly. I cleared this with the platform manager, telling him that the man had worked hard, effectively and was in part, one of the reasons that the department had met its targets.

The news returned that the taxi had caught up with the train at Stonehaven, the taxi driver being well aware that the traffic getting into town to the main station was its usual late afternoon rush, i.e. stopped just about everywhere. The technician arrived home to find his wife was recovering well,

Two days later I received a very unpleasant phone call from some numpty in the HQ Human Remains Department. Why had BP wasted money on a taxi fare for a contractor? Keeping my temper in check, I explained that the person had a family emergency and the taxi ride had enabled the person to use his return railway ticket, rather than BP incur the expense of a flight. I then received a load of earache, the man was 'only' a contractor, blah de bloody blah.

I informed this waste of space that the man was a member of the human race, had shown exceptional performance in his efforts to bring the shutdown programme to success and it was the right thing to do to look after anybody who had contributed above and beyond the call of duty. Anyway, I had informed the Platform Manager who had approved my request so what was the problem?

It was this change in the company that started to work my sub-conscious. The memory of the early hectic days was fading fast, but there had been big changes in BP's Dyce HQ, as new managers built their little empires. The building was fast filling up with non-productive staff, people who had control over the offshore team without actually knowing what the hell it was we all did.

Salary increases were being delayed. Cost of living increases were not being allowed for. One of the other platforms sent to Dyce HQ, a round robin letter requesting extra payment for dangerous offshore working conditions. The civilians in the onshore HR Department sent back a comparison, using very complicated data, proving that offshore, there had been no fatalities, few injuries and no medical evacuations due to ill health, whilst onshore, the data suggested that it was more dangerous working in Dyce HQ than serving with the US Army at the height of the Vietnam War.

After four years valiant service with BP, the chance of a second promotion looked slim. The remaining three platforms were all fully staffed up, with little chance of being reassigned to one of BP's new projects. The heavy hand of normalisation, turning offshore into standard onshore conditions, had almost completed its work.

With the cost of living rising by the month and salary rises delayed, it was time to consider options. Also, Johan was starting what was to become a long illness. She had an allergy to salt and our closeness to the sea was becoming a big issue.

So, knowing that the industry was going to grow and with friends encouraging me to think about changing jobs, I started to consider. The pluses and minuses were obvious, they balanced beautifully, but I had the urge to progress and BP had become that plateau.

15

GOING CONTRACT

Chevron 'Ninian Central'

I LEFT BP, THANKFUL FOR THE experience of being one of the North Sea early birds. Now I had to make my way in the commercial world, look after my family and provide for them. I raked around the marketplace and made contact with an in-house personnel agency working for the mighty Chevron Corporation.

There were two project teams being formed, one for the Ninian South platform and one for the Ninian Central platform. The topsides for both platforms were similar. The South platform topsides would be installed offshore on top of a steel jacket being built by McDermott's at Ardersier, Scotland, by the usual crane barge method.

The Central Platform would be constructed complete with its topside on top of a massive concrete base that included storage for the produced oil from the three planned Ninian platforms, ready for offshore loading onto tankers. When constructed in Loch Kishorn, Scotland in 1978, the Ninian Central Platform at 600,000 tonnes was the world's largest man-made movable object, which was towed around the North of Scotland into the North Sea and fixed at its current position on the seafloor.

I was offered a good contract, the salary was a good percentage increase and the terms and conditions most attractive. I was posted to London, living in digs during the week and flying home for a long weekend once a fortnight.

I entered the world of Chevron Oil, a mammoth oil and gas producer with its own strange ways and even stranger customs. The project offices were located on the second floor of premises at the bottom end of South Molton Street, a side street leading up to Oxford Street; prime territory to be sure.

I had a window seat so I could look down at the comings and goings of London's busy workforce. Being summer, the lady office workers would dress for the warm weather and the view from above was most agreeable.

There I met.... the independent contractors. Chevron, in its infinite wisdom, insisted I would be part of the Southern platform team, which would be mostly London based. I explained to my agent the situation at home and I would really appreciate being assigned to the team in Scotland on the Central Platform. No dice was all I was told. During lunch times in the pub, I learned about the contractors that worked through their own limited company, which was different from being self-employed. One's small limited company was paid gross, plus VAT and I became an employee of my company, taking a salary, and putting spare funds into a company pension scheme. All this was a steep learning curve.

I befriended Raymond, a cockney from the east side of London. He was in the know, whatever was going down in the Big Smoke, he knew about it. One Thursday well before lunch time, he shimmied over to my desk to tell me that McDermott, in Wembley Park, had landed a contract for an offshore hook-up they didn't expect to receive. Now there was a mad panic to find bodies to fill spaces on the project team chart that up to now had been the work of fiction.

He gave me the name and telephone number of the manager I had to call. So, nothing ventured I made the call. 'Come lunch time,' said the voice. I was fortunate. Chevron had called a big meeting, which was bound to run through lunch time. Raymond said he would look out for me, so with my CV in hand, I slipped out of the building and made my way to the nearest underground tube station. Remembering to take the fast train I quickly arrived at the offices of this major American contractor.

The manager met me at the lift on the third floor, took me to the coffee machine before we went to his office. Through his office door window, I could see an empty room full of empty desks and empty drafting boards with just two draftsmen pretending to be busy.

The manager went through my CV, looked up and said, 'Not bad, are you any good?'

I replied, 'Not bad, I know how to get things done which is what counts offshore.'

End of interview. The manager asked if I had an agent, I mentioned the name Peter at an agency in Sevenoaks, a name he obviously knew. He confirmed a contract would be sent straight away and when could I start. I told him I had a staff contract, but my employer had never issued me with a contract of employment, contrary to current legislation. I told him I would speak carefully to my current employer, repeat my current circumstances and tell him I was prepared to work a weeks' notice.

The manager nodded his head and said, 'Good man. See you a week on Monday then, you'll be back in Scotland in no time at all.'

With that, he was gone and I had to rush back to my office.

My employer took the news with stoic calm and said he would make the right noises to his client. That evening, I rang Johan with the good news, but she didn't understand any of the detail, apart from my return to Scotland.

And so I entered into the world of being a contractor, complete with my own limited company with which to sell my services and a trusty agency to look after my needs and guide me in what was a strange world apparently full of opportunity with the chance to work hard and escape from the 'greasy pole' that is ever present when working as a humble staff person in any organisation dealing which the mighty oil and gas industry.

16

MCDERMOTT-HUDSON

(1977 - 1980)

MCDS, AS MCDERMOTTS WAS USUALLY referred too, was awarded the *Dunlin 'A'* Hook-up contract more or less out of the blue. The company was more interested in a much larger hook-up and so their bid for *Dunlin 'A'*, an oil platform in the Shetland Basin, was awarded unexpectedly by Shell UK.

I started on the Monday morning as promised and by Friday lunch time I had been given an air ticket to Aberdeen, an advance of expenses and a pre-paid hotel reservation.

The taxi ride to Heathrow airport beat the rush hour traffic, so I found myself on the mid-afternoon flight drinking a welcomed gin and tonic. The flight arrived on time and I rushed over to Dyce railway station and caught the next train home.

Johan was delighted, asking a thousand questions. After a calming conversation, she became happier with the change of fortune, although she still struggled with the fine detail. I rang the hotel to tell them I would be staying with them Mondays to Friday.

I drove to Aberdeen early on the Monday morning, actually found parking close to the office in West North Street, and met with the project manager, one Mr. Jerry Pursley from Texas. Receiving a warm welcome, he spared ten minutes of his frantic schedule to bring me up to date, did I need an advance of expenses? Just make myself at home.

I found a desk, put my jacket on the back of the chair and looked around. There was a wall chart showing the layout of the *Dunlin 'A'* platform, constructed out of concrete with a steel cellar deck with legs to mate up with concrete structure below the water line. Mounted on the steel cellar deck were the production and utility modules, including the accommodation block with its helideck perched on top.

Lunch time came and some of the other early birds collected me on their way to the pub. I half recognised one of them, yes he did see me in Wembley Park, but he was leaving as I was arriving. We got chatting. According to my new friend we had landed a plum opportunity. Everything was chaos, the boss was a good hand, but he was no fool and needed all the help he could get.

The contract was sketchy, the scope of work contained therein only accounted for twenty per cent of the expected total, Shell UK, was in a tearing hurry due to the rapidly rising price of oil and everyone was going to make a great deal of money. This guy started to make my head spin, so I vowed to learn the new game and its many rules, spoken and unspoken, as quickly as possible.

So many memories come to mind, but my friends were correct. The project would turn out to be a good move. On Friday my car had to spend the weekend with the main agents when a component they did not stock failed to arrived. Jerry offered me a lift up to Elgin, which I accepted.

Jerry was a very interesting man to talk to. I mentioned the girls in the office, all unusually pretty. In his slow Texas drawl, he told me he didn't hire ugly women. I discovered he had been yanked out of the McD's fabrication yard at Ardersier to head up this project. The Ford Granada he was driving was obviously a site car, underpowered, covered in mud and showing advanced signs of communal abuse. As the traffic cleared, it became obvious his passion was driving very fast. He was an exceptional driver as everything seemed to be in slow time when the car speedometer showed warp speed.

He told me he had a Porsche 911, kitted out for rallying in the forests and he had a sponsor. He dropped me off at Mosstodloch and said he would take me back to Aberdeen Monday morning if he could pick me up where he dropped me off.

'Thanks a lot,' I replied.

'See you Monday morning, six a.m.?'

Crikey, he was keen. Guess he had a lot to do.

The ride back to Aberdeen was a classic demonstration on how to drive fast on a road empty of early morning commuters. The driver makes everything appear to be very slow. I remember this beat-up Ford Granada, as it swept magnificently through that beautiful long curve through the trees that is the Huntly By-pass, started to exhibit a slight vibration at the back of the car. I asked Jerry had he noticed?

He smiled and said, 'The back end is on about ten per cent break-away,' The car's speedo showed a hundred and five miles an hour. That ride into town took nearly fifty minutes out of my best time. Strewth!

I spent the week studying the design of the platform. The Dunlin Field was originally discovered in July 1973 in a water depth of 151 metres (495 ft). So, nearly four years later the development was in full swing. The platform's concrete gravity base was sitting firmly on the seabed. Installation contractors had moved on from their early days by constructing two monster semi-submersible crane barges called *Balder* and *Hermod*, with two massive cranes that could lift five thousand tons. A world first.

These crane barges used ballast control to do the actual lifting. The two cranes would provide a certain amount of lifting force, then when all was ready, massive internal ballast pumps would cause the barge to quickly rotate about its centre of buoyancy to snatch the load from the transport barge. It was all very clever. No wonder these hugely expensive marine units became a success.

I believe it was the *Balder* that installed the large cellar deck onto the concrete gravity base, followed by installing the topside modules and accommodation block.

Then, I received the call to go offshore. Not as easy in my previous existence with BP. First, there was the Aberdeen to the Shetland Islands flight in a twin-propeller commuter aircraft. Landing at Shetland looked tense, as to one side of the aircraft a steep rocky ridge, towered above the aircraft, seemed awfully close, with the open ocean on the other side.

In the Shetland heliport, all was chaos. Shell had many flights to many platforms and the aircraft were making at least three round trips a day. A delayed or late returning helicopter would bring a knock on effect on the schedule for the whole day. My crew change was scheduled for Shell Flight 18. After a long day in a badly equipped heliport, we eventually took-off on Shell Flight 31. Not impressed.

On my first arrival on the *Dunlin 'A'* platform, I was assigned accommodation in the main accommodation block. Others were assigned accommodation on the *Nortrol*, a large semi-submersible support vessel anchored alongside.

The accommodation was quite reasonable. I changed and showered in time for the evening meal. The Project Engineer (PE) in charge made himself known and advised the evening progress meeting would be in half an hour. The meeting turned into a bit of a bun fight, with competing interests reaching for the same resources. Some asked for the overall plan, but there wasn't one. The planning guy winced. Just where was the information he needed.

The PE looked at me. I shrugged my shoulders, what did I know? I did, however, ask if a 'scope of work' survey had been completed. The PE asked why? I replied the beauty of a concrete platform was that it could be floated into place practically complete. Now here we all were, try to organise a hook-up of items not fully complete before load-out.

'Yes, we all know that,' said everyone around the table. One of the other contract engineers, who had also come up from Wembley said, 'Well it's happy days. We get to fix what should have been done onshore, then we install everything that should have been completed onshore, then we rattle through the hook-up, and the job is complete.'

The PE in-toned, 'We have a target date to meet Gentlemen.'

'That's why it is necessary to survey the work-scope in the smallest detail', stated the contract engineer, 'then estimate it to the last minute. Then any changes, client cock-ups that need fixing, and there will be a few, a new estimate adds to the time required.'

The PE was not convinced, but an edict from the beach instructed this would be the way ahead. In fact, it was the only way ahead. The McD's hook-up team discovered that, in its haste, the client had ordered the larger items of the plant using specifications from other projects and many did not fit the specific requirements of the *Dunlin 'A'*. A huge amount of rework looked likely.

I watched all this tooing and frooing, from the back of the pack. This hookup was going to be one long hard slog, our timesheets were going to record our magnificent efforts to meet impossible targets, for which we would get paid our basic hourly rate plus the overtime uplift. Nice one. My bank manager was about to stop whinging like he always did.

After a hectic two weeks offshore, I was more than ready to get home. Jerry Pursley asked me to stop by on my way back offshore in two weeks time. An easy call, as it was much better to arrive in Aberdeen before the next day's flight to the platform. Johan complained she would miss me for an extra night. I told her it was an extra days pay and my expenses would cover the costs involved. She cheered up at the thought of the extra pay. Being a good wife, she realised that paying off the debts for the house purchase and all the other items to make a happy home was sound management.

*

AFTER A BUSY but enjoyable break, it was time to go and see what the boss wanted. Arriving late afternoon, I found Jerry, as always, in a relaxed positive mood. The pile of urgent paperwork on his desk suggested otherwise.

He welcomed me, and his lovely secretary brought coffees for all and closed the door behind her. Hum! I thought a closed-door chat with the illustrious leader? Jerry smiled and handed me a slim volume of a technical nature, entitled DW121.

'What do you know about HVAC?' he asked. 'Not a lot,' I replied, wondering why he had opened with this subject.

'Well,' he continued, 'by the time you have completed this scope-of-work, according to that single sheet of paper inserted at the back of the document I have just given you, you will become my proud expert.'

I looked at him over the top of my glasses, frowning.

'Just ramrod the whole thing through. Be bolshie if you have to, there are some very serious issues. One; certain modules need area pressurisation. No pressurisation means no certificate to drill will be issued to the client. You don't need me to expand on that subject.'

'Two; the plant ventilation system was thrown on the platform at the last minute. If it is installed, it's installed incorrectly, otherwise, it is just lying around on the deck. The issuance of the Production Certificate is another vital matter. Production areas are shielded from the weather so ventilation is vital to ensure the number of air changes. This, as you know, affects the area certification.'

'So, you're ex-navy, just take charge and have fun.'

'There's a rate increase in all this?' I asked.

'Good question,' he replied. 'Time for your frantic dash to the airport.'

We shook hands and off I rushed to the waiting taxi outside.

I arrived back on to the platform to brief the PE. Fortunately, he had been brought up to speed with the difficult task that had been dumped on my lap. I requested two assistants, general workmen from the motley crew he had on the platform. I was assigned an ageing very short gentleman by the name of Jimmy, from Glasgow, such an unusual name. And a tall gangly youth from god knows where who hung around him like a bad smell. Good start, I thought.

I had a long chat with them in the dining hall, showed them the drawings I had, and what it was we had to achieve. Jimmy wasn't a dumb as he looked. Pretending to be dumb had led to an easier life, more simple tasks, but I discovered he was a very skilled steel erector and there was a lot of steel and air trunking that needed a good erection.

We marched to the first module. The sections of trunking had been dumped on top of each other, in grave danger from all the activity that was going on in this area. I requested the large section with the ninety-degree bend be brought down from on high and set-up on trestles.

Using the soon to be famous DW121, I showed them how to fit the internal air vanes to direct the flow of air around the corner. The two of them wandered off to get the permit-to-work document, their tools and the vendor pack that contained the air vanes.

I spent the rest of the time checking and marking the sections of trunking before wandering over to the planning office to ensure that the work area would have all other activities stopped whilst we bolted long sections of the trunking together ready for lifting, hopefully after the evening meal. Some sections of the trunking had shutdown vanes with their actuators on the outside. These all needed checking. One piece had a 'T' section so that smaller trunking could be added later on to feed other areas or enclosed spaces.

I prowled around the work site, talking to the other work crews and getting promises from the scaffolders to work some promised overtime in the task of some heavy lifting and shifting.

To my immense surprise, this part of the work scope went well, and by late evening the trunking had achieved its permanent home. The area foreman was pleased he had, at last, the space he needed for his many tasks. Next, the work measurement team rushed in to record the progress and get the details processed and converted them into a money format for the monthly billing.

*

TALKING ABOUT THE monthly billing, it is described as the most important activity of any construction team engaged in a project. Receiving part payments as the project progresses is normal, and payments are made against progress achieved. If the project is being well controlled there is a system of measurement that compares progress achieved against progress that should have been achieved, according to the overall project schedule.

The *Dunlin 'A'* project was divided up into its component parts, lump sum for an original specified amount of work contained in the bid; cost plus, which is man-hours used in completing the task plus a mark-up of fifteen per cent and rates. Rates were agreed with the client before an item of work was commenced. For instance, to install a pressure gauge the time awarded may be three hours work time. Take less time, result happiness. Take more time, money is lost, happiness turns to recrimination.

Thus, we meet the stars of the show, the cost engineer and the quantity surveyor. The quantity surveyors come in their different disciplines. E.g. electrical, to perform the actual measuring.

The cost engineer applies the data using the agreed rate for the work that has been completed and turns this data into money, then adds it to the monthly billing report. Now, this is the game, perhaps I should not call it a game, but never mind.

So, hang on while I describe what happens. The good book, the Page & Nation Norms, is a big volume that gives a time for any particular task, in the singular.

Perform two tasks at the same time i.e. install two cables, instead of one, a bonus is achieved. Pull ten cables at the same time, its happy days. The cost surveyor has to physically measure the length, normally with the co-operation of the clients cost surveyor. The two would agree on the length and the number of cables pulled, and the data written-up. Now, remember, this is in the age before the computer, iPads, et al. All data is handled handraulically, using sheets of paper forms.

Enter into the fray, one Bart Henderson, a man of many facets. A tall grey-haired man with a stoop, he was in his seventies I believe, who could measure anything to the advantage of his client. Bart came from the Western Isles in Northern Scotland. Poacher, gamekeeper and all things in-between.

He could drink anyone under the table in double quick time. His favourite tipple was a quarter gill of five-star brandy mixed with similar ten-year-old malt whisky, which was his version of a rusty nail. They are quite delicious.

Frequently, we use to meet in Elgin's Royal Hotel, close to the railway station on our way into Aberdeen. He could drink three of these delightful beverages to my one. Damn, they were strong.

Bart had a huge range of stories, the best when he served aboard *HMS King George VI* in the battle of the *Bismarck*. He was a signaller on the bridge with the admiral and the other senior officers.

Before the final battle commenced, he used to say, 'Och ey, ye ner saw such a feared bunch of bastards in all yer days. Shittin' their breeks' they was.'

As the final moments of the great German battleship came, 'Ye ner saw such a braw brave bunch of bastards in all yer days.'

I could imagine his story had some truth. The *HMS Hood* had been sunk very quickly only a short time before. No wonder the admiral had his concerns. Even my school teacher, Mr Barnes was there on *HMS Cossack*. He used to describe the torpedo attack carried out on the great German ship at very high speed. Crashing through the waves caused secondary damage. Ship's boats were ripped away. Even steel lockers welded to the deck vanished into the cold dark waters of the Atlantic Ocean. We school boys would be spellbound by this story. He described the action in graphic detail. It sounded very thrilling or totally hair-raising, depending on your point of view.

Anyway, back to Bart, who would measure the electrical work as it was completed, always accompanied by the client's cost surveyor. When measuring long cable runs, Bart, being the senior citizen, would give the end of the measuring tape to his young client and read out the numbers to be recorded.

One day, the young man said, 'Uncle Bart, if I work for the client, Shell UK, should I not hold the tape measure and you take the end of the tape to the far end for me to read out the numbers?'

'Och ey me loon.' Bart answered, all apologetically. 'Yon ave' a point there.'

I watched as the next cable run was measured. As Bart walked away down the long dark passageway, he'd gather a fist full of tape in his large hands before holding it tight for the young man to record the numbers. Classic, absolutely classic.

Before I leave this wonderful man behind, just one last memory. Production platforms are prone to stray electrical currents, so every item not welded to the main steel structure requires an earthing lead. An easy example is a small stairway bolted to the deck. *Dunlin 'A'* was so equipped and had hundreds of them. A typical installation consists of the earth cable bolted between two welded earth studs.

Bart, whose job it was to measure the earthing leads noticed that the agreed unit rate did not include two small items, namely one washer and the blob of protective grease. He gently pestered the Shell UK rate setting team for weeks. He was such a nice old guy, he could charm birds off their trees. One day, just to humour their favourite senior citizen, a revised rate sheet for this minute item of work was issued with a smile and a well-earned, 'There you go, Granddad.'

At the next monthly billing, McDs issued an amendment item, concerning the billing for earthing straps, a cool quarter of a million pounds. 'We canny 'ave money like that a-lyin' on the ground unharvested,' he told me on the train going home. Wonderful man.

*

IT WAS DURING this time of frantic activity in the oilfields of the North Sea, that certain unwanted practices by the client companies became apparent, late payment of invoices. Employment agencies were not being paid, their invoices held up by minor errors that took forever to resolve, entirely unnecessarily. Agents had to pay their contractors, otherwise, their contractors would be long gone.

The same nonsense was happening with vendors supplying equipment and services. My ducting vendor, a company called Rigblast had the same experience. The owner of the company was Raymond James, and he was a blast. One of life's real persons. We were destined to meet later on.

The pace of work offshore was increasing rapidly and project supply boats were running on very tight schedules. In fact, a supply boat was due to arrive at midday and scheduled to leave with the vital materials early Sunday morning.

My vendor had a substantial amount of ducting and other equipment packed and ready to go. Everything should have been moved to the dockside on the Friday morning, only it hadn't. I was preparing for an early start to my weekend and about to slip out of the door when I was asked to see why nothing had arrived on the dockside. It was on my way, so I said, 'No problem.'

When I arrived at the site, the main gate was shut, locked in fact, and the transport left waiting outside, their drivers complaining at length.

I saw Raymond who ordered his staff to let me in. Stepping out of my car a pensive Raymond came up to me and ignored my greeting. Why was I here?

I told him I wasn't sure, how could I help?

He told me that he was not going to release any equipment until he got paid, which is nothing I could help with. I checked his unpaid invoices and could see that Shell UK was playing the pay invoices late game to the max. I rang my office, as they didn't know what was going on. Next thing I know, I am talking to the Shell UK head of project. He was aghast, no delays could be tolerated.

I told him all I knew, mentioned very briefly the general problem with late payments in the city and here was a vendor making a stand. He asked to speak to the vendor. Raymond had a fizzy fit and didn't mince his words. He'd paid good overtime to his staff to finish all the orders on time, his bank manager was giving him a hard time, and enough was enough.

Threats flowed from the Shell UK manager, causing Raymond to lower his voice. This was getting serious. I moved away from the conversation. I sneaked into the gatehouse and was given a cup of strong coffee. A foreman I knew joined with me, I asked, 'You guys are going bust are you?'

'Close,' came the reply through clenched teeth.

'Merde,' I thought, this is getting serious. Was Raymond fighting this battle for others as well as himself? A lot of people could lose their jobs and the Trade Unions were very close to the city council.

I looked over at Raymond. He was smiling although his words on the phone remained strong and defiant. I'm not sure what happened, but this kerfuffle was well on its way to Shell UK's upper management. I got a thumbs up. I phoned my boss, gave him the few details that I had and he bid me have a good weekend.

The vendor obviously received his money, as when I passed his premises early Monday morning, his yard was clear. Good for him! I met him in the pub later in the week. His story was most interesting. It's a pity I cannot share.

*

THREE OFFSHORE TOURS of duty later the ventilation system had been completed and Shell UK received a permit to drill. So that was a success I was happy to achieve. But there was more. Jerry gave me another scope of work to bring the platform ventilation up to a new standard. It concerned all the air intakes of the many ventilation systems, sited flush with the steel side of the platform.

Hazardous area charts for the platform showed one metre around the exterior was considered a hazardous zone. The air intakes had to be extended outside of this zone and they had to point downwards to reduce the force of the winds hitting the side of the platform.

And so, I quickly entered into the world of ventilation ducting design and their support structures. With no drafting support offshore, I became competent making fully detailed drawing isometric sketches and sending them to the beach so that the purchasing department could place the orders.

There were quite a few air intake extensions required, and so I spent a few weeks onshore guiding this work through the ordering system and being at one with the chosen vendor

Eventually, all the ventilation work was completed offshore, and the platform's ventilation and pressurisation system was tested and fully certified on a day when there wasn't a breath of wind. Phew, that was lucky.

During the next fortnight offshore, the platform was considered mechanically complete and the *Dunlin 'A'* team was dissipated among McD's other projects. I was transferred to the next Shell UK extravagance, The *Cormorant 'A'* Onshore Project team.

*

THE 'CORMORANT ALPHA' Project was an oil producing platform that also collected crude oil from the many platforms in the Shetland Basin. The platform was an important hub, as it could pump a million barrels a day of crude oil to the Shetland Islands, where it was processed in a major receiving centre called Sullom Voe.

It came at a time of great change in the way the industry worked in Aberdeen as I recall below. This project for Shell UK was another that had been awarded to McDermotts Inc.

The project offices were housed in a large warehouse located in King Street, Aberdeen. The large open space was equipped with dividers between the many different design teams. The senior management were buried in the underground offices. Stacked at one end of the warehouse, was Portacabin City, where the Shell UK team lived, overlooking the toiling masses below.

Once again, I was working on platform HVAC installations. My desk ended up embedded in the cordoned-off section that held the group in the story below. No idea why. It was a very surreal experience.

*

THE MEMORY OF the Pipe Stress Engineering Group, a group of lunatics, I mean highly intelligent and experienced pipe-stress engineers (a breed in its own right) dedicated to driving our American masters crazy.

Pipe Stress engineering is a highly specialised part of the piping design process. Large oil platforms have complex piping systems carrying, at very high pressures and volumes, hot and cold process fluids (oil or gas) as well as fire water systems with big pumps and the injection system where powerful pumps inject fluids into the oil reservoir to maintain field pressure.

Thus, these engineers are the best of the best. These engineers had a truly wicked sense of humour and had developed the highly unusual habit of talking in Clanger Speak.

The Clangers was a children's TV programme where the cast, who looked like moles living on the moon spoke in whistles of varying tones. The programme was a big hit with adults, especially fathers after a few beers following a hard day's work.

As per the cast in the TV programme. the team leader was known as Major Clanger supported by, Mother Clanger, Tiny Clanger, Small Clanger, and of course, the Soup Dragon.

They could converse, in Clanger language, on the most technical of subjects and when the American team leaders tried to engage with them on the serious issues that existed in this project they would find between themselves in between Clanger Language and American.

Major Clanger would translate the discussed details into English which wasn't too helpful as the American floor walkers, as they were known, all came from Texas where the English vocabulary is half of what it is in the UK.

Like I said it was very surreal.

One day, Soup Dragon, the designated tea boy, invented a new way for his team members to order their coffees. The coffee machine dispensed the three ingredients in powder form, the individual ingredient being dispensed by a lever that clicked each time it delivered one portion into a handheld paper cup. A push button then supplied the hot water to mix with the ingredients in the handheld paper cup.

At the frequent rest periods for coffee Soup Dragon would hand out three dice to be rolled on a desktop. This resulted in some very strange coffee's being ordered, from the very weak, upwards. It had to happen when one day Tiny Clanger rolled three sixes. Roars of laughter all around, the dreaded eighteen click special.

When Soup Dragon returned with the drink the contents of the cup were as close to concrete that is possible. That Tiny Clanger actually drank the mixture was a surprise but he was duty bound to do so. His system was never the same afterwards.

*

The Beginning of the all inclusive rate

IN THE BEGINNING, there was God and he was kind. At this time, staff and contractors alike worked a 37.5 hour week with overtime paid extra, and everyone received expenses for living away from home.

On request, an advance of monthly expenses was available if, at month's end, an expense form with receipts was submitted for approval.

The project personnel felt submitting a monthly report a chore best left for later if management did not complain. But the monthly advance of expenses continued apace.

This led to certain members of the project team to consider an advance of expenses as beer money with the occasional fish supper to assist in the ceremonial stagger back to the B&B.

At the rear of this huge warehouse sat the piping designers, a group of people whose workload comprised of recording the incoherent thoughts of the piping design engineers into drawings that allowed the process of review and checking to take place. This checking allowed, as we say, rude matter to be corrected into due form.

The lead piping designer had mastered the art of filling out the monthly expense report. He never missed a month and was thus considered by the American in charge of expense reports as something of a saint. I too became saintly. Anyway, this guy excelled in his work and his expense report was a true work of art that would rival any of the famous monastic manuscripts. The Book of Kells for example.

And, secure in the knowledge that as far as expenses were concerned, I was one of the saintly ones.

However, at this time, the oil industry in Aberdeen was extremely busy and the city's economy, especially the hotels, pubs and restaurants, was floating on the wave of cash flowing from the many expenses systems.

Unknown to many of this great merry-go-round was the VAT system, still in its relative infancy. With regard to expenses, any submitted receipt in the monthly expense report had a serial number. A copy was held by the issuer of the receipt, obliged by law to keep the copy for inspection by the VAT man.

The VAT man was well aware that companies running expense systems were recovering their VAT costs, as they were entitled to do. What the VAT man also knew was the huge discrepancy between VAT received and VAT being recovered. This meant only one thing. Expenses were being fiddled (surely not) and false expense claims with even more false receipts were flooding the city.

My usual eating establishment was owned by Carol who was the niece of a famous lawyer in Aberdeen who warned of the impending holocaust by the VAT man and double checked her company books to ensure an easy life.

The VAT man girded his loins, mobilised his army to Aberdeen and set-up shop for a truly long operation. As a quick diversion, I should mention there was an even bigger VAT scandal being uncovered in one of the farming towns south of Aberdeen involving huge sums of money. This became known as the Great Tatty Scandal.

And, so it came to pass that the era of the all-inclusive-rate for contract staff, operating their affairs through their limited companies, came into being. The Project Director issued the directive of dread; that all outstanding advance of expenses (and there were some truly outstanding advances) should be covered by the submission of long overdue expense reports before the end of the month. Just two weeks hence.

The drinking classes went into a panic. An industry was quickly set up where the drinking classes would scour hitherto unvisited restaurants and hotels targeted for the great receipt books robbery.

A gang of master forgers at the back of the warehouse was set-up to produce receipts to order, in a huge variety of handwriting, all produced by the same hand.

It did not take long before a second edict was issued by management; 'Anybody found passing forged receipts would be sacked on the spot.' To be fair, with the VAT man breathing down everybody's neck this was serious business.

The drinking classes had to surrender and repay all outstanding balances as management watched their funds flowing back to whence they had come. The game was over.

*

THE *CORMORANT* 'A' project continued on its merry way. The terrible twins turned up, two American planners that had sometimes graced the *Dunlin* 'A' project. They were both real live Texans, who shared an apartment and watched the soap opera Dallas without fail every Wednesday evening before going hunting at the Grab a Granny Night in the Palace Theatre dance hall.

Jim Nail owned farmland with gas fields underneath. Quite why he worked in the North Sea was never revealed. Paying alimony was the most likely reason, but this was never confirmed.

Ed Mussler, the more sensible of the two, was a planning engineer from Melbourne Beach, Florida. He preferred to work at the Cape, or Cape Kennedy, for NASA, but when things were slow he would pack his bags and head for the North Sea.

At Miami Airport, when he checked his luggage, he would ask for a window seat to London, but could they send his luggage to Chicago. The check-in girl told him they couldn't do that. He replied, 'Hell no, you've done it the last two times.' Ed always had an answer to most things.

Jim Nail would, after taking a shower, would drown himself in Giorgio aftershave, which at the time was very expensive. Get within few feet of Jim and be prepared to be knocked out. Together they were a comedy act, both at work and in the wild west that was Aberdeen in its heyday. I became good friends with Ed Mussler and in the years to come, I visited his home in Florida. His wife came from Georgia, with an all-original Georgian accent that was so strong, it was hard not to laugh out loud. One didn't, of course, as she was a totally genuine person.

One night, during an inconclusive evening at Grab a Granny Night, Ed Mussler left early. He was bored, there were no ladies he could even begin to be interested in.

At two a.m. in the morning, Jim Nail returns with two ladies, age unknown due to the excessive makeup, propelling one of them into Ed Mussler's room. Ed woke up and told her to fuck-off. She considered his words as a come on.

'But honey,' the woman cooed, 'I can do anything you want.'

'Good, let's see you vanish,' as Ed Mussler rolled over and went back to sleep.

*

ANOTHER MEMORY OF note came on the occasional working Saturday, when either Glasgow Rangers or Glasgow Celtic football teams came to town to play Aberdeen FC, whose stadium was not too far away from our base.

Their football supporters travel in hoards, heavily escorted by the police. From the railway station to the football ground, the hoards, barely in control, was a force to be aware of. The main gate to the warehouse complex was firmly shut and guarded. There were valuable cars inside, including my pride and joy, a SD1 Rover 3.5 litre. Even more valuable was a Fiat Coupe 132 spider, with a Ferrari engine. Nice wheels

Of the two groups, the Celtic supporters seemed to be the more human. We were all glad when it became time for the match to start, and the end of our working day was always fifteen minutes before time.

*

IT WAS DURING the summer months when the project hit the buffers due to a lack of material. With so much construction activity in the North Sea, the vendor supply chain was struggling to cope with an avalanche of orders.

One week, the onshore team decamped from Aberdeen to Peterhead, where the project warehouses were located. The stores were controlled by an old acquaintance of mine called Neville, a hard-working, no-nonsense professional. He complained to me, on the quiet, that a lot of material was being stolen and he had an idea how. Could I help him as a witness the next time a supply boat returned to Peterhead Harbour, usually carrying skips loaded with scrap or waste material?

Two days later, a supply boat arrived and the skips were delivered to the warehouse complex. Neville had arranged for a trusted employee who drove a forklift truck. Neville waited for the afternoon tea break, then signalled his employee to use his forklift truck to up-end each skip in turn.

As the first skip was up-ended the scrap and waste material cascaded onto the ground, revealing six brand new six-inch valves used for the platform's firewater system. Neville pushed a fast dial button on his cell phone and within minutes, the police had arrived. There was danger, unscrupulous hardened criminals were involved. Few people remembered that dark sombre building up on the hill on the road to Aberdeen. The Peterhead Maximum Security Prison.

Having discovered and stopped the theft that was bringing stress to the project, the team, holed up in the Waterside Hotel, known as the fireside hotel after someone set fire to his room smoking in bed. The team got to work with a long list of commodity items that required sourcing from anywhere they could be found.

It was at this time that I met one Harry Troup. Harry came from Wick, a small town in Caithness with a fearsome reputation for drinking. Harry Troup was that man. He told me he was looking to sell a very nice bungalow in Morayshire, just inland from Forres, a lovely little town that always won the annual small town in bloom competition.

Harry explained his complicated personal life. He was a divorced man with four girlfriends, all pregnant. It was time to sell and move to safety. Would I be interested? He didn't want the hassle or the costs of lawyers and estate agents. I jumped at the chance and shook his hand on the deal. Johan was suffering living by the seaside and I had been thinking to move for some time.

That weekend I took her to see the bungalow, she just loved it. I phoned Harry to confirm. I was not to know, that Johan, being physic, knew it would be her last home. We moved within weeks as fortunately selling the cottage by the sea was an easy task.

*

AS WINTER APPROACHED, I spent all of my time in the office in Aberdeen. It was becoming more obvious that my wonderful wife Johan was not well. It was even more obvious that the local GPs had no idea what they were dealing with. During the winter months, I would work extra hours during the week to be allowed an early start to the weekend. I generally slipped away just after lunch.

I had the Rover fitted with winter tyres. Deep treaded, Scandinavian tyres from Sweden, with a much softer rubber compound. They worked wonders. I just had to get home on the weekends to help keep the household together.

There are three places on the Aberdeen to Inverness road that are bad for collecting snow, blown by the strong northerly winds. If I kept the speed of the car somewhere between forty and fifty miles an hour, it would plough through most snow drifts, the steering was very quick so slipping and sliding was easy to catch. Good anticipation was the key to driving in the snow. I rather enjoyed it.

It would be other motorists, usually with no idea what to do in these conditions, which would cause the rescue services the most trouble. I had few problems with new snow. Ice and hard packed ice needed a great deal of luck along with skilful driving.

When I did get stuck, a very useful feature of the Rover was the small choke lever between the front seats that controlled engine speed at start-up. Rarely seen these days. The rescue services always had doubts whether they could get such a heavy car on its way again. I explained I would very gently increase the engine revolutions, so the power went into the automatic gearbox, without sufficient force to cause the back wheels to rotate and start slipping. Then, when they started to push, the back wheels would turn without slipping and all being well, the car would very gently accelerate away, and I would gingerly continue my journey. I did this a number of times. Very effective.

When I got home, I would visit our doctor, strongly asking what could be done. The pressure worked. Johan's mother Margret came down from Thurso so that she could spend a week in Aberdeen's Royal Infirmary for a series of tests.

She then endured the battery of tests, some of them quite invasive. The result? They knew what it wasn't. A big help! Her heart had enlarged, so its pumping action was very inefficient, causing all sorts of problems. I took her home to rest, but she was very down in herself. From being a super fit championship highland dancer to being semi-invalid was hard to come to terms with.

Still, the new home, up on the hill behind Forres did bring some improvement, and matters started to return to normal.

*

ONE MORNING, AT the bottom of King Street in Aberdeen, a major emergency was declared. The smell of gas was everywhere. The police closed the street and cordoned off the whole area, frantically trying to trace the sources of the leak.

During this frantic hoo-ha, a delivery driver left the worker's café where he had been taking breakfast and walked to towards his tanker truck smoking his usual cigarette. The police screamed at him to put out that 'blankety blank' cigarette. Some brave policeman rushed up and knocked the driver flying and stamping on the cigarette.

'What the F…?' said the driver.

'There's a gas leak, canne ye nae smell it,' yelled the policemen.

'Aw, din' worry loon, there's a valve wiv' just a small leak on mau' truck.'

The road tanker was carrying liquid oderiser, to be delivered to the British Gas Terminal in Peterhead, where it would be injected into the gas stream supplying the UK market.

*

Back to the office

ONE DAY DOUG Calum, the project engineer for the group I was assigned to, asked me if I could complete the design for a ventilation plant room to feed the four pump modules yet to be installed on the platform. I asked if the design contractor had any information. Seemingly not. The only two drawings that existed was a schematic of the cellar deck panel where the twin ventilation fan assembly would be mounted and the underside of one of the pump modules where the ventilation supply was to be delivered

I looked at the first drawing. It was two years old, a first revision, marked, 'For Information Only'. The drawing regarding the underside of the soon to be installed pump module was also suitably vague.

'Not a lot to go on,' I offered, at which point I was presented with all the vendor information regarding the twin ventilation fan assembly.

'Priority?' I asked.

'Medium,' I was told, whatever that meant. I asked for an offshore survey visit, which was flatly rejected. I raised a number of points, but the result of the conversation was just to get on with it. Which I did.

I did a lot of checking, as the area in question seemed quite empty and empty spaces on platforms get filled up very quickly, with other stuff people forget about.

First, I wrote a brief document called a Design Premise, generally known as a design promise. Cynicism rules OK. It described the intent, the references and hopefully the operation. The document was passed to all departments for comment. This is called 'arse covering'.

So, I slept on it and next day fixed how I would make the design. I collared a spare draughtsman's drawing board to hide behind and started work. Within three weeks I had a good layout, a suggested scope of work for construction and sent it out for comment.

Later, I filed all the 'no comments' that were returned and gathered the drawings for each item to enable the purchasing department to do their part. Two weeks later, I was on my way to see my good friend Mr Ray James, with a package of information and a purchase order.

It was time for lunch, so we slipped to somewhere just out of town to talk shop and agree between ourselves the details to achieve success. Next, it was necessary to compose a fully detailed procedure for the installation of the new plant room. I had allowed for the lack of confirmed design detail regarding the area of the work, so this document would be vital to achieving a successful installation.

The fabrication and delivery of the new plant room proceeded at an orderly pace and all seemed to be well.

About a week just after the installation of the new plant room had started, that the large rotating device in the perpetual ceiling was hit by a 'grande quantité de merde'.

My floor walker, Mr Calum, came to interview me. His face said it all. I immediately knew what had happened. We went and sat in a quiet room with hot strong coffees, not a good sign. He described the enormous fuck-up, which I believe is a technical term.

The ducting had been delivered with one flange attached and the second flange supplied loose. The concept allowed for the installation of a section of ducting to be bolted to the preceding section and then after measurements had been taken, as described, the extra length of material could be removed and the loose flange fitted.

The offshore workforce, the bears, after cursing everybody on the beach and the idiot who had sent all this junk offshore, had just welded the loose flange onto the end of the ducting and then started the installation. The ducting didn't fit because every piece was too long.

The problem? Offshore workers do not read the installation procedures. The procedure I had taken two weeks to carefully craft into perfection and had been issued to all and sundry 'for comment and approval'. I knew full well I would not be permitted to go offshore to oversee the installation.

I handed my interrogator all the signed off procedures and calmly sat back. I also had document transmittal notices to prove the platform had received their copy of the procedure. No doubt they would be trying to find where they filed it. In the bin, most likely.

Inside, I was fuming, ready to explode with anger. How dare these people make a mockery of my work. Mr Calum then realised the truth of the matter. Now, the workforce would have to make the best of a bad job, at the company's expense. I washed my hands of the whole sorry saga. I knew full well that the offshore workforce thinks everyone on the beach is mentally deficient.

There was to be a meeting. I offered not to go, I couldn't trust myself to keep a civil tongue and the offer was accepted. Later, I called my vendor in case the client asked him to send his specialist team offshore to fix things. His men were all spoken for. I smiled and kept the information to myself.

So, the storm blew over. Whatever happened offshore happened, 'Frankly my dear I don't give a damn,' as the saying goes.

*

DURING THE FOLLOWING weeks good progress was at made at work and I met a young Londoner, a very interesting chap. I was asked if I could drop him off at another office close to my vendor's premises. It seems he had been grounded, as not one car-hire company in Aberdeen would rent him a car.

Apparently, he had been training to be a Formula One driver, but he didn't make the grade. He did not reveal why. He studied to become an engineer and passed with flying colours. The problem, I discovered later, was that he would be driving along quite happily and calmly when his brain would switch to F-1, drop two gears and red-line the engine. A friend of a friend was with him when it happened. Scared the living out of him, especially in the middle of Union Street, Aberdeen's main thoroughfare.

Apparently, the last time he hired a car, he was travelling down a country road, his brain had flipped, accelerated very hard and the car had crashed at some frightful speed, demolished an electric fence, cattle had escaped, and he was lucky to be unscathed. It was by no means the first time this had happened.

It was such a pity. He was such a nice chap when he was normal, and not doing his Mr Toad routine.

A few weeks later, I was transferred back to the company HQ. A mega bid was in the offing, and this sounded interesting.

*

I FOUND MYSELF office-bound, travelling from Forres early on a Monday morning, returning on the Friday evening. This suited my family needs. My wife's long illness imperceptibly increased. Her good days were fewer, the bad longer. During the week I employed a kind lady to act as a home help, which helped enormously. At the weekend, I had the chore of attacking the garden, which had been beautifully laid out by Harry Troup's drinking buddy, the Forres town gardener. I should have found a gardener, but they are a rare breed at the best of times.

*

STILL, KEEPING EMPLOYED was the name of the game and the Valhalla bid was just the ticket. Valhalla was an oil field in the Norwegian sector of the North Sea, consisting of three linked platforms, the Wellhead platform, the Process platform, and the Accommodation platform. The Accommodation platform had already been let, but McDermott's bought the winning company and so bagged the whole shebang.

Normally, a bid would be of little interest but this was the first time the client had asked for a fixed lump sum to design the jackets (the structures on the seabed), the topsides for each platform, construction of same, plus load out and installation of all three platforms, then commissioning of the whole. The bid had to include weather downtime and any number of everyday disasters that affect the offshore industry.

Get the numbers wrong and your shirt gets lost for all time. The first part of the work required receiving and sorting all the design drawings and documents, thousands of them. Then four copies of everything were made. Our local reprographic company was overjoyed and overloaded with the work.

Then, two sets of drawings were marked up to show the onshore scope of work and the offshore scope of work. Copies were again made of all everything, and the onshore scope of work drawings and relevant documents were sent to head office in the USA for them to chew on.

Then, the offshore scope of work drawings were copied and given to everyone in the team to work on.

My part of the bid was relatively easy (instrumentation and controls) in as much the scope was easy to quantify, making up tables and adding proven man-hours for each item and then just add up the numbers. Add a few factors obtained from past experience and hey presto an upper and lower figure came into view.

The American in charge of the bid was one Eddy Clay. He was easy to work with as he knew his stuff inside out. He appreciated hard work and listened to the detail that was found in this huge mass of information. The team was short of an electrical engineer, so I recommended by chum Brian from days on the Dunlin Project.

Brian arrived in short order to start on the estimate for the electrical scope of work. He confused a few people by spending four days just reading the contract. It was just as well he did as it had some sneaky details that were going to have a big impact on his work

It was at this stage when the bid team knew that Eddy Clay had his own number (don't ask me how these guys do this but it comes from massive experience in their field). The work being done by the bid team was to double check for no missed or hidden items. I re-read the contract for my scope and found little that was new.

Brian completed his work a few weeks later and whoops his estimate was nowhere near the thoughts of Mr Clay. His number was way too high by a long way. The inquest began. I looked had a quick look through Brian's numbers and could see where he was coming from. His estimates considered the scope of work to be completed offshore, which is always expensive.

Brain explained that all of the interconnecting cables of any type had to be installed offshore because the separate cellar decks and modules had no roof and it was impossible to install the supporting cable tray and their cables before loadout.

Well done Brian. Not many people would have spotted this.

*

THE END OF THREE YEARS AT McDS – FINAL THOUGHTS
TALKING ABOUT OIL-RELATED companies preferring staff employees, it is the goal of all Management and HR departments but it's a myth. In the world of design and construction of front-end engineering, everybody is a contractor whether they like it or not.

Individual contractors, like myself, we come, we complete the contract to its last day, we get paid, we ignore the client's greasy pole, the politics and the usual bloodletting sessions that go with it, and then we slip out the back door to pastures new.

It is a simple and efficient system. It gives the ability to enjoy one's work to the full. It's the 'I built that, now let's go build something else, somewhere different,' syndrome.

The system allows for the right people to be recruited at the right time, for the correct remuneration for the skill being supplied, and it does not upset the company's staff structure.

It was round about this era that the large contractors and design houses stopped carrying their staff on overheads in between contracts. It was just too damn expensive. No point having a large cast of top hands if there is no work to keep them busy. Letting go of long-term staff personnel can be an expensive business.

A delightful story comes to mind on the Dunlin Project. The onshore manager, called Raymond, had just the one staff guy in his offshore team, the electrical engineer called Richard. Raymond was always asking why the rest of us didn't go staff? The company had a bold future ahead of it. Right?

Most of the team were sat around the coffee table, winding up Raymond, (it was a fun thing to do, and he didn't mind, or so he said) when Richard rushes in, grabs a cup and asked, 'Raymond, I've just finished two weeks offshore, so I now have two weeks break?'

'Yes, my son, that is correct,' said Raymond, smiling at his favourite person.

'And, you're due me two weeks holiday, which I should take soon,' continued Richard.

'Yes, my son, that is correct,' said Raymond.

'Oh good,' replied Richard, 'Here are my outstanding timesheets and expenses, my request for two weeks holiday with pay and with two weeks break that equals one month, so here is my notice to quit and leave the company. Must rush, I have a train to catch.' With that, he was long gone. Amazing.

Raymond sat there in shock. His prize engineer had just jumped ship. Unfortunately, someone laughed, out loud. It was a cruel thing to do. Raymond was an OK manager, just following the company line.

*

HAVING FINISHED, THE bid team went on to bid another project for a small inshore project in the Moray Firth. Duty done, a new contract was awarded at a fabrication yard in Fife using a long disused shipyard in a very poor part of the county.

I ended up being sent to the site where little of any interest occurred except for the unusual tale regarding one of the client's management team. This gentleman drove a Ferrari Dino. It seemed to attract the local ladies on the lookout for better days.

How he came by this desirable motor car had an interesting story. It seemed our hero had been working a very unusual scam, if that's the right word, by working two weeks offshore on one project and during his two week rest period he was working two weeks offshore obviously for a different client. He was madly in love with a lady singer from Glasgow and spent all his hard earned cash chasing the dream. What a waste of money.

Anyway, with Christmas soon to arrive and with my wife still struggling with her long illness the forthcoming seasonal holiday was going to be a welcome break. However, the company, being full of Christmas cheer, decided that it was the right moment to downsize its team of contractors and to build a new team using staff personnel. That worked a treat. Didn't just, I don't think. I took the offer of two weeks' pay in lieu of notice and collected some expenses and slipped quietly away

Anyway, I was done, and it was time for something new. I packed the Rover and headed for Perth where I stopped for a stiff lunch and a couple of drams before heading up the A9, that marvellous road that passes through the Highlands of Scotland. It was a dreary day, the traffic was the usual pain, so I just played all the good music I could find in the car and took it easy.

I stopped in Aviemore to phone home my time of arrival and raided the tourist shop for presents and boxes of pure-butter Shortbread. My arrival home was subdued and Johan looked tired and unwell. She worried about me getting a new position. I told her not to worry, there was always work if you looked for it. The custom is simple, as one door is slammed in your face, so you ruthlessly kick another one open.

17

ST. FERGUS, SCOTLAND

(1980 - 1982)

AFTER THE NEW YEAR, I took time looking for a new job. The employment agencies were slowly getting back to work and I enjoyed just being at home. I managed a little cross-country skiing with good snow in the forests and the exercise did me the world of good. The roads to the north were OK, so off to Thurso to visit Jim and Margret before the school term started.

A few days later, a call from Aberdeen sounded promising, so back to Forres, then Aberdeen the next day to start with a new company. They had a few odd jobs to keep me busy.

One included a visit to a huge linoleum factory to repair instrumentation during a shutdown. For years, train passengers arriving at the Fife town of Kirkcaldy knew they were nearly there by a peculiar lingering smell. The distinctive odour emanated from the linoleum works whose products were exported around the world from the end of the 19th to the mid-20th century. But now, the world's oldest and largest linoleum factory, had its future very much in doubt. Built in the 1880s, it was the last of six factories making linoleum using linseed oil.

But what next? The company salesman was a genuine Aberdeen wheeler-dealer, so I figured he had many pies in which to dip his fingers. I awaited the future with interest.

I was invited one day to lunch with a client to talk about the huge gas plant project north of Peterhead, at a village called St. Fergus. The plant would receive the gas from UK's massive Brent Field and eventually, from many other North Sea fields.

The Brent Field was restricted in the gas it could flare, unable to reach its full oil production potential. The UK government mandated North Sea gas should come to shore and this important project was late. It would take some time to understand the issues, which were huge.

The lunch went well and the next day a visit to the gas terminal took place at St. Fergus. The site was undergoing a major change of personnel working for the prime contractor, Ralph M Parsons, an American design, construction and installation contractor.

The client needed someone to take over the control room, a strong concrete building, half underground, in fact, a blast-proof structure.

The requirements were trawled over but without much firm detail. I said I was up for it, whatever it was, recalling my offshore experience. I would simply apply the same procedures and energy to get the job done.

I started on Monday for Parsons, checked-in with gate security, received badges to enter the site and ordered supplies for my office in the building, my base for the next two years. I received the grand title of Engineering Coordinator – Central Control Room: St. Fergus Gas Terminal.

I spent the first week finding my feet and somewhere to sleep, a reasonable two-bed apartment somewhere in Peterhead, away from the fishing port with its fishy smells.

The site was the usual mess, mud everywhere. Portacabin City sat on top of a small rise for the management personnel. The area quickly acquired the name Up the Hill, presumably from a Sean Connery movie, playing the part of an army prisoner being bolshie in army detention camp, with all the usual violence that goes on in army detention camps.

Then I did the round of introductions. The client engineers were immediately forgettable, but the most important person was Mr Gerry Cotton, Parson's Resident Engineer, the man responsible for the day-to-day control over all site activities. He had managed the two adjacent gas plants sites and thus had great knowledge. He was also an ex-RN Engineering Officer. He was a calm quiet man, but if he entered into any conflict he would surely prevail.

I was taken down to the control room, entering via the garage to the main floor. To one side was the supervisor's office, which I put my name on straight away. Along the far side stood four large control cabinets for the process plant outside, Offsites, to the left, then Modules '100' and

'200', Module '400' and finally 'Unit 800' to the right.

On my side of the building at the far end, next to the double steel doors, was the mysterious Computer Room, still empty and a useful space for a good pool table.

Down below in the basement? Well, it was a mess, full of cabinets not bolted down to the floor, cabinets waiting to be removed and junk everywhere. The side rooms were all similar.

*

SO, WHERE TO start? Good question. Complete a scope of work survey, what else? It was vital to understand all the issues on-site. Here I ran into secrecy, so they must be something fundamental going on.

I looked inside the Fire & Gas Control panel and saw the problem. Different voltages. Oh dear, surely not a conflict with the client's DEP.

The Design & Engineering Practice, (DEP) was the client's mammoth document on how to do stuff. Some of the sections of this document required you to face Jerusalem whilst reading the holy words. I jest of course, but now you have the underlying ethos.

The DEP mandated 24 volts DC and 3-15 psi instrument air. The on-site process plant was controlled by instrument air, using thin multi-core tubes that connected the control room out to the plant via on-site junction boxes. No explosion risk in the presence of gas, of which there was going to be a great deal coming down a 36" high-pressure pipeline from the offshore Brent Field, high up in the Shetland Basin.

This site would supply twenty-five per cent of the UK gas market. That's a lot of gas. Now came the pressure to get the project heading in the right direction and from what I was hearing, the control room was seen as being the crunch issue.

*

DURING THE FIRST year at St. Fergus I managed to get some racing at the club, Royal Findhorn, using the tide tables to arrange my weekends.

In July 1982, I took holidays in July to take part in the National 18 Championships on the Isle of Man. I wanted to take Johan and the two girls but a long road journey would not be good for Johan. One of my girl crew, the beautiful Marie, came up with the solution to the problem.

She would fly to the IOM with my family. It was a wonderful offer.

My friend Bobby couldn't bring his boat to the IOM so offered to crew and assist with the drive down to Morecambe. The next day the ferry to Douglas, the IOM capital, would complete the journey.

And so, everything was arranged and on the Wednesday 29 July 1981, Bobby and I set off on the long road south. The roads were remarkably clear and we had a smooth run. Despite the speed limit for towing, the Rover managed a steady seventy miles an hour where the road was clear and traffic was light.

It wasn't until we had driven passed Glasgow that we realised that our easy drive was a result of the nation watching the royal wedding, Charles and Diana. I had forgotten all about it. The Diana saga was overdone, causing me to lose all interest.

A close friend summed up the whole sorry saga as 'HRH Prince Charles, having received orders from above, required our future King to marry the nearest thing to a virgin that was available and produce an heir'. That the saga continued to its eventual conclusion came as no surprise.

Late afternoon, Bobby and I arrived in Morecambe, parading down the promenade as slowly as possible, towing a thousand pounds of racing dinghy and luggage, just to look at all the attractions. There was some confusion finding the correct road to Heysham and our B&B for the night.

After breakfast, we checked-in at the ferry terminal. The harbourmaster's team decided to load the commercial traffic first. The ferry was not roll-on / roll-off, so we were treated to a display by drivers who had no idea how to reverse an articulate rig. Some of the attempts were rather amusing.

The load-master came up to me, asking me the easiest way to load the National 18 and the car. Now I am quite good at reversing with a big dinghy attached to the car. But the load-master had other ideas. The dinghy was unhitched and his men manhandled the National 18 down the ramp and onto the ferry. It took just a few minutes to reverse the Rover on to the ferry and reconnect the National 18.

The sea was calm as the ferry crossed the Irish Sea, time for a decent lunch and a couple of beers. On arrival at the port of Douglas, we were one of the first to unload, make our way to Port St. Mary, unload the National 18 and put the mast up. That done, we checked-in to the hotel which was actually very nice. The next morning, as Bobby set about getting the dinghy ready for racing, I went to the IOM airport and picked-up the family and the lovely Marie.

The week's racing was good, although we could have had better results. But there was time off during the week after the racing each day to enjoy the IOM. I had always wanted to drive around the IOM TT race course. Johan kept a close eye on my speed. She was not up to being thrown around in my powerful Rover. She was ill, but the holiday was doing her good. Just had to take it easy.

There is a lot to see on the IOM; we did get to most of the attractions. The class dinner was held in the Douglas Casino, a posh affair with the dance floor next to the casino. Bobby was a bit short of cash. He said, 'Come with me and watch this.' He sidled up to the roulette table, watched the table for about ten minutes, then dropped twenty quid onto red, it won and he was gone.

Johan came through and I tried the blackjack table. The game started nice and slow, so within minutes I was holding my own. Then the dealer changed for a lady that could deal so fast, it overtook me. I left the table as soon as my winnings were taken back.

And so, the holiday was a success, everything went well. Johan enjoyed being somewhere with the family all together. It was to become the last time. I never thought it would be. Whether she knew I will never know.

*

The Instrument Air Saga – back to St. Fergus

WHEN WORKING ON-SITE, one has to gauge each contracting company working on their part of the project. Haig & Ringrose Ltd were the electrical and instrumentation contractor, based, in all places, Middlesbrough, located in the deep north-east of England. Experienced site warriors, best to be careful.

The instrument air system was constructed using large bore bronze pipework. The workforce, known as the 'bears', had almost finished this work, so I was told. So I went to inspect. Oh dear. Someone had been using large pipe wrenches, their teeth marks were everywhere, like dinosaur teeth marks; same effect.

Bronze is a soft metal that requires loving care when screwing the sections and bends together. At the time, a 2" ninety-degree bend cost ninety quid each and you could buy a good suit for the same money. I asked for a pressure test and it leaked like a sieve. The bronze fittings had been over tightened and badly distorted.

To cut a long story short, it was a mess. I consulted with the client's engineer, who merely told me the contractor must rebuild with new bronze fittings. That was never going to happen. The lead time for new components was huge and the contractor had a 'Get out of jail free' card, but I never found out what it was.

To get it repaired I handed out a work change order to silver solder every joint. Later the system test passed with flying colours. Oh, the cost of the silver solder, thirty thousand pounds, plus labour.

*

A FEW MONTHS after my arrival at St. Fergus, a new manager was appointed to look after the electrical and instrument work-scope on the site. A two-faced person, forever smiling with those shark's teeth of his, the Born Leader was more interested in making himself look good in front of everybody. A back-stabbing bastard with it, a storyteller and empire builder; I clocked him instantly for what he was.

I welcomed him to my control room, gave him a brief run-down of the issues. I could tell he was going to stay well clear, which suited me down to the ground. The control room had bad karma. I never worried souls about my control room. It was going to be my favourite project and I was going to succeed.

'Did I not need an assistant to help with the electrical work-scope?' asked the Born Leader, 'The building would soon need a night shift and seven day a week supervision,'

A helpful suggestion indeed, which I had brought to the table weeks ago. I answered, 'Yes. That would be helpful.' The Born Leader confirmed the position, then in a throwaway remark he said, 'Best find someone who can work with you.' Nice guy, Eh!

I rang my Glasgow friend, Brian, from our Dunlin days; did he want to join a long-term project with good pay? He arrived soon after. I gave him the tour, he looked into the Fire and Gas control panel and said, 'Oh dear, the design is completely fucked.' A truly precise technical evaluation.

I smiled, led him to my office, gave him a coffee, shut the door, to explain, 'The story, as far as I know, is that the main contractor told the client that their DEP wouldn't work on a site this big. You just can't get a 24-Volt DC signal down a standard sized cable over long distances.

Their design was to use British Standards, that is to say, send the 24-Volt DC signals to the Electrical Interface Building next door, that operates a relay and then another signal at 110 V DC is sent down the standard size cable to do whatever.'

'Next problem, this site does not have fail-safe shutdowns, as is the norm offshore, so for every safety action, two signals must be sent down separate cables and the building is not big enough to house all the cables needed. Now Parsons thought they had a document, an amendment to the contract, which is why they went ahead in the manner you see today.'

'Now, just about everything has to be ripped out, the DEP is King and vast numbers of engineers and their draftsmen in London are burning the midnight oil generating a completely new design. So while we wait, there is time to get our sorry act together and to get ready for a fast ride and healthy time sheets.'

Brian asked where he could get a bed. I suggested the spare bedroom in my newly rented apartment; we could do a deal with or without VAT. Brian smiled.

*

BRIAN GOT TO work, giving me time to deal with the other trades in the building. There were five in all. We worked well together. Then, one day Gerry Cotton dropped by to see how things were. He never mentioned the Born Leader. I wondered why.

I updated him on progress. The basement had been cleared out, the floor sealed to keep the water table, just a foot under the floor, at bay. I had a draft planning schedule waiting for news from our London Office so as to put some detail in all the different boxes.

Gerry told me a lead designer from London office would arrive on-site to act as the go-between and shine a bright light into the many dark corners that existed on this project.

I also told Gerry I was going to keep all the building entrances locked-shut, except for the entrance that passed my office. Please, could he clear that with the client?

He asked, 'Why?'

'Have you ever served on an aircraft carrier that was about to leave on a long commission, leaving the weeping wives behind, or sailing two days before a Cup Final?'

Gerry smiled, he knew what I meant. Anyone looking to extend the contract could, with a handy hacksaw and a spare five minutes, put the project a back a long time.

*

THE NEXT MONTH, a Raymond arrived from London office. A Cockney with an accent that came complete with a Berlitz phrase book. He was to be the source of much entertainment and inside information.

His most entertaining moment came during the long VAT strike. The sensible ones put the VAT man's money to one side. Not our Raymond.

One day, he turned up on-site with a brand new Rover SD1, 2,600cc, in brown, so it must have been a cheap deal. I asked from whence the funds came, as he said he was always boracic lint (skint).

'Dunno guv,' he said. 'The money was there so I bought it cheap, like.'

The follow-on event arrived when Raymond received his VAT return going back to the start of the industrial action. During a coffee break in my office, he told his audience, that he had sent the VAT return with a covering letter and a photograph of the car keys. The VAT man, enjoying the moment of humour, had sent back a photograph of a pair of handcuffs, with a notification giving him thirty days to pay. London humour at its best.

Outside, we did what we could, dragged the redundant cables out of the building, back-laid them in the cable trenches and buried them forever. New cable started to arrive outside the building and with no idea as to their intended destination, we left long ends coiled-up on the ground.

A fussing client demanded a large tin shed be built over the area. A work-order was signed and by the end of the week, the Veranda had been completed. Inside the control room basement, all was bare, a great space to start a snooker club. The request for a championship standard table was rejected.

I had the basement floor repainted with a two-pack sealant, to make it doubly watertight. Good stuff it was too. Four tins of it found their way into the back of my car. Not sure how.

Then, one day, when Brian and I were taking a coffee, Raymond wandered in with a new layout drawing. 'Careful Guv,' he said. 'It's kind of new.'

I replied, 'The bloody ink is still wet, dripping all over my Savile Row suite.'

'Death row suit, more like it,' smiled Raymond. 'This illustrious drawing has 'Issued for Construction', in the revision box.'

I passed the drawing to Brian for forensic examination of a fraudulent stamp. Brian took out a magnifying glass to examine it intently.

'Looks ok, could even be a true story. Let's take in down into the basement and check it out.'

Jimmy, the electrical foreman, joined in on this path to Valhalla. The drawing showed the installed positions of the first tranche of relay cabinets, due to arrive soon. With chalk in hand, Brian marked out the positions of the new cabinets. He asked Raymond for the list of cables per cabinet. It didn't look good.

'OK, gentlemen, Colin and I will have to put our heads together and we'll come back to you,' said Brian. And so Brian and I went away, 'to think again'.

It took a while to come up with the Master Plan, but when it was complete it served us well.

Day-shift would be reserved for work items that needed movement and access. The night-shift would be reserved for sedentary activities, most of which was termination of over half a million cable cores. The error rate for this work had to be zero, otherwise, the commissioning teams who would follow in our wake would need a tremendous amount of time fixing any errors.

Another odd thing was forced upon us by common sense. When the new cables were brought into the building, it was vital to reduce the amount of space they needed.

It became necessary to remove the outer plastic sheath and the braided wire armour as the cable entered through the under-grade cable windows. Now the cables lying in the cable trench outside the building had an array of many colours, depicting what service they were providing. Reds, blues, greens, yellow, whites. But once inside the building and 50 mm of the wire armouring clamped to the earthing frames, all cables became uniformly black.

Another Brian, one of the client's electrical engineers mentioned the fact. It just so happened that I had a Work Change Order in my jacket pocket.

'Here you are Brian,' I said. 'One in number WCO for a huge box of multi-coloured electrical tape to wrap each cable with the correct coloured tape. Oh, and you had better send down your man-hour estimators to crank-up a new rate for handling cable in the control room basement, say ten minutes a metre. Nice addition to the calculation of the lad's bonuses.

Brian of Shell smiled, the control room basement was too small for all the new cable coming into it and there wasn't a damn thing anybody could do about it.

Next, I arranged for a workers tea hut to be parked outside the back side-door. Gerry Cotton needed little convincing, my argument went like this. The workers had two breaks a day, plus their lunch time. Their facilities were located next to the Hill complex, that depressing jumble of temporary buildings a half a mile distant.

They were allowed ten minutes walking time for each direction, or twenty minutes in total for each break, which, over the day, equalled one whole hour, just for walking.

The client didn't like the idea of the costs until a simple spreadsheet was laid out before them. The workforce loved it, somebody was actually thinking about their welfare. Walking in the rain, getting soaking wet just to get a mug of coffee and a bun. That sucked.

A full-sized Portacabin arrived. Alex, my dedicated building cleaner took charge of the tea hut. Jimmy, the electrical foreman, found a source of electrical power and I left the workers to it.

Soon, the Tea Hut had a beat-up fridge, a two-ring cooker and a microwave, all acquired by fair means or foul. The wall heaters were on day and night. Getting into warm overalls every morning is a rare treat for a site worker. It is here I must say that this part of Scotland sticks out into the North Sea. It is always cold, it is always damp and humid and that's on a good day. It's a miserable location.

I also ordered strong lighting installed in the basement, as the termination of so many cable cores needed the best conditions to ensure accurate work. The client's safety man came to complain until I told him it was to maintain a good environment, warm and dry, for all the sensitive equipment inside the new cabinets now arriving on a weekly basis. Had I mentioned it was for the benefit of the workforce, well you know what would have happened. There is a phrase in the contracting industry, 'You can't do enough for a good client and when that client is found?'

It is here perhaps I should mention our workforce and what a mixed bunch I had to work with. Jimmy, the electrical foreman, came from

Fraserburgh, a fishing town right on the corner of the North Sea coastline. Brrr. Then there was a few other ex-fishing folk from the same area.

Next, came the locals from inland, farming stock. Then, there were the Jocks from the central region, mainly Glasgow, then the site warriors from Newcastle, the Geordies and next the gentlemen from the South of England. Talk about the United Nations. With these vastly different and sometimes very strong accents, no wonder the Americans supervisors on-site were confused.

These workers were all experienced site warriors and so Brian and I played the game. We always asked them for their opinion on all matters relating to the need to shoehorn-in so much equipment into a control room basement that was shrinking in size each day. Still, we looked after their needs and they gave us their best work. I was so proud of how Brian and I achieved this.

Another problem to be solved was cats. The whole site had become invested with wild cats, always looking for somewhere warm to sleep. The cable trays located up in the ceiling of the basement fitted the bill perfectly.

A site meeting addressed the problem, but the do-gooders complained about removing kitty in a kind and humane way, plus finding homes for them on the Cote d'Azure, or similar.

I told the meeting that one of my electricians nearly had his eyes scratched out. The newly installed cable trays reeked of cats piss and the unions were about to shut the site down.

Gerry Cotton glowered across at me and said, 'There's a bank holiday weekend coming up. Use the Sunday to fix the problem'. I took his meaning. The day before the start of the weekend, I ordered a team of my electrical guys to make removable wire screens for each incoming cable window and promised them everything would be OK by the time they returned after the weekend.

I called Alex, my faithful building cleaner and gave him a proposition, which he accepted straight away. I also told him I didn't want to know how, OK.

When Brian and I left for the long weekend, the building was closed down and locked, leaving the key with Alex. Brian asked what methods he would use. I smiled, replying that our part-time crofter was, in his day and an excellent poacher. The barrel of water in the basement was one clue, plus other items best not mentioned.

'And payment?' asked Brian. 'Some slight of hand on his timesheets perhaps?'

I smiled and bid Brian a good holiday weekend.

*

Kirsty the Dog

IT WAS NOT long after the family moved into our new home at Rafford, when the wife announced the latest member of the family. A very small puppy, a Labrador taken from a dog rescue home. It needed a lot of looking after to restore the poor thing to full health. Previous dogs had come and gone. The last one was a pedigree Basset Hound, but it was too inbred. It would snap at the children and a dog that bites children had to go.

I mandated no more dogs. Should've saved my breath. So here was Kirsty, a wee ball of black fur. Johan promised it would not be a big beast, as it had pedigree. I mentioned the size of its paws, clearly a large percentage of the whole. Working away from home during the week I was unable to observe its meteoric growth. Within six weeks it sure did have pedigree, lots of it too. A collie's head, with one floppy ear, an Alsatian's tail that could sweep any coffee table clean in one swipe and a Labrador's body with Alsatian's shoulders, all in dark black. Apparently, it was a bitch. Well, it was here, so I stopped bitching about it.

It was wonderful with the two girls, who would sometimes pull its whiskers out without complaint. If the children were playing in the front garden, Kirsty would settle down for a spot of sunbathing. One day an unwanted salesman approached the house. The sight and sound of a dog baring its teeth, practising its low growling technique persuaded the salesman to try his patter next door.

I liked to walk Kirsty in an open field. One time, she dropped to the ground, spotted a hare and then whoosh she was gone. The hare was very tasty and when I got to the remains there was little left.

My favourite memory about Kirsty was the evening I arrived home late. The snow was on the ground. The street lighting made everything look flat and grey. As I pulled in to the driveway I noticed a rabbit sitting in the middle of the road. As Johan opened the front door, Kirsty hurtled past at full speed after the rabbit.

It was some time before she returned, licking her chops, a small piece of rabbit fur hanging from one side of her mouth. Johan mentioned that she must have forgotten to feed the dog that day.

Early next morning, a lovely clear crisp day, with a frost and a little extra snow, the little girl that lived just around the corner knocked on the front door and very politely asked Johan, 'Had anybody seen Thomas, her pet rabbit?' Whoops.

We both dressed for the weather and joined in the neighbourhood search for Thomas. With six neighbours searching high and low, I wondered when Johan might reveal the secret. Ten minutes, later a shout of joy came when Thomas was found trapped between the thicket hedge in my garden and the wire fence that marked the boundary of our two properties. Phew, that was a close one.

*

BRIAN AND I returned after a long weekend. We were looking around in our favourite basement when the ground shook with the most violent thunderous sound from outside. We rushed up into the control room, where we found others similarly interested in what had happened.

The phone rang, the voice said, 'The client's pre-commissioning team have just managed to wreck one of the main incoming pipeline 36" 'Slam Shut' valves.

'This should be fun,' I thought.

There were two of these gigantic assemblies, welded into the main 36" pipeline. In the world of high-pressure gas systems, confirmed safety isolation requires two valves in series to ensure separation of the onshore processing plant from the huge inventory of gas contained in the long pipeline coming from the offshore platforms.

(Note: in the event that the supply of gas and the associated gas liquids, at the offshore end of the pipeline became shut-in, for whatever reason, the high-pressure inventory in the pipeline could keep the onshore processing plant operational for about two weeks.)

We waited for the morning break, saw our workforce was busy, so time for a nice walk in the park and a breath of fresh air. When Brian and I arrived at the incoming gas pipeline station, a crowd of engineers were looking at something of a disaster, which it was.

The long spindle that operated this massive 36" SSV valve was badly bent. The force required would have been considerable, as it consisted of high strength stainless steel. The SSV was operated by two hydraulic systems, one to perform the closing stroke and one to perform the opening stroke. Large hydraulic cylinders provided the reserves of pressure.

There was no explanation of what had gone wrong, but the vendor, who was keeping well back from the mêlée, told me that the idiot in charge' (the vendor's technical description) had closed the SSV valve and thought he detected a slight seepage. He had then recharged the 'Close' hydraulic cylinder, fiddled with the safety interlocks and then used the 'Open' hydraulic circuit just sufficiently to lift the valve away from the fully closed position.

Then, he stopped the opening sequence, and activated the 'Close' sequence without realising that the hydraulic force from both the 'Close' and the 'Open' hydraulic cylinders would be applied to the valve actuator, at the same time, when it was in the almost fully closed position.

There was a huge bang and the most enormous event that, according to the valve vendor, should have been impossible to achieve.

The SSV valve consisted of an all welded body, so cutting it out of the 36" pipeline was not possible. These valves, sourced from Italy, had a two-year delivery time. To make matters worse, retesting the pipeline line with a new valve, to certification standards, would be hugely expensive. Adding to these considerations, was the fact that the sea pipeline from the Brent Field, was full of gas and would have to be depressurised, so any retest would cause a very large quantity of an expensive commodity to be vented into the sky.

Brian just shook his head at the whole nonsense. This little affair could put the site back a considerable amount of time. We slipped away, back to our ordered world.

*

THE FOLLOWING WEEKEND I programmed the basement battery room for completion. A new charging unit had been installed. Raymond produced a set of drawings that gave every hope of being final. The capacity of the battery system was sufficient to enable the process plant to be safely monitored and controlled for a period of three days, which was the length of time it would take to ensure a complete shutdown and venting procedure.

Care was needed, as the batteries had been pre-charged to ensure long-term storage. Jimmy, the electrical foreman, had assembled six large reels of very thick copper cable, plus all the tools and fittings to make the connections. It was Brian's turn for a weekend at home in Glasgow, so I supervised the first few hours of the Saturday, then told Jimmy I would see him on Monday.

The short weekend at home flew by, but at least the garden surrendered. The vegetable patch, which I had grassed over, had its first cut. Johan was grateful for the rest and I took over from Sheila, our home help, who had the weekend off.

Monday morning, I returned to the site and for once I enjoyed the drive over. The farmers were starting their run-down as autumn approached and the roads were clear of their slow-moving impedimenta. Back on-site, the work in the basement had gone well and the battery room cleaned out of all debris by the ever attentive Alex.

Brian arrived Monday lunch time, as did three bottles of whisky for my office. Ask no questions, get told no lies, but clearly, the electrical cable scrap had been converted into a nice handout for everybody. Another week of frantic activity passed and according to my spreadsheet, we were marginally ahead on my programme. This spreadsheet of mine was kept under wraps, as the client's planning staff had their own version that showed that we were always behind. This worked in my favour, as when I asked for more resources, my requests were rarely denied.

*

ONE DAY, ABOUT mid-morning, a Shell PR person came rushing into the control room in something of a panic.

'Are your men working, is the work-site clean and tidy, etc, etc?' he breathlessly asked. I looked at him, tried not to smile and sternly told him, 'My men are always busy and the worksite is always as clean as it can be. What's the occasion?'

'VIPs,' was all he could manage, as he rushed out the back door. I straightened my tie, found my jacket and went to unlock and open the big double doors at the far end. Brian dropped down to the basement just to check all was indeed ok.

Coming towards the building I could see Gerry Cotton escorting the client's Site Director and two senior executives. The first one was a thin short person with a pale almost sallow complex. The second executive was a tall grey-haired distinguished looking gentleman who looked as though he was the master of all he surveyed.

I welcomed Gerry as always, who returned the greeting, smiled and made the introductions of the two executives. The thin gentlemen turned out to be the American Ambassador to the United Kingdom, a very senior position in the diplomatic world.

The second executive was equally important, Mr Jack Fleming, the project director for the entire Shell UK Gas Project, which included: the 36" pipeline from the Brent Alpha platform, all of the facilities at St Fergus, the pipeline to the British Gas Terminal next door, the overland pipeline to a processing plant in Fife, the process plant in Fife, a tanker loading terminal on the Fife coastline and a pipeline across the Firth of Forth to the BP refinery. Some responsibility.

That these two executives were on the same social level was obvious. Mr Fleming requested in his dry American voice a 'brief but short' description of the control room and its functions. I drew Mr Ambassador's attention to the four large control panels in front of him and these related to the four process areas out in front of the control room on the site.

I calmly explained, going from left to right, the first panel controlled the incoming gas and the associated liquids to be separated into two separate streams in the Slug Catcher, that huge array of horizontal pipes at the shore crossing, the next panel controlled two units that dried the two separated streams, the next panel controlled the unit that processed the gas being sold to British Gas. The last panel controlled the processing and export of the liquids being sent to Fife for further processing.

I stood back to let Gerry fill in a little more detail, but he assured his clients this control room was on track to finish on time due to an enormous amount of hard work by one and all. Thanks, Gerry.

I found out later the Ambassador was due to visit somewhere else, not sure where, but the weather in the form a dense fog necessitated another venue and there must have been a lot of American money tied-up in this huge and most important project at St Fergus; the biggest in the world at the time.

I wonder where they went for lunch?

*

THE FOLLOWING WEEK went well, with few problems and thankfully no interference from anybody. The night shift was going well. The policy of having only sedentary work performed at night, with just one technician assigned to his personal cabinet ensured the standard of workmanship remained high and progress terminating the electrical connections was going well. The technicians took great pride in their work and they enjoyed the responsibility.

It was my turn for a long weekend. I slipped away shortly after lunch on Friday and enjoyed a clear run home. Johan was up and about, but clearly, she was taking matters very easy. Her condition had changed drastically. Two weeks ago she had ballooned out to almost twice her normal weight and now she was as thin as a rake. The doctor had been to see her that morning, told her the worst was passing and she should look forward to a period of slow improvement.

At bedtime, she would wait until she felt she was ready to sleep. Some nights, the light of the new day would be creeping above the horizon before she felt safe to go to sleep.

I would stay up as late as I could, but St Fergus was draining my energies and I would slip away to bed just after midnight. Saturday and Sunday came and went, there was little to do as Johan did not feel like venturing outside except to sit in the veranda and enjoy the garden.

Monday morning, I returned to site at St Fergus and found all was well. Monday was the usual merry-go-round, but progress remained satisfactory. All was well. The coming weekend would be my thirty-seventh birthday, with Johan's thirty-sixth birthday just six days later.

Tuesday morning, I arrived a trifle late and was met by a very sombre Brian. He sat me down, put a strong hot coffee in my hand and confirmed what I knew he was going to say. Johan had passed away during the night, adding the children were being looked after by the next-door neighbour.

I sat stock still for some time just looking at the floor, as Brian turned away the early callers. Someone escorted me to my car and seeing that I had come to myself, bid me a safe drive home. I always imagined I would wish to drive as fast as possible. What for?

I fired up the Rover to let it take me home. It knew the way just as well as I did. The car kept a calm steady pace and in no time I had passed over the River Spey. A warning light told me I needed more fuel, so I pulled in to the next service station. The owner, seeing my sad demeanour, offered to fill the tank of the car, allowing me to sit and reflect. I confirmed his thoughts; he said the usual kind words and brought me my change.

I reached home, pulled into the driveway and went inside. I found Johan at peace; it looked like she was sleeping. Most of her beauty had returned. One eyelid was half open, I tried to close it but it remained. I lay down beside her for the last time and kissed her cheek. She was nine days from her thirty-sixth birthday.

It was not long before the front door opened and Mary, our neighbour returned with Carolyn. Her younger sister had been packed off to school, but Carolyn had elected to stay behind.

Doctor Anderson, our GP, arrived. He had little to say. So much for a period of slow improvement. Explaining why Johan had died was no help, what was the cause? Nobody was going to help me with that question. I never found out.

I phoned her parents in Thurso. Yes, they had heard the news and they were just about to leave. I shouted to Carolyn that Granddad and Nanna where on their way and please could she make a bed for herself in the third bedroom with her sister and change the sheets on her bed.

Then, the undertaker arrived. I left him to do whatever it is undertakers do. I found two trestles to place in the veranda. Johan would rest there until it was time to go the Chapel of Rest, the day before the funeral, which would be Saturday lunch time.

I took a break and a long strong coffee heavily laced with whisky. Sheila, our home help arrived and got busy. Lunch was coming and the grandparents would need a meal after the long drive down from Thurso.

I phoned Brian, passing him the details about Saturday, the name of the church, Rafford Church, where the funeral would take place. Everybody was welcome to come to the house before and after when refreshments would be offered.

Then, there came the long sorry task, phone book in hand, to gather family and friends together. My parents were unable to make it in time. That was a blessing. My family had not visited Southampton since we had left for the Far East. Family from Fife were shocked at the news, but Margret had already been busy. I left Brian to contact our work friends and I contacted the rest.

Sheila made some hot soup and a thick sandwich. I gulped another very large dram and went to bed for an hour, leaving Sheila to look after the comings and goings of our neighbours, comforting Carolyn and looking after Kirsty.

Late afternoon, Jim and Margret arrived safe and sound. A long journey without much conversation I guessed. I took them through to the veranda and left them with their only and much-loved daughter.

I poured two stiff whiskies and took two chairs for them to sit on. James thanked me for the whisky but he could say little. He was as silent as the rest of us. Eventually, they came through to the living room. Margret took the offer of a strong cup of tea. Eventually, Jim asked about the arrangements and just nodded his head. I asked if they were hungry; they said they would wait a little while.

Sheila took the children into the kitchen to give them their supper. The clock struggled round to seven pm. Carolyn said the two of them would like to visit Alice across the road. They returned one hour later, had their shower and went to bed. Alice arrived and started a general conversation with Margret taking her mind away from the tragic event. It cheered her up a great deal. It was time for Sheila to go home; her family would be waiting for their supper. She said she would look-in tomorrow to see how she could help.

I turned on the TV if only to have something break the silence in the room. I chatted with Jim, but nothing of importance. Tomorrow would be a better day following a good night's rest. It was time for my shower and to get some rest. I was grateful Sheila had already changed the bedclothes and made the room tidy.

When I made to bid Jim and Margret goodnight, I found Jim was sitting in the veranda nursing a large dram. I gave him a hug and said goodnight. Margret was busy getting ready for bed.

I left them to it and slipped between the sheets. Tiredness overcame me for which I was most grateful and slept until morning.

*

THE NEXT MORNING Sheila arrived early made breakfast for the children and packed them off to school. She had written a note for the teacher, saying to call if there were any problems and they could be brought home as best suited the situation.

I took breakfast then sat down to make a list of the many important things to do. I went out to the veranda, Johan's body had lost all its warmth, how peaceful she looked, free of the pain that had blighted her final years.

When Jim and Margret had finished their breakfast, Jim and Margret wished to visit the churchyard, which we did. A place had been marked out near to the top end where one could look over the hedges to the farmland on the other side of the road. The tall overhead pine trees made a soothing sound in the cool northerly wind. It was a very tranquil place.

We met with the vicar in the church and after the usual condolences went through the necessary procedure and paperwork. The grave would be dug three deep with assurances the area was safe from any disturbance.

Next, came the visit to the stonemason's workshop. Together we chose the headstone with the inscription, 'From the Kingdom of Fife to the Kingdom of Heaven, Eternal Rest', with Johan's name, birthday and passing day inscribed below.

Margret became a bit weepy, so I took her home. Sheila brought her a strong coffee with a drop of whisky to help her along. I took Jim down to Forres and parked outside the off-licence I had come to trust.

We exchanged greetings and commiserations with the owner and got down to business. What to purchase? There was no list of who would come. I guessed that we should provide for forty persons. The vendor suggested a box of whisky, which was on offer, perhaps one box of gin mixed with vodka, mixers for same, a box of mixed wines and six crates of various beers.

By Thursday, everybody was slowly coming to accept the tragic event. Flowers and cards of condolence were arriving from all over Scotland. A huge bouquet arrived from St. Fergus, signed by Shell and Parson's personnel alike. The most distressing thing I remember was the amount of time Jim spent talking to his daughter. Occasionally, Margret would join him. Everybody left them to their grief. I was glad the two girls were at school and keeping their spirits up with their school friends.

Friday morning was another sad day as the undertaker came to take Johan to the Chapel of Rest. If nothing else, it allowed Sheila with the other ladies to prepare the veranda for the wake. Jim asked for a traditional Scottish funeral and being ready for guests before and after was most important to both him and Margret.

Friday evening Brian and his wife Rosemary dropped by on their way to a B&B in town. Others came and went, keeping the kitchen busy serving tea and strong coffee.

Saturday became frantic. The family from Fife arrived, took refreshments and being the fun people that they were, spent time trying to keep the atmosphere as light as possible. Work friends who had travelled to Forres that morning came to say hello, took a cup and then made their way to the church. Club members and other neighbours had called beforehand, wished everyone the best and said we would all meet at the church in Rafford.

By eleven o clock, the hour was near. Jim and I took courage from an unopened bottle of twelve-year-old malt whisky. There would be precious little left for anybody else.

The family arrived at the church to be greeted by the vicar. The grounds outside the church were full of cars. The congregation took their seats so that we could enter. As the family entered the church, the sight of Johan's coffin, surrounded by a flood of colour from the many flowers was almost too much to bear.

Arm-in-arm, I help James and Margret leading the family, with Sheila, our wonderful home help, standing with Carolyn. (My younger daughter stayed at home due to her young age.)

Jim and I stood tall and strong. The whisky was doing its work.

With pride, the family took its place in the front pews. We held hands during the service. Other members of the family from Fife were behind, giving their silent support to enhance a wonderful and moving ceremony. With some many friends from so many different parts of the country, the funeral took place with grace and style. The vicar led a wonderful service throughout, impressing everyone with his solemn grace.

At the end of the service, we all took one last look at Johan's serene face before the coffin was closed. Jim and I, along with the other bearers, slowly and with care, took Johan to her final resting place. The churchyard was quiet and tranquil. A lovely place for Johan to rest in everlasting peace.

Duty done, everybody made their way back to the house. Sheila and the neighbours had slipped out of the church when the congregation was at the graveside. Everything was ready, piping hot tea, coffee, sandwiches, cakes and pastries. The long shelf along the veranda windows were laden with drinks of every type.

The wake relaxed everybody after such a solemn funeral. The funeral had been completed with style; everybody had played their part to the best. Time to unwind a little, grief would come during those solitary moments, but now to meet and greet everyone and enjoy, yes, enjoy, the coming together of so many relations and friends.

*

SUNDAY WAS A quiet day. Jim and Margret stayed for another week with Jim taking special leave from Dounreay, giving Sheila the week off. I guess we were still in shock. How could this tragedy happen? There were no answers, but what had happened had happened.

Now, I wanted to start planning the future for my two daughters but waited later in the day before Jim and I started to discuss the best way forward. We eventually agreed that the two girls should be with their grandparents, at least until Christmas.

So, arrangements were made for them to return to Thurso. It was familiar to them and in the interim, I would find an au pair to live-in after Christmas, allowing Carolyn to come home to re-join her class in the Forres Academy, where she was doing very well. This would be important, as the last two years of secondary school are the most important.

I would spend Christmas and New Year in Thurso and then return with Carolyn. I left Jim and Margret to think it over then contact the schools in question. Monday morning I left to return to St. Fergus and used my busy schedule to shield me from my inner thoughts.

Everybody was very kind upon my return to work. I was told to take it easy. With the work progressing so well, this was an easy call. Gerry Cotton came down to see how I was and expressed his regrets that he couldn't get me any paid time off.

I thanked him for the thought. The last six months had been very heavy in the pocket, but now I could recover my finances. Time would fly in November and soon it would be Christmas. The weekend arrived and both Brian and I left Jimmy, the electrical foreman, in charge of the building. I had to get back to Forres to help Jim and Margret get packed for their return to Thurso with the two girls and the dog. With fond farewells, I was left in an empty house, with jobs to do, for which I had no energy to do them.

I spent the day in the yacht club preparing my two sailing dinghies for their winter storage in my large double garage. Club members helped me get the National 18 on to its road trailer. The Phantom being as light as it was, it took little time to do the same.

I took the Phantom home first and stored it up under the overhead beams. I returned to the club, took a big lunch and a few drinks in the bar, hitched the National 18 to the back of the car and made a slow return home, sure that the local bobby would be down at the Forres Football Ground for a Saturday afternoon local derby.

Sunday was a day of rest. I found a few boxes and started to pack a few of Johan's clothes, but there was no rush. The task was too emotive anyway. In the afternoon, I chose to drive back to Peterhead in the daylight. Winter weather was with us all and with snow forecasted to be coming in from the North Sea, it was the best thing to do. North Sea snow is very wet and heavy, sticks to everything and then turns into solid ice.

That night, I turned in early; my emotions still trying to come to terms with Johan's passing. I took the doctor's wise advice, not to keep things bottled up. I also took my own advice with a stiff dram as necessary. Fortunately, there was a sufficiency of whisky left over from the wake. It sure came in handy at times.

It was only later, that I came to realise that Johan, being physic, had indeed understood for a long time that she would not overcome her illness. It never occurred to me for an instant that she would not recover.

By chance I had chosen Rafford as a good place for her to recover her health, never realising I had chosen a quiet place in the beautiful countryside of Morayshire for her to spend her last days. So now she rests in peace. At least we all did well by her at the end.

*

IN THE RUN-UP to the Christmas break, the work on-site did not slacken. In fact, so well ordered was our little world, there was little to do except keep an eye on our workforce and help them where we could.

There was, however, one part of the work scope I had kept back from my planning. The main process plant was controlled by very fancy pneumatic controllers. The pneumatic tubes entered the control room basement along with all the electrical cables. These tubes were enclosed in a plastic sheath, the same as electrical cable.

Each tube connected to a three-way fitting stacked on the end of the long line of twenty racks that filled that side of the basement. From the top of this termination, each separate individual tube disappeared up above to connect to their controller.

Because of the huge volume of gas to be delivered to the British Gas terminal next door, the client had invested in what was, for this era, a very fancy piece of kit, an optimising computer, reckoned to give another five per cent output, something well worth having.

The third off-take allowed for another tube to be routed around the basement to the computer interface room to convert the pneumatic signal into an electrical signal for the computer to process.

The installation of these tubes was a substantial piece of work, however, with a bit of careful planning, a way to reduce the time needed had been thrashed out between myself, Brian and Jimmy, the electrical foreman.

And so, on Saturday, two weekends before Christmas, all other work in the building was stopped.

The many drums of multi-tube cables were set up in the control room. By bundling three or four multi-tube cables together; each bundle disappeared through strategically placed openings into the basement, with Jimmy's entire squad spread along the cable trays to complete the work of pulling everything into place. The task was completed by midday Sunday, leaving just the termination work to be completed more calmly on the night shift.

On Monday, the Progress Sheets went up to The Hill to be fed into the great progress monitoring system that the client used.

With the weekend fast approaching the site's workforce were looking forward to being paid for their extended Christmas break. My workforce wondered about their bonus. They need not have worried. On the following Wednesday morning, the senior electrical manager, a bearded Scot from Perth, by the name of I. McKay, came into my office. Brian served him a coffee and we waited for him to say something. Christmas Greetings, perhaps.

There was a pregnant pause, then I. McKay said and here I quote with great accuracy, 'You complete bastards.'

We smiled hugely. We both liked I. McKay; he was a good man to work with. Very droll, at the best of times. But his words were not quite what we were expecting.

Brian suddenly picked up on why such profanity had been uttered with such honesty.

'There's a problem Ian?' I asked with great sincerity.

'You've bankrupted my company. There's panic in head office. The directors have to find an extra five quid an hour, for the last two weeks, for every electrician on the site. Over an extra three hundred thousand pounds is needed, in cash, so we can pay our workers bonus on Friday before they break for the Christmas and New Year.'

Brian and I realised that our ploy to grab a big jump in overall progress in the control room would have a positive effect on the site worker's bonus, but we were not privy to the inner workings of the system. Oh dear, what had we done?

Well, the client was delighted at the reported progress and so were our bosses, but we never thought such a fuss would be created.

'Another coffee?' asked Brian.

I. McKay replied, 'See you two, I don't know. Anything to put in the coffee?'

A half bottle appeared and all three of us had another coffee.

'Going anywhere for the Christmas break?' I asked.

'Very funny,' replied McKay. He upped and left, shaking his head, only to be replaced by a smiling Gerry Cotton. Brian hid the half bottle and refreshed the coffee machine as Gerry made himself comfortable.

'Mr McKay full of the joys?' he asked.

I replied, 'There seems to be a moment of some tension. They need to find some cash for the boy's Christmas bonus. Perhaps flog the company Rolls Royce at the Wednesday auction at Blackbushe.'

Gerry smiled, 'You two have done wonders, but I need to see your planning schedule, the one you keep for those that understand such matters.'

I retrieved my planning sheets, the ones I had started at the beginning of the contract and had taken me over two months to get settled down for the long haul. Crikey, it was nearly eighteen months old and it had stood the test of time. It had just over a million man-hours identified on it.

Gerry knew about it, of course, but he asked how I had it been put together.

I replied, as with other experiences with this client, every item of work, or activity, was given its own reference, then the quantities added, then add the man-hours for each item as per the Page and Nation norms that I used on the Dunlin and Cormorant projects, numbers proven by real work experience.

Now, just over a hundred weeks on the project, we were running just one week behind on my schedule, which was about right considering all the changes that had to be dealt with.

Gerry smiled, 'The client still has the control room as the last vital area to finish.'

'Well, we will see.' I replied. 'I have five trades in the building. The heating and cooling systems are being commissioned as we speak. All the civil works are almost complete, just need some painting finished. The lighting systems are all finished and working, as are the telephones plus the other comms' circuits. The backup battery system is finished and tested. Just waiting for the fire engine to put in the garage I guess.'

Gerry smiled.

Brian and I took Gerry to the computer room, where the geeks were having great fun generating Top of the Pops graphics. Apparently, it was the only software that ran the machine hard to its limits.

'So when will the client pre-commissioning team start their work?' asked Gerry.

'Oh, the Born Leader's new army?' Yes, he's been here, poking around being a bloody pain in the backside. I chase him outside every chance I get. He's only trying to build his new empire.'

Gerry replied, 'Yes, he was always trying. Anyway, I'm happy. Mr Eddy McDonald, our volatile site director is happy. How about the design team from head office?'

'I believe they are delighted. Raymond has been a godsend if you can believe that. Mr Jens, the principal engineer is happy. His Rottweiler, Mr Perkins is growling less and the rest of that team are just about to clear up the last of the confusion regarding cable numbers.'

'So, well done you two, so have a Happy Christmas and New Year.'

We thanked him for his visit. I walked with him the far entrance. Gerry asked how I was at home? I replied, 'I was OK when I was busy; otherwise, it was not good. I have an au pair coming after New Year, so my eldest will be back at her old school. The other one can stay in Thurso to finish of her Primary School programme.'

'So Christmas and New Year in Thurso. I hear they drink a lot,' said Gerry.

'The locals are professional grade, but I'll take it easy,' said replied. 'Lots to plan for the New Year.'

With that he was gone, his hand held radio phone calling him urgently to the 'Offsites' area next panic. It seemed that the client's pre-commissioning team were in the middle of their self-destruct programme.

Later that week, Brian and I watched our workforce getting paid for the holiday. Between two weeks money, bonus plus living allowance, not forgetting their travellers, these guys were going on a well-earned break with thousands in their pockets. We wondered how much of their pay would actually reach their happy homes. There were many pubs between St Fergus and wherever home was.

I thanked Brian for all his hard work and told him to travel home safely

*

I HEADED FOR home and rested a couple of days. There was a pile of mail to throw in the bin, or read, as appropriate and prepare the third bedroom for the au pair, due to arrive in the New Year. Her name was Marianne, from Denmark. The au pair agent lady said she was an attractive girl from a good family. She would pick her up from Aberdeen Airport and bring her to my home on the 3rd of January 1982.

I told her I would return from Thurso the day before with Carolyn.

I was concerned about the weather. Driving to Thurso in winter required a good knowledge of what the weatherman was going to provide. There had been a lot of snow down south, but as Christmas approached there was a general thaw and the roads north were clear. The Rover was fully equipped with snow shovels, blankets, et al. I loaded up with a lot of Johan's clothing for Margret to sort out and find a new home, mostly amongst her relatives in Fife.

One uneventful journey later, I was back where I started, spending time in Thurso.

*

THE RETURN TO Forres encountered some seasonal weather. I just took my time, drove carefully chatting to Carolyn. There was little to say about Thurso, everybody just getting on with life. What else was there to do?

We arrived at Rafford to find Sheila had put the heating on and made dinner for us all. What a godsend this lady was. I missed having Kirsty with us, but Jim thought it best she stayed in Thurso.

Another lonely night passed peacefully and the au pair arrived just in time for lunch with the agent, an attractive professional person, living in the wilds communing with nature, somewhere over towards Nairn.

The Danish young lady was indeed very attractive, very Scandinavian, slim build, blond hair and a fresh face with freckles. She was eighteen years old and this was her first time living away from home. She had nice manners and her English was much better than I had hoped, but the English language is very common in the Scandinavian countries.

She understood the details surrounding the recent history and said she would do all she could to help. I explained my schedule and hopefully, I should be home most weekends. After our meal, I left the girls to talk amongst themselves.

Sheila and the agent left. I had a few minutes with Marianna and gave her the expected do's and don'ts. I was very pleased to see Carolyn settling down with Marianna. I needed this new domestic arrangement to work and work well.

I returned to St Fergus and met up with Brian who had enjoyed his long break. Now it was back to work. The workforce was due to return the next day, so we spent the morning having a good look around, just to check the work was up to standard and there were no loose ends to ruin our planning.

January turned into February and our workload was finishing quickly. The client's construction engineers started to hand over parts of the control room to the client's pre-commissioning team led by the Born Leader, now resplendent in his new overalls and shiny hard hat. He started generating the odd problem or two, which had the effect of delaying the end of our contract.

Later that week, a nice surprise. An invitation to dinner at a well-known Newburgh hotel just down the coast. It had a fine restaurant and an à-la-carte menu that was a favourite with lovers of fine food. The invitation came from Parson's Mr Eddie McDonald, our very own volatile project director. His nickname, Razor, a splendid piece of London humour that originated from a television cult series called Turtle's Progress, broadcast between 1979 and 1980. The series dealt with a petty criminal named Turtle and his minder, 'Razor' Eddie, a sharply dressed minder who was handy in a London gangland environment.

This nickname for the man with the responsibility for delivering this huge project had come about during the early days at St. Fergus. Parson's started with what they thought was their best team, mainly Americans relocated from the Middle East and their prize staff persons from the London office.

Things had not gone well at the start. Exposing expat Americans from the Middle East to the conditions in north-east Scotland was never going to work with a trade union workforce, most of which had come from other major Scottish projects. It became the mismatch of all time. The staff from head office had little site experience, which only added to the possibility of things not going well. Then there was the conflict with Shell's DEP.

Eddie McDonald had been appointed to sort matters out. He was a tad volatile, but a very sharp cookie. He had decimated the original team with his usual style, (hence the term Razor), then turned to the contract market to get those persons who could do and turn matters around. I liked him a lot, the few times that I ran into him.

A bus was laid on at 6 pm; picking-up the people he considered had given the most effort to turn his project around. He had succeeded, the project overrun was slashed and now he wanted to show his appreciation. Good for him. I wish it was common practice in the industry.

The bus dropped everybody off at the hotel to be greeted with a glass of best bubbly. Good start. Then everybody was presented with the extensive à la carte menu, choose what you wish. Impressive. We were told to choose any bottle of wine, one between two and coffees would be served with your choice of liqueur.

Being hidden away in our own secure world, Brian and I did not know many of the others, but it soon became apparent that the best of the best had been procured from the many employment agencies in Aberdeen and London. What a good night we had.

Razor Eddie was in fine form, entertaining the crowd like the professional he was. Nobody I saw abused such magnificent hospitality, which was as it should be. I even forgot my worries and cheered up a great deal. It did me a world of good.

The food was the best. I had the venison, Brian the steak. The hotel was famous for its sticky toffee treacle pudding. How I found the space for it I don't know. I forget the wine Brian chose, but the coffees with twelve-year-old Speyside malt whisky went down a treat. The bus returned everybody back to Peterhead. Brian and I slept soundly, that's for sure.

By the first week in March, the work in the control room had finished. We had hoped to be sent to the next project site in Fife, but that team had been fixed and with a more modern design, that project became, well, more modern.

I had a few companies interested in my CV, but I had no end date to give them.

Come the Monday morning, I was invited, for the first time, to attend the site's monthly progress meeting. Gerry Cotton had kept me out of this firing line throughout the project due to the politics that surrounded the control room. I learned later, that the other areas of the site knew the control room was going to be the last to finish.

Gerry, as the Resident Engineer, played a canny game, wheeling and dealing with the different entities inside the Parson's empire.

I arrived at the meeting in my usual jacket and tie which I always wore when working in the control room and slipped unnoticed into a comfortable chair at the back of the room. With the seniors all gathered around the conference table, the meeting got down to work. Most of the process sites were behind the control room progress, but not badly so. Many were catching up fast, but Offsites was well behind, for many reasons.

Gerry Cotton chaired the meeting, sitting next to client's site director. Each section head had to give a detailed description of exactly where they were in terms of progress and what measures were in place to improve matters.

Then, Gerry came to my part. He introduced me to everybody and asked for my report. I replied, 'Well, gentlemen, I think I can say we have finished unless there are changes I do not know about?'

The meeting went silent, a voice at the back expressed the opinion 'That just couldn't be.' Somebody else muttered an, 'Oh shit.'

I assured him it was, then remained silent. My being at the meeting was a cute move by Jerry well aware, as far as I could tell, the various programmes for the other site areas had been adjusted to the control room end date as shown on the client's master programme schedule, which was three maybe four weeks behind my spreadsheet. No wonder Gerry took so much interest in it.

So that was that. I can't remember when Brian left, but he had a happy hunting ground to return to in Glasgow. The next day Gerry called me to his office to discuss my end date. Knowing my situation, he was prepared to offer me a one, possibly a two month position out on Offsites, the last place in the world I wanted to go to.

I smiled and suggested three weeks pay in lieu of notice. Gerry smiled back and said he could manage two weeks pay in lieu of notice at the end of this week. I agreed to that. I would have three weeks money to come. I rang my agent in Aberdeen to tell them the news, but they doubted they had anything for me.

On Friday, I said goodbye to my team, now greatly reduced, then visited Gerry Cotton with my paperwork and time sheets to be signed. We shook hands, I received his thanks and with that, I left. I quickly went into Peterhead to remove the remainder of my belongings and to settle up with the rent. The drive home was quite sober. I had enjoyed the work over the last two years, safe in the knowledge I had actually achieved something. The St Fergus contract had gone

well, the last major site contract I would be involved with. What lessons I had learned and as one of the last of the original intake in 1981, I had beaten the contractor's ditty, that goes:
Those that try and do their best go down the road with all the rest.
Those that loaf and lazy about get to see the contract out.
I had seen the contract out, now for something new.

18

TWO SHORT CONTRACTS AND A BIG SURPRISE

BY THE TIME I GOT home, it was mid-afternoon. A letter was waiting for me, please call as soon as possible. It came from a well-known engineering consultancy. When I called to give my name, the receptionist put me straight through to the general manager. We quickly exchanged pleasantries but the manager asked my situation. I told him and he sounded relieved, asking could I start as soon as possible. I asked for the time duration of his requirements. He thought six to eight weeks. This sounded promising, as short-term usually became long-term in the contract world.

I offered Monday and the manager sounded relieved. We agreed on an hourly rate and I suggested that we leave the paperwork until then. I rang a B&B I knew and was pleased they had a room for me. They also had a secure car park to store my trusty Rover.

Carolyn asked if I could stay for the week, at least. It pained me to tell her I had to take this offer to build my reserves, sadly depleted by the sadness of the last six months. The au pair was doing just fine and Carolyn was glad to be back at her old class in the Forres Academy. She had some catching up to do, but she didn't think it would be a problem.

Early, Saturday morning, I picked some spring flowers from the garden and took them to the churchyard. It made me feel better, but the deep sadness remained. In truth, I had to keep busy at work, if only to occupy my thoughts on the future. Life goes on, invoices, bills plus other unwanted correspondence continued to drop through the letterbox and thud their way onto the doormat.

Monday morning proved an easy drive to Aberdeen. The traffic was the usual mess and far too many people seemed to know about the backway into town I normally used. I dropped my car off at the B&B then took the bus into town. I met with the General Manager, a Mr Shaw and concluded the short-term contract between ourselves. This was to be an 'in-out' contract as the company saw a falling market and they were the process of retreating back to the south of the country. I managed a slight increase in the hourly remuneration.

The project. Shell's Brent 'A' platform was to receive a new module to be a part of changes to the overall gas system. It had to be the size of a forty foot container, open sides and weigh less than twenty tonnes to enable the platform crane to perform a snatch-lift off the back of a supply boat. The structural design was complete and I was required to make the equipment layout, specify the equipment and complete an offshore survey to check on all the related matters to its installation.

So, I set too, everything seemed straightforward. It would be the week after next before I could complete the offshore visit. I settled down, read all the specifications, the contract from Shell and began stroking a sharpened pencil across virgin paper.

Wednesday evening, I went to my favourite bar and met up with the owner of my favourite ventilation ducting company. 'Come for a late lunch on Friday,' was an offer I readily accepted. I bought my round and made my excuses as I had a busy schedule the next day.

Thursday evening, I went to the lodge but the place was half empty. Many of the brothers were either police or ambulance service and a high-value prisoner had escaped from Peterhead Prison. Apparently, the escapee was an Australian, ex-French Foreign Legion, therefore considered highly dangerous.

Entry into the city was locked down tight. The traffic jams exceeded all records held by any UK motorway. Three days later he was found in a farm barn halfway between the prison and the city. He gave up without a struggle, being cold, hungry and very tired. So that was the fun of the first week. I must say I was impressed how efficient the various public services were in containing the escapee.

The weekend at home gave me the usual jobs. I told Carolyn and the au pair about my forthcoming visit offshore. The visit to the platform was the usual grind, the drive to the airport in the rain, the flight to Shetland, it rained all the way, the flight to the platform, still raining and when I arrived on the platform there was a bit of a fuss over beds, in which I prevailed.

The new half-module would be located at the back of the drill rig pipe-rack, now largely unused. I managed to get the information I needed although this did involve waking up slumbering supervisors of the various disciplines who should have known more about their platform than they did.

I returned on Friday, reaching home safely and on time. It didn't take long to finish the required design work, so I thanked Mr Shaw for his business and after seven weeks I had completed a good job of work and made a few bob in the process.

*

NEEDLESS TO SAY, during my tenure in Aberdeen, I had been scouting around for the next opportunity. This came in the form of an invitation to join the Bechtel Corporation, who had been awarded, by the USA Company Conoco, to manage the world's first tension leg platform (TLP).

I am always attracted to being involved with something new. So what did I know about the world's first TLP? Well, the industry magazines had published many articles about extending production facilities into ever deeper water.

A TLP is a platform designed to float like a modern drill-rig that can be towed, complete, to its service location. Then, long tethers, looking remarkably like up-graded drill pipe, are lowered to be connected to strong piles on the seabed and these are used to keep the platform in position. The tethers are attached at the top of the columns in four corners of the platform. When ready, ballast water is pumped out of the hull, then the tethers take-up a tremendous amount of tension. The platform becomes firmly secured with only limited movement when the North Sea weather imposes itself on all and sundry.

Vickers Offshore had been working on the TLP Concept for eight years since 1974. The topsides design was completed by Brown and Root. The topsides were built at the McDermott Ardersier yard, in Scotland. The hull was fabricated at the HiFab Nigg yard, which is where I ended up.

Bechtel proved to be an experience. They only hired staff personnel. That sounded like a good deal until the small print revealed the duration was 'by project only'. End of project equalled goodbye unless you were needed for something else, which meant a new contract.

This avoided some pesky Government legislation, but like I said before, in this industry everyone is a contractor. Oil companies sell oil, design and construction companies sell man-hours and vendors sell their product. This sort of clarity is generally overtaken by company bullshit, which is believed by those who do not understand.

So, what about the Hi-Fab at Nigg Bay? Well, it exists at the end of a peninsula that forms the north side of the narrow entrance into the Cromarty Firth, in its day a very secure anchorage for the Royal Navy. Just one-kilometre distance is the south side of the entrance on the Black Isle, a lovely part of the world when it's not raining.

The site is equipped with a large dry dock, one of the largest dry docks anywhere. The *Forties Alpha* jacket was fabricated in this dock in 1973/74 before being floated out to the field on a huge barge.

The site is also famous for mud. Huge puddles abound. In other words, it's just another miserable damp construction site at the end of nowhere.

The TLP team was housed in the usual Portacabin, meals were served in a Portacabin, in fact, if there were no Portacabins, there would be no North Sea oil.

Still, the salary was OK, considering, and accommodation at the Kincraig Castle Hotel included the evening meal, where the food was just the best. The owner, a butcher to trade, used to produce and hang his own meat in a special building.

His staff consisted of a very nice couple. The lady was the divorced wife of a very senior British diplomat based somewhere in South America. Her humour was priceless. One dinner, she started to serve a very nice Scottish wine. Nobody had heard of Scottish wine this good. We enquired for more details. She informed, 'French grapes, Scottish feet' and left us all smiling. Lovely lady.

The Nigg Bay project construction site had seventy plus carpool. The pool cars in question were 1.3 litre Vauxhall Astras, which doesn't sound too grand, but when the driver is not paying for the petrol and new tyres, it is not a slow motor car by any means. And wow, does it go around corners, of which Scotland has a great sufficiency.

The client had them supplied on lease terms, but the insurance companies declined insurance cover, so Conoco Corp set-up their own insurance scheme to save money.

This led to a most interesting story, as told to me by Norman. Norman was a new hire who came to work for Conoco as my immediate boss. Somewhere in the past, as a technician, he'd worked for me. So, always be nice to your workers, you never bloody know who is going to turn-up.

Norman's boss was a very nice man, very clever, but erratic at times. His story begins. The main road from Tain towards Inverness was blessed with the entry into a small town that comprised a long dead straight section of road. I can't remember exactly where but it was somewhere in the Invergordon district and with the many road improvements since this event occurred, I cannot be sure exactly where.

Anyway, this long straight section of road encouraged the brave, the foolish, plus the reckless, to travel at well above the speed limit. The problem was, at the end of the very straight section of road was an all original, instant, right-hand corner, a very sharp corner. Road signs mentioned the fact. It nearly caught me out once.

The story continues, Norman's boss, let's call him Mark, had a very bad crash on this corner. His Astra demolished a waist-high stone dyke wall, travelled a further fifty odd metres, demolished two greenhouses in adjacent gardens, then rearranged, quite badly, a householder's garden shed, amongst other things.

Fortunately, Mark was uninjured. Quite why he had the accident was not exactly revealed. He was a fast driver and he did like a drink, but the two were not related otherwise, the police would have said something.

So, two days later, the Conoco Car Insurance Claim Form arrived in the office. We all sat back to see what words of wisdom Mark would communicate to his head office in London.

Mark completed the claim form in surprising detail so that the injured parties could be fully reimbursed for their loss. At the end of the claim form was the box that asked the obvious question, 'Please state, as accurately as possible, the velocity of the vehicle at the moment the crash occurred.'

Mark looked around, smiled and wrote 32 mph. Sniggers were stifled all round.

A week later, Conoco head office returned the claim form, including a letter stating that the police had determined the velocity of the vehicle at the moment of the crash using their expert knowledge and a cunning computer programme that crunched data faster than you could crunch a car.

The letter continued, 'Sir, in taking the data from the police report we conclude two possibilities, which we would like you to confirm.'

'Possibility 'A', states, the damaged caused by your accident, your vehicle would require to weigh approximately six and a half tons. The makers of the car state that no such model exists in their range of vehicles.'

'Possibility 'B' – the best calculation that can be determined suggests your velocity was somewhere in the region of 65 to 75 mph. Please, can you confirm which possibility best suits your circumstances?'

There was laughter all around, but it was a serious point being made with humour. To all our surprise, Mark chose Possibility 'B', returned the claim form and as far as we know, that was that. Amazing.

The administration side of the project was run by the Colonel, an ex-army officer from one of the support and logistics regiments. He tried to keep strict order, but against the willful ways of the average site person, it was a hard task. Being an ex-army colonel of more than twenty year's service he had not fully assimilated the ways of the civilian and was never likely to.

However, after a few brief tense encounters, we got on quite well. I called him 'Coronal' and he called me 'Navy'. I used to pull his chain on occasions, just to keep him straight.

One day, I showed him my medals awarded for the Borneo Conflict. He asked was I ever in danger. My reply was, 'Only in Bugis Street, Singapore, trying to get rid of some transvestite looking for a free meal.'

I also showed him Johan's grandfather's diary of the WW1 Dardanelles expedition, where boredom was the biggest danger. The diary is a very interesting read.

One day, a new Astra arrived on-site, which the Colonel bagged to save any arguments. I was visiting his office with the week's paperwork and he asked me for the keys to my Astra, which was somewhat second-hand, to say the least. He gave me the keys to his Astra, still shiny and unmarked. 'Thanks, Coronal,' I said.

He invited me for coffee to tell me there had been a bad accident. One of the welding inspectors had died in a crash. He was not one of the lunatic welding inspectors who thought Arton Senna was the slowest driver ever born. This chap had been working late, probably too tired, wet roads, no excessive speed, but the accident black spot he entered claimed another victim. Left a young family behind too.

Three weeks later, four ex-police heavies arrived on-site. Ex-Hendon Police College driving instructors. Everyone had to undergo a morning or afternoon session on defensive driving. My turn came and for some reason, I had to use my Rover. The instructor gave it a look over, then said, 'Nice car, well kept too.'

He asked if I knew the local roads. I told him I frequently travelled from Inverness up to Thurso. Perhaps he should try it sometime. There are some serious challenges on the A9 to Wick. But if he was looking for something more interesting today the B9176, the Sluie, would be of interest.

The Sluie bypassed the dreary coast road that wound its weary way past dreary Invergordon. It went up over the hills, through a forest and in winter with some snow, provided a nice challenge to the careful driver wishing to hone his winter driving skills. So that was the road used for the driving lesson.

The instructor taught me how to get the big Rover through a corner in a very smooth balanced way. It was good to learn how to increase my driving skills. Just one small problem presented itself; it was hard on the tyres. Police drivers do not pay for the tyres on their patrol cars. I was getting over thirty thousand miles before it became necessary to spend large bucks on new rubber. I enquired what mileage the police were getting on a similar vehicle; less than ten thousand miles I was told.

The instructor told me they used the big Rovers as unmarked patrol cars and how effective they were. I smiled, telling him I could spot an unmarked police Rover quite easily. 'How?' he asked.

I told him the Grampian Police always used steel wheels on their 3,500cc SD1 Rovers. The standard car always had alloy wheels. Plus the fact that police patrolmen tended to have square shoulders, mostly because of their uniform. I recalled once I was heading down the Dundee road from Aberdeen in something of a hurry and almost whooshed past a dark blue Vauxhall Carlton when I spotted the occupants were err, kind of big in the shoulders. I rapidly lost a lot of speed and hung-back behind it.

When the police car pulled into a lay-by, the driver gave me big smile and a wagging of the finger. No doubt he had phoned ahead to his fellow patrolmen from the Dundee Force.

*

MEANWHILE, WORK IN my sector was very slow. There were many welding issues with the very special high strength steel being used in the construction of the hull. The lower sections of the TLP hull came from Japan. They were lowered into the dry dock by the ultimate Tonka toy, a Lampson Crane, which could lift two thousand tons on a short lift.

Lampson is an American company. The easy way to describe this marvel of engineering is to place two heavy military tank chassis in parallel with a third chassis behind, which articulates and provides steering. Mount a suitable crane on a strong structure connected to all three units and there you have it. It was a magnificent beast, most impressive.

It was very interesting how these parts of the lower hull would form a large, almost square, doughnut. They fitted together perfectly so they could be welded together. Then, there were six circular towers, three spaced along each of the two longer sides. Four towers were being fabricated at the Nigg Bay yard, plus another two at a shipyard somewhere near Edinburgh.

The problem was the steel, a very high strength killed carbon steel. Welding this steel required a lot of pre-heat and pre-heating a large tower in the open in not so sunny Scotland was difficult. And so the welding, when inspected, showed a propensity for cracking and given the safety margins needed on this first-of-a-kind design, the issues had to be addressed.

This meant the group I was in had to sit around most of the day with little to do. I was not keeping busy, so I started to dwell far too much on my family problems. Within two months, I was in bad shape. I rang my family doctor and he suggested an appointment late Friday afternoon.

I had had a word with the Coronal and slipped away for a long weekend. The doctor's examination did not go well. I was told to take two weeks rest at home, some strong medication to help with the grief that kept returning and an exercise programme. I asked the doctor to inform the Coronal and let him take care of matters concerning my absence.

I had two weeks at home, most of it spent either in bed or taking long walks, trying hard to get the stress of the last two years out of my system. The first weeks were very tough; just where the hell was I? Still, taking two weeks to calm down was a very wise move indeed. I did some maintenance work on one of my dinghies and that helped quite a lot.

Marianna did what she could to help and Carolyn enjoyed having me at home. It took most of the two weeks to recover, but recover I did. When I returned to the site at Nigg, some progress had been made, but still, my group had little to do.

The months dragged on through the winter. Then came a slight problem in that Marianne discovered the nice young boys in the local RAF station and they certainly discovered her. The fact that Carolyn came from school one day and found a Danish au pair snogging with some airman on the floor behind the big sofa should have prompted me to take much stronger action than I did. I didn't want to call her father, but that was a mistake.

And so, the inevitable occurred, the world population was going to increase by one in eight months time. The au pair agent gave me a hard time, which was her mistake as I set to putting her to rights and Marianne went home to her parents. What happened next I have no idea.

Another au pair called Allison arrived in the household and everything settled down once again.

It was during the Christmas shutdown I was relaxing at home when the phone rang half-way through a fascinating programme on nuclear power and its future in the UK. With the UK governments that come and go, I was surprised that any programme could conjecture on the future of nuclear power in our country. MPs have more important things to be involved with. Their expenses for example.

The caller asked very politely did I want to join a team of specialists to oversee a project in Brazil building offshore platforms. I grabbed the TV remote controller, pressing the off-button, twice. Was I interested, yes, but my home circumstances was going to take some fixing. The caller seemed to be most insistent that I do my very best, as his company would just love to have me join them. Hum, I thought, is this a true story?

To keep the conversation going I made positive waves and on receipt of a written offer, I would do all I could to satisfy his requirements. To my surprise, the paperwork duly arrived by express mail.

I had a long conversation with Johan's parents. It was a big ask to leave them in charge of the children, but Jim insisted I needed a new start and one must be bold. Surprised me, I can tell you.

19

MATTHEW HALL

Rio de Janeiro (1983 - 1984)

THE FIRST WEEK IN FEBRUARY 1983 found me travelling to London in the employ of Matthew Hall Ltd. based in the famous Tottenham Court Rd.

It would be a busy week, getting work visas from the Brazilian Consulate, visiting overpriced medical centres to check for various illnesses very few people had ever heard of, then receiving inoculations against all conditions and complaints, except poverty.

The volunteers going to South America were told that a number of UK banks had stumped-up loan finance for the development of a number of offshore oil production platforms in the Campos Basin, in the State of Rio de Janeiro. It would be our job to see how these projects progressed. There was, so we were told, a consortium of four companies, three Brazilian and one, ours, from the UK.

The deal offered included; a good tax-free salary, doubled when offshore, accommodation, a medical plan, membership of a sports and social club approved by the company, plus a monthly allowance of US$100. For the single men, an air ticket home every sixteen weeks. Any business flights would be provided by the company. What was not to like? Well, it was not going to be all sunshine and beaches. Anybody who thought it would be was, err, stupid.

What did seem strange when we were issued with a very useful indefinite visitor's visa for the USA. I used it once when I left Brazil. It got cancelled on the spot.

After a week skulking around London, the Aberdeen contingent returned to Scotland and told to prepare for our outbound journey via Amsterdam. There were dark rumours the directors of the company had made a visit to Brazil on Concorde, which if true, meant that the UK banks were paying a hefty fee for our services.

Ten days later, the Scottish contingent of Matthew Hall mustered at Aberdeen airport clutching one-way tickets to Rio de Janeiro. KLM was to be our host for the next fifteen hours; business class would have been nice. Fat chance, but the overnight flight from Amsterdam in a Jumbo Jet was quite comfortable.

We arrived at Rio and waited for some time while a visa agent took our documents and papers then disappeared into the Brazilian World of Immigration officialdom. That done, we passed the Arrivals Duty Free, which in 1983, resembled an American Cash & Carry outlet. Refrigerators and every other type of white goods were on sale. The duty-free allowance was US$500, and the objective of the Duty Free shop was to collect as much hard currency as possible, of which Brazil had a huge shortage.

Most of our group bought a box of Red Label at an amazing price compared to the UK. I don't like Red Label and I couldn't be bothered lugging more luggage. A bus took us all to a hotel one block back from the far end of Leme Beach, at the bottom of Copacabana. The hotel was OK, seen worse. There were a number of young ladies sitting around in the downstairs bar looking lonely and hopeful.

One of our number was a Macurian by the name of Big John and the second thing he did in the hotel was to drop his luggage on the bedroom floor. Strange behaviour, as on the journey out, he had told how his young wife, and I mean young, had just had his baby and would be unable to travel for some time. Later we learned that Big John had broken some kind of record, the time between leaving the airport and getting horizontal samba lessons in a hotel bedroom. The previous holder was most put out.

The group was given four days to rest-up and acclimatise, although Big John had already done that. Welcome to Brazil.

*

IT WAS A Saturday and someone had organised tickets for Maracanã Football stadium, the cup final between Flamengo FC and Santos FC. Eight of the Brazilian national squad would be playing. How could we miss the chance? The tickets were not the best, somewhere on the upper terrace of the stadium. Their location was never found.

Our group ended up lost on the lower level, under the overhang of the terrace above. The stadium had a formal capacity of a hundred and fifty thousand souls, but this match had at least two hundred thousand spectators. We found a VIP box full of Americans, so we asked nicely if we could sit on their back wall. Sure, no problem, have a beer they said. Nice guys. The sitting was just a touch awkward as one had to lean forward to get the overhang out of one's eye line. Otherwise, it wasn't a bad place to watch the match.

What happened next, during the game, was well beyond anybody's previous experience.

The first thing to notice was the seats directly under the edge of the overhang were still empty, about three rows deep around the entire circumference of the stadium. Slowly but surely, as the time for the match approached, hesitant spectators, producing a strange array of plastic attire, took the vacant seats. Can you guess what was going on?

All around the pitch was a deep moat. Four scruffy individuals made it across to the pitch side carrying a number of articles. The police did not intervene. OK, Now what?

Two of them started to light a small bonfire, as the other two started to construct something which turned out to be a hot-air balloon made from thin lengths of bamboo and very light paper. As they progressed with their industry the crowd cheered them on.

As the match started, the noise was just incredible. As the hot air balloon was held over the fire, a length of line was attached to the balloon. The balloon reached operating temperature then rose magnificently into the air with a huge Flamengo FC flag hanging from it. Even more noise from the entire stadium.

As the balloon rose upwards into the sky, the balloon self-ignited, resulting in a large ball of flame, with large football club flag hanging from it; last seen accelerating very quickly in the direction of the flight path of the local airport, Santos Dumont.

From my angle, it looked kind of close. The airline pilots didn't seem to waver; perhaps it was normal because this is Brazil. What was not a hundred per cent normal was the city in the grip of a drought. Everywhere was very dry. Where was Nero when you needed his music?

Almost at the same time, less than a minute into the match, a goal was scored. Two hundred thousand spectators roared and shouted.

Make that one hundred and ninety-nine thousand, nine hundred and ninety-nine. I was just stunned by the noise, unbelievable.

After the half-time interval, the match got down to serious business. It was close, who was going to win? The crowd shouted their encouragement, offering no doubt, many interesting suggestions. On the far side of the stadium, on the upper level, I saw the Santos FC football supporters in their brightly coloured strips.

They took to hurling large quantities of team-coloured paper tape over the edge of the upper level, thus spoiling the view of the spectators below. A thoughtful spectator produced a cigarette lighter and a fire started. The crowd seemed to enjoy the spectacle. As the fire started to spread, a genuine British fire engine, a very old Denis in excellent condition, arrived on the pitch to extinguish the flames.

The crowd at the front of the upper level started to urinate on the fireman below. The lead fireman whistled to his man controlling the firewater pump, which went to full pressure. The fire-fighting team almost swept a number of those taking, or rather giving, the piss to their deaths. More jeers and whistles from the crowd.

The football players concentrated on their match. The final score was 4-2 on aggregate to Flamengo. The entire spectacle was surreal.

My stay in the hotel stretched to just over two weeks as the real estate lady trailed me around a number of apartments. I eventually choose an apartment at the end of Botofogo Beach, a huge building in yellow with thirty floors. An apartment on the twenty-ninth floor seemed suitable. It looked down at Flamengo Park, the local municipal airport and Guanabara Bay, with fabulous views. The elderly windows rattled in the rain and let in a lot of noise from the two major highways that passed the building on either side, but Rio is a noisy city whereever you go to.

Still, it was comfortable, nice furniture and a huge bathroom, with a marble bath that took over forty minutes to fill-up. The apartment's location was handy for the many bus routes and being some distance from the poor areas, safe. In fact, on one side of the complex was the official residence of a senior police chief, with its own security guard.

The work experience was not as expected. The Brazilian's were going full tilt at the project. This was their third project for the Campos Basin and surely they knew what they were doing. Best to sit back and get involved slowly.

The main problem with this 'too good to believe contract' was that us UK specialists had to work the same long hours as the Brazilians. Getting up in the middle of the night, OK 6am, to catch a bus at 7am and then cross to the other side of the Guanabara Bay was not mentioned in London.

Let me explain the daily journey. Guanabara Bay is large, all 400 sq. kilometres of it. There is a bridge that crosses the bay from Rio de Janeiro city to Niteroi, a biggish city on the other side. When Rio was the Capital of the Country, Niteroi was capital of the State. The bridge is named after a deserving president named Costa e Silva, which translates to 'it cost a lot of silver to build it'. It's almost fifteen kilometres long, not including the approach roads. Not only is it long, it's huge, so huge that an unloaded super-tanker can pass under the centre span with ease.

There is also a very busy ferry service. Each day ten million people cross from one side of the bay to the other, usually at the same time. If you don't believe, best check it out. Enjoy the experience. We sure as hell didn't.

*

Life in the Office

WELL, LIFE IN the office was certainly different, plus there was the problem of Culture Shock. This is a well-known phenomenon that I had never heard of. During my time in the RN, wherever I went, the local population spoke English, as they should.

Now, our language was not that common in Brazil, but it was used extensively in our industry by our fellow Brazilian colleagues simply because our industry is so international. The company took steps and employed briefly, a lady teacher to help us through the maze. The dedicated expats, especially those who had served in the Middle East, sat in silence and generally thought the whole process was unnecessary. What was wrong with just shouting at your maid: works everywhere else.

However, we Brits were on parade and there were a few of our number that did not take this into account. The first thing to recognise was the fact that Brazilians can be very nationalistic. It is a very patrimonial society so, despite their smiling faces they can be quite formal.

The big difference was remuneration. The Brits were on mega bucks compared to most of the Brazilians, even up to quite a high level of their management. The clue was in the fact that our US$100 bucks a month living allowance was a high wage for the Brazilians, especially as the Brits were provided with good quality accommodation in Rio de Janeiro's Zona

Sul region on top of the allowance. That alone put our senior engineer's remuneration way above the Japanese Brazilian project manager.

And of course, Brazil, like the USA, is an immigrant country so underneath the surface there are many different cultures, not only from foreign countries but from the many different states in Brazil. It's a big country, you can put the whole Europe into the outline of Brazil, with space left over.

Our group had no direct control over the activities of the Brazilian group. We Brits were not universally welcomed by some, but most of us got on well together, which is as it should be. If one had a friendly disposition, there was generally no problem. Language could be a problem and to be fair, many of us tried to learn the Brazilian Portuguese, which is very different to European Portuguese

Those that had learnt French at secondary school had an advantage. As for me, it was far too late at age forty, with a minimal aptitude for the language learning process. There was a great story regarding a very educated Scotsman who was one of our Project Engineers. He had the language skills, so he attended the consortium monthly meetings with the client Petrobrás, the state oil company and their hierarchy, all senior oilmen.

So this guy, on behalf of the consortium, gave a very eloquent presentation to the Petrobrás seniors and when he finished he thought he had done quite well as he saw a lot of smiling faces. During a natural break for coffee and that other thing, he asked one of the Petrobrás people he knew reasonably well and asked why everybody was smiling. He was told, 'They all know where you are learning your Portuguese,' which obviously meant the night time horizontal classroom syndrome. Classic.

So, the Brits were in Brazil to impress. Some certainly did that. I'm quite sure it's not what the UK Company director had in mind though. Heavy drinking at lunch time, in some hole-in-the-wall under the local viaduct, would have been one activity frowned upon. Still, if our people were not under the cosh working hard, but just trying to make the day go by, what else would happen? But having a fully fuel short-arsed Scotsman going around the office after a lunch time session asking his Brazilian counterparts for the Portuguese words on how to perform oral sex on a woman, was, in my opinion, beyond the pale.

*

DURING THE WEEK, the group caught the company bus early in the morning and by the time we got back to the Rio, it was always dark, even in mid-summer. The bus would drop-off the single men at the Taberna Atlantic on Avenida Atlantica overlooking the beach and close to the thirty-story Meridien Hotel, Copacabana.

The Taberna Atlantica became that home from home. The Brits made it quite famous. We acquired our own waiter called Macae. Actually his real name was 'something-de-something-de-something else de Francisco', but Jock Fraser asked where did he come from and the answer was 'Macae', the Petrobrás base and port for offshore support, about a hundred kilometres up the coast. From then on, this was the old guy's name, even for all the years after the Brits went home.

It was necessary to understand the system for the beachside Tabernas. The waiter, in practical terms, purchases the food from the restaurant owner and sells it on to the customer plus ten per cent. Don't pay the waiter? Not a good thing for a person on poor income.

The singles group indulged in a lot of activities that I avoided. Drinking too much was the first, the beer was cheap, the local rocket fuel from sugar cane brandy called 'Agua Dente' even cheaper. The cheaper version could have methanol content, as the distilling process is not always the best. I always asked to see the bottle first. The Brazilian like it mixed with lime juice and a lot of sugar, called *Caipirinha* and they are extremely potent. The good quality products are very nice, triple distilled, best consumed neat or *puro* with ice to split the aromas.

During the drinking session, some would eat, others got blitzed. I always ate first, with a couple of glasses of Choppe or draft beer. Following the drinking session, the singles group would gravitate to the other side of the main road to a bar called Mabs, where young ladies of all shapes and sizes, and many differing hues, would linger looking hopeful and available.

The leading light in this procession was an Irishman called Wee Jimmy, a tough little blighter who used the statue of Christ the Redeemer to navigate his way around the city when his navigation skills had been degraded by the devil's brew.

Jimmy was famous for a few social firsts, like waking up at midday on a Saturday to find, Monday's young lady, through to Friday's young lady, all staring down at him, wondering what next. He'd thrown a hissy' fit, then thrown them all out. His first steady girlfriend was Regina 2, whose father was a very senior police person. When he threw her out one night in an alcohol-fuelled moment, Regina 2 was very upset and his demise was expected in the short term.

He ended up with Regina 1, known as rock hard, due to the interesting medical enhancement she had done to her breasts. Meanwhile, Big John also played the game until six months later, when his wife and child arrived. Anybody spilling the beans was promised a facial rearrangement of a severe kind.

Most of the married single status guys had live-in girlfriends. The fun game was to remove said girlfriend and any possible trace of her existence before the wife and/or family arrived during the school holidays. Forensic skills were required. Needless to say, there were a few moments of tension between all parties.

*

FALLING IN LOVE Again. Eventually, I soon tired of this never-ending show and looked for more suitable company, which arrived in the form of Flavio. Flavio and I shared the same responsibilities at work. He had worked in the USA for a number of years so his English was good. He lived near Sao Paulo, but unlike the UK where travelling men get accommodation assistance, when working away from home, the Brazilians were on their own and he spent his evenings in some hovel in Niteroi.

Many times, I had offered him the use of my second bedroom during the week. He could even commute on the company bus. Well, it took a long time before he accepted the offer. His acceptance came at the end of the week when his accommodation made him quite ill. Offering a fellow worker a bed just for the weekdays seemed the natural thing to do.

With Flavio's arrival, the bars of Copacabana were left behind, as we explored the other districts, mostly in and around Flamengo, with its magnificent park alongside the shore of Guanabara Bay, a safe area with a welcome lack of favelas. A solid middle class and working class district.

At the weekends, I would visit the Clube Federal, parked on top a mountain at the far end of Leblon, the last and most expensive of the beach districts in the city. The company paid for the membership, but I would pay the monthly charges. There, one could swim, play tennis and meet up the British married couples with their delightful children.

If you thought it was only the single men enjoying the sins of the flesh in Rio de Janeiro sex charged environment, the married couples were not much better. I heard rumours about wife swapping. Without being too unkind, most of the wife's would hardly rate a crate of decent London IPA.

Then, there were the husbands who would drop their family off at the club, then take their car to be serviced. On a Saturday? Some cars seemed to have a very intensive maintenance schedule. One husband had a rather embarrassing moment when his highly maintained car broke down due to, the mechanic said, 'a distinct lack of maintenance'.

The 'garage', I later found was downtown and called the Green Frog, a male boutique dedicated to the art of restoring the male species to its former glory. Depending to which floor the customer repaired, to services ranged, on the lower floor from the sauna and whole body massage and hairdressing, to other services depending on how high the customer wished to reach. Many years later, I found where it was, when visiting a ninth-floor office of a Christmas Tree manufacture and looked out the window. The view overlooked a veranda where the girls took a break from their various activities to have a cigarette.

Wives who complained at length telling their better half, 'They were going home to mother', would find their bags packed and a flight ticket back to Blighty. But then, this was Brazil.

It is a fact, that in warm climates the population has more of one sex than the other. Eskimo's are the opposite of hot Latin countries. This reminds me of a story some years ago when Johan started to take driving lessons in Morayshire. Having confirmed where the instructor could and could not put his hands, they got on quite well.

One day, the instructor revealed that his son worked on a drilling rig that was being relocated to Brazil. The father asked his son if he was taking the wife and kids. The reply, 'You don't take a sandwich to a banquet.'

Anyway, came the seventh day of June, 'A date that will forever live in infamy.'

Flavio pestered me to take him to a pub in Ipanema, your trendy café society area of Rio. The pub was called Lord Jim's, owned by an American with a British wife from Hampshire.

I never really had the urge to go, it was normally full of Americans trying to play darts, but the girls there tended to be bi-lingual secretaries interested to practice this strange language called English.

So, I said, 'OK, let's go and get it over with.' We'll take the bus and off we went. When we got there the place was empty. I ordered the beers and looked around. Sitting over on the window seat were two ladies deep in conversation. Brazilian ladies are always deep in conversation – it's what they do.

Flavio and I were leaning on the bar looking out of the window, when one of the ladies looked up, smiled at me and what a smile it was too. I smiled back and then she spoke to her friend. Something was going on here. I sent Flavio across to ask the smiling lady two questions, would they like to join us and does she speak any English.

Flavio returned smiling. The answers were yes and no. We went and sat down with them and Flavio made the introductions. Lights were illuminating brightly, gosh I thought, not again. Her name was Sonia Montenegro Vieira, a professor no less, with a good job and salary. Strange, I found out later she was just ten-days older than Johan.

Flavio also found out that this was the first time they had visited this bar. Sonia had never even heard of it. Flavio told them this was also our first visit to Lord Jim's, so our meeting was a thousand to one chance.

And so the great romance began and by the end of this book and beyond, it is still alive and well.

*

IN THE RUN-UP to the Scottish summer school holidays, I thought about whether I would fly to the UK, or perhaps the children could come to Brazil. I had the first of my air ticket money in my purse and the Portuguese airline, TAP, or 'Take another Plane', offered a good deal for school kids.

The company travel agent cut the deal for me, so the two girls came to Brazil. Jim and Margret thought it was a good idea and it would give them a break too. I had wondered what I would do with two children for the two weeks. Fortunately, the problem solved itself.

My first date with Sonia was the evening after we first met. The Meridien Hotel had a French restaurant on the top floor, with fabulous views along Copacabana Beach. With a flurry of my English/Portuguese dictionary, we arranged to meet in the lobby of the hotel.

The restaurant was very classy, the French food was fine dining, or small portions, which was just as well, as Sonia thought we were only meeting for drinks and had eaten before leaving home. Subtle music was played by a jazz combo that was truly the best. I listen to a lot of jazz, mainly because father listened to nothing else. The pianist, a very old

Negro musician, was playing a mixture of Art Tatum and Oscar Peterson, the two world greats. A very memorable experience.

Sonia was delightful company. I told her, as best I could, that the children were coming to Brazil on holiday and the company travel agent was suggesting a tour to the south of the country to see the waterfalls at Foz do Iguacu, then the new super dam at Itaipu that sat astride the mighty River Parana not far away. Both are world wonders.

On the way back, we would stop-off at Curitiba, then go to Santos and back to Rio de Janeiro by bus. Would she like to come? Sonia said she would check her work programme, but her smiling face said, 'Yes'. Brilliant.

*

JUST AFTER I met Sonia, I ventured into the world of driving in the city of Rio de Janeiro. I bought what I could afford, which wasn't much. I acquired a VW Brasilia, which is an estate car version of the VW Fusca, known to one and all as the VW Beatle. It is a poorly made car that comes with the same engine at the rear. It had four wheels on the outside and four seats on the inside. It is the ultimate example of the well-known maxim, 'a second class ride is better than a first class walk' and it is theft proof. No need to wonder why.

It came in a muddy version of gold, and it hadn't been polished since new. It had, however, been regularly washed, by the rain. Like I care. My first drive was just before midnight, which went well as I didn't hit anything or get lost. I insured the car via the company insurance agent and he gave me a good deal on the premium.

One day, I am driving with Sonia to Clube Federal by way of passing the Botanical Gardens. The Imperial palm trees reach into the sky to an incredible height. My speed is low, well lower than the municipal buses, who all drive as thou the devil himself was chasing them. Quite why the devil would chase a Brazilian bus driver is a question I let fall.

An impatient driver, the norm in Rio, pulled out in front with no warning, no indication, no nothing. I cannot swerve to miss him as an overtaking bus, at warp speed, is poised to send us all for an interview at the pearly gates. The resulting crash wrecks my car and the other car has a front wing and steering that are badly damaged

The driver of the other car is most upset that I didn't miss him. I tell him that the accident is his fault. He agrees one hundred per cent, but that does not alter the fact I should have missed him. Brazilian driving lesson number one. It's the mentality. Sonia cooled things down and took all the necessary particulars. My VW Brasilia is towed away to become spare parts for other VW Brasilia's that are still whole.

Fortunately, no one is hurt, well the other driver's ego is severely dented, like I care. In the office on the following Monday, paperwork in hand, I start the process of making an insurance claim. Everything goes quiet and the insurance man disappears. Now what? It turns out that the company's insurance agent has been trousering the premiums. I am in effect driving with forged documents, which is a serious offence. I could have been in deep-do-do had the police arrived on the scene.

I receive a generous settlement, which does two things. It makes me happy, as I can now afford a better second-hand car and I become an accomplice in a cover-up. But then, this is Brazil.

Next weekend, Sonia and I take a look at a very nice second-hand VW Passat, in red. It has air-conditioning too and with summer fast approaching that is the bonus of the day.

*

IN THE WEEKS up to the Scottish school holidays, we spent our evenings and weekends together. During the week Flavio would come along, but there were no late evenings in a land where everything starts late. Sonia was living with her brother and she had an early start each day, as did we all. My second courtship became a mirror image of the first one and I loved it.

I became a bit nervous the day when the children were due to arrive. There was no real problem in their travel as the airline staff would escort them safely. However, on their arrival at Rio de Janeiro, there was an excessive delay in them coming out from airside.

Eventually, they made it, Carolyn was glad to see me and rushed-up and gave me a big hug. I asked what went wrong. In a calm voice, she told me that the airline staff had processed them through immigration OK, but there was a big confusion getting their luggage.

Carolyn told me that nobody was listening to their requests and nothing seemed to be happening. I asked her what did she do next?

'Oh,' I just found a clear space and start crying and sobbing big time holding onto my sister. The ladies at the baggage desk all started rushing around in ever decreasing circles and the problem was solved very quickly.

'Works every time,' she said smiling.

Wow, what a clever girl, soon to have her sixteenth birthday.

It was late when we all arrived back at my apartment, where we all met up with Sonia. The introductions took about ten seconds, after which Daddy became redundant. An early night was needed by everyone and Sonia slipped away home.

The next day was a slow day. My daughters had survived a long three-leg journey from Inverness to London, then to Lisbon and finally the long flight to Rio de Janeiro. The two girls slept late and so did I. I was so pleased to see them both here safe and sound.

After a late breakfast, we took things easy as there was just two days before the long flight to Foz do Iguaçu. The first holiday together since when? It took a while to remember, the holiday in the Isle of Man.

Carolyn looked through the holiday programme. A flight to Foz do Iguaçu via Curitiba, stay at the Hotel das Cataratas, the red hotel, very close to the waterfalls. I told her that the waterfalls would be awesome, as Brazil was under the effect of a very strong *El Nino*. The rainfall down south had been exceptional. Good weather was promised in the forecast, hopefully, a true indication.

Then, there was the new dam, Itaipu Hydroelectric Dam, the world's largest, destined to supply the cities of Sao Paulo and Rio de Janeiro. As Foz do Iguaçu was very close to the three borders, a visit into Paraguay was included, but not Argentina, not sure why –something about some offshore islands somewhere.

Next, would be a short return flight to Curitiba and then spectacular railway journey to the coast, then back to Sao Paulo by air followed by the bus down to Santos and stay at a beachside hotel, then take the bus back to Rio de Janeiro.

'Is that all,' Carolyn said, as she ducked my not so lightning backhander. We laughed, glad to be together. I told her if she was a good girl she would win a big prize.

'What big prize?' she asked hopefully.

'A week in Skegness.'

'And second prize?' she asked.

'Two weeks.'

There were plenty of things to do before the holiday travelling around Brazil. The two girls needed a few summer clothes despite the fact that June is mid-winter in Brazil. It would be good for them to look their best in some new togs and the prices were very reasonable.

They also needed to adjust to their new surroundings. It was common sense to learn how to be a traveller and not a tourist in this huge strange country. Always be aware of your surroundings, wearing nothing you would want to lose.

Two days later we had an early start. Sonia arrived with the taxi and we all piled in. Getting out of town to the main airport was a lot easier than the millions of workers trying to get into town. Sonia took care of the checking-in process and after a quick coffee and a snack, we boarded the flight.

The flight to Curitiba took just over an hour and a half. On the flight, an attentive cabin crew served the first of many snacks, always a 'misto frio' and a glass of guarana, a very popular soda made in Brazil from the fruit of the same name. (Misto frio is a non-toasted cheese and ham sandwich.)

That they continued serving passengers despite the bumpy ride was impressive. I spoke to the pretty air hostess and asked, 'Excuse me, this Boeing 737 seems to be much larger than I remember.'

She replied, 'This is a Boeing 757, we have the first two in South America from the American production line. We used them to transport the many workers at the new dam project in Iguaçu.'

Before landing at Curitiba, we were all served another misto frio, and a glass of guarana. After the shortstop at Curitiba, the pretty airhostess asked if we would like any refreshment. I asked for a misto frio and a glass of guarana, full in the knowledge that's all they had. Sonia and Carolyn laughed out loud. Daddy's humour was getting into gear.

We arrived at the hotel in time for a quick look at the waterfalls. Never seen so much water since Mother insisted I put some in a glass of rum I had acquired on Daddy's birthday.

After a restful night, the tour continued. The waterfalls were seen in all their glory. The waterfall consists of a 'throat', (el Boca) on the Brazilian side, followed by a river that has a number of separate waterfalls along the Argentinean side of the river. There is just one additional waterfall on the Brazilian side. This fall consists of the drop to a ledge, about ninety metres wide, followed by another fall into the river below. This ledge has a walkway for the tourists to get soaking wet on whilst looking up at the main fall itself.

The guide showed us what was left of this walkway, which stands on pillars about one metre tall with handrails about one and a half metres elevation. At the height of the inundation, the water depth on this flat ledge was apparently one metre above the hand railings. The walkway was virtually destroyed; its remains were very badly damaged.

It was impressive all the same. The river was very angry, the water was full of mud and there was so much spray that the main fall was hard to make out. In fact, there was so much spray that the helicopters that scare the living daylights out of their customers, at a hundred bucks ago, by flying into the throat of the main fall and pulling up and out through the spray, stopped flying.

The four of us repaired to the café that is just upstream of the main fall. The large notice says, 'Don't feed the Fish' is congruous, as the fish would have to be Olympic standard to catch any food and then not be swept over the fall.

In the afternoon, the tour took us to see the Itaipu Hydroelectric Dam (Foz do Iguacu). Much had been written about this dam, the world's greatest 'white elephant' and other complete rubbish.

It had been built in an amazing four years, not including the generators, of which there would be twenty in total, sixteen on the Brazilian side and four on the Paraguay side. The whole project was colossal. Putting a dam across the mighty River Parana could be nothing but colossal.

With no generators installed, the river flowed over the spillway, way over on the far side of our viewing position. At the end of the spillway was a 'kick', throwing the water high into the air, a measure to aerate the water and diminish the erosion of the river bed. The thunder of the flowing water is loud and all invasive.

Note: I have seen satellite photographs of this spillway, which are quite clear.

Brazil gets eighty per cent of its electricity from hydro-power; some of these projects attract great controversy from the environmentalists. However, this dam provides power to the most productive regions of the planet, Sao Paulo State and Rio de Janeiro State, which can't be a bad thing. Some weeks later, a most impressive photograph is published in the Brazilian magazine Veja of a thousand-ton rotor for the first generator being lowered into place. On top of the rotor, were a large number of persons clearly enjoying a social event, but then this is Brazil.

We return to the hotel for an early night. The children are still playing catch-up from their long international journey. The next day after breakfast comes the bus tour. Not too early thank goodness. The journey to Ciudad del Este, Paraguay is thankfully short. We see the real South

MEMORIES AND FORGETFULNESS

America, a one-horse town that the horse left long ago. It is the centre of huge export market smuggling everything Brazilians want to buy on the cheap. This trade makes the border crossing take longer than it should. Still, we look around, take some photographs and head back to the bus which is thankfully parked next to a café.

*

THE FLIGHT BACK to Curitiba brought nothing to record, but what a nice city. Founded by immigrants in the seventeenth century, it has prospered greatly. Many Volvo motorcars were to be seen, an expensive import. Having checked-in to the hotel we enjoyed a gentle walk around the well laid-out centre of the city.

The hotel manager recommended an Italian restaurant located in a residential district. So, nothing ventured, we all piled into a taxi, another Volvo and wow what a super experience awaited. The décor, the ambience, the food was just the best. Our holiday was improving by the day.

The next day, tickets in hand for the ride of a lifetime, the *Serra Verde Express*. This proved to be a German-built rail car, with massive 'add-on pak' disk brakes on the four corners of the car. The route climbs steadily out of Curitiba, then in the space of a few kilometres, it drops five hundred metres, going down a single track that literally clings to the side of the mountains. The views are enormous.

There is a small siding on the steepest section of the track. The rail car pulls into it and stops. Everybody gets out to look at the views; one is easily well over two hundred kilometres to the east. I look up; there is nothing but the mountain stretching towards the heavens. I look down at a sheer drop of many hundreds of metres. The route is like a switchback as it twists and turns through the mountains. Just who surveyed this route? Apparently, the Jocks on mules that did not have a death wish to fall off the ledges that were eventually joined up to make the railway possible.

My informant on such matters is a fellow middle-aged Brit who we met on the flight up from Foz do Iguaçu. He is David, the manager of a sugar estate in Haiti. The estate is huge and they use a lot of movable railway track to transport their product to the processing factory. He is accompanied by a younger lady from the Dominican Republic. She has lightly coloured skin and the biggest set of Bristol's I have ever seen. Unsupported, they droop not one centimetre. Her thin low cut tee shirt is also noticed by, err, everybody. Apparently, she has good conversation, but she ignores Sonia who can understand most of what she does say in her version of Spanish.

I search for my camera, but Sonia has purloined it to take photographs of the children standing in front of the magnificent views. One magnificent view is confined to memory, still working well, if slightly dimmed by the many years.

The guide tells the group he is sorry we will miss the experience of a lifetime, which is when the tourist railcar is hiding in this siding and a freight train passes-by heading north to Curitiba. The trains carry heavy freight and need four huge diesel engines to haul it. By the time it reaches this siding, the train has little speed, the engines are on maximum power, their turbo-chargers are white hot on the point of exploding and the whole mountain shakes.

I muttered something about, 'Oh what a shame, I would have really liked to have that experience.' Carolyn digs me in the ribs, knowing full well we are all ready to imagine this treat but to experience it, hum, perhaps not.

We continue our journey and the rail car stops at a siding in Morretes, a small town. The location is called Ponte de Ferro. There is an old stationhouse selling banana juice in plain brown beer bottles that have been improved to 88% proof. I try an offered sample; sure would cure a toothache, that's for certain.

I noticed a waiting freight train ready to depart with four huge diesel engines being wound up to full operating temperature. The noise becomes incredible and the ground starts to shake. The signal goes to green and nobody, but nobody has seen a heavily loaded twenty-wagon freight train disappear that fast down the track, the driver desperate to build his speed before he hits the slope on the journey up to Curitiba.

Sonia takes the girls around the back of the station, where they sell yummy snacks and coffee that is too strong. I ask for a big cup of hot water to dilute the beverage otherwise the children can't drink it. With the amount of sugar in the coffee, the girls will get a big high and end up in the overhanging branches of a tall tree.

The journey continued towards our destination, Paranguá, a famous colonial city and port. Our journey ends in the tourist sector of the city, which means there are lots of stalls selling stuff, local foods, basket wear, et al. The visit is enchanting. At the end of a very pleasant day, a comfortable bus arrives and our group piles in. The road back to Curitiba sweeps magnificently up the mountain along a new road.

At the hotel, we collapse in the bar to refresh ourselves. My two daughters are holding up well, but the holiday has a tight schedule. It more like an assault course, but I explain that trying to see Brazil in two weeks is a tough call. Anyway, I assure them that in Santos nothing is planned other than a day on the beach

The next morning, our travel arrangements work well, but it is late when we arrive in Santos. Another early night, after a visit to the bar for suitable drinks and something to eat for both children and adults.

Santos is Santos. It's mid-week so the beaches are empty. At the weekend they will be full to overflowing. So we relax and it does everyone good. The two girls assault the ice cream seller on a regular basis and splash about in the sea. Sonia sits quietly with me by her side, getting some sun on her very attractive legs. Later, I join in with the swimmers, Sonia can't come because, in the first place she declines to get her hair wet and someone has to guard our clothes, bags and documents on the beach.

That night is barbecue night, a genuine Brazilian Churrasqueira that serves their meat in traditional style, on the ends of long swords with a waiter who slices the cuts to order. Sonia attacks the salad bar. I attack the man with the yummy sausages. The children enjoy it all too.

The next day is the long ride in the bus back to Rio de Janeiro. Long distance coaches in Brazil are very comfortable. This one takes the back way out of Santos to climb the escarpment up to the Dutra, the main Sao Paulo – Rio de Janeiro road. The coach passes through some beautiful countryside, but when it reaches the Dutra, everyone drifts off to sleep.

There is a mid-journey stop at a Posto. I remind the children to stay close. The bus spends only a limited time at the Posto so be quick in the loo and then there is time for a quick snack. We re-board the bus at the bidding of an impatient driver. Sleep returns to us all.

As the coach descends the escarpment into Rio de Janeiro the magnificent views are interrupted by the rain. The smell of brake linings being burnt by overloaded trucks as they crawl very slowly down the steep slope invade the coach. The road is very sinuous, any mistake and there are no escape lanes to help.

We arrive back at the apartment and say goodbye to Sonia as she has to rush home to get ready for whatever. For us, the next day is do nothing day.

With only three days left of their holiday, I take things easy. It is winter in Rio de Janeiro and the weather is cool and calm. After a slow morning, the three of us take the rack railway up to the statue of Christ the Redeemer. Considering what's going on below in the city, there must be a lot of redeeming going on.

The views are spectacular as always. One can never visit this place too often. We eat in that evening, I have some British grub left over, baked beans and other UK delights. The custard goes down a treat.

The end of the girl's holiday is in sight. There was so much left to see, but they have seen plenty in a short time. In the morning we go to the Clube Federal for a swim and have lunch. In the afternoon, we meet up with Sonia and her mother Risette, a wonderful grey haired lady long in her years.

We all enjoy afternoon coffee and sweetmeats at the local café and then head to Sugar Loaf Mountain. There are two cable car rides to the top, which is always exciting. The cars sway in the afternoon sea breeze. It's quite an experience. On the second ride, we look down at the brave rock climbers roping their way to the top of the mountain. Rather them than me was the general opinion.

The next day is the last full day and a special treat for Carolyn. I have organised a party in Clube Federal for her 16th Birthday. My, how grown-up she looks. Our friends and some of Sonia's family are there too. It's a splendid occasion in a wonderful setting.

*

SUNDAY, THE DAY of their return to Bonny Scotland and my two daughters thankfully lie-in during the morning, getting as much rest as possible. As they sleep I have done what packing I can. I have a special bag for them to keep in the cabin full of little treats for them both. I telephone Jim and Margret to tell them all is well and the girls have had a great but busy holiday. They will need to rest to get over their great experience. I slip some duty-free into Carolyn's suitcase. A bottle of whisky for her grandfather and two presents for Margret.

It's time to go, the girls are dressed and ready for their long journey. Lisbon is their first stop, an easy nine hours. Then to London and finally to Inverness. The girls are happy; they start chattering on their way to the airport. Sonia is chatting away too. I am so pleased to see that everyone is getting on very well together. Hopefully, my sad days are over; thanks to Jim and Margret making the opportunity come true.

I reveal to the chattering classes Sonia and I will see them in Thurso for New Year. This is news for all three of them. I endure the usual pain of parting at the airport. The airline lady who will escort them to the aircraft via the immigration desk is given a word or two from Sonia. I understand most of it and relax that they are in good hands.

With tears and kisses, they disappear airside, as I promised to call as soon as they get to Rafford. They arrived, safe and sound with no problem. I felt very relieved at the news.

*

Carnaval Time

CARNIVAL TIME IN Rio de Janeiro is famous and rightly so. It is the most amazing spectacle I have ever seen. The MH team's arrival in Brazil was just after the 1983 event. Each day the company bus would pass through Tunnel St. Barbara and proceed along the elevated road to the Niteroi Bridge passing the Sambadrome.

The city had decided to remove the existing temporary stadium, constructed from scaffold and board that, mostly, leant against the wall of the Brahma Brewery. The city fathers turned to the famous Brazilian architect Oscar Niemeyer to design a permanent stadium.

With just over a year to build a ninety-thousand seat facility, the contractor certainly took his time just to clear the site, over five months. As construction started the MH team members who had the task of progress measurement got to work and the conclusion was the stadium couldn't be built in time.

However, this is Brazil, and the two things that are never going to happen in Rio de Janeiro is the election of a corruption-free Governador and State Assembly and Carnival to be late.

Mind you, it was a close run thing, but Brazil does not do early, they just cannot do it. In the last six weeks more progress was made than the previous six months, always the sign of a good project.

The second memory comes from the 1984 Carnival. Carnival is a huge event that also covers the weeks before the actual start, always on a Wednesday, through to the weekend. Traffic becomes a nightmare, the city is full of tourists and prices rise. What's not to like?

Most sensible residents of the city bugger off and that's what I did with my new intended. The colonial city of São Joãl del Rei, in Minas Geriâs, also holds a carnaval parade because carnaval is just that, a street parade.

With luck, we managed to find a position to watch that did not involve parting with any funds. We mingled with the Blocos, as each competing samba school is known and wow, what a lot of pretty girls, all with a can of beer in their hand having a great time. It was all very natural.

At the head of each Bloco is a very ornately dressed couple with the Samba School's flag. They are followed by the Samba School's carnaval queen and her assistant. Then, follows different blocs of dancers in a huge variety of dresses depending upon the theme.

There will be a percussion band; the larger schools in the Rio de Janeiro parade can have up to six hundred. They make a wondrous noise. But the singer with the microphone has the power to be heard over anything else that goes on. In a BBC TV programme some years ago, a lady without any hearing informed that being deaf was not a problem when attending Carnaval.

We watched three schools start their parade and one of the schools had a Carnaval Queen who was the spitting image of Audrey Hepburn at eighteen years of age.

The other untold delight about the city of São Joãl del Rei is the original railway station and the railway line to Tiradentes. It is the oldest working railway in the world. Engine #1 sits in the station as a static display, an American Baldwin built in 1881. And more surprisingly, it is oil-fuelled. A short walk down the track is a genuine engine roundhouse, full of old engines, most of which could work, but of all things, I found a 1950's UK built Deltic diesel engine in bright red. Absolutely magnificent.

We took the journey back into the past, the smell, the steam and no grit to get into the eyes. We wandered around Tiradentes cobbled streets, enjoyed the coffee and other delights, then caught the last train back to town.

The drive back to Rio de Janeiro was quite interesting. Having struggled down the very poor road that was the main north-south highway, I reached a section of new dual carriageway that had been constructed along the side of a valley.

The car picked up speed and as we swept along a long slow curve my partner said, 'Where's the road?' I looked twice then saw a big section of the dual carriageway was down the bottom of the hill. Late braking occurred. I must have been dreaming.

What had happened was the *El Nino* effect. Huge amounts of rain had found fissures in the red earth, which become quikothropic and a huge slab of hill-side had descended into the valley. A temporary road had been carved out to reach the other side of the great divide and it took weeks to wash the mud from underneath the car.

Our arrival back in Rio was well timed. A group of MH team obtained tickets for the super-championship, which is run after the main event. An amazing experience, as only the top schools take place. The sound of the samba infuses into every molecule of the body. It can take you over which is a little scary.

*

Time to go Offshore

THE RETURN TO the office was exciting, or perhaps it wasn't. There was some good news when an invoice arrived on my desk from the company travel agent for the holiday we had all enjoyed so much. When booked a month ago, I was offered a discount and a firm price in the local currency. But, the price in US dollars looked very reasonable, so no problem. And now one month later, with the Brazilian currency being devalued at a straight-line rate of two point five per cent a week, I am also another ten per cent ahead. I pay this invoice willingly.

It is here that I should explain the Brazilian currency system. Our monthly living allowance of US$100 was adjusted each month for devaluation. When I arrived in February 1983 the allowance received was about Cr$340,000 cruzeiros and when I departed in May 1984 it was about Cr$1.2 million. But the financial system in Brazil was such that there were multiple indices that related everything to the relevant indices and if you had a bank account, the rate offered for savings included an adjustment for the devaluation so that the price of most things stayed, more or less, the same when compared to the US dollar. For example, house prices were always quoted in USD. There was also a very efficient black market. People could make a lot of money out of inflation. For the poor people without banking, the value of their income dropped accordingly, so this money was always spent just to try and survive. I remember some years later an old farmer, who lived in the back of beyond, died. His relatives found a sack of old money, dirty torn notes, with a face value, in US dollar terms, of over two hundred thousand dollars. Had they been able to change the notes for the latest Brazilian currency the value was peanuts, I forget the amount, say twenty bucks.

I am also informed that the project is moving ahead at a rapid rate. The jacket has been installed on the seabed and the Heerema crane barge, *Balder* is due to arrive back in the harbour at the weekend. There is to be a reception on-board during the change-around. This sounded interesting. Friday evening is the time for the project party when all the other partners will be there too. I make my excuses to Sonia, as this will be a boy's night out.

Our team muster at a landing point near to the Niteroi ferry. The transfer to the *Balder* is carried out by a large harbour workboat. Now, we all know the *Balder* is huge, but when we go under its deck, it becomes very dark. The night sky is eliminated.

The workboat goes alongside the ladder to reach the top of the port pontoon. It's a stiff climb. Now we have to climb up into the heavens to reach the main deck. It's a long, long way. I climb the ladder and dare not look down. The darkness is more than scary. There is just a single light at the top of the stairs to guide me.

As we reach the empty main deck we find it empty. We are guided to the tables and bars leaning against the main superstructure that houses the accommodation and other facilities. There are boxes upon boxes of best twelve-year-old blend whisky, a very famous brand.

'Can't drink all that,' says someone.

'We could try,' says another.

It's a jolly evening, and the Brazilians are impressed with the size of the cranes, which start to move. Slowly but carefully, the main deck becomes loaded with more structures and piles to be installed offshore. I realise this barge is a 24/7 operation. Time is always money. As the reception comes to an end, the main deck is almost full and so are we all. Great snacks, cold beer and it seems that the *Balder*'s stock of whisky has not suffered too badly.

Shortly after we arrive back on dry land, the *Balder* is almost ready to depart. Her tugs are fussing around her, a sure sign.

At work on Monday, comes news of our mobilisation date to go offshore by way of an accommodation semi-submersible called the *Safe Jasminia*. She is a new ship undergoing her first annual inspection. We are programmed to sail Saturday week, so the British team gets split into two and take it in turns to enjoy a week off.

With the details I have been given, I plan to visit the family in Thurso for the New Year. I explain to Sonia that I will spend three-weeks offshore during Christmas and on the 28th December, I will fly to the UK and ask, hopefully, if she would like to come. She agrees immediately, so

I contact the company travel agent to see if he can get two seats at good prices to Aberdeen. Carolyn will get a friend to extract my trusty Rover from its slumbers and come to Aberdeen to pick us up.

More good news, I will be onshore for my birthday, when I will be a young forty years old. Sonia's birthday is just a few days before, so she organises a joint party. We are very happy together and the party is a big success. The family phone from Scotland and a solitary birthday card makes through the Brazilian postal system.

Soon, it is time to go offshore. Everyone in the UK camp is looking forward to the extra pay. Offshore hook-ups and commissioning are usually good for about a ten to twelve month period. We did not know at the time, but disappointment lurked on the horizon.

The *Safe Jasminia* is ready, having passed its inspection. The company bus takes us all to the other side of the bay to Niteroi and then by launch to the semi-sub. It is a stunningly nice day, but very hot and, unusually, very clear. The other half of our offshore team will be on the beach, no doubt commiserating at our misfortune.

I check-in on-board the *Safe Jasminia*, the cabins are very nice. I share with Ron, an ex-RN CPO, a former gunner. He is married to Mavis, they are both near retirement age. Mavis does duty as the onshore agony aunt for the UK wives who think their husbands should be more romantic in this exciting country called Brazil. They do not understand the competition. Brazilian women, to the average British male eye, are a cut above. This is because the Brazilian girls are in competition for the few suitable males available to them in their section of society. What doesn't help is the gay community in Rio de Janeiro which is huge. With so much delightful 'totty' around, the 'boys' are practising being a British public schoolboy, shirt lifting for all they are worth. Amazing.

Big John's wife was a frequent caller on Mavis. Ron and Mavis lived in a beachfront apartment just a stone's throw from the Taberna Atlantica. Big John has a serious drink problem, he only has one mouth. When he is fuelled up, it's best to keep clear. He is actually on-board with the team. We watch him detox his way back to being a decent bloke.

At last the ship gets underway. Two harbour tugs are busy fussing around as the *Safe Jasminia* manoeuvres to pass under the huge Niteroi Bridge. Most of us are on the helicopter flight deck, cameras in hand. We are joined by our two Aberdeen master-mariners that are part of our team.

As the *Safe Jasminia* makes its way towards the open sea, somebody mentions a sight not seen before. We all look to the west. The sky is totally black; it's the blackest sky I have ever seen, a mega Tempestade. On a scale of one to ten, this one is way off the scale. I have seen a few of these storms in the city and they are bad news. Daylight is vanishing fast and it is going to become very dark. If nothing else, nature's fury is beyond impressive.

Safe Jasminia slowly starts to pass Botafogo Bay. We learn from our two Aberdonian Master-Mariners that the semi-sub is not configured correctly for the on-coming storm.

The vessel is very high out of the water. The twin hulls should be submerged. They are not. To our right, Sugar Loaf Mountain towers above the vessel and almost disappears in the tempest. To the left, the Fortaleza de Santa Cruz da Barra looks far too close for comfort.

The flight deck is cleared in record time, as the *Safe Jasminia* exits the bay into the open sea and waits for the storm to vent its energies on the City of Niteroi. Eventually, it passes and the Petrobrás ocean-going tug takes the tow. The tug is an old British built ocean tug, proud, traditional and timeless. She is also very powerful as the *Safe Jasminia* starts the short journey to the Campos Basin.

After the evening meal, our team settle down to a marathon card session, playing 'Hunt the Lady', although sailors will know this card game by another name.

A word from the beach reveals that Rio de Janeiro has taken a big hit from the mega-storm. Even the Clube Federal was flooded and it sits high up on the side of a mountain. The flooding in the city was bad. Many favelas that cling to the side of Rio's many slopes have been washed away, their inhabitants suffering badly from injuries, loss of life and their precariously located homes.

The *Safe Jasminia* arrived at the platform, called *Cherne II*. It is a standard eight leg platform with topsides to process a reasonable quality crude oil. However, there seems to be a problem with one of the Safe Jasmina's mooring winches, of which there are eight. It seems to be a big problem, as its repair is taking a long time.

It's not a problem for team Matthew Hall, who mutter 'Shame, now shut up and deal.' The card game has been going flat out since we left Rio de Janeiro and it is still going strong. More of our team have joined-in as there is naff-all left to pass the time.

Hooray, the *Safe Jasminia* technicians have repaired the winch and we are now alongside the platform but there is a problem with the gangway. Shame, I am dealt a pat hand for a change and rush into the lead. It does not last long.

The next day is a work day. After an English breakfast, we all head to the platform to look around and become familiar with the many systems undergoing installation. The progress is rapid, too rapid, as a lot of come-along-later items are still to be finished.

This is where we have to learn what is going on. The Brazilian throw things together and book that part of the work as complete. Uncompleted items go to a 'punch list'. The objective is to book progress to enhance the monthly invoice. We remind ourselves that the currency is in constant devaluation. The punch list crew comes behind to complete the work. Given the circumstances, it's as good a system as any.

The next day is the end of our first tour of duty. Little gets done in the morning as we all change and prepare for the helicopter flight to Campos. The flight is late, no surprises there, but we miss the connecting commercial flight back to Rio de Janeiro's Santos Dumont airport, the local airport that nestles on reclaimed land between the shore and the Brazilian Naval School which sits on what was an island.

After much toing and froing and murmurs of discontent, we are shown to a long distance bus which is 'semi-leito', the Portuguese for reclining seats. It is getting dark and the driver arrives. He is of short stature and looks about a hundred years old. We all groan, this journey is going to take all night. It doesn't, the bus leaves the airport at pace and quickly accelerates to warp speed.

I am sitting in one of the front seats and I am amazed this driver can see in the dark and miss, with ease, every unlit bullock-drawn cart. After two hours the bus comes to a rapid stop at a Posto called Restaurante Oasis, which is one of the main stops used by all the long-distance bus companies.

As we arrive, the overnight buses from Rio de Janeiro to Salvador, Recife and Belem are just leaving. These are interstate journeys that will take days to complete. The drivers will change out regularly every four hours depending where the next Posto is located on the long road to the top of Brazil. It is all very organised.

The buses are comfortable and the drivers are dressed in uniform with company tie. They are more than a cut above the lunatic highly stressed underpaid municipal bus drivers in Rio de Janeiro. The long distance buses are the latest, well equipped and a much higher standard than the ones I am used to in the UK.

The coaches are all equipped with variable tyre pressure systems so as to match the roads they have to drive on. Some roads are dirt roads and in many places after the visit of *El Nino*, many of the main roads have been washed out in places where stream and rivers have overflowed.

Ten minutes after our arrival at Oasis, the bus driver is impatient to get going. We dare not leave anyone behind, as we are in the middle of nowhere and it is very dark outside. This is Brazil.

The bus arrives at the Rio main bus terminal in three hours and thirty-five minutes. In all the years I have driven the same journey, I cannot match this time, even in daytime. Impressive to say the least.

*

THE NEXT FEW month's pass at pace. Sonia and I settle down to a steadily building relationship. We visit Flavio's lovely home in an estate just outside the city of Pindomonhangaba. It took me a long time to pronounce this name correctly so that Brazilians would understand what I said. His home has a nice swimming pool that needs to be prepared for the summer months.

Flavio and I spend most of the day cleaning and scrubbing and taking refreshments from small glasses on a floating tray carrying his latest beverage and a large insulated box full of ice. Flavio buys cachaça in bulk from a distillery not far away and bottles the cachaça with different favours. I liked the lemon one the best. It was a pleasant way to spend an afternoon.

After resting from our labours, we relax and watch the sunset over the distant valley as his wife prepares the evening meal on the barbecue, a traditional Brazilian churrasco. The meat is cooked to perfection and there is not too much damn salad to ruin the intake of the non-vegetarian experience. I had a surprise for Sonia and wait for the right moment.

*

DURING ONE OF the earlier drinking sessions at the Taberna Atlantico, our very own educated Scotsman reveals he has a nice trade in precious and semi-precious stones, which are a good price in Brazil. He has ornate high setting rings made up for onward transportation to the UK via the fingers of lady friends that he trusts. They forward them to his partner in London, who breaks the rings down, extract the stones and uses the gold to become part of a new delight for a lucky lady.

Once he brought a Dutchman to our table, a Mr Kurtz, who is part of the project, but which part I have no idea. For sure he's one of the seniors. Mr Kurtz invites the team to visit a trade jeweller at the top end of Copacabana. We all elect to go the next morning as it is a Saturday and it sure beats Saturday morning chores, especially supermarket shopping.

The next morning, we meet at the Taberna for breakfast and then grab several taxies to the destination. On arrival, we all find ourselves in a dingy ninth floor corridor that is a non-descript as it is possible to be. I notice the door is constructed of solid steel. A look up into the corridor ceiling reveals concealed cameras pointing in every direction. Mr Kurtz rings the interphone at the entrance. A door opens down the corridor. A man beckons us to use the other door, also made of solid steel. We all enter a very small space as the steel door closes behind us. Then another steel door opens and we enter the premises.

The owner of the business is on hand to give a guided tour of his extensive stock. I make the connection between the owner, Jewish and the Dutchman, from Amsterdam.

His talk on coloured diamonds is very interesting, but it his talk on aquamarine that is the most interesting. Brazil is the sole source for this elegant stone that comes in differing qualities from 'cheap as chips' to 'if you have to ask the price you definitely can't afford it'.

We are shown a cabinet of trays. The top tray has large almost clear stones, about US$10 a carat, as the owner proceeds down the trays, the colour of the aquamarine stones increases. They also get smaller. The bottom tray has few stones, the largest is three carats, the smallest just one carat. These are twice the price of the most expensive diamonds and I guess these are trade prices. The three-carat stone is removed from the tray into the light. The depth of the colour is endless, like a swimming pool of the clearest bluest water with no end to its depth. It's a humbling experience.

I ask my friendly Scotsman for ideas on an engagement ring. I might have mentioned the possibility before. He takes a small package from his pocket opens it to show me a very attractive ring in emeralds and diamonds. Six hundred bucks is the price. I ask its UK value, only to be told a lot more. The owner, who has obviously supplied the ring tells me 'a lot more' is a conservative estimate. I say OK.

When we leave, I purchased a stone chess set, which is quietly ornate, classy and an economic price, compared to the UK.

*

SONIA IS LOOKING her best when I present the engagement ring. She smiles a special smile. She has waited patiently for the moment. We have both become expert at reading each other. It is a magic moment. Flavio produces a decent bottle of wine. Up to now, Sonia has been teetotal. That changes, but after twenty-five years, she has never over-indulged.

The weekend passed with visits to Campos do Jordâo, which is up in the mountains. It is a weekend retreat for Brazilians from Sao Paulo. It is known as their version of Switzerland. Judging by the swanky houses in the Swiss style they appear to have more of their fair share of wealth.

The city is overloaded with chocolate shops; their clientele are teenagers busy showing off their woollen leg warmers, which are all the rage. There are shops selling Swiss Cuckoo clocks, made in the local factory. In the centre of a large square is a substantial ornate clock on a tall pedestal complete with a large secondary dial to show the temperature. A red line on this dial records the lowest temperature at minus five centigrade some five years ago.

Flavio takes us both to the telefèrico at the edge of the city for an exciting ride through the air to the top of a hill for the views of the city below to take photographs. Then we take the car down a narrow road, a dead end, which has a vast array of wireless aerials and telecoms dishes of every description.

Exciting stuff, really. Flavio mentions the view behind us. Wow. Sonia and I find ourselves looking down on the Dutra, the main Rio to Sao Paulo highway. It is sixty kilometres distant. I take out my road map and pick-up on a couple of recognisable places. It is a very clear day and the view is over two hundred kilometres long. No wonder the aerials cater for every service, including the state and federal authorities.

The next day, after a restful day at the poolside, as the sun descends over the valley, we all jump into Flavio's car, as he takes us to a traditional market fair. It is an amazing experience. There are the usual funfair stalls, many different kinds of rides for the brave and the children, stalls selling wonderful sausages that comes as a big coil sat on a very hot hot plate.

The vendor keeps the sausage in a constant swirling movement otherwise it will be reduced to ashes in seconds. At the same time, his assistant prepares very fresh French rolls with lashings of butter and a spicy tomato and onion sauce. The sausage is whirled round and round, then a precise length chopped off that disappears into the prepared French roll. I try one; it is moreish. I try another one; damn that was good.

I look for a stall selling drinks. The best stall is surrounded by the young folk, laughing and shouting and generally being very happy. The stall only sells fruit juice, made from a vast range of Brazilian fruits displayed behind the vendor. I marvel at the joy of the crowd and there is no alcohol in sight.

Next morning, we thanked Flavio and his wife for a wonderful weekend and make our way back to Rio. On the drive back, the Federal Road Patrol pull me over for a spot check. Sonia does the talking and it is not necessary to slip a large value note in amongst the car documents.

*

MY NEXT ONSHORE break is enhanced by my fortieth birthday on the 23rd October. Sonia trails behind me just under one year by a few days, four to be exact. The party for both anniversaries is held in her brother's very nice apartment in Flamengo. There are two ten stories apartment blocks located on the side of a small hill with views fine views of the statue and a traditional part of Flamengo, Parke Guinle. Sonia's brother is a businessman. He is also a macho shit to any woman with the slightest hint of independence, including his elder sister.

Anyway, life goes on and all is well. When I arrive back on the platform for the long three weeks over the Christmas period, the hook-up is proceeding quickly, too quickly. It doesn't look as though we will get any offshore stints in the New Year.

The only moment of interest is when the drillers junk the hole they have been attempting to finish. To remove the junk (broken drill pipe) the drillers import a specialist with his fishing tools. After much effort, the drill rig winch extracts a long length of very bent drill pipe just before lunch time. The drill rig team leave the well open, with just the weight of the drilling mud holding any hydrocarbons in the bowels of the earth where they belong.

I look down at this scene with interest. The well gives the occasional burp and the safety team broadcast that no smoking or naked lights are allowed on the upper deck of the platform. A cordon of plastic tape defines a safety boundary.

Meanwhile, it is barbecue for lunch. The chefs have opened the galley door on the far side of the platform accommodation block that leads to the outside walkway, chopped a fifty-gallon drum in half, found some supports for it and turn it into a barbecue grill with about half a ton of charcoal to cook the meat for lunch.

The grill is, to say the least, very hot. Meanwhile, the open well in the centre of the platform continues the occasional burp (of hydrocarbon gas). After my lunch, I return to my comfortable lower bunk on the far side of the *Safe Jasminia*. I am still sharing a cabin with Ron, the ex RN CPO, who is our group's safety representative. He is almost fast asleep. I have never reached my comfortable bunk for my lunch time zizz before Ron.

I mention the open well in the centre of the platform and the BBQ on the side of the Platform's accommodation block. He assures me that all is ok because we are sleeping on the outboard side of the semi-sub and the barbecue fire is 'intrinsically safe'. This is a great aside, I will explain.

In the world of hydro-carbon safety, faulty electrical circuits cause explosions. Generally, in an area considered to have hydro-carbon gas free in the air, all electrical components are housed in an explosion-proof box. These are heavy, strong and expensive.

Intrinsic Safety (IS) is a protection technique for safe operation of electrical equipment in hazardous areas by limiting the energy, electrical and thermal, available for ignition. This energy is limited to the energy required to flutter your eye-lids at a pretty girl. Thought you would like to know, about the pretty girl.

I smile a huge smile and turn-in for an hour, it has been busy morning watching the Brazilians spend the British bank's money.

Christmas dinner on the platform was the usual traditional fare, only with a double portion of black beans or *feijoada*. Black beans are the staple of Brazil. They even serve black beans with more black beans. Black Beans have nutritional facts. Per cup, 227 calories, 15 grams protein, 15 grams fibre, 0 fat, 64% folate, 40% copper, 38% manganese and 35% vitamin B1 Thiamine. They are not made by Mr Heinz. So why don't I eat them? Don't know, perhaps I will start tomorrow.

Matthew Hall (MH) has a member of staff known as Black Beans. He is a Scot, very serious and always looks morose. Actually, he's a nice guy. He came to the Taberna one evening, so one of the MH drinking team asked why he is such a miserable son of a bitch, thereby lowering the level of etiquette at the table to an all-time low.

He tells everybody, 'You too would look fuckin' miserable if during divorce proceedings your wife's lawyer (in Aberdeen) was one Frankie le-Favier,' the first 'no win-no fee' lawyer in Scotland. His sympathy rating climbs at the news. Other divorced men around the table mutter in their beer how lucky they were.

The three-week tour of duty finally comes to an end. Back in the apartment, I am almost ready for the long flight to Scotland. Sonia comes and stays the night. Her luggage is dropped in the hallway, ready for the off. The next day we rest and get a little sun. It is a hot day, thirty-six degrees centigrade and climbing.

The taxi arrives and we are off on a big adventure. I wonder how my favourite in-laws will react to my new intended. The only consolation is that it was Jim's idea to venture into pastures new. The check-in is OK but Varig staff are very picky about baggage weight. British Airways does not do this. A BA check-in lady told me long ago, luggage complains, freight never does. They take freight off the flight if necessary, so the story goes. The journey is OK. It is not too uncomfortable. On arrival in London, the transfer to the Aberdeen flight is smooth and it seems we are being closely followed by our luggage.

As Sonia leaves the aircraft to walk to the terminal she is wearing a very warm fur coat. I ask where the hell that came from, as I didn't see it during the journey. Apparently, she has borrowed it from an aunt. I am impressed.

Carolyn is waiting, as promised, with my comfortable Rover. It impresses Sonia, a car like this in Rio de Janeiro does not exist unless you throw a lot of money at the German car makers. The tax on imported cars in Brazil is very high. What could possibly be wrong with aspiring to a new VW Gol, Brazil's version of the original VW Mark 1 Golf.

I enjoy the drive up the A96 to Forres. I notice that the promised improvements have not been implemented. This would require the Scottish Roads Authority in Edinburgh to actually know where the A96 is. Many years later I met the head of this authority, a university 'Hooray' with a plummy accent, who couldn't find his arse even if he used both hands.

It is great to be home, how I miss it. Sonia and I are both tired from the long journey. In the morning Sonia complains she found it hard to get to sleep. I ask why? 'It's too quiet,' she tells me. Carolyn laughs.

The next day comes the special day. The drive to Thurso is a steady journey. The roads are ok, well gritted against the overnight frost. North of Inverness I take the short cut over the Sluie Road. It has nice hard packed snow that is easy to drive on. The winter scenery is enchanting and Sonia and Carolyn love it.

The drive becomes more difficult at Helmsdale and Berriedale where the road drops to sea level and then back up to the top of the cliffs that line this coastline. These very sharp declines and inclines must always be driven with great care, even in good weather.

As I leave what is left of the A9 and head north across the corner that is this part of Scotland Sonia is introduced to some truly wild country. The snow makes it look very scenic, but to cross this land on foot is very dangerous. There are peat bogs everywhere. Occasionally a peat bog will give up that which it has swallowed, sheep, humans, sometimes they are very old and quite well preserved too.

As we arrive and cross the Thurso River Bridge, I tell Sonia that this bridge was built before the age of the motor vehicle, but the local Laird saw the future and spent his money on a wide two-lane bridge built in the 1880s. Every other bridge in Scotland of the era is a single track and very few have survived the many years.

As we arrive at Jim and Margret's home, I toot the car horn as Carolyn jumps out of the car to be the first to introduce Sonia to her grandparents. It becomes a great homecoming. The duty-free is quickly liberated from its protective containment. I become both pleased and amazed as Sonia very quickly becomes as one with Jim and Margret. Losing a daughter and now they are gaining. It is all very emotive. I hide behind my glass of whisky.

Soon, I shall need a lie down to recover from the long flight. The drive to Thurso although enjoyable required great concentration. Instead, I get a strong cup of tea and homemade shortcake. Later that evening, the girls are sent to bed as Jim takes us down to his home from home, the Thurso Club. It is classy, exclusive and UKAEA members are very few on the ground.

There is not a lot to do or see in Thurso during the winter. Our days were spent being together and catching up on the world in general. The weather provided more snow, so Sonia, the girls and I took to nice walks in the countryside. One morning I discover the Rover needs some TLC, so Jim and I drive out to Halkirk to visit a garage that can fix almost anything. The owner of the garage shows us his new pride and joy, a two-door coupe XJ12 Jaguar fitted with a factory fitted soft-top and the colour is classic squadron blue. It is indeed a very fine motor car.

The Rover is now a hundred per cent and as we drive back to Thurso Jim takes the opportunity to ask if there are plans for a wedding. I explain the situation is not easy as there seems little chance of the expats continuing to live in Brazil except possibly on Brazilian rates. The Brazilian engineers are just as capable as ours so what will happen is not clear.

Sonia has a few years left to go at the university before she can retire, so best to enjoy the moment and let things fall into place. As my friend, Brian used to say, 'What's in front of you will not go by you.'

After a wonderful holiday, it becomes time to head back south. Sonia and I would spend a few days in my home at Rafford before trundling through to Aberdeen for the flight home. During the change of flights in London, it is necessary to change terminals, so our baggage could not be checked through to Brazil.

The Varig check-in became a major pain about baggage weight per suitcase. We have to move away to rearrange our luggage. Items are swapped between suitcases to even things up and the food items I have purchased to hold a traditional New Year party in my apartment are transferred to by cabin bag, which fortunately does not get scrutinised. I check its weight away from the Varig people, the tins of baked beans, black puddings and the haggis increased its weight to a mere twenty-two kilos. Whoops.

When we board the aircraft to Rio de Janeiro a strong drilling engineer kindly helps me by lifting it into the overhead bins. Apart from that moment of stress, we settle down to the long flight.

*

The Final Days in Brazil

AFTER OUR ARRIVAL back in Brazil there are a few days to rest before going offshore. The New Year party in my apartment was a great success. To enhance the menu, Flavio cooks a Bahian dish with fish. I watch and wonder, as this dish has so much Brazilian pepper in it I cannot think how anybody would eat it, at alone enjoy it. At the last moment, Flavio pours three tins of highly concentrated coconut milk into the mixture. The fish dish is absolutely delicious.

The first offshore tour of duty in the New Year starts and the team learns that this might be the last one. The Brazilians are insisting we are no longer needed. Progress over the holiday has indeed been impressive. Politics takes a hold to which we are not a party to, but word eventually filters out that the tour of duty in February will be our last. We are given dates on which to plan our demobilisation. The company offers a standard return flight to Aberdeen, or they will supply the same amount of funds if we wish to take a confirmed holiday route back to the UK.

Whispers have it that the company have been unsuccessful in gaining a new project on which to keep us all working, in other words, goodnight Vienna.

The next break period became a bit of a watershed. Sonia and I talk things over and the practicalities presented themselves in a stark manner. She still had six years before she can retire and understands that I have to return home to look after the family.

We put these matters to one side, determined to make the most of the time we had left together. Meanwhile, all options would be explored. During the weekdays, I raked around to gather as much information about the best way to demobilise. The idea of a holiday route home was attractive, so what did I discover?

Well, as luck would have it, I was put in touch with a big Irishman, called Tam, who was part-owner of a travel agency. Their main business is sending Brazilians to Rome to see the Holy See.

First things luggage. The company offered $300 bucks to send extra suitcases home as accompanied excess baggage on the journey home.

Tam lifted the thickest book I have ever seen from a dusty shelf and poured over its contents, then told me he could send two large suitcases to Aberdeen as freight for a third of the extra allowance. Good start.

The holiday route home? I enquired about Rio de Janeiro to Florida, to see my friend from McDermott days, Ed Mussler, at Melbourne Beach, then to Haiti to visit my knowledgeable friend on the subject of railways, Mr David, and then to Aberdeen by whatever route was best. He came up with a blinder, Rio to Miami, then to Orlando, returning to Miami, then to Port-au-Prince, then club class with Air France to Paris, then to Aberdeen. He added it all up and said, 'If you give me your extra luggage allowance, the airfare money to Aberdeen plus another three hundred bucks from your pockets then it's a done deal.' It certainly was.

*

THE LAST TOUR of duty offshore became a bit of a farce, with little to do. Maintaining a low profile was the best option, which all the team adhered to. The platform had been completed in record time and our part in it was, well, hard to quantify.

On our return to shore, the company had generously given people the option to choose how much time they needed to settle their affairs. Since November, Sonia was staying with me during the weekends. We were not sad but faced the future, whatever it would bring.

I still felt, deep inside of me, that one day we would marry, just when was the question? First thing I had to do was to drop off my excess luggage at the travel agency. Tam gave me the exact time it would arrive in Aberdeen, precisely one day before I arrived.

I gave a lot of things I no longer needed to Sonia to pass on to a charity and Flavio took the rest. I took them both for a farewell dinner at the Casa Swiss, where I said farewell to Flavio and wished him well.

The next morning, Sonia and I were both reflective. She elected not to say goodbye at the airport, which I thought was a sound idea. She could be with her family, especially her dear mother who was visiting from Campos. Driving home from the airport alone would have been very sad.

I was sad to leave Sonia behind, but I had my family to go home to and the small matter of finding new employment. In the meantime, there was the excitement and experience of visiting USA and Haiti. The flight to Miami passed as well as can be expected. I even managed to get some sleep which I rarely do on an aeroplane.

I was met at Orlando by Ed Mussler, who hadn't changed a bit. We nattered all the way to his home on Melbourne Beach. His wife welcomed me with the strongest Georgian accent I had ever heard. At first, it was hard not to smile, even laugh. But she was a kind, gentle and totally honest person who deserved much respect.

I was very well received and looked after. In common with most properties in the area, Ed had a swimming pool. He also had huge bins full of the pinkest grapefruit I have ever tasted. Ed's wife worked as a school teacher and Ed promised to take alternate days off from his labours at the Kennedy Space Centre.

So, first full day in the USA was a late lie-in, then a swim in the pool, followed by a walk to the beach that stretched for miles in either direction. There was something strange about the beach, but what was it? It was empty, the opposite to Rio on any sunny day. The 'Snow Birds' had flown home and the tourists had yet to arrive for Easter.

The next day Ed took time off work to show me around all the small places up and down the Inter-coastal waterway. Great fishing spots and wonderful scruffy bars. The conversation in Ed's favourite bar was priceless. The six men were locals, the baker, the butcher, etc and Shirley the high school sweetheart of two of the men. Shirley is middle-aged but still attractive in a raw sexy kind of way. She fancies the baker, Albert.

'Hey Albert, you wanna come home with me this evening. I could sure use some action.'

Albert replies, 'Hell no Shirley, I've a bin screwing you for over twenty years. I need a rest or a change. Your sister still in California?'

'Huh,' says Shirley. 'Another night in the motel. Girl's gotta make a living somehow.'

Ed backs me away, it's time to go. After a hard day, we repair to his swimming pool and make wonderful refreshing drinks with his pink grapefruit with added spirit.

The next day, a visit to Space Centre. It is an awesome experience. The simulated Saturn 5B rocket launch in the Moon Shot Control Room is unbelievable, especially the sound. The audience is told that at T-minus-30 seconds (I think that's the time they said) the rocket either takes-off or blows-up.

The following day Ed drops me off at Vero Beach to catch the tourist bus service to the Epcot Centre, which is also very impressive. I visit again many years later only to find it's been dumbed down so much it was not worth going. Even then, it's still too technical for the Mexican and Cuban kids.

I spend the weekend with Ed and his wife and all too soon, its back to Orlando for the two short flights to Haiti. David meets me at the airport, which is just as well as Haiti is the opposite end of the spectrum compared with Miami.

The visit to Haiti confirms it is indeed a very poor country. David shows me the nice, but small apartments the UN built for some of the local population, in the hope that Haiti's government would follow the example and continue building more badly needed homes. The senior members of the government moved into these properties that perchance over-look the beach. Nice for the weekend.

David is also a keen sailor so we enjoy time on the water. I also try a windsurfer with noticeable lack of results. The water in Haiti is wonderfully blue and crystal clear so falling in was a great opportunity to get a cool swim.

That evening over a few drinks, the rum in Haiti is the best I have ever tasted, I ask David about the lady he was travelling with Curitiba. Apparently, they did marry, but now she is visiting her mother in the Dominican Republic. He further adds that she may not return. The young girl that is his maid, has her own bedroom, but there is no bed in it, which leads to advanced speculation.

Still, I did enjoy my visit. David gives me great assistance at the airport. I stocked-up with more of the rum and slip gently through Immigration. What a treat it was to be shown to my club class seat. I looked out of the aircraft to see hundreds of people milling about on the tarmac. I assumed they were there to wish their loved ones goodbye and 'bon voyage'. Actually, they all get on the aircraft. I am told later that there are over five hundred. I checked during the night and saw no reason to doubt the information. Human sardines and as for the aroma: Phew!

*

Back to Blighty

THE JOURNEY TO Paris was very comfortable and the Air France service first rate. Reality returns on the flight to Aberdeen, where I arrive tired but on time.

I met up with Carolyn who has organised her friend to bring the Rover. I dumped all my luggage in the car and then head to the customs shed before they close. I made it by just ten minutes. Today, the Customs are kind and my suitcases that came directly from Rio do not attract their attention. By now I am keen to relax in the back of my car surrounded by a lot of luggage. Carolyn lets me drift off to sleep and my snooze lasts until the Rover passes the church and the graveyard. I must remember to get flowers the following day.

Having been paid until the end of the month, it was time to rest after my travels. The house needed some TLC and so did the Rover.

20

MARATHON OIL

Aberdeen (1984 - 1986)

IT WAS JUST BEFORE THE end of the month when my agent telephoned, offering me a position with Marathon Oil in Aberdeen. Yes, was the answer, working for the client oil company is always a sought-after option.

So I joined the instrument maintenance team and found three other engineers working in the group. Two of them spend all day talking about Aberdeen Football Club and what the manager called Fergie should have done. This was the same Mr Ferguson who went on to manage Manchester United with some success. The team was led by a senior engineer who I called Billy Whiz, as he is always rushing about. Nice guy, always happy and funny with it. The work was steady, if repetitive, supporting the offshore team who had the task of maintaining the North Sea's biggest and heaviest platform *Brae 'A'*.

The produced crude oil was not sweet and lite but laden with the worst of unwanted fluids and gasses. Many extra systems are needed to deal with them. Still, it's a big field, so even with the difficulties, it's worth developing.

The processed oil was pumped to the Forties Field and then to shore. The gas, after the nasties had been removed was pumped to St Fergus. It was steady work and I was able to come to Aberdeen on a Monday morning and with luck, I could slip away on a Friday afternoon before the weekend panic.

During the week I stayed with friend Allister on a paying guest basis.

MEMORIES AND FORGETFULNESS

His company was great and life in Aberdeen was tranquil. We used to meet one of the ex-Matthew Hall Captains who I knew from the Clube Federal when he wasn't getting his car maintained.

He gave up trying to get obtain suitable employment locally and joined in the B&B Industry with his wife. The last I heard he became divorced, from a somewhat volatile lady. After Brazil, both their temperaments changed, unfortunately in opposite direction.

I had the odd liaison with members of the opposite sex, but nothing serious was ever going to develop. At weekends I always retreated to Rafford and when the tides were good, I got as much sailing in as possible.

During my time with Marathon, I had two visits offshore. The first was in 1984, before the great oil price crash of 1985. There were so many people on the platform if I had not been a member of Marathon staff, I expected to be given a hammock and told to 'sling my hook'. Even worse, I could have been dumped in the accommodation known as the Leper Colony.

The second time would have been in 1986. As I checked-in I met the same receptionist who, with humour, offered me any bunk, in any cabin, in any corridor. The platform crew list had been cut by seventy per cent. So, what was going on?

Two major events hit Marathon Oil at the same time. The dramatic crude oil price drop brought the price of oil well below break-even and the company went into saving money mode. Deferring maintenance tasks from one year to the next actually costs more, but the thinking was that when next year came the price of oil should have risen.

The other major event? The owners of Marathon Oil was US Steel, who had their own troubles and they needed their other companies to generate profits to help keep the company directors receiving their bonuses, no that's not right, to help stop the company from laying off American workers.

There were two issues that did not help the operational finances. The first was a very sophisticated spare parts re-ordering system, designed to keep stock levels tightly controlled at set levels, depending upon the number of items actually in use on the platform.

But the platform staff, who couldn't be bothered to be at one with this computer-driven system, when they could not find what they were looking for they simply wrote out a new stock number, added the description of the item and sent it to the onshore purchasing department as a 'I must have this tomorrow' urgent request.

Somebody figured out what was going on, so a team was sent to the company's Peterhead Support Base for two weeks, to pour through the stock held list and match up all the duplicates. It was amazing how badly treated this clever system was. The best example I found was when I presented the team leader with fifteen expensive 1,000 barg (15,000 psig) safety pressure gauges in a big box. He asked how many of this type of gauge was actually used on the platform. Answer? One, the gauge used to show the export gas pressure.

What was worse, all the other disciplines discovered similar mis-ordering, costing many millions of pounds. It proved one thing, give highly trained offshore staff the latest technology and human nature will win through and make a complete mess of it.

Four months later, rumours started to spread about staff reductions. This was not just in the company, but the whole industry was looking very closely at staffing levels and managers were being forced into getting a grip on the numbers. I know that Shell, on the other side of town, was seriously overstaffed. Word had it that every staff engineer had a contract engineer to keep him company and find his slippers when needed. They actually let go five hundred secretaries cum typists, and I ended-up wondering what they would do with all the spare desks and chairs.

The next assignment came from the top floor. The accounts department decided that the stock of spares in the Peterhead Support Base, base value £55 million, had been written down to almost nil. The cost of running the base was £15 million a year, so if the 'worthless' stock was scrapped, the company could shut down the base in whole, or part, and save a lot of money.

This was the bombshell of the decade. Middle management was up in arms that brand new parts, that would get used one day, were destined for the bin. The battle raged in the corridors of power, but orders became orders. And so, back to Peterhead for the wake.

I must say, at this point going to Peterhead was enjoyable, because the team stayed in the best hotel just outside the city and it was steak for dinner every night, not forgetting seafood starters, the yummy puddings and drinks that never appeared on the weekly invoice.

The best story of this nonsense came when two crane rings were scrapped. I watched as the blowtorches did their work. Now, crane rings are the most vital part of any crane. It's the big circle of steel with teeth cut on the inside edge. The driven pinion wheel engages with the teeth, to enable the crane to rotate.

The engineer-in-charge of the cranes begged, pleaded, even cried, all to no avail. The words, 'The crane vendor is no more, they went bust two years ago,' meant nothing to the accountants driving this stupidity.

Three weeks later, one of the main cranes on the platform became U/S. The crane ring was worn and the safety guys shut it down. Panic on the platform and onshore. The crane engineer was inundated with requests for a new crane ring.

'What was he going to do?' A senior meeting was held on the top floor of the building. The crane engineer presented all his information to management and simply asked what they wanted him to do next. 'Fix it,' came the answer.

The crane engineer, enjoying every moment, supplied the only solution; to have a bespoke crane ring manufactured at a cost of some millions in a favoured location and he would have to oversee this vital task performed exactly to specification, otherwise the crane would never receive the new certification without which no crane driver was going to risk his life. (The North Sea industry lost a lot of cranes and their drivers. A fact that received very little attention from anybody.)

Anyway, the end was coming. My department lost the two football experts thereby breaking the rule 'first in - last out'.

The American manager of the adjacent department gathered his troops on the Friday morning and said, 'OK guys, I don't how I'm a going to do without you all, but starting Monday I'm going to find out,' A voice from the back said, 'That's the trouble with you Americans, you can never come right out and tell us straight.' Everyone laughed, took a week's pay in lieu of notice, before proceeding to the pub.

I was the last contractor in my department to get the heave-ho. The staff guys started taking the piss until I told them, 'You will be next. We contractors, have a month to hoover-up whatever dross is left in the labour market. Be prepared for a long cold winter boys.' They knew I was right; their faces said it all.

I was forewarned, so on my Friday, I drove down to Hampshire to see my parents. The Rover was ready for the long journey. Outside, t'was the second week in June 1986, with snow, sleet and hail that followed me down to the English border. So much for global warming.

And so, the 1985-86 oil price crash enabled the oil industry to shoot itself in both feet. Thousands of highly skilled engineers and other trades were shown the door. Three other doors welcomed this flood of highly skilled resource, the Channel Tunnel, a big refinery project in the north-east of England and the massive rebuild at the Sellafield Nuclear Facility on the north-west coast of England. These people left the industry, took their knowledge with them and many never returned. British management at its very best.

*

DURING MY STAY at Marathon, my immediate boss, Billy Whiz, showed an interest in sailing. He was that sort of guy, always looking for something new. So I invited him to come sailing in the National 18 and he really enjoyed it. He decided to buy a racing dinghy and keep it at Stonehaven SC, which was not too far from where he lived. He became quite the competent sailor in a short space of time. As I said, he was that sort of guy.

In 1985, the championship for the National 18 was held at the Plas Menai National Outdoor Centre, on the Menai Straights, North Wales. I managed to borrow Bobby Steven's National, but he was unavailable to crew as he did in the IOM two years earlier. Billy Whiz volunteered, so I drove down with my regular crew and Billy drove down in his company car, so he could visit relations after the event.

During the racing, I took things easy with a scratch crew, and in light winds we did not do too badly. Midweek, the wind increased, blowing down the straights with a lot of back eddies. We were doing quite well on a dead run, when Billy, as third crew, shouted out a gust of wind was about to hit from a different angle. Something got caught-up, the spinnaker could not be released quickly enough and over we went. Crew number two fell into the water and swam to hold on to the bow. I sat on top of the dinghy, but where was Billy, under all the sails. Oh my God, what to do? I was just about to jump in and cut him free when he popped up on my side of the boat, shouting and laughing he was OK.

The rescue boat came alongside, to assist in the recovery. The more modern National 18s floated very high and with three sails in the water, recovery would have taken a long time. Still, the rescue boat soon had us upright and so ended our race.

Back in Aberdeen, another memorable experience came the day I was sitting quietly at my desk when I heard the unmistakable sounds of Roger, formerly a senior member of the MH onshore team in Rio de Janeiro. I never saw much of him as he lived on the island close to the main airport. He was living with a lady called Vanda, an African Brazilian from the south of the country. He had arrived from London and the couple had a small boy.

Roger was the opposite of his partner, white, middle class and university trained in the mystic arts of process engineering. I was invited to visit their rented apartment. Vanda looked very young and a little lost. It was to her credit that in just a few years living in Aberdeen, she mastered English to a high standard, completed a three-year course at the local university and received an appointment as the Brazilian Representative for North Scotland, a post normally reserved for, in this case, a Scottish national.

She also galvanised all the Brazilians living in the area and every year organised a very Brazilian Carnival Party that became, in the era, quite famous. Vanda was to play a very important part in my life.

21

THE SURVIVAL PERIOD

Glasgow & Aberdeen (1986 – 1987)

WITH THE CULL IN ABERDEEN reaching its peak it was time to find pastures new. There were mouths to feed, including the mortgage company. After the visit to my parents in Hampshire, my trusty agent found a position for me at Weir Pumps Ltd in Glasgow. They had been contracted to build a full-size test loop for the Sizewell 'B' Nuclear Power Station, using the American Pressurised Water Reactor.

The test loop would simulate the exact conditions of an actual reactor cooling loop as it removed the heat from the reactor to make steam for the generation of electricity.

So, it became very useful to have my experience at Dounreay on my CV. The technologies are completely different. Now, in case you are wondering, water will remain as water at very high temperatures if the pressure is correspondingly high, very high in fact. And the velocity of the water flow was also very high, which brought a lot of issues I won't bore you with.

Entering Weir Pumps, at the time, was like going back in time. Everybody sat at their desk, in rows, in front of an elevated desk where sat the supervisor of that section. Comfort breaks were set at exact times, indicated by the ringing of a little hand bell.

Lunch break was the same. I kept looking around for Charles Dickens, who would have been sat at the back taking notes for his next book. It was a strange environment, there was little to actually contribute and to save everybody's face, my Aberdeen agent called after a few weeks to go to Aberdeen and take a short-term contract with Shell.

WHEN I REPORTED for work at Shell UK, who should I be working for but one Jim Perkins, the Ralph M Parson lead instrument engineer that led the redesign of the St. Fergus process plant.

Yes, he was that Rottweiler, but he needed to bring a lot of people into line to get that job done. His bark could be as bad as his bite, but if you knew what you were talking about and defended your position, Jim would give you the respect you deserved.

He never did explain why he had left Parsons; lack of work was a reasonable guess as the industry slowed down.

Our task was to conduct a design audit on a Shell Fulmar Gas project. I remember little about it except for the many interesting conversations with Jim and the eight weeks money, which came in very handy.

*

NEXT, I ENDED up at a company called Oilfab Engineering Services. Another short-term contract, but I was still working when others were not. The longer it lasted the more chance the industry would recoup and start anew.

The company had been contracted to produce a design for the St. Fergus Gas Terminal. The concept was simple, well for me anyway, as I understood the issues. When the gas terminal sends its product to British Gas to reach your home to keep you warm or cook dinner, the flow of gas is measured in terms of energy: that is the volume delivered at the specified calorific value of one thousand calories per standard unit. The very complicated meters, mass spectrometers that do this were located in their own building always under lock and key. It's all to do with the money. If the gas specification goes higher, you are giving away free energy, if the numbers are lower, British gas had very stiff penalties.

So far, so good, but when a cold snap hits the UK and British Gas is struggling to match supply with demand, the Shell plant was constrained. However, by taking the gas directly from the incoming pipeline after it had been dried and connecting it directly to the gas export pipeline going into the British Gas site, the volume could be increased by ten per cent and as this gas would be well above the contracted calorific value, Shell would receive a suitable premium.

If this sounds simple, well it wasn't. I had landed on an interesting project that required the mustering of my brain cells and inviting them to think hard. With hard work, some luck and ringing-up my friends for any ideas and advice they could offer, the task was complete.

To my surprise, when this welcomed contract finished a few months later, I had the chance to enter into the world of subsea engineering, which with just a couple of breaks, would see me reach the end of my shelf-life many years later.

22

GOING SUBSEA

(1987 - 1990)

ONE DAY MY AGENT RANG me up and said 'JP Kenny Caledonia needs you to fill a senior controls position.'

'Who the hell are they I ask?'

'Subsea engineering outfit, a fun company to work for and good rates'.

The last word got my attention as it was bound to do. JPK, as I shall call them from now on, was formed by a group of interesting people. Not a big company people but people who were expert in pipeline engineering and were prepared to have fun doing it. I think this explained their love of the odd half pint of beer now and then.

John Kenny and his partner Dr Paul Davis built this company with the help of the Three John's all pipe-liners to a man. This was a new world for me and it gathered my interest.

In the first four years in Aberdeen, I was involved with eight interesting projects, which involved working on two or three projects at the same time.

This is not as hard as it sounds because projects ebbed and flowed and it was a case of keeping busy. John Kenny and Dr Paul had the gumption to enter the Russian market just as the country was changing rapidly. Many great stories came our way.

One of the better ones came in Moscow, where business was fuelled by waves of vodka. One evening, they were resting after a hectic week. John said to Paul that they should jot down some details so they could fill out their expense forms, but he had absolutely no idea where the hell they had been. Dr Paul couldn't remember either.

Their secretary and interpreter, Natasha One, a very nice lady, was asked her to put her coat on, pop downstairs and ask their KGB minders where they had been that week so they fill-out their expense forms. Poor Natasha was very nervous about this request, but eventually she did what she was asked.

John watched from the hotel window, as the KGB men realised the request was serious and buggered off, leaving our two heroes laughing.

My first project was for Mobil's Ness Field development, a subsea tieback to the Beryl "B" Platform. I didn't do any subsea work but I was landed with a load of issues to bring oil with a different tax break onto an ageing oil platform. Very interesting work which went well.

Another interesting project was an LNG import feasibility study for a confidential client. No prizes to guess who. In the very north of Russia is a massive offshore gas field, which if developed was looking for customers. The JPK London office would handle the overland gas pipeline option and myself another engineer would handle the option of importing the gas in liquid form, or LNG.

So what did we two know about LNG? Not a lot. Books out and heads down. Actually, the technology changes very little, so that was a help. The study considered the importation of twenty-five per cent of the UK market, so taking the average liquid volume carried by an LNG ship and a trusty calculator, we could work out the number of ship movements and the number of vessels required.

Although the project gave three ports to ship the LNG from, Murmansk was the only real option. A lot a detail was required which was never going to be made available. It was the home of the Russian Red Feet for goodness sake.

My next-door neighbour in Rafford was stationed at RAF Kinloss, home to the Nimrod fleet of submarine-hunting aircraft. His department handled the information retrieved from the aircraft after each mission. I asked him what anybody knew about Murmansk.

It seemed that there was a lot of information, including photographs. Who took them I asked? Oh, the navy, from one of their silent submarines, which they took at night through the periscope. Would I like a copy? Difficult to put them in an official report I said, where all the sources had to be referenced.

Thinking about Murmansk and its tremendous WW2 history, Dr

Paul was visiting the port and came across a large wooden crate that had obviously been abandoned for a very long time. His curiosity got the better of him. The extremely faint stamps on the side were in English. He persuaded the Russians to open it up, and found a brand new WW2 Hurricane fighter aircraft. He tried to get the crate closed up and offer some cash for it but to no avail.

I believe this story was repeated in other parts of Russia. At the end of WW2, serviceable Hurricanes were extremely rare. After the Battle of Britain, most were shipped to North Africa for dessert service, or to defend Malta. Those that survived ended-up in the Burma conflict and those that survived that were scrap.

Another Russian project that came our way was for USSR Ministry of Oil – Piltun-Astoskskoya Early Production Project on Sakhalin Island on the very eastern side of the country.

The energy industry on this island reaches back to the 1930s, but offshore in the Sea of Okhotsk large reserves of oil are promised. But Russia was seriously short of hard-currency and there was a small accumulation of oil close to shore that could be developed as a tie-back using subsea technology

My boss, Phil the Jacket, or Jacket for short, as he always wore Boss clothing, took the long journey to Sakhalin via Moscow. This was a story in itself. From Aberdeen to the Island of Sakhalin crosses nine time zones. On the last of many stops, travelling west to east, the aircraft landed to refuel and strict orders were no blinds to be opened on any window.

Phil had a quick peek but was seen. His reprimand was short, the language barrier took the blame, but this airport was very close to the Chinese border and there had been a lot of military action along it.

When Phil returned, the design team solved most of the issues, like building a process plant for the crude oil some distance inland to avoid any possible contamination of the caviar industry.

The given environmental conditions were plus twenty-five to minus thirty-six centigrade. Some range. The Russians were able to transport all they needed in their Antonov 124 aircraft using Aberdeen airport. But how to get fifteen kilometres of subsea umbilical to Sakhalin Island?

This stumped everyone until I came up with the solution, which was to ask the Russians to donate one of their Red Fleet destroyers, remove all the super-structure from the funnel aft, leaving a large deck area for a collapsible carousel to carry the umbilical to Sakhalin. Everybody laughed, but calmer consideration agreed that it would be one way, perhaps the only way. The project was stolen by others, mainly the big Japanese companies with USA backing.

We did, however, have two visitors from Sakhalin. The first was the political boss of the island and JPK pulled out all the stops. I was roped in as driver/organiser. The highlight of the visit was a day at Gleneagles for a major golf tournament.

John K and Dr Paul, our honoured guest, Natasha 2, Phil, who had already met the guest on the island, and myself, are all gathered together on the hole nearest to the hospitality tent that awaited for us all.

Ian Woosnam, a short-tempered Welsh golfer, chipped to the green and was trying to settle down for a long putt, when our honoured guest, a well-built, not to be argued with sort of guy, was having a loud conversation in Russian with Natasha 2 trying to keep-up with the explanations of the game. Mr Woosnam shouted something out loud, clearly very upset and our honoured guest was about to respond before Phil and I hurriedly guided him to the hospitality tent and the many opened bottles of vodka. I explained to the steward who our honoured guest was, a very senior VIP, whose power on his island absolute. Phew!

*

IT WAS LATE 1987 when six young Russian engineers arrived in the UK to work for JPK.

John Kenny was busy developing the market in Russia and had a white Russian working for him, a nice and very clued up person called Nicholas, or Nick to everybody.

This was at the time of Perestroika (restructuring) and Glasnost (openness). Three young men were assigned to the London office and three came to Aberdeen, Boris, Igor and Olaf. It was assumed that these youngsters, in their early twenties had Party approval at a high level to leave the country.

Despite all the changes in Russia I doubt if the average Russian could get a passport and work permit for the UK without a few strings bringing pulled. Anyway, this subject was never going to be revealed.

Anyway, of more importance, Boris was the son of a leading Russian sailor and Igor was an Olympic crew for the Olympic 470 class. One windy day, when club racing had been cancelled I took Boris and Igor for a blast around Findhorn bay in twenty-five knots of wind. These guys were so good as crew, I never felt more comfortable. However, we didn't stay out long, the oncoming storm clouds taught prudence.

These three engineers were very well trained. What they couldn't get to grips with was UK supermarkets. Nick, who would stay with them on his visits from the London office, found they were spending their living allowance in the local corner shop, rather than the much cheaper supermarkets.

Nick discovered if they went to a large supermarket the sheer number of choices for any single item was very confusing. Just think how many different types of bread you can buy. In Moscow at the time, there was either one type of bread or none at all.

After their visit to Findhorn and its Royal yacht club, I came up with the idea that the RFYC should visit Moscow. Boris told me that his father's club had state supplied Carter 32' yachts and two teams of five would be no problem.

The club Commodore liked the idea, but who would sponsor? However, it would be the first visit to Russia by a foreign yacht club, which would be a magnificent achievement. I had a word with John Kenny, he liked the idea and it all took off from there

So, in 1990, the RFYC went to Moscow for what turned out to be a truly memorable experience. The Russians came to RFYC the following year.

The Russians laid-on a huge amount of hospitality, so much so that on the return to Aberdeen I got the shakes on the plane from London up to Aberdeen. When the stewardess asked if I would like a drink, I asked for three vodkas, not my normal drink, in a glass with orange juice. With shaking hands, I was just able to drink it. The first time and the last time I ever had this experience.

During the visit to Moscow, the club members had to go to the UK Embassy, to collect a sum of money in rubles to help pay our expenses. No idea where this money came from, but I do remember the Embassy doorman and other members of staff acting strangely towards us. Like they came from the Planet Mars. Weird!

The racing was good, but local knowledge helped our hosts to victory.

During our stay we visited the apartment of Boris's father in Moscow. Very 1920s but with triple glazing, it was warm and cosy. The house in the country, a dacha, was more attractive, quaint, comfortable and quiet. Very pleasant.

*

THE SECOND RUSSIAN visitor was Dr Astafyev, the chief engineer of the Sakhalin Oil Company, a cultured thoughtful person, who had a daughter that painted. He came to visit the companies in the Aberdeen region producing the equipment for subsea production. I was again tasked with organising his visit. First, two items, hire a large Ford limousine a Scorpio Ghia and a new set of swimming trunks.

Dr Astafyev liked to swim before breakfast, so I was invited to join him every day. It was a new experience, getting up at six in the morning to drive to his hotel, swim for forty minutes, then take breakfast. The good doctor was an active guy, so each morning we arrived at the office at 8.30 am, for the daily briefing, then collect one of the three young Russians engineers as interpreter and set-out on a visit to the vendor of the day.

Afterwards, back to the hotel, more swimming and then dinner with the company managers. It all went rather well until the last day when a visit to the umbilical factory in Leith Docks, Edinburgh, was planned. Goody, a night in Edinburgh, or so I thought. I asked Boris to come that day, to which he readily agreed.

Driving down from Aberdeen to Leith Docks is a chore first thing on a Friday morning, especially after the early start, the swimming and big breakfast. I managed a good journey time; what a nice car this was to drive at other's expense.

Dr Astafyev was impressed with the Forth Road Bridge and the Forth Railway Bridge. The traffic into town was less than impressive, although I knew the back way, which helped a great deal. The tour of the umbilical factory went well as the factory makes all of its own components from raw material.

A slight moment of concern came when Dr Astafyev did not believe a 5,000 psi quarter inch hose could withstand a pressure of four times that before bursting. The plant manager laid on a test. Dr Astafyev, looking very pensive, hid behind something thick and heavy. The test went well, but the good Doctor kept his distance.

Then came lunchtime and the party repaired to The King's Wark a beautiful bar and restaurant situated close by. The charming building is steeped in history dating back to the 1400s and its food is the best.

At the end of a long lunch, I mentioned it was time to go to the hotel and rest up before seeing the sights of Edinburgh. Boris told me that Dr Astafyev had invited everybody to dinner at his hotel in Aberdeen, which would include more swimming at eight of the evening.

Now, I had to get this party back to Aberdeen and Edinburgh rush hour was going to be a factor. How I wriggled the car out of town I will never know. Fortunately, the traffic cops were absent and I had a very fast run back to town with everyone fast asleep after such a magnificent repast.

As I reached Aberdeen, Boris told me there was a pre-dinner reception in his apartment, where we found Phil the Jacket, Nick the white Russian, the other two youngsters and the boss of the company and his wife.

They had started early. Clearly, the young Russians had smuggled quite of lot of Russian vodka, the real stuff that becomes like a syrup when chilled to the correct temperature.

Dr Astafyev quickly joined in the vodka drinking session and I collapsed on the floor absolutely worn out. I could hardly move. Boris gave me a glass of his vodka, the lemon one and it slipped slowly and steadily down my throat. Now, normally at this stage of the proceedings I would have gone fast asleep for at least four hours. That didn't happen. I ended up in the bloody swimming pool doing Mike Phelps impressions and then eating a big dinner. In all, a great day out and the end of the visit. On Saturday I slept until midday.

*

THE NEXT PROJECT was the Buchan Alpha 9th Well for BP. The platform was a former drill rig that needed a big makeover to get it fit for the conversion. The field was marginal but BP made it into a success by the cunning method of being so late in completing the conversion the price of oil had risen to make it all worthwhile.

Originally designed for eight subsea wells, modifications for a ninth well required shoehorning a lot of equipment into spaces that were difficult to use. Oh, and the platform was not going to shut down, no matter what, to enable the work to be carried out more safely. *(BP did actually shut down the platform after some hotshot managed to connect the production from Buchan Alpha to the receiving platform's flare tower, with burning crude oil falling all over the sea and deck, oh dear.)*

The onshore design work went well, but muggins here ended-up offshore trying to turn rude matter into due form and what a struggle it was. Working all the hours and with little sleep the team only just made breakfast each morning.

On this fateful day, the BP project leader, known as Pluto – he was a dead ringer for the cartoon character – marched into breakfast and held up the galley shutters so we could put a hot breakfast on our plate, As we sat down to eat, Pluto looked across to the deep water divers who had just come out of their Saturation Chamber and shouted, 'Good morning Frogmen, (which they hated being called) what's the matter with your miserable faces.'

The reply? Said one of the divers looking up at the live TV news, 'You won't be so fuckin' cheerful when you see this.'

I stood up went to look at the television and didn't believe my eyes. The news report was covering the *Piper Alpha* disaster. Had it not been for last night's fog we could have seen this tragic event, live, but we had slept through it.

It could have been us. During the previous evening, there had been a gas fire onboard that was quickly extinguished. Something else I didn't know about.

Shocked, the team completed its breakfast and soon got back to work if only to take our minds away from the North Sea's first major platform disaster. Much has been written about *Piper Alpha* and I cannot add anything new except speculation and that is not for this book.

*

WHILE I AM on the subject of tragic events, my favourite person Jim Anderson, Johan's father, died of a heart attack. In 1986, Jim had retired from Dounreay to my home at Rafford which was under used. So, after many years in Thurso, Jim and Margret said goodbye to their friends in Caithness and moved to Morayshire to enjoy their retirement.

Jim was good in the garden. His method of pruning overgrown trees and bushes will not be found in any weighty tomes on the subject. Jim would cut and cut hard. He used to say, 'the plant will either live or die'. None died and what had been a beautiful garden was restored.

Jim was always at risk of a heart attack, as he had a spot of coal dust on his lungs.

In 1988, Jim's health took a turn for the worst. The signs were there for all to see. I was working away from Aberdeen, forget where. What may have saved him had he been admitted early to the hospital in Elgin.

Instead, the modern thinking was to let patients stay at home where it was familiar to them. Stopped too much stress and all that rubbish. When he died, he was sick in every room in the house as his body literally exploded. Poor Margret had little help to clean-up the mess. Bloody know-all doctors.

We all gathered at Rafford then went to Kirkcaldy, Fife, where he was cremated and his ashes spread in the beautiful gardens of rest.

The next body blow was when Kirsty, my wonderful dog passed away. She had been ill for some time and quite old. Again, I was away from home, but this did not decrease the sadness.

Sometime later, I helped Margret to return to Fife to live with her cousin. She was unable to stay in Rafford. There was no bus service into town and she never drove.

*

FOLLOWING THE *PIPER Alpha* tragedy, the North Sea industry rushed to fit platform safety valves, designed to stop the back-flow of highly compressed gas into a platform with a fire, major or otherwise. Many valves were installed low-down on the platform structure, but many were subsea, the optimum location. I worked on few of these projects, the most memorable was for the Ninian Field SSESV (subsea emergency safety valve),

It was memorable for the hard work it took for the client to see common sense on quite a few matters; a severe case of young university-trained client engineers not willing to listen to the older more experienced members of the industry. All I can say is if they are prepared to waste a lot of money when they didn't need to, why do they complain at great length about the invoices they received. Of course, the fitting of these extra safety valves was a 'dead money' project. I believe over a billion pounds was spent in the North Sea for not one extra drop in oil.

As for the murky details of this project, perhaps another day.

*

IN LATE AUGUST, 1988, new work was thin on the ground in Aberdeen. London office had work, and they were also losing people. I was asked to go to London and help out. There was a big bid in progress and whoever had departed had left a half-finished job in a very poor state. I was able to turn this around with the burning of some midnight oil. Then BP awarded JPK a part of a consortium project for a UK FPSO project (Floating production storage and offloading).

This type of project was becoming popular in the industry, as a little used tanker could be converted to produce and store oil before offloading onto a shuttle tanker. This opened up the possibility of developing small fields quickly and cheaply and then moving the FPSO to another field in due course.

The project was housed in the old Craven 'A' cigarette factory in Camden Town, famous for, if nothing else, its Greek bakeries. The building was more than old, tall high windows performed the opposite job to double glazing. The heating was either on or off, usually the opposite to that which was required. A warm day in winter was a very warm day in the office, and vice versa. The building management took great delight at being contrary to all requirements of comfort.

The project stalled because the FPSO ship was based on a tanker. BP Shipping bagged the rights to say what goes and what didn't go. BP Production was completely different in their thinking. After two months of discussion, or was it concussion, the project looked doomed. A previous FPSO project for BP had gone the same way and eventually finished three years late.

On the 21st of December 1988, JPK held their annual Christmas party at the Kempton Park Race Course function rooms. Halfway through a very good evening, rumours started to swirl around about a big event in Scotland at a town called Lockerbie. A jumbo jet had been brought down.

Little was known until the full details became known the next day when Dr Paul came around the office to tell everybody that the project had been cancelled and BP would pay two weeks money in lieu of notice. He came up to me and said, 'Colin, return to the Aberdeen office, in the second week in January, there will be something for you, can't say what.' And with that, he wished me a Merry Christmas.

Everybody left the office that morning. I rushed back to the B&B to collect my belongings and headed up the road to Scotland. It had to be the A1, as the main A74 was blocked at Lockerbie, in fact, half of the dual carriageway was in a big hole along with the remains of the jumbo jet. Whatever was going on in Lockerbie, it was going to be chaos.

The drive north on the A1 is never pleasant and it was twice as busy with Christmas traffic and now the diverted Scottish traffic. My trusty Rover chugged up the road, sitting behind endless queues of slow moving traffic. It was also a cold miserable day. I followed the A1 all the way to Edinburgh. Never again.

*

MEMORIES AND FORGETFULNESS

IT WAS DURING these later years that I had a not too serious relationship with the opposite sex. The lady was having a real hard time with her ex-husband. The family home was in Inverurie, north of Aberdeen. It was far too big and to get to work she had to rely on an ageing Alfa Romeo that had advancing tin worm.

During a Christmas break when she was not at home, a sharp cold spell froze the water pipes in the loft and when the thaw came, the water near on destroyed what was a modern build house. The floors and all the wall panels had to be removed. Fortunately, the house insurance covered most of the building and contents.

The downstairs flooring had just been replaced when I had a brilliant idea. She wanted to sell, but it would be ages before the house was ready. She had told me that a couple did look at the property and liked the house very much but the wife was very picky about the kitchen and dining room layout. I suggested that she ring the couple straight away and I would sell them the property. I received the queerest look of all time, but she phoned and the couple came round within the half hour.

When they walked in the house they were upset, what kind of nonsense was this? I calmed them down and told them that if they liked the house, now they could have any layout they wanted. The builder doing the work was known for providing an excellent finish and when all the repair work and modifications had been completed, they would have their dream home, brand new.

The husband picked up on it straight away. He steered his wife into another room to explain and she came back smiling. Soon after, terms were agreed and everybody was very happy.

23

GETTING MARRIED

(1990 - 1992)

IN 1990 ROGER AND VANDA were living in a very classic residence in Aberdeen that Roger bought at the very bottom of the market. He then proceeded to refurbish the property in his spare time and what a wonderful job he made of it. All the original beautiful woodwork had the paint stripped and the staircase up to the third floor was a delight to see.

I used to visit when I could and when I heard that they would be going to Brazil for Christmas and New Year I asked Vanda a big favour. When she reached Rio de Janeiro please could she call Sonia's brother's residence and ask after her.

This went well and I got back in touch with Sonia, as during the time apart contact had slowly faded. I was doing well at JPK but felt the need to see her again. I arranged to visit during the Easter holiday.

So, putting my best foot forward, I took a ten-day break and flew to Brazil. By this time Sonia had her own place in Leme at the end of a Rua sem Saida. It was like I had never been away. The time was right to make plans. Sonia could come to Aberdeen in August until December when we would both return to Rio de Janeiro for Christmas and New Year. It was all very romantic.

After the holiday in Brazil, I went back to work and the time flew. Running my part of three projects at the same time kept me very busy. There was also plenty of overtime, so the pennies mounted up.

With Sonia due in August I rented an apartment in town. I also started to look around the housing market in Aberdeen. My time at Rafford was coming to an end and when I married Sonia, which would happen in 1992, a new home will be the best all around. My daughters had left home, so the time had come.

Sonia arrived in August 1991 as planned and we lived very happily together. With a large Brazilian contingent in Aberdeen, she was not alone.

Having discussed all the issues we planned a big re-engagement party in October and celebrated our two birthdays at the same time. The party was a big success and we welcomed Margret who had travelled up from Fife on the train.

I had ordered a new home in Stonehaven and Sonia and I used to visit to inspect progress.

The next two months flew by and Christmas arrived quickly. I saw my family before I returned with Sonia to Rio de Janeiro. Good news, Sonia received news that she can retire early and finish her post at the university in April 1992.

Having consulted with the family, the wedding was fixed for the middle of June 1992. The New Year fireworks on Copacabana Beach were spectacular. The Meridien Hotel is my favourite display. It is called the Waterfall, a massive bank of white flares placed horizontally on the roof behind the front of the hotel. The white flares almost reach the ground, thirty floors below. Nowadays, this display has been banned, health and safety, so they say. My, how the million people on the beach loved it

The holiday came to an end and it was time to return to the office. The new house would be finished in February and Rafford was an easy sell. Then my schedule became a rush. I said goodbye to Rafford and the house was stripped.

The National 18 had been sold to a sailor based at Tamesis Club, one of the oldest sailing clubs in the world, on the River Thames. I enjoyed racing there when working for JPK in their Staines office. It's a lovely place but the wind is everywhere and that's when there is any.

Back in Aberdeen, I moved quickly to organise a wedding. The church in Stonehaven and the reception was easy. Vanda took care of the wedding cake. She knew a lady who worked from home. What age did I want the cake to be, six months, a year or any year up to ten, where the price of the cake was close to the price of gold. They were clearly very special cakes.

The subject of the wedding car became very stressful. I could not find anything with class and a white Volvo estate wasn't going to cut it. Feeling fed-up I joined the office for their usual Friday lunch time session. Our chief piping guy, Big Dave, a man who liked his drink and drove a V12 Jaguar S-Type that never attracted the attention of anybody, slipped me a piece of paper.

It had a name, a Mr Scroggy and his home telephone number is from one of those little villages that hang on to a cliff edge further down the coast. With trepidation, I made the call and just about understood what the man said. He reminded me of Johan's uncle all those years ago, the one that only spoke his version of English after having spoken only the Gallic for most of his life. Yes, he had a car, a 1978 Rolls Royce Silver Shadow in mid-blue and it was available for the date and time of the wedding. I felt so relieved at the time.

I just had time to move into the new home when I was awarded a plum posting in Dublin. Some city, wow. I was very lucky to rent a wonderful apartment in Balls Bridge, a very upmarket area. The street had quite a few embassies for the smaller countries around the world. Even better, all the buildings were classic Georgian style and extremely elegant.

What impressed me the most about Dublin was the evenings when I liked to go for a good walk and then pop into one of many public houses for a glass of local Guinness. I remember never being able to sit on my own without the locals inviting me to join in their conversations and what conversations they were too.

And what of the project. Well, it was an EU funded project to bringing gas from the main trunk line on the west side of Scotland to a site just north of Dublin. It was a big pipeline too, destined to become one of the mainstays of gas supply to the Irish Republic.

Of the many sectors I was asked to deal with, the main one was to take over the contract for the purchase of the high-pressure ball valves located at the pressure let-down station. The core of the contract was for highly specialised types of large ball valves rarely seen and only used in special cases.

Dealing with the vendors of this particular product was an eye-opener. Imagine the most persistent seller of time shares or double glazing, only ten times worse. Only by carefully reading of the contract documents was it possible to make a short list of vendors who actually compiled and eliminate the rest for mostly under-bidding this high specification product, which is always a recipe for disaster. Even then, to bring success to the project was extremely hard work. A useful lesson though.

By this time, I was driving a VW Passat GT with the sixteen-valve engine and mechanical fuel injection. It was an excellent car and I should have kept it as now they are very rare.

Mid-May arrived and it was time to take holidays, drive from Dublin down to Rosslare to catch the evening ferry to Fishguard in Wales and meet Sonia at Heathrow the following day. I enjoyed a reasonable dinner on the ferry and found somewhere to sleep before the arrival in Fishguard. The ferry disembarked just as the sun was about to show some interest in the day. Fully fuelled I made rapid progress in the calm of an early morning and I was glad to join the motorway before the good people of Wales started their day.

Taking the M4 motorway in my stride I arrived at Heathrow an hour before Sonia's flight was due to land. At least it was on time. And then the happy moment came, we met in the terminal and didn't she just look radiant, even after a long flight. And what a lot of luggage. A rather overloaded car made it out of the car park as I searched for the exit road. Sonia asked if we were going directly to Aberdeen, which would have been a long day for her and an even longer day for me. She was pleased to know I had reserved a hotel for two nights in London then we would be ready for the long drive to Aberdeen.

The next few weeks was a blur of action and organising. The Brazilians in Aberdeen played their part and my good friend Irene made a wonderful job of decorating the double garage of our new home to be the centrepiece of the wedding party to be held after the wedding reception. The dining room became overloaded with presents and outside the back door of the kitchen was piled high with crates of refreshments for what would be a grand party.

Next, the cake arrived and what a splendid cake it was too. Vanda fussed over it like an expectant mother, while husband Roger looked for a cold beer in the fridge. And so, everything fell into place. Tarpey, his massive beard, and wife Linda arrived and I managed to squeeze him into my silver grey suit so he could stand next to me at the altar as best man.

Andrei, one of the three Russian's, arrived from London and I quickly managed to find somewhere for him to sleep for a few nights. My brother and his youngest son, arrived with a video camera to record the proceedings. Carolyn arrived with mum-in-law Margret and last but not least, my parents had made their second long journey to Scotland for their son's second wedding. In all, it was a grand gathering.

The Brazilian ladies clustered around Sonia well aware this brave lady had travelled a long way to get married with none of her immediate family to support her. Her mother was too frail and the others, well, they were no loss, to be frank about it.

There was a hen party in the house and the men retired to the hotel, which would provide the venue for the wedding breakfast. I shared a room with someone and the next day, the 27th June 1992, err it would rain, just a little. Nothing would spoil the day.

After a late breakfast, Tarpey and I made the church in good time. I had all the paperwork ready, including Sonia's UK visa to enter the country for marriage. My father did the honours by collecting the official photographer, taking him to the house to collect Sonia and waiting for the magnificent Rolls Royce to arrive and bring them to the church.

Sonia arrived in the church to receive the admiring oh's an ahs' from the ladies, her trousseau in blue was just stunning and where did she get that hat, hand carried all the way from Brazil.

The ceremony was meaningful, the sermon short and the taking of the photographs took the usual length of time. Then, with the wedding reception just across the road, I persuaded the immaculately dressed lady driving the Rolls Royce to take us across the road by way of a quick wiz around Stonehaven on the bypass road. What a wonderful ride. I noticed how well prepared the Rolls Royce was, flowers on the back window shelf, the small decorative umbrella in the front of the car and everything just as it should be. Thank heavens for my friend Big Dave and Mr Scroggy the owner of the Rolls Royce.

The wedding breakfast was a big success. I used to eat in this hotel quite frequently. The owner, Herman the German, was more than capable of mixing it with his customers and he did make the best lasagne it was my pleasure to order.

Roger made a great speech and Tarpey, my best man equalled it. I had a speech, but abandoned it for something more me and kept it short. It was that very special occasion and I do not think my writings give it the class I would have liked.

But more was to come. Following a short break for everyone, the evening continued at home. Irene and the Brazilian wives all pitched in and I was left with nothing to do. I cannot remember half the detail, but the party ended a special day for a special lady now my beloved wife. What a lucky person I was.

*

MEMORIES AND FORGETFULNESS

A FEW DAYS later, I closed up the house, packed up the car and headed for Dublin. It's a long five-hour slog to the ferry terminal at Cairnryan and fortunately, the Seacat service to Belfast is fast if the weather is good. The onward journey to Dublin is a tad over two hours depending on the Irish Border, still being guarded by the British Army.

I was never tempted to spend time in Northern Ireland, I'm sure some parts are quite beautiful, but its history does not attract. As we crossed the border my bride asked an expected question, where would be the honeymoon. 'Dublin', I replied.

Sonia didn't know what to think. That was until we arrived at the apartment I had recently rented in Gray Street, Balls Bridge. The apartment was owned by an Irish businessman in the oil industry. Big spacious and well appointed. A beautiful park could be accessed via a pathway between two of the buildings.

We unloaded the car then took a taxi into town and headed to the Dury Street area. Sonia's eye lit-up and marvelled at all that was going on. I said 'One honeymoon, as requested, about nine months.' And that is how it turned out.

The work was fun, but other memories include the night a neighbour banged on our door, having prevented my car being stolen. The 'crooklok', that unsung hero of preventing car thefts, had slowed the robbers down long enough to get caught in the act. The police arrived amazingly quickly, but with so many embassies in the area, including the US Embassy at the bottom of the road, it was not too surprising.

I asked the policeman why anybody would want a six-year-old VW Passat. He told me, to break it for parts and the engine. The VW 1800cc 16v engine was highly prized by the formula racers. It is worth more than the car. Fortunately, the damage was light and repairs were met by the insurance.

The next memory occurred when I came home from the office and Sonia was on a big high. I asked and she said, 'I was taking the bus into town talking to a young lady in my poor English. I asked oh how are you?

'Oh, I am fine thank you.'

'And,' I asked.

'The young lady was Brazilian and worked at the Embassy.'

'At which point in time the bus was flooded with high speed Portuguese and nobody could hear themselves think,' I said.

'Sim.'

We had a fantastic time in Dublin. It was during the referendum to join the European Union. Vast billboards had the very subtle message 'There are Six Billion Reasons to Vote Yes.' Brilliant.

Sonia, now living away from Brazil for the first time, immersed herself in all there was to do in Dublin. At weekends, I would go with her to revisit her favourite places.

Then, there was the cheap long weekend visit to Paris during a national French holiday. It took three hours to get up Tour Eiffel. Reason: Italian tourists, millions of them.

The next long weekend was the visit to Galway at the end of the season. No cheap hotels, Italian tourists, millions of them had booked them long ago.

I had to book a five-star hotel full of American tourists. Eight o'clock in the morning they are up and out, cameras at the ready, in their white bobby socks and trainers. We would go to breakfast at the death and the chef had to cook everything fresh. Brilliant.

*

WE ENJOYED DUBLIN so much but when it was time to depart I was transferred to the JPK Staines office. I rented a small 3rd floor bijou apartment in a traditional River Thames three-story property, right on the river's edge. The River Thames is a fascinating river to watch. Just so much goes on. Great pubs too.

I could walk to the office and Sonia loved taking the train into London for the day. The project was for the Hamilton Brothers, an American outfit. More of the same, head down, churn out the work, and collect the pay.

24

BACK TO BRAZIL

(1994 - 1996)

BY THE END OF 1994, the work ran out, again. With the help of friends in the company, the time came to try and enter the Brazilian market. Petrobrás was very busy and moving into ever-deeper water. I had contacts that would enable me to approach a Brazilian company who had an ex-Petrobrás E&P director as one of their directors.

Sonia and I returned to Brazil to live in her apartment. So I found myself in the lion's den that was Petrobrás. Nothing has changed. Initially, it went well and the ex-E&P director took me to visit the top floor of the Petrobrás HQ, to meet most of the directors.

Lunch there was also an experience, as the Petrobrás directors all sat in small groups, watching each other intently. I had a good friend, George, a Ukrainian Canadian. Unfortunately, he is no longer with us. He was a director of Brazil's Oil & Gas magazine. His contacts were invaluable. I ended up in the Petrobrás building close to Maracanã football stadium and by chance, Sonia's university was on the opposite side of the road.

The general manager of the subsea installation design group had the need for a deepwater pipeline engineer. I had someone in mind from the JPK Staines office, but internal politics meant that the Houston office grabbed the control of my nascent operation. This proved to be a big disconnect from the persons prepared to support my initiative.

Anyway, terms were agreed and JPK Houston sent down an engineer of Chinese origin. He looked and felt out of place the whole time he spent in Rio de Janeiro. What didn't help was all the Brazilian's kept calling him, 'O Japanese,' mainly because the only Orientals in Brazil are indeed Japanese, of which there are a large number.

He was replaced after a few weeks by Roy, an all singing and dancing American from upstate New York. He fitted in just fine. Recently divorced, he found himself in Valhalla as far as the opposite sex was concerned.

The main thing though was that he was effective at work and the client welcomed his efforts. Through his efforts, the business also sold computer software and generated other leads to be followed up.

I also help to manage a subsea equipment bid. A friend of Sonia, Mauricio, had been relocated from Aberdeen back to Rio de Janeiro where he took-up the general manager's position.

At the time Petrobrás was ordering a large amount of subsea equipment and invitations to bid were rarely ignored. The bid concerned subsea production manifolds and Mauricio asked for assistance with the subsea control's side of the project.

The decision to bid was rather late, but some hard work managed to get a reasonable document out in time. The experience of the meeting, where bids from all the vendors are received in a quite formal manner was most interesting.

As the documents were handed-in, one vendor at a time, every page was initialled by the vendor and the client. Each separate commercial proposal was double wrapped and every vendor had to sign over the sealing tape to ensure it was not opened until the second meeting when the technically acceptable bids were chosen on the basis of price.

Everybody attending this submission meeting was hanging around, drinking the coffee and eating the biscuits. It was not long before the assembly turned into a sort of a party, people circulating amongst old friends and as always the level of many conversations rose to the point where the client asked for quiet. All this took rather a long time and the coffee ran out. Damn.

The meeting when the commercial documents were examined by one and all to ensure they had not been tampered with went more quickly. The bid I was involved with came in second place. The winning bidder just quoted the same price for a previous manifold bid, which was impossible to match and I know for sure money was lost.

A very sad event occurred when Mauricio lost his life when his plane took-off from Sao Paulo's city airport and one engine deployed its thrust reverser. The result was a horrible crash and no one survived. There was a lot of delay in the following investigation by the authorities. Word was there was a large stash of Bolivian Marching Powder on the aircraft.

The end of my initiative to create a market in Brazil came when the Houston office sent their chief engineer down to make a visit of the Petrobrás directors and senior managers, most of whom I knew reasonably well. The whole thing descended into farce. The person concerned swopped his business class airline ticket for two economy tickets and brought his hideous vegetarian wife with him. Brazilian restaurants do not cater for 'veggies'.

This couple caused more chaos than I care to record here. She got robbed of a Walkman on the beach, which turned into a Federal case and her husband actually cancelled a meeting with the head of the famous Petrobrás R&D division to attend to the matter of a thirty dollar item.

His final act, driving the nail deep into my coffin, was the morning he came to the company's office to meet with the ex R&D director of Petrobrás, my mentor, dressed ready for the beach. The ex-director showed him the door and later I took the full force of his displeasure. This idiot had no idea how powerful this person was in the industry as a whole, let alone his country. I almost died on the spot.

Sonia and I were invited to a meal by this person, but he forgot his credit card. He said he would repay me and thirty years later I am still waiting. What a complete shit.

25

BACK TO BLIGHTY

(1996 - 1999)

I RETURNED TO LONDON AND WAS invited to join a Norwegian FPSO project called Varg, for Statoil PLC. The project was based in ABB's offices in Sutton, in Surry, South London. My office on the top floor in the north-east corner of the twenty-story building had fine views of all the aircraft using Heathrow Airport. Fascinating to watch.

I managed to find a suitable apartment for us both, a brisk twelve minute walk away. The train station was next to the office, and there was good shopping to be had and wonderful pubs that sold London's favourite IPA, my favourite beer.

On a Friday, it was possible to leave early before the weekend crush on the roads, so it was an easy call to visit the parents in deepest Hampshire. The project lasted a just over a year and I tasked with the topsides safety and broadcast systems, which caused a certain amount of revision of past skills.

The project went very well except for a very tragic event. The project manager was under severe stress by his company. He worked far too many days with excessive hours, and to compound his worries he had a very difficult marriage break-up to contend with.

One morning, just as everybody was arriving at the office, the building security staff would not let anybody into the office. The crowd outside the office grew at a rapid rate as each train disgorged its passengers all heading for the one building.

What was going on? The police were present in some numbers but they were not for crowd control; these were the investigative specialists. Everybody was also barred from spilling over into the car park. Eventually, everyone was ushered into the building, but told not to use the telephones. For what?

It turned out that the project manager had arrived very early and made it up to the top floor, defeated the safety mechanism that prevented the window near my desk from opening and had jumped, trying to land on the company director's parking space. Everyone felt for the early morning security staff, as they thought it a bit strange when the project manager rushed in, then five minutes later they heard the sound and they just knew what it was. Horrible.

The project work in the London office did not last too much longer after this tragic event. The work was well on its way to completion and the client took the remaining work back to Norway.

*

Ralph M Parsons, London - 1997 Esso "Fawley" Refinery.

SO, AS ONE project dumped its people on the street, so the fleet of foot found somewhere else to go to. Now it was mid-way through 1997 and it was a lot cooler than the summer before.

I found myself back working for Ralph Parsons on an oil refinery project for Esso's Fawley refinery near my hometown of Southampton. The project was to add a new plant to process one of the many take-offs from the refining process.

The chemical, I forget which one, was in big demand in Europe. This additional plant would propel the refinery into profit for the first time in many years. I have no idea why oil company refineries seem to make a loss. I guess it's the way they like to run their business.

The design team even got to visit the refinery. Half the day was spent in a safety briefing and it was very interesting to know the issues. I wonder why anybody would live within two miles of a working refinery, as it uses a lot of heat and pressure to persuade all the different molecules contained in crude oil to become something else. It's up there with trying to change a woman's mind once it's been made up.

The project had a slow start and Parson's discovered they were overstaffed about ten minutes after I came to the same conclusion. Without previous experience of refinery work, I did both parties a favour by suggesting, very politely, that I had another offer so after the shaking of the hands and with a week's pay in lieu of notice I was on my way to a BP Project, the like of which I had never heard before.

*

AMEC Process & Energy (1997) BP Marine Vapour Recovery Project
I FOUND MYSELF working on a BP project to be installed in Bonny Scotland, close to Edinburgh. In the Firth of Forth at Hound Point, BP operated a loading and unloading terminal for its tankers. The terminal connects with underground pipelines to the Grangemouth refinery.

When an empty oil tanker is loaded with product, the air in the tank is ejected into the environment. This air is loaded with VOCs, or Volatile Organic Compounds, which stink. However, the rich landowners close to the terminal were fully informed, especially about the stink. And in proud traditions of rich people, they complained to their buddies on whichever local council had the powers to interfere with anything they wish to interfere with.

Amec collected the contract and after years in the industry, everybody knew Amec. It was quite a good company actually. I met a few people I hadn't seen in years and the first lunch in the local pub proceeded in the usual manner.

A team was formed and ended up in Paul Street on the eastern edge of the City of London, overlooking the Ferrari Concessionaires. (I do like the F-400 saloon, but the cost to keep it running – wow.)

I met up with an old friend Geoff who was the rotating engineer specialist. The project was different simply because a normal oil processing plant is based on containing high pressures, high rates of flow and even higher temperatures

This project considered collecting the VOR gas at very low pressures, obviously cold and the flow rates were similarly low. BP were in a rush, there must have been pressure from the wealthy, so the work proceeded rapidly. My part of the project took just a few months and as luck would have it I managed to return to good old JPK in Aberdeen.

*

BACK IN ABERDEEN, it was a busy two years with six very interesting projects, one for Petrobrás R&D department CENPES, in Rio de Janeiro with the opportunity to make good friends with the two engineers that

MEMORIES AND FORGETFULNESS

came to assist in the project.

Sonia was happy to be back in Aberdeen. Vanda was still ruling the Brazilian roost and there were a few good parties. The last carnival party I went too was very exciting. Quite how Vanda got away with wearing 'that costume' is a subject I shall leave for another day.

On the social side, I combined with my brother and his latest girlfriend to take my car to visit the continent. I had sold the VW Passat after ninety thousand miles of excellent service and ended up with a 1995 Vauxhall Omega 2.5 CDX saloon. This car was amazing and had features even the motoring media's favourite BMW doesn't have. It covered long distances very easily and the boot space is huge.

I picked up my brother and his partner from his home in Stirling and then next day drove down to the east coast port of Harwich. We stayed in a B&B for the night and after an early breakfast took the catamaran service to Hoek van Holland.

This is a very big catamaran ferry carrying hundreds of cars and big trucks. It is also very fast and we arrived in the early afternoon and had time to make it down to the historic City of Cologne. We stayed just the one night.

Next day we enjoyed a very scenic drive along the River Rhine. For some reason our stops for refreshments seemed to be very close to Germany's best cake shops, where diet plans disappear instantly. Another overnight stop in a small village proved most enjoyable and the evening dinner of local fare was a real treat.

The next day was a long day on the road. My brother had organised a house swap holiday in Vienna. The year before we had all visited Barcelona on a house swap holiday and it was very successful.

The autobahn to Vienna is full of diesel vans with Hungarian plates. My car cruises comfortable at ninety miles an hour and the Hungarians are in a hurry to leave us in their dust. Most of the autobahn is only two lanes and the heavily loaded Omega takes just a little time to get back up to speed. But this little time is far too long for the impatient Hungarians.

Still, the long journey is OK, we stop at good quality service stations and lunch at a motorway stop was reasonable. I didn't realise that Vienna was so far to the east.

The disappointment comes when we reach our destination. The apartment is on the top floor of an old Hapsburg building that looked like it came from a Harry Lime film. There is only one formal bedroom and Sonia quietly makes it plain she isn't going to stay.

My brother is upset as we move out. I told him it was just bad luck the owner of the apartment did not give a better description of the facilities. I found a very comfortable back street hotel for the remainder of our stay.

Our programme divided and we agree to meet for the evening meal, except my brother will cook the evening meal in the Hapsburg apartment to save money. Sonia and I leave him to it.

Our first evening we explored by foot and arrived at the gardens outside the town hall where there is a big fair. There is also a showing on a big screen of an original version of the movie West Side Story which was most enjoyable. Our evening meal is also very pleasant in one of the many cafes in the area. One the way back to the hotel, Sonia and I run out of energy and it looked like rain. The Bristol Hotel is close, so we slip in for a nightcap and a taxi ride to the hotel.

The taxi driver is Egyptian, a charming fellow who has lived in Vienna for many years. My brother wants me to take the car to Budapest so I ask for advice. The taxi driver warns against it. He recalls that when his clients takes the same journey the taxi always has two drivers as the car cannot be parked without serious risk. If left unattended, it will vanish like a puff of smoke. In Budapest, the taxi is continually on the move. I thank him for his advice.

I meet up with my brother the next day and apologise my car cannot go to Budapest. He seems upset and discounts the Egyptian's advice. I stand my ground and my brother and partner disappear in a huff and take the local train to Budapest. Much later he apologises as he found out something I already know, which is if you visited one Hapsburg city you have visited them all.

I found Vienna was not to be as expensive as the people make out. You just need to be careful where you eat and drink. After four days we have visited most places and the highlight was the wonderful lunch in the rotating restaurant high in the sky on the east bank of the River Danube.

The next day I collect my brother and his lady and take the road along the north bank of the River Danube. It proved to be a most enjoyable day out. We raided a supermarket and sat on the river bank watching the barges slowly head up the river to Prague. They all seem to be carrying a car on top of the cargo hold. What an excellent way to get to Prague. Having been forewarned I fill the car with five-star petrol to the very brim. The petrol in Prague is known to be just two star at best.

When we reach Prague I find the hotel that is just off the main road. But it is located in that part of the city built by the Russians, very gloomy. But the rooms are OK and parking is inside the grounds behind a stout concrete wall. There is a metro station very close by. Despite my initial impressions, the hotel is a good deal.

This was my first time in Prague, but it would not be the last. Everybody had a great time, but where Vienna was not as expensive as expected, Prague was by no means as cheap as we were led to believe. Still, it was good value and the Bohemian beer was most delicious.

Soon, it was time to head north to catch the ferry from Holland back to the UK. The car had sufficient petrol to reach the German border, but I bought a few gallons in Prague just to be sure. The car soon lets me know it did not like the cheap petrol. But, the going was slow, the road a very busy two-lane affair badly in need of rebuilding.

I stopped inside Germany as soon as possible and filled up with best premium five star, then found the autobahn and settled down for a fast run up to Holland. Using cruise control as much as possible and holding the speed down to just under ninety miles an hour, my over-loaded Omega made Hoek van Holland from Prague in nine hours, including stops, and consumption returned a respectable thirty-one miles to the gallon.

We soon found a B&B for the night and caught the ferry the next morning. It was late when we arrived back in Aberdeen, feeling refreshed after the holiday ready for the next challenge, whatever that might be.

26

BACK TO BRAZIL AGAIN

JPK Inc. Houston and Brazil Office (1999 - 2000)

AT THE END OF 1999. I found myself back in Brazil as Technical Manager and Project Coordinator for the Petrobrás Campos Basin Leak Detection Project bid. Aberdeen had panned out and it was time to pack the camel and move along.

By this time, John Kenny had sold the company to the Wood Group, based in Aberdeen, a fast-growing company in many fields of operation. Wood Group had also purchased Mustang Engineering in Houston and they had been invited to bid for the Petrobrás project.

The backdrop to this bid came when Petrobrás had two accidents, one close to Rio de Janeiro and another in Rio Grande do Sul. Both involved large oil leaks and both attracted large fines from the local authorities, ever eager to help themselves to free money.

The Brazilian government insisted that Petrobrás start a project to protect the environment or to prevent Petrobrás having to pay out more fines is what they really meant.

I was hired to be the Brazil end of the bid and to coordinate the work. The somewhat extensive scope included leaks from the offshore transfer of crude oil when loading transport tankers, leaks when transport tankers discharged their cargo and any leaks when one platform, floating or otherwise, transferred its production to another facility for onward transportation.

The bid documents also specified non-intrusive measurement and detection from a US company called Clampon Inc, based in New Jersey,

USA. They had a clever piece of technology that could measure flow in a pipe by clamping their device around the pipe and using ultrasonic techniques.

It was a fascinating bid and I had to go to Houston to visit Mustang Engineering Inc. and advise what the team approach would be. The head of the Electrical and Instrumentation group gave me many lessons and insights.

As car ownership is as fundamental as having a pair of legs, the most valuable lesson was on driving in Houston. Being cool was good, road rage was not good. This manager told me of the four hundred people that worked for him, eighty per cent 'carried' in their car or truck.

'You mean they have a weapon in their vehicle,' I asked.

'Yep,' was the lengthy reply.

My visit went well and I returned to Rio de Janeiro. By using my Brazilian contacts I acquired two valuable associates who knew Petrobrás well and a small but effective team was formed.

Each bidder's personnel were taken to visit an offshore fixed platform, a floating production platform and the two main onshore receiving terminals, one just down the coast and the huge terminal near to Santos that fed two giant refineries that supplied fuels, lubricants and chemicals to the most productive state in the world, Sao Paulo.

I was very pleased with the documents that were produced and so was Houston office. The seniors from Mustang Engineering came for the bid review meetings in Brazil and I had to look after their needs and get them to meet the team I had put together.

Even more interesting was the visit of the two owners of Clampon Inc, two Jewish heavyweights who arrived with their wives determined to splash the cash in the up-market shops in Rio. Sonia took care of them and was left exhausted. The two owners liked the documents I had put together and on the quiet told me the Mustang Bid looked very good if the price was right.

I also heard, via the back door, the same comments. But then my friend Betty, a member of the team, who knew Petrobrás well poured a little cold water on our prospects. The meetings with Petrobrás went well, then we all went home to wait.

One of the Mustang managers called me at home asking had I heard anything. By this time I had put two and two together. The opposition had been working their chums in Petrobrás very hard and Petrobrás wanted a cheaper price to which they agreed.

So, I told the Mustang manager the good news and the good news, which was Mustang had submitted the best technical bid and Petrobrás was very pleased with it. The second piece of good news, via my friend Betty, and I have no idea how she knew, our bid failed on price. To soothe my caller's nerves, I told him that the project was a 'dead money project'. Petrobrás having satisfied their government's instructions to start the project were not about to go 'hammer and tongs' at it.

And so it was, the winning company, a real shady load of buggers I might add, got zero support for their work and I believed they lost a lot of money or went bust, I never did find out. Still, a lot of hard work had produced some good result for myself.

As the end of the year approached, one of the Three Johns called me at home and asked if I wanted to move to Houston and work for a company called Pegasus, where a number of ex-JPK managers had escaped to. What an opportunity.

And so, the camel was packed yet again and off to Houston Sonia and I went. We returned to the UK for Christmas, stopping off in Lisbon for a little festive shopping and so on the 6th January, a Saturday, we arrived in Houston with just four suitcases.

27

PEGASUS INT. INC

Houston (2001 - 2006)

HOUSTON WAS FUN AND AN easy place to live. I had set aside five working days to set-up house and home, but it only took two. To be fair I had already chosen an apartment, close to Sonia's friend Cristina, wife of Roy, that I found a position for in Petrobrás.

Houston has a huge apartment rental market, just sign here and move in. Furniture takes a little less time and the buying of the car is very easy. Houston is car country, bus services are correspondingly less frequent, but Houston is so spread out, public services have little chance. In summer it's too hot and humid to walk and walking is not always safe.

I checked in with the office and found all was well. The company was busy and the number of Brits was slowly increasing, coming mostly from the Aberdeen office. Having straightened out the apartment, I was back on my travels back to Rio de Janeiro to help with a bid review for the UK's Enterprise Oil, only this time I travelled in business class.

Houston did not have a direct service to Rio, so the first leg was up to New York and then down to Rio de Janeiro. I was sitting next to the manager of Continental Airways and he was a happy man. He told me that business class was full, so the flight was paid for, which means the revenue from economy class goes straight to the bottom line. Useful information.

The review team, all from the UK, holed up in one of the better hotels on Avenida Atlantica, but there was little time to enjoy the view of Copacabana beach. The work is very interesting and adds to my experience. An ex-Petrobrás tanker is to be converted to an FPSO and there are four main bidders. This is serious work and great care is needed in the evaluation of their bids.

The CEO of Enterprise Oil is a fun guy, very professional. Halfway through the project he takes everyone for an evening meal in one of Rio de Janeiro's best churrasco's.

All too soon the work is done, but the return journey is a direct flight on Continental's new route to Houston.

I get home rather tired, but I am glad to find that Sonia is well and happy. She has been networking with the local Brazilian ladies so she is not alone.

*

NEXT UP, I get an assignment with one of Houston's largest contractors working on an Exxon project in Angola, one of their first. I was sent as a specialist in umbilicals. I know about umbilicals hanging from an FPSO in deep water. The contractor had already placed the order for the product, so first things first I am sent to Oslo for the kick-off meeting with the vendor, a vendor I will meet many times over the next ten years.

On the return journey through Paris, some obnoxious airport official at the gate to the aircraft asks for my return ticket from the USA to my point of origin. As I have yet to receive my work visa, he has a valid point, but he's also a complete shit the way he goes about his business. I get handed to another shit, there is no shortage of this type of person in Charles de Gaule's favourite airport. I cut to the chase and rudely tell them I have a return ticket from the USA back to the UK, but it is in my Houston bedroom. I also tell them I am on company expenses, so a few days in Paris while this matter is sorted out is fine by me. I stare this person down. I can see that he cannot be bothered to fill out all the paperwork he is about to generate, so with little grace, I end up sitting in a comfy business class seat drinking a pre-flight cocktail.

*

BY EARLY AUGUST, my work for Exxon is done and I end up in Unocal's deepwater group in their Houston HQ on I-59 South. I love it. I make good friends with Charlie and we do good work together.

On the 11th of the following month came the dreadful event in New

York. I watch it live on the huge TV monitor in the main conference room. I am amazed at the calmness of the Americans. They are all sad rather than angry.

I later heard that one of Pegasus's client engineers was on his way to the JFK airport when the news comes over on the radio. He beats a path to the nearest car hire company before the dreadful new is common knowledge and he gets to drive home to Texas. Everybody else gets stranded, some for many days.

Later that day, during lunch time, all the news about the various attacks are known and it's a strange experience that there are no aircraft flying in the sky.

*

OVER THE SIX years we spend in Houston I get to work on many interesting projects. I also take-up tennis every Saturday morning before the sun becomes too unbearable. I haven't played tennis since goodness knows when, probably school days. We play doubles and I usually double up with the company's personnel guy. He also plays league tennis during the evenings, so he just needs me to get my serve going and he will take care of the rest. There is a real mix of characters playing and it is all good fun.

One day, the sky to the west goes very dark black. I suggest we finish immediately and get home before the tempest drowns everybody. I get told to shut the hell-up and serve. My old boss from Aberdeen days is also a member of this group. He looks nervously at the sky too. The tennis court is far out on the west side of Houston and we both live in Up-Town some twenty miles away. When the tempest hits, the roads will flood in minutes.

I serve out the game then everybody scurries to safety. I make it on to the main highway, I-10, and drive like the wind. The tempest is chasing me and everybody else. I get to within half a mile of my home when the tempest wins the race. Blinded by the rain, I just make it into the apartment complex and park the car under cover just as the golf ball sized hailstones begin their merry pattern making on any vehicle left in the open. The roads flood and Sonia and I are stuck indoors for the rest of the day.

*

IN THE SUMMER of 2004, Sonia and I flew over from Houston to visit the family in the UK. The star attraction of the visit was the 200th Anniversary of Steam Exhibition in York at the National Railway Museum. It also gave me the chance to visit with Tarpey and Linda in Lincoln. Quite why a navy man would end up in RAF country was never really explained. But it was a nice quiet town not too far south from Lincoln.

Tarpey also had many projects on the go, which is why the reformation of his home took such a long time. Sun dials could have been used to measure progress.

Anyway, the year before he had completed that Everest of the cycling world, the journey from Land's End to John o' Groats. And now he was struck down with lung cancer. Try as hard as they could the NHS were unable to arrest its morbid progress.

On the journey to York, we stopped off to see Richard and wish him a speedy recovery, which in our heart of hearts looked increasing unlikely. The car journey across country from Hampshire to Lincoln can best be described as tiresome. If you like crowded roads and even more crowded roundabouts this is the journey for you. Its hard work, even if it is quite pretty.

A hot cuppa and cakes welcomed us both, and I spent a bit longer talking to Linda before going up the stairs to Tarpey's bedroom. That was my loss, those precious few moments.

He was sat up in bed, thin as a rake, his beard as strong as ever, smiling and waiting for my visit. We started to converse, his conversation was always most interesting.

After only a few moments together, suddenly, blood started to flow from his mouth as he slumped backwards into the pillows. I rushed downstairs to phone his doctor. The doctor's tired and overworked receptionist told me doctor would be with us in fifteen minutes.

'Lady, Mr Tarpey does even have fifteen seconds,' I shouted and I slammed the phone down to join Linda at his bedside. The doctor arrived very quickly but by then the last signs of life were leaving him. Linda and I went down stairs let the doctor do his work. I comforted Linda as best I could. She was very brave, but the time she knew would come had arrived, and now was the time to plan the arrangements for a fitting farewell.

Richard had been my oldest friend since 1961, we had served together on *HMS Albion*, man and boy for almost four years. We had sailed together, won the Southampton Town Regatta, my first race, by a fluke, and spent the winnings, mostly in the pub.

He had the most fascinating conversation, could always see the other side of any discussion. An expert on the British Railway history of steam and was secretary of a railway magazine for many years. He had made hundreds of models of steam engines.

His death was a great loss to us all.

*

THE NEXT EVENT I witnessed was the Enron saga. The whole of Houston is fixated on the story as it unfolds. I am still working at Unocal and a guy in the next cubical has on-line trading, with instant execution on the stock market. Late one afternoon Enron shares drop from $30 bucks to 30 cents in a matter of hours. He watches his screen intently. By the end of the day, the shares have died, down to 20 cents.

I learned later that he bought a shed load of shares at that price and put an automatic sell notice at 30 cents. Next morning he came back to work and he is one very happy bunny. The 'dead cat bounce' took the share back up to 35 cents before the stock exchange took them from the market. Rumours abound on how much he made, but it was substantial. All the employees of Enron who had millions of dollars' worth of company shares in their pension fund are in shock. Some take their own life.

Now we all know that the very clever persons that put this Ponzi scheme together are very dangerous persons to the community at large. The rest is history, very sad history.

*

DURING THE SIX years we lived in Houston we were both very happy. Sonia had her own car and passed her Texas driving licence in English as the Spanish they used was too confusing. She made friends with the Brazilian Consul General's wife as they are both dog-a-holics.

We were honoured to receive a couple of invitation when the Consul General held receptions for the other consuls in Houston, I believe there are over eighty of them. The most interesting person I met at the first party was the American who worked for the State Department. His job was to liaise with all the Consuls in Houston. I said to him, 'Too many pies, not enough fingers,' He liked that comment.

I also got to learn some of the goings-on after the 9-11 tragedy and the new rules about banking that were imposed on foreign consulates. It was all very interesting.

The work was very interesting too. Lots to do and working for the small Texan oil companies, without all the big company BS, demonstrated what could be done if your team knows what to do.

I remember an executive called Bob, who could do wonderfully complicated calculations in his head. Way over everybody's head, his calculations could even be correct. If nothing else it was a great show. On one project, he worked his team to the point of exhaustion. Their reward, a brand new Volvo salon car, I think they were all yellow.

By far the most interesting experience was when I was asked to go to Israel in 2004 and produce a document called Safety & Operations Emergency Procedures, which the client, Noble Inc, an American company, had to present to the relevant government authorities to obtain a license to produce. What did I know? But to quote from Mr Pursley all those years ago, I would know a whole lot more when I had completed the task.

I flew to London and took the weekend to visit my father who had been admitted to Salisbury Odstock Hospital for tests. The front of the hospital was new and looked very grand.

The old general hospital in the city had been demolished years ago. It was where my mother learnt to be a nurse. According to her, the training was twice as tough as becoming an army commando. Judging by the way she terrorised the world, she could be right.

The reality of Odstock was, that by the time one found the car park, the main part of the hospital was the old 8th Army Air Force Burns Unit from WW 2. Same buildings, only with double glazing. Dad was in a mixed ward and hated it. If you weren't ill when you were admitted, you would be on discharge.

There were no signs of anything tragic about to happen, so I made my way back to London and took the flight to Tel Aviv. The flight was very tranquil until the aircraft started to make its descent when it made a very sharp ninety-degree course change to the north and then one minute later, it returned to its original course. The air stewardess told me it was just a safety precaution, with air traffic control making certain the aircraft was under their control. SAM missiles anyone?

The work in Tel Aviv went well. The hotel overlooked the beach and in the evening, if you didn't mind all the layabout guards pretending to protect the Israelis from whoever it was they thought was going to ruin their day, or evening, there were some truly average restaurants and bars.

I spent four weeks in Tel Aviv, so I had some time to explore. One part of the city had a population of Russian Jews, who eat pork. To rear the pigs, they had to build platforms to house their animals, but the platforms were made of open planks of wood with a uniform separation. So the pigs lived on the straw, the straw became contaminated with their dung and the straw with the pig's dung falls on to the hallowed ground that is Israel. Think about it, what a lot of nonsense, same as talking to a wall.

One weekend I visited the port of Jaffa. Archaeological evidence shows that Jaffa was inhabited roughly from 7,500 BC. Its modern history is well over three thousand years old and you can feel the history. It is a strange feeling to stand in the port and think of all the events that have happened in this time.

Mid-week I had to attend a meeting at the Ministry of Energy in Jerusalem where my client had to present the documents on which I had worked. There were a few changes, but all in all, there were no outstanding issues. There was no time to visit the tourist areas, but the city seemed rather, I don't know, downbeat I guess.

Project finished, time to go home. I stopped off in London and went to see my father. He was back in hospital. The situation did not look good and Sonia flew over from Texas to help me look after mother.

At the hospital a week passed as more tests were attempted but they revealed nothing. The doctors knew less and less. Father sensed he was about to become a burden on my mother and decided to stop eating. He complained there was no liquid to give him any relief, no taste in his mouth, so I suggested Lucozade. Its fizzy taste would satisfy his craving for some taste in his mouth and the glucose would give some strength.

I phoned the office in Houston and explained the situation. No way could I come home in the immediate future. They gave me my sick leave that had accumulated since I joined the company. Mother, now in her early nineties needed transport to/from the hospital. The doctors still could not decide what was wrong. Five days later the chief doctor ushered us all into a separate room to reveal that father had Amyloidosis, which they had never seen before.

The prognosis was poor, the only centre of excellence for this illness was in Boston USA and the treatment was highly invasive so the patient had to be fit and strong to survive it. So, with regrets, the family was asked to take him home and await whatever would happen next.

Shocked, was not the word. How could this wonderful strong man, one of the best craftsman have this unknown illness? The ambulance brought him home the next morning. My brother's two sons arrived that morning. Sonia and I took a couple of hours break to visit the shops in Salisbury. When we returned it was all over. It was all very sad. He was only eighty years old.

The funeral was a very sad occasion and I was left with my memories. My parents had been married for over sixty years, their anniversary party in the village hall was a blast. But they used to fight like cat and dog at times. My favourite memory was the day Sonia and I arrived from somewhere, the parents had just finished arguing about nothing in particular. Sonia went into the living room to calm mother down and I retreated to the double garage where father had his snooker den and beer brewing factory.

I asked, 'Father, has my mother always been like this?' His reply, never bettered was, 'Why do you think Hitler invaded Russia?' I smile every time I remember this magic moment.

*

THE NEXT TWO years passed very quickly. One magic moment came when I was called to a peer review meeting at one of the major clients. The project involved a long subsea step-out, about 26 miles. These meetings are called early in the morning. A buffet breakfast is provided to ensure the invited attend.

There were thirty people around the conference table, all munching away, of which only three people had anything to contribute. The subject is unimportant but I was one of the three. My client was the person answering the questions by the chairman. Somebody had made a rather ambitious statement on how cheap it could be to transport the equipment, the long umbilical being reviewed, from Europe to the USA.

I said nothing, which is unusual for me. My client turned to me and asked my opinion. He may have guessed my answer. I told the meeting this very heavy item could only be transported by the installation vessel itself and that was going cost. Ships that install stuff in very deep water don't come cheap. Reality check.

The project I did like a great deal was working for my good friend

Richard writing an operations manual for a rather interesting subsea development. I had to learn a lot before I could write about it. I had previous experience on similar projects, so I was able to improve on my work. As Richard was overworked, I was given other vital procedures to generate. I even got to go offshore to supervise the procedures. A good engineer should always produce a procedure on the basis he will be the one to do the work. Concentrates the mind wonderfully.

The project I didn't like was the day one of the Three John's flew in from London all cock-a-hoop, to tell one and all that our company was going to support Bechtel in India. I was to be the lead engineer in my sector. My previous experience with our new client came back to me.

The team on this major gas project began commuting Houston to Mumbai, which involved two international flights, back to back, both ways. Mumbai, previously called Bombay, is a shithole. I could write pages about what is wrong with the place so let's leave it at that.

It was very tiring wading through huge piles of project documents in the unconfirmed knowledge that the Indian's had already cut a deal with their vendor of choice. That I could well have come to the same conclusion as they did is neither here or there.

Not once in four long visits to that country did our hosts offer any hospitality. Just goes to show where we stood in the pecking order of things. The only local person I really liked was Little Sammy our driver. Team members were expressly forbidden to drive. If there was an accident, the locals, seeing we were European, would rush to the scene, cover everything in paraffin and set fire to you. So we were told. True or false, who knows?

One day Little Sammy, who drove a nice mid-sized Honda, turned up with a locally made car that was the worst car I have ever been in. Where was the Honda? Getting a new automatic gearbox fitted, the sixth that year. We looked inside the bonnet and it was clear the engine was all original. Nothing to see here.

On the journey back to Houston, following my fourth visit, I took seriously ill and almost requested a diversion to Dubai. I had a huge fever, shivering with cold. Two hours out from Amsterdam, my fever flipped as I started to sweat profusely. In Amsterdam, I took advantage of the hot showers provided airside, changed my clothes, took breakfast and then enjoyed a very comfortable journey on the KLM service to Houston.

*

Struck Down

I TOOK A day off after the long journey back to Houston and went to the office the next day. I made it to lunch time but hell I was ill, time to visit the medical centre not far from the apartment. The doctor diagnosed a severe cold and gave me some tablets. I thought the examination was not as thorough as it should have been.

The attempt to do a day's work the following day ended when I collapsed in the office and someone was kind enough to drive me in my car back to the medical centre and this time a more professional looking doctor from one of the USA's Latin countries. He listened intently to my recent history, completed a blood test and conducted a real examination. The blood test results confirmed his diagnosis and the next thing I remember was being given a massive injection.

Sonia drove me home and put me to bed, where I stayed for just under a week.

When I was able to return to the office the news was not good. Bechtel wanted our team to move into their offices, modelled on a Dickens workhouse, dark and cramped and we were advised that future flights to India would be in economy class.

Not for me. I asked to be transferred to another project but new projects there were none. Then, an agent called and asked if I wanted to work for a client company and move to Rio de Janeiro. Sonia said yes before I could get a word in edgeways.

The company was not pleased with me jumping ship, but there was no way I could go back to India. My health was seriously at risk. I told them I had contracted double pneumonia and going back to India would most unwise. In fact, it took the best part of two years to fully recover.

28

CHEVRON

Houston and Rio de Janeiro (2006 - 2007)

FOLLOWING A CHANGE TO THE Brazilian Constitution, a new government agency was formed called the ANP and Petrobrás was removed from being the Government agency and a national oil company at the same time.

Petrobrás kept its producing fields and a large number of potential projects called Blue Blocks. The rest were returned to the ANP to be auctioned off.

Chevron entered the Brazilian market with the purchase of an oil field called Frade. It's a blue block that Petrobrás had delayed in developing due to issues. The field required some imaginative thinking, so Chevron had the larger slice of the pie, as Petrobrás watched and paid its minority share of the development.

I was given the position of lead umbilical engineer and the product would be made in a local factory in Niteroi. So far, so good.

The project team gathers in the huge downtown office of this monster oil company. I soon found out it had its own way of working. The project is waiting for final sanction so not a lot is happening. I meet up with my old chum Charlie, who is heading up the subsea control system work. We agree the layout of the subsea system will work, but great care is needed with choosing the different vendors.

What is a given is the subsea control system vendor, a well-respected company indeed. What I am concerned about is the supply of the subsea electrical cable, that will be bundled in the umbilicals, has been changed. The umbilical vendor has plants based in the UK, the USA and Brazil. The vendor is very competent, but to improve their margins they make their own electrical cable. The plant in the UK makes good cable, but I have inside knowledge about the USA made cable and a Brazilian friend of mine who is heading up a project in the Gulf of Mexico has had substantial problems.

I share my concerns with Charlie very much on the quiet. He is new to Chevron as I am so it is best to make haste slowly. The problem is this, subsea control systems have to be perfect when installed, otherwise redemption costs are very high.

The project manager (PM) assures everybody that everything will be OK. Charlie and I are not so sure. The project manager is a know-all and cannot be told what he wishes not to hear. He is also has a difficult personality, his nickname is not pleasant, so I shall not repeat it. He is also in the middle of a divorce, and everybody is on the side of the long-suffering wife.

While we wait for project sanction everybody has to rewrite their specifications all to no good purpose. The PM picks on minor details and in the process upsets many people. His man management is dreadful. He has a nasty habit of hiring specialists and then not signing their contract until the ultimate last moment.

He crawls all over the umbilical specifications that I didn't produce in the first place. A lot of minor changes are forced upon me without actually changing the meaning of the words as if the vendor is actually going to notice. Vendors build their product their way and that's it.

One of the rebels in the piping department writes a spoof memo and pins it to the notice board that reads, 'The cat sat on the mat.' The revision now reads, 'On the mat the cat sat. Who gives a fuck as long as the cat's arse is attached to the F..... mat.'

Everybody laughs and the PM is most upset. A witch-hunt ensues and everybody points their finger at everyone else. This drives the PM mad.

The crunch-time came when I was sent to the USA vendor's plant in the Florida panhandle for the kick-off meeting. The location is not the easiest place to get to and the airfare is a disgrace. I arrived at the beachside hotel in the early evening to be met by Howard, the vendor's account holder. He comes from the north-west of England and we had a very nice dinner and conversation.

The next day, I arrived at the factory ready to hold the expected contract kick-off meeting. A tour of the electrical cable plant proved useful, but some of the equipment was home made when my information was that the imported cable twisting machine should have been fully integrated. Still, a manufacturing run was underway for another client.

That done, the working documents for the contract were not ready for the review meeting. Nor did the vendor have any samples to guide me. This was not good. Reviewing the Quality Plan, the manufacturing schedule and the Safety Plan are all important before manufacturing can start. These are the documents that the client's inspectors work too.

I left the vendor's premises well before the expected time. I still had to drive a long way to get to the airport, then catch the flight to Houston. In all, it was a long day.

Next morning I completed my trip report and gave it to Charlie. It spoke the unvarnished truth and it could do little else but be negative. The PM, when he received his copy, was most put out. A Brit doing down on an American company. He did not like that at all.

I was asked to rewrite it, difficult as it is necessary to be truthful. I rewrote it in some flowery words, keeping the same message in a less blunt manner. The fuss blew over and I never heard any more about it. The PM chose the site quality inspector himself and received a report more to his liking.

Not long afterwards Sonia and I were transferred to Rio de Janeiro. Sonia's pet dog, in its cabin bag would not fit under the business class seat in front of her, so the unusual situation occurred where she had to sit in economy class every time the aircraft took-off or landed. Queer way to run an airline, but that's Continental for you.

*

SETTLING DOWN ONCE again in Rio was easy. The country manager did not like the area in which we lived, as it wasn't safe. I assured him that it was very safe as the apartment was one hundred metres from the Governor's official palace, in which the army housed a hundred of its finest fighting troops, not forgetting the Policia Militar which had one patrol car in the grounds and one at the top of the road.

His reply, 'Well you're contractor, so it doesn't matter.' Go USA.

I bought a car for the daily commute to Niteroi and the one time I took Charlie I pointed out the famous shop that sold lottery tickets. Seeing that we were in a very nondescript part of the world, Charlie asked what was famous about it. I told him, a grandfather had won a mega-lotto, but his family considered he didn't distribute the funds fast enough and he suffered a bad accident by walking in front of a speeding vehicle. The fact he was wheel-chair bound led to suspicious thoughts amongst the locals, but not the police apparently.

The umbilical factory was the same as I remembered it. After introductions, I settled into my office and met with my locally employed inspectors. There was a project meeting about the supply of materials and their USA factory had already shipped the cable to be used in the test piece used for fatigue trials, a process that takes some time.

I mentioned the fuss around the supply of the electrical cable and their chief engineer had doubt written all over his face. Anyway, the project proceeded in the usual manner. Once a week I met up with Charlie who was based at the subsea control systems vendor in the industrial northern part of the Rio de Janeiro where one definitely does not slow down when driving.

Charlie, being the hero that he was, would work late. I told him driving back to his wonderful apartment on the Lagoa wasn't a good idea, but he never had any problems. Pure luck.

*

I REMEMBER ONE day when the team from the umbilical factory had an interface meeting at the control system vendor's facility on the other side of the bridge. During introductions, the young engineers of both companies seem to know each other very well. I twigged it. They had all studied at the same university, the Centro Federal de Educação Tecnológica Celso Suckow da Fonseca - Cefet/RJ, where Sonia used to work as a senior in the planning and training department. I asked my vendor's team leader was I correct. 'Yes,' he replied.

I said, 'My wife was a senior in the university management. Perhaps I will get her to check you lot out.'

He laughed, then saw I was serious. He frowned, then we both laughed together, but it sure did make them all think.

*

LIFE SETTLED DOWN, the project was on track, so everyone was happy until the day the first batch of electrical cable arrived from the USA. Everyone gathered around as the specialists tested the many characteristics it had to pass. Their glum faces said it all.

I flipped open my cell phone to call Charlie. The message, get yourself here, pronto.

Everyone looked at me. After all, I had been to the factory where this stuff was being made. The accompanying certification showed the cable had passed all testing in the USA, so what had happened in between?

I took the vendor's PM to one side and told him, very much on the quiet, most of the story. He was not amused. I told him I had tried sort matters before they became serious and almost got fired for my pains. Best he writes to his company and get it all official.

Charlie arrives, puffing and panting. I told him what had occurred and asked his advice.

'Get it all down on paper and get the vendor to send the notice to Houston as per the contract.'

'All in hand,' I said. 'Best to duck.'

'Why's that?'

'Shit can spread far and wide when propelled into a big fan. We are clear, so don't worry,' I counselled, in the full knowledge that was not how the PM in Houston worked.

So, there was a big fuss, the project would be delayed. Now what?

Three days later 'Now what' arrived in the form of first class BA tickets to Bonny Scotland with the message, 'Get it sorted.'

If you have ever wanted the experience of flying in first class you will either need a healthy bank account, or, in my case, an oil company at one with its travel agent Wagon Li. This part of the aircraft was empty, but business class was full, nice upgrade. Also, oil companies do not pay the full fare, they get special rates as the airlines want their business.

The transfer in Heathrow was a mess, but first class passengers get looked after. I must win the lottery one day. At Edinburgh airport, the hire car company gave me a very nice Mercedes Benz.

The next day, a wet Monday, I got to grips with the situation. A Mr Sutherland was the company expert, also the industry expert in this area of subsea electric cables. I learnt a lot. I was told, confidentially, that the people in the USA had been told what to do, but they decided to do their own thing. Now they were going to pay the price.

The vendor's jungle drums had obviously been busy over the weekend and various actions were considered. I agreed with some and questioned others and then wrote a report and sent it to all the seniors involved and life moved on.

*

WHAT HAD NOT moved on was my contract. When I was working in Houston my agent, a UK company, had stated they could not support me in Brazil. It was a market they had no intention of getting into.

Chevron gave me the name of another UK agent that would take on my contract as they were based in Rio de Janeiro. The problem was I was working in Brazil, being paid in the USA. The time came to transfer to the agent's office in Brazil, but once again the same problem came my way. The Chevron PM, with the unfortunate nickname, delayed signing the paperwork.

To make matters worse, thinking I needed more technical support he had sent a young engineer called Rick from Chevron's advanced technology group. Rick was no doubt a bright laddy, but he was also a smart arse who liked to play politics. It was time for me to think about the future.

Just before I went on holiday to meet the family in Lisbon, I was in the position of not actually having a contract, which among other things would make my presence in Brazil illegal. I had words with Charlie who told me all would be well when I returned to work on the Monday after the holiday.

They weren't. I telephoned my new agent and they knew the score. The lady asked if I would be interested in going to Paris, same job title, better pay, mostly tax-free.

'Please send the documents,' I replied.

On Tuesday, Charlie told me my new contract would be ready on Thursday, meanwhile do not go to work. I went anyway, just to clear my desk and to smile sweetly at Rick, who looked confused.

Tuesday morning I signed up for Paris, then told Charlie I was on the move.

'You have to give your notice,' he said, not at all pleased.

'Charlie,' I said. 'I do not have a contract, but I can stay for a week or so while I get ready to move to France.'

And that is what happened. The PM in Houston went ballistic by all accounts. He had played his little game and lost. Without realising it, I made him look stupid, which is something one should never do. No matter, my time in Brazil was getting shorter by the day and there was no future.

Poor Charlie took it in the neck, despite his words to the PM, 'The man had no contract, he was in fact unemployed. What do you expect?'

Young Rick wasn't too pleased either. His hints that he was going to take over came true. I left him to play with the Brazilians. That will teach him.

29

TOTAL SA

Paris (2007 - 2008)

MOVING TO PARIS WAS AN exercise in flexibility. With little of the language it took time and patience to get to where I wanted to be. The lady in the office was a big help as Total had a working agreement with the local hotels and more importantly, the apart-hotels. Quite why apart-hotels are not more common in the UK I have no idea.

I moved into a one bedroom apart-hotel and it had all I required and it was only a five-minute walk to the office. For leisure, the main Total HQ in La Defence had a magnificent swimming pool underground, very Roman in style.

Paris is the most visited city in the world. Sonia and I enjoyed Paris, but then we enjoy most big cities. Paris tourists do impose themselves on the local residents.

I led the way and Sonia followed later with Bob, her pedigree Shih Tzu. Eventually, we found a nice apartment to the north of Porte Maillot. Renting requires care and prices can be expensive. Still, it was comfortable, but in winter it cost a fortune to heat. Just where was this global warming we hear so much about?

Paris had a few notable moments during my stay. That year France did not win the FIFA world cup final. The next big occasion was the Rugby world cup. The French engineers in the office were certain France would collect the glory.

I remember very well the gloomy faces in the office when I returned from a long weekend in England. The Boss of the department, a big no-

nonsense installation manager, with rare humour, asked me to tell him all about cricket.

France and its capital city is blessed with a superb public transport system. I never needed to hire a car. In Paris, parking is very difficult everywhere. On the other hand, the TGV gets you to anywhere you want to go, fast and with a 'seniors' railcard, it is not expensive either.

I took Sonia to Mulhouse, way over on the eastern border to see the national car museum, which is a must see. It has a very interesting history and a big collection of Bugatti's including three Type 41 Royales. The museum is now listed as a National Heritage site.

The national rail museum near-by is also excellent. The section of the museum regarding WW2 is outstanding. The French Resistance caused their occupiers many serious problems, and they lost a lot of people, especially train drivers.

So apart from the pleasure of living in Paris, not a lot was happening on the work front. This huge project for a deepwater field in Angola was waiting for final sanction. When it came, I was replaced by the guy with the same job title from the project in front that was cancelled and Total moved people on to the project I was working.

So I had a quiet year enjoying Paris and I even managed to extract a favour from my boss for a two month notice period. I spent my time wisely and courtesy of a Brazilian who I had briefly met on the Chevron project, I landed a similar position on a BP Angolan project in Staines, near Heathrow airport. It's a small world.

30

BP

London and Angola (2008 - 2010)

THE DAY I LEFT PARIS, Sonia took the flight to Brazil and two hours later I was on the flight to London. The BP project was housed in a building that once housed HMG's Revenue Office in Staines. Bad karma? Not a bit of it.

I was lucky to find a very comfortable first-floor apartment overlooking the River Thames and by chance there existed a footpath that wound its way around the houses to the medical centre, the county offices and my office for the next two years.

There I met my Brazilian chum Marcelo who had been head-hunted by BP. The Angolan project was manned by both BP and JP Kenny and included four FPSO's to be developed in sequence.

I was once again working for the subsea department looking after deepwater umbilicals. Given the complexity of the project, the first FPSO would be producing from four separate subsea fields. The figures were impressive; the total weight of all equipment on the seabed would be twenty thousand tons.

I did enjoy this project, with monthly visits to Oslo to hold the progress meeting with the umbilical manufacturer. My all-time favourite restaurant was DS Louis down on the waterfront. It is old shipping office, with a huge collection of nautical artefacts and a monster of a polar bear parked in a corner stood fully upright.

I had known the personnel at this vendor for a number of years and it was always a pleasure to meet them again.

Had some fun too, the best was with the BP Health and Safety guy, who held a meeting on driving in Oslo during the winter. The message was, always take a taxi, the locals know what to do for the best in the snowy weather.

I asked, with a much irony as possible, if the Moroccan taxi drivers, who were very common in Oslo, had been trained to drive on snow instead of sand. The BP guy was not amused. I think they are paid to be miserable.

There was one visit to Oslo where the weather was in between snow and rain and a truly horrible virus gripped the city. I caught it, by lunch time I was unwell, by the time I embarked on the return aircraft I was just hoping to make it back to London. The aircraft was caught up in the queue for de-icing and I just collapsed. The aircraft had to return to the ramp, I was taken down the stairs at the end of the ramp into a freezing cold ambulance and then to Oslo's new very modern hospital.

At the hospital, my blood pressure was near zero and I had never felt so ill except for the time when I came back from India. The upside, as I slowly recovered, was the Swedish nurses, all wearing full bacterial protection suits and headgear. All I saw was blond hair and blue eyes.

Still, I made it back to London on the Saturday morning, to be fussed over by Sonia.

Angola is a queer place to do business and part of the umbilical supply had to be made locally. And so a visit to Angola was necessary for the kick-off meeting with the vendor.

Getting to and from Angola is a different experience to most places. Most of the international airlines fly just once a week. I flew down with Lufthansa, but our return was via Johannesburg. Angola was still recovering from a very long war, but facilities were better than expected. We saw a lot of Chinese workers building new infrastructure. The Portuguese language is the main language in the country so my chum Marcelo and I did well during the meetings.

I even got to swim in the sea, it was very pleasant. The flight back via South Africa was a long day. The flight to South Africa was late and the BA flight to London had no business class seats by the time we arrived for the connecting flight. I stayed the night and caught the flight the next day, which was just as well.

During my next visit to Oslo, I checked in at the Raddison Hotel. I like this hotel but there is something quite odd about the way it's positioned. I found out later that the land belongs to a Muslim organisation. They sold half the area to the hotel company on the condition the building faced Mecca. Interesting.

The other reason I liked the hotel is that it has a swimming pool on the top floor. Very cold water, so dive-in and get swimming. All I got was a massive pain across my chest. I struggled out of the pool and took a hot shower, but the pain returned when I returned to Heathrow late in the evening and I was rushing up a freezing cold ramp from the aircraft.

I checked in with the local health centre the next morning. I needed a stent somewhere, so they gave me a spray to keep me going while appointments were made. The first examination was weird, as they couldn't find anything wrong. Just open the window, I said, its minus four centigrade outside, that should do the trick.

Anyway, due process didn't take too long and I ended up in Tooting of all places on a Saturday morning at the main teaching hospital getting fixed up. So far so good, even today.

Fitting in other long-term medical maintenance, like a new hip, with my work programme took some careful planning. The NHS did a good job, but all that is wrong with UK society is seen in these big hospitals. There are so many different nationalities it is very difficult to get everyone on the same page. And management is nowhere near where it should be.

Hospitals need strict discipline. My mother, fast approaching her ninth decade, threw a hissy fit at the doctor when she discovered I had bed sores. In her day, that was a sacking offence. I guess the doctor learnt a lot that day. Can't argue with old style matrons that went through WW2.

31

THE END OF A WORKING LIFE

(2010 - ???)

MADE IT; SURPRISED ME I can tell you. The BP Angolan project was reduced to just the first FPSO and JPK had a large number of engineers and support staff released from the project.

With little else to do, I took time out and returned to Rio de Janeiro. It was sorely needed respite from the many years of hard work. In 2012 I was lucky to get a job offer in Houston, but after a few months that panned out and so more time off.

I did enjoy Houston as we always do. We have many good friends there. The result of six stable years in the same place.

So, what are the good points about Houston? It's just so easy to live there. My favourite outing is the 'Classic Wheels and Wooden Keels' weekend at the Clearlake YC. It's at the eastern end of the NASA -1 highway.

The Wheels and the Keels are the best, with some much needed love and money lavished upon them. Most of the cars are 'Trailer Queens' and hardly if ever get driven far on the open road.

The most impressive was this 1937 Cord, a present to the President of Uruguay from the President of the USA. There was a revolution, but the car was saved by the driver. Eventually, it returned to the USA. The cost for the paint alone exceeded US$30,000 dollars.

My time in Houston extended when out of nowhere I was asked to help a Chinese company with a FEED study (front-end engineering and design) for a subsea tie back which pleased the misses no end. That completed, five months hard work then back to sunny Rio de Janeiro. It took a further two years before the Chinese moved to the execution stage, by which time I had retired.

During my winter stays in Rio de Janeiro I liked to go sailing, racing the Olympic heavyweight single-handed dinghy (the Finn) and became involved with the 2016 Olympics.

I signed up to be a technical equipment inspector, which involved lots of revision of class rules and other details. Some dinghies are made by a sole vendor. However, the Olympic Finn can have every individual component made by any company or home builder. Thus every component must be weighed, measured and checked for compliance. The standard is so high, even a small modification outside of the rules can give an advantage.

Test regattas were held in 2014 and 2015 and it all went jolly well. I had to learn a lot, as the management of the sport is very technical.

Dividing my time between the UK and Brazil seems to have taken up most of my time and now I am just waiting for a final return to Europe. Still, need to keep busy otherwise the day begins and ends with taking all those damn pills the doctors seem to think I should take to keep going.

Writing this book has been fun, just the same as writing my previous three books.

Memories came flooding back, and I was glad they did, but I am surprised how many memories I have forgotten, but that is to be expected. But it is most annoying, it really is.

With no parents surviving, there is no one to ask. I recommend the use of a diary, I really do.

Finally, on the family front, my Mother passed away on the 9th Oct 2011, just one day before her 98th birthday. She was buried in the same grave as my father. She had died peacefully in her sleep, which is the best way to go.

That she died in October was fitting as she was born in October. My first wife, Johan was born and died in October. Her father died in October. Sonia and I were both born in October, as were my grand-daughter Charlotte and her step sister Rebecca.

Sonia's mother, Risette, died in 2012 after a long illness.

So Sonia and I are first in the queue for what's next. I think we will wait awhile for the next event.

END

www.ingramcontent.com/pod-product-compliance
Lightning Source LLC
Chambersburg PA
CBHW071331080526
44587CB00017B/2792